MISSISSIPPI'S AMERICAN INDIANS

Heritage of Mississippi Series / VOLUME VI

MISSISSIPPI'S AMERICAN INDIANS

James F. Barnett Jr.

University Press of Mississippi
for the Mississippi Historical Society and the
Mississippi Department of Archives and History
JACKSON

Publication of this book was made possible through a grant from
the Phil Hardin Foundation.

www.upress.state.ms.us

The University Press of Mississippi is a member of the Association
of American University Presses.

First printing 2012

∞

Library of Congress Cataloging-in-Publication Data

Barnett, James F., 1950–
Mississippi's American indians / James F. Barnett Jr.
p. cm. — (Heritage of Mississippi series volume vi)
Includes bibliographical references and index.
ISBN 978-1-61703-245-5 (cloth : alk. paper) —
ISBN 978-1-61703-246-2 (ebook)
1. Indians of North America—Mississippi—History. 2. Indians of
North America—Mississippi—Government relations. 3. Indians of
North America—Mississippi—Social life and customs. I. Title.
E78.M73B37 2012
976.2004'97—dc23   2011041573

British Library Cataloging-in-Publication Data available

For Sharon

CONTENTS

ACKNOWLEDGMENTS

Without the help of many people, this project would not have been possible. I am indebted to James R. Atkinson, Sharon W. Barnett, Samuel O. Brookes, John M. Connaway, Jack D. Elliott Jr., Patricia K. Galloway, and Elbert R. Hilliard, who read and commented on portions of the manuscript as it developed. Robbie Ethridge, Evan Peacock, and Brantly Willis served as readers for the University Press of Mississippi and provided essential critical reviews. Ethridge also graciously sent me the page proofs of her new work, *From Chicaza to Chickasaw*, and suggested a reorganization of my manuscript that was most helpful. For various forms of assistance, I am also grateful to David Abbott, Rebecca M. Anderson, Clinton I. Bagley, Charles R. Barnett, Ian W. Brown, Lara R. Brown, H. Clark Burkett, Earl Cotten, Jessica Fleming Crawford, Joseph V. "Smokye" Frank, Chris Goodwin, Hiram F. "Pete" Gregory, Hank Holmes, Grady Howell, Jay K. Johnson, Rachel Lynn Jolley, Avis King, George E. Lankford, Sarah J. Laramore, Mary Lohrenz, Kay McNeil, Kathy Moody, David W. Morgan, Stanley Nelson, Sharon R. Ogden, Carol Barnett Robertson, Janice B. Sago, Gordon Sayre, Stephanie Scott, Jean S. Simonton, Vincas P. Steponaitis, Anne Webster, and Christine Wilson. In addition, thanks are due to Nancy McLemore, Beth Richard, and Paul Smith of the Willie Mae Dunn Library, Natchez Branch, Copiah-Lincoln Community College, for assistance with interlibrary loans. Details are tiresome but critical, and I appreciate Robert Burchfield's thorough copyediting work. Finally, I want to thank the Heritage Series editors and Craig Gill and the staff at the University Press of Mississippi.

MISSISSIPPI'S AMERICAN INDIANS

INTRODUCTION

When I began work on this Heritage of Mississippi Series volume, I was completing a book about the history of the Natchez Indians (*The Natchez Indians: A History to 1735*). In my Natchez study, I made use of recent reevaluations of Natchez political structure suggested by anthropologists Marvin T. Smith and Karl G. Lorenz, which depict the Natchez as a confederation of three, and possibly four, different ethnic groups. It seemed that the "confederacy" model better explained the documented interaction between the Natchez and other tribes and Europeans. In the early history of the American Southeast, one does not have to look far to find impetus for the formation of tribal confederacies; the coming of Europeans to the continent set chaotic and terrible forces in motion that gave confederacies of small native groups a better chance at survival.[1]

The formation of confederacies implies instability and dynamic interaction among societies, a scenario that aptly describes the rapidly shifting world in which all of the Mississippi tribes found themselves by the late seventeenth century. Of course, the recognition of confederacies in this area is nothing new—ethnohistorian Patricia Galloway has described the seventeenth-century formation of the formidable Choctaw confederacy. Likewise, smaller confederacies coalesced on the upper and lower Yazoo River and along the lower Tombigbee and Alabama rivers at about that same time. Many of the groups joining forces were immigrants into the Mississippi region. The Natchez and Yazoo coalitions included refugee groups from collapsed Mississippi period chiefdoms to the north in the Middle Mississippi Valley, while similar refugee groups from disintegrating chiefdoms in present-day eastern Mississippi and western Alabama formed the Choctaw confederacy and the grouping of small tribes north of Mobile Bay. Behind the urgency to unite for mutual protection was the pan-southeastern Indian slave trade initiated by the English in Carolina. At the same time, European diseases spreading among the tribes reduced their numbers, providing additional motivation for banding together.[2]

The sources of information about Mississippi's American Indians include archaeological reports, historical documentation, maps, and, to some extent, ethnographic data collected in the late nineteenth and early twentieth centuries. Sadly, only in rare instances are the words of the Indians themselves preserved. The vagaries of preservation limit what can be recovered through archaeology, and the native societies of interest here were quite different from those extant when trained ethnographers arrived on the scene. On the other hand, the colonial and early U.S. narratives are potentially much more informative. These writings provide a window upon a bygone world and its inhabitants; however, the narratives should be used with caution.[3] With few exceptions, this information comes from individuals whose interests lay in controlling the native people for military purposes, Christian indoctrination, profit, and political gain. European observers interpreted what they saw in the context of their own experiences, prejudices, and religious beliefs, which generally consigned the American Indians to a lower level of humanity and tagged them with the appellation "savages." The narratives also come at a high cost—the native societies we encounter in the letters, journals, and military reports were dwindling rapidly because of the presence of the Europeans observing them. The dynamics of European encroachment generated desperate migrations and dangerous alliances with agents representing French, English, and Spanish interests. The region's ethnic landscape grew even more unpredictable with the introduction of Africans into the Louisiana colony during the early eighteenth century. It follows that the tribal groups discussed here were quite different from whatever they might have been before Columbus sailed. Instead of pristine forest societies, the writers who generated the narratives observed traumatized social groups attempting to adapt to the changing world. As we will see, those Mississippi tribes that survived into the nineteenth century did so by reinventing themselves.

In a history of Mississippi's American Indians, terminology becomes a potentially sensitive issue, and there is no set of politically correct terms that are immune to ever-changing perceptions and attitudes. My overriding concern in language usage is clarity of communication. In this sense, the word "Indian" has certainly stood the test of time. Of course, everyone knows the story of how Columbus mistook the people of the Caribbean Islands for eastern Indians; however, North America's indigenous peoples seem much more comfortable with the word "Indian" than with the new age expression "Native American." In this book, I use the terms "Indian," "American Indian," "native," "native people," and "indigenous people" interchangeably, keeping in mind the diversity of groups within the broader label. Likewise, "tribe" has not met with universal approval, but the term is closely associated with American Indians and to attempt to avoid it altogether would have made for an unnecessarily awkward narrative. Today the Mississippi Choctaws refer to themselves as a tribe, as do numerous other state- and federally recognized American Indian groups.[4] Here, I use the word "tribe" in its broadest sense to denote a single ethnic group, such as the Pascagoula tribe, or a multiethnic group, such as the Natchez confederacy. As such, "tribe" is used interchangeably with "group" and "nation" to identify a community of families or villages inhabiting a shared place. Unlike today's formally organized tribal groups, however, the Mississippi tribes of the past were not fixed entities, but instead were always fluid coalitions changing to take advantage of events unfolding around them.

In recent books about the southeastern Indians, perhaps the most conspicuously avoided terms are the expressions "mixed blood" and "full blood," which differentiate between individuals born to European and American Indian parents, and those whose parents were both American Indians. This distinction is critical to understanding Choctaw and Chickasaw politics in the late eighteenth and early nineteenth centuries.[5] In this book, I steer clear of the euphemisms used by some writers who substitute *métis* (French) and *mestizo* (Spanish) for "mixed blood." These are curious choices since both terms translate to "mixed blood" (and also can be understood as "half-breed" or "half-caste"). Also, foreign-language expressions such as these carry potentially confusing ethnic implications. The ethnohistorian Greg O'Brien has suggested the term "bicultural," although this conjures an image of a person equally steeped in the cultures of both parents. As we will observe, such individuals were nearly always the offspring of European traders living with Indian women in strongly matrilineal societies. I would argue that, culturally, these people were Indians with European surnames.[6]

The names of tribes and individuals in the narratives present a different set of problems. Tribal names, especially for the smaller groups, were often supplied to Europeans by native informants who were not members of the groups under discussion. Therefore, the recorded tribal name may not be the name by which members of that tribe called themselves, but another name, sometimes derisive, used by neighboring groups. For example, the ethnologist James Mooney points out that members of the Biloxi tribe called themselves "Taneks" (meaning "first people") in their Siouan language. The origin and meaning of the term "Biloxi" are unknown. Neighboring tribes used the expression in reference to the Taneks in 1699, and, without the Taneks having any say in the matter, Biloxi became their ethnic identification.[7] It is worth noting that, within confederacies, constituent groups considered their identity to be that of their own group. Patricia Galloway has noted that the French sometimes viewed constituent groups within confederacies as separate tribal units, for example, the Concha group within the Choctaw confederacy.[8] Like tribal names, variations abound in spellings of village names and the names of individuals, and translations from French or Spanish sources into English introduce still further variations. Confusion also arises in distinguishing between personal or warrior names and office titles. Galloway has pointed out perhaps the best-known example of this in the famous eighteenth-century Choctaw called Red Shoe, a title equivalent to "war chief" carried by several other individuals mentioned in the narratives.[9] As will be seen, names like Red Shoe held meanings to the Indians who used them that were often quite at odds with the vivid images that these words invoke for twenty-first-century English-speaking readers.

For some of the Mississippi tribes, such as the Amylcous and Bayacchytos, their names are all we have to point to their existence. As we shall see, the Mississippi region was for a time a refuge of last resort for many small tribal groups in the late seventeenth century, and an unknown number of them undoubtedly fell victim to disease or slave raids and vanished before La Salle, Iberville, and the missionaries arrived. In the pages that follow, readers will encounter familiar tribal names long associated with Mississippi, including the Natchez, Chickasaws, Choctaws, Yazoos, Biloxis, and Pascagoulas, as well as lesser known tribes such as the Chakchiumas, Ibitoupas, Taposas, Ofos, Koroas, Tious, Grigras, Moctoby/Capinans, Choulas, Colapissas, and Etouchocos. My study also includes tribes that may not be readily associated with Mississippi, but nonetheless figure importantly in the region's history, such as the Alabamas, Tunicas, Quapaws, Taensas, and Houmas.

As might be expected, using Mississippi's state boundary lines as the geographical limits of this study presents problems. The native people of this region dwelled upon a much larger stage. Therefore, in order to create a meaningful narrative it is necessary to look beyond these boundaries, especially when discussing critical developments in the Lower Mississippi Valley and along the lower reaches of the Pearl and Tombigbee drainages. Some of the tribes associated with Mississippi dwelled on the state's periphery, technically outside of the boundary lines. This is especially true of the Mobile Bay area, adjacent to Mississippi's southeastern corner. Here several small tribes coalesced around the French colonial settlement, some of whom eventually joined the sprawling Choctaw confederacy. On the Mississippi River, tribes on the west bank, particularly the Quapaws, Taensas, Chitimachas, and a branch of the Koroas, interacted in important ways with the groups across the river.

Similarly, we must ignore the thirty-first parallel, which defines the southern borders of Wilkinson, Amite, Pike, Walthall, and Marion counties, in order to discuss the historical roles of the Colapissas, Houmas, and post-1706 Tunicas.

At present, scholars recognize four distinct language families represented in the Mississippi region at the beginning of the eighteenth century: Muskogean, Natchez or Natchezan, Tunican, and Siouan. Muskogean languages, spoken by the Choctaws, Chickasaws, Alabamas, and several others, were the most widely spoken among the tribes under discussion here. Scholars further distinguish Western Muskogean from the Eastern Muskogean languages spoken by some of the groups in the Creek confederacy. The ethnic groups that came together to form the Choctaw confederacy spoke a variety of Western Muskogean languages that were probably not mutually intelligible. A group from southwest Mississippi that coalesced in the southern part of the Choctaw confederacy known as "Sixtowns" may have been Natchez speakers.[10] As the Choctaw confederacy took shape, the version of Muskogean spoken by the people living in the northern part of the tribe's territory eventually became the accepted language throughout the Choctaw homeland.[11] By the mid-1700s, as small refugee populations sought protection by attaching themselves to larger groups, the Chickasaws also became a multiethnic assemblage comprised of a core Chickasaw population and adopted remnants of other tribes, including some Natchez, Tunican, and Siouan speakers.[12]

Natchez is considered a language isolate, although both Natchez and Muskogean languages lack the "*r*" sound, indicating a possible distant connection between these language families. The Taensas, whose villages were about twenty-five miles upriver from the Natchez, are the only other tribe in the area securely documented as Natchez speakers. The Avoyels, a small group living on the Red River near present-day Marksville, Louisiana, may have also spoken Natchez. A colonial reference to the Avoyels as "Little Taensas" implies a linguistic connection with the Taensas and, by extension, with the Natchez.[13]

Tunican is named for the Tunica tribe, first documented along the lower Yazoo River in 1698. The Tious and Grigras living with the Natchez in the early eighteenth century were probable Tunican-speaking groups. In contrast to Natchez and Muskogean, the Tunican languages had the "*r*" sound, a distinction noted by French colonists. Another probable Tunican-speaking group, the Koroas, lived several miles downriver from the Natchez when La Salle visited the area in 1682, but they left this location prior to 1700. The Yazoo language included the "*r*" sound and thus may have also been related to Tunican.[14] Other possible Tunican-speaking tribes in the region include the Chitimachas and Atakapas.[15] Groups speaking Tunican languages have sometimes been identified as immigrants into the Mississippi region from present-day north-eastern and west-central Arkansas.[16]

Mississippi's Siouan-speaking tribes, the Biloxis and Ofos, along with the neighboring Quapaws, were immigrants with ties to Siouan groups in the Great Lakes area and in the upper Ohio Valley. Historians attribute the movement of these Siouan-speaking groups into the Lower Mississippi Valley to the violence associated with the expansion of the Iroquois confederacy in the seventeenth century, which itself was instigated by competition between colonial Europeans in the Northeast.[17] As mentioned above, the Biloxis are saddled with a tribal name provided by their neighbors. The story behind the Ofos' name is similar. They are sometimes referred to as the Ofogoulas. The "goula" suffix is a variation of the Choctaw word "*oklah*," meaning people. "Ofo" itself is a variation of the Choctaw word "*ofi*," meaning dog, hence the enigmatic Muskogean appellation "dog people." The Ouispés were a tribal group whose village was sometimes placed near the Ofo village in colonial maps of the lower Yazoo River. Some scholars have suggested that these two were the same ethnic group identified variously by a Tunican name (Ouispé) and a Muskogean name (Ofogoula). They have both also been identified with the Siouan-speaking tribe called the Mosopeleas, first documented in southwestern Ohio.[18]

Language affiliations for many of the other Mississippi tribes are uncertain, in part because these groups routinely conversed with the French in the Mobilian jargon, a lingua franca based on Western Muskogean. The origin of Mobilian is a matter of debate. The jargon may have developed as a way for native populations in the Mobile and Gulf Coast area to interact with each other and with the incoming French.[19] The historian and archaeologist Hiram F. Gregory points out that the use of Mobilian would have also supported taboos against sharing one's language with outsiders.[20]

Within the restrictions of Mississippi's boundaries, documentation exists for as many as twenty-three different native ethnic groups residing in this region in the early eighteenth century; however, only one, the Mississippi Band of Choctaw Indians, remains today. My purpose in writing this book is to illuminate the story of what happened to bring about such profound change. In doing so, I emphasize the diversity and complexity of the native societies that lived here. Likewise, this study reaches beyond description, drawing on the work of ethnohistorians such as Patricia Galloway, Greg O'Brien, and Robbie Ethridge to interpret the interactions between the many tribal societies and their relationships with the Europeans who came to live among them and ultimately to dominate their lives.

The book's chapters are organized in a more or less chronological narrative, beginning with the evidence for the earliest prehistoric inhabitants of the region, the Paleo Indians, and ending with the forced removal of most of Mississippi's American Indians in the early nineteenth century. Chapter 1 is about the sequence of prehistoric cultures of the region. From the waning of the last Ice Age, early southeastern Indian populations successfully adapted to climate fluctuations and a changing environment. Hunters and gatherers found ways to thrive in the evolving forests and prairies. The Mississippi River and the state's other familiar drainage systems assumed their modern courses, and the Gulf sea level rose to form the present coastline. An increasing concentration on agriculture and technological developments such as clay pottery and the advent of the bow and arrow culminated in the ostentatious mound-building civilizations that flourished here in the final centuries before European contact. Mississippi's prehistoric past is a rich mosaic of archaeological cultures, and this broad subject, covered here in summary fashion, deserves its own book-length treatment. My review of this material will hopefully steer readers to the many books and reports in the bibliography that explore this subject in detail.

In the second chapter, I sketch the record of early European contact with the native people of the Mississippi region, from intermittent Spanish exploration along the Gulf Coast in the early sixteenth century through the beginning of French Louisiana at the end of the seventeenth century. Called the Protohistoric period, these two centuries are a time of mystery. Debates continue over causes of the sweeping demographic changes that occurred between the De Soto invasion and La Salle's Mississippi River voyage. Woven into the De Soto chronicles is our first glimpse of the probable ancestors of some of the region's eighteenth-century tribes such as the Chickasaws, Chakchiumas, and Alabamas, along with accounts of powerful Mississippi Valley chiefdoms with exotic names like Quizquiz and Quigualtam.

In Chapter 3 we see how the Indian slave trade initiated by the Carolina English triggered intertribal violence across the Southeast. Human slaves and deerskins became the currency that pulled the Mississippi Indians into the Atlantic market economy, the source of a seductive new material culture that included guns, ammunition, gunpowder, blankets, metal tools, liquor, and European clothing. During this volatile period, the French followed up La Salle's adventure by establishing a colonial foothold on the Gulf Coast, setting the stage for sixty years of competition with England for control of the Mississippi region. Positioned between these two European powers, the Indians of the Southeast incorporated the ensuing client warfare into their social and political traditions and found ways to profit by playing the colonial administrations against each other. It was a dangerous game fraught with potential for disaster. In addition to the human loss through fighting and enslavement, the slave trade helped to spread the Southeast's first documented smallpox epidemic from Virginia across to the Mississippi River. This dark period in Mississippi history came to an end in 1715 when the Yamasee War brought about the collapse of the Indian slave trade.

Chapter 4 covers the rise of the deerskin trade and more than forty years of bitter client warfare among the Mississippi tribes. This period saw the privatization of France's colonial venture and proliferation of French settlements in the Lower Mississippi Valley, an initiative abruptly halted by the violence at the Natchez and Yazoo posts in 1729. These clashes led directly to the futile French campaigns against the Chickasaws in the 1730s. French and English competition for the allegiance of the Choctaws, the most powerful military force in the region, helped to fuel the catastrophic and enigmatic Choctaw civil war, a unique and still poorly understood episode in Mississippi history. The French and Indian War finally decided the European contest for North America in England's favor and signaled the beginning of the end of the Indians' game of playing colonial powers against one another.

The final decades of the eighteenth century are covered in chapter 5. The departure of the French from the area after the Treaty of Paris compelled Mississippi's tribal groups in opposition to the English to migrate across the Mississippi River to that part of Louisiana under Spanish dominion. The exodus included the Biloxis, Pascagoulas, Houmas, Colapissas, Tunicas, and a large number of Choctaws. Choctaws and Chickasaws remaining in their homelands endeavored to sustain a dwindling deerskin trade and maintain their status as nations. The American Revolution swept England out of the picture, and the Spanish soon lost their hold on the region, leaving the Indians to face an American government intent on westward expansion. For the first time, the chiefs had to contend with treaty conferences and initial talk of land cessions.

Through the sequence of treaties spanning less than forty years, described in chapter 6, U.S. commissioners such as Thomas Hinds and Andrew Jackson employed bribery and threats to coerce the Choctaws and Chickasaws to surrender all of their tribal land in Mississippi. (Appendixes provide the text of the Treaty of Dancing Rabbit Creek and the Treaty of Pontotoc Creek, the respective Choctaw and Chickasaw removal treaties.) While contending with the relentless demands for land cessions, the tribes provided the U.S. government with military support in the Redstick War and made use of Protestant missionary schools to better prepare their children for an uncertain future. The options of the Chickasaws and Choctaws began to diminish when the Mississippi state legislature supported the federal removal effort with acts in 1829 and 1830, which placed the tribes under state law. The federal officials who orchestrated Indian removal claimed that they were saving the tribes from annihilation. This sentiment may well have been genuine, but by opening up a vast amount of agricultural land in the Southeast, Indian removal meshed conveniently with the United States' accelerating economic engine fueled by the cotton boom and the profits of the interstate African American slave trade. Economic considerations aside, removal also assuaged racial concerns of whites who nurtured the stereotype of the drunken and intractable savage. In the end, whether altruistic, greed-driven, or purely racial, the political forces rushing to effect removal found it expedient to disregard the degree to which the Indians had conformed to the lifeways of white frontier society.

Article 14 of the Treaty of Dancing Rabbit Creek between the United States and the Choctaws provided a way for tribal members to remain in Mississippi and receive land allotments. Although relatively few Choctaws were able to overcome bureaucratic obstacles and take advantage of this provision, those families that stayed in Mississippi formed the community that eventually became today's Mississippi Band of Choctaw Indians. In the epilogue, I summarize their story of perseverance against racism and poverty, a story shared by Mississippi's expatriate tribes who managed to hold on to their identity as Oklahoma Choctaws, Louisiana Choctaws, Chickasaws, Houmas, Tunicas, and Biloxis. During the nineteenth and twentieth centuries, the U.S. government tightened its control over American Indians through a series of laws that reneged on removal treaty promises and further eroded tribal languages and traditions. I provide summaries of these laws, which reflect Washington's cumbersome attempts to manage the so-called Indian problem.

Although chapters 2 through 6 covering the colonial and early American periods are presented as a history, I found it hard to tell this story without departing occasionally from the historical narrative to discuss cultural issues such as appearance, social organization, settlement patterning, and ceremonial activities. The history of these people is, after all, more than just a timeline of confrontations, commerce, epidemics, wars, and treaties. The reader should not view these cultural accounts as static portraits, but rather as snapshots of traditions in transition. They are important because the spiritual and social lives of the Natchez, Chickasaws, Choctaws, and Mississippi's other native groups had a bearing on their interaction with each other, with Europeans, and finally with citizens of Mississippi and the American government.

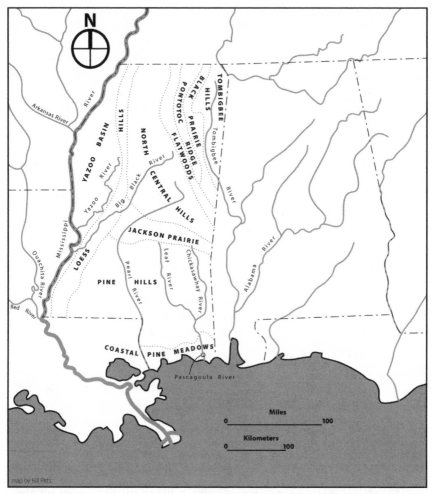

Figure 1. The Mississippi region showing major river systems and physiographic zones. (Based upon Cross et al., *Atlas of Mississippi*, 3–7, 20–21, 81–84)

Chapter 1.

MISSISSIPPI INDIANS IN PREHISTORY

The intriguing story of Mississippi's native people before historic contact is the hard-won result of a century of archaeological investigations. The amount of information that has been compiled about the state's prehistory is truly remarkable given the widespread destruction of archaeological sites from agricultural and urban development. Archaeologists have found that Mississippi was home to a succession of prehistoric American Indian cultures stretching back at least 12,000 years.

Mississippi's diversity of physiographic regions and its network of rivers and streams influenced prehistoric settlement patterns, resulting in three distinct centers of cultural development within the state: the Mississippi River valley, the upper Tombigbee River valley, and the Gulf Coast (Figures 1 and 2). During much of Mississippi's prehistory, these three regions were more connected with cultural developments occurring outside of the state than with each other. The Mississippi River was, of course, a major factor influencing settlement by creating in the Yazoo Basin a floodplain environment favorable for hunting, fishing, and gathering, and, in late prehistoric times, for agriculture. The vast bottomland forest, characterized by cypress, gum, and oak, which once covered the floodplain, stood in contrast with the predominantly oak-hickory forest supported by the Loess Hills that form the eastern border of the Yazoo Basin and extend southward into Louisiana. The Loess Hills, composed of fine-grained, wind-deposited soil, offered advantageous settlement opportunities for exploiting both the uplands and the floodplain. To the south of the Yazoo Basin, the Loess Hills are sometimes referred to as the "Natchez Bluffs," reflecting late prehistoric and early historic cultural development in that area. The drainages of the Big Black and Pearl rivers form important settlement locales in the central and southern part of the state, rising in the North Central Hills and traversing the Jackson Prairie and Pine Hills physiographic zones. To the south along Mississippi's Gulf Coast, native settlements exploited the rich estuaries of the Pearl, Pascagoula, and smaller streams. In the northeastern quadrant of Mississippi, the north-south-aligned

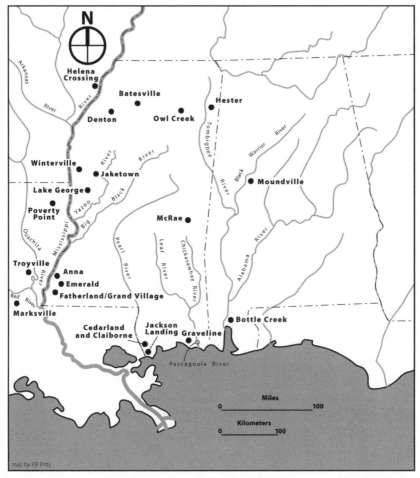

Figure 2. Locations of some of the archaeological sites mentioned in the text. (Based upon Blitz, "The McRae Mound," Figure 1; Blitz and Mann, *Fisherfolk*, Figure 4.8.; Brown, "Prehistory of the Gulf Coastal Plain," Figure 1; Galloway, *Choctaw Genesis*, Figure 2.2.; Kidder, "Prehistory of the Lower Mississippi Valley after 800 B.C.")

Pontotoc Ridge forms the state's interior divide between the valleys of the Mississippi and Tombigbee rivers. Prehistoric settlement in the northeastern part of the state was influenced by five contrasting physiographic zones that extend generally north-south, paralleling the Tombigbee River valley. In this area, the Tombigbee Hills, Black Prairie, Pontotoc Ridge, Flatwoods, and North Central Hills are distinguished by a variety of soil types that support contrasting vegetation zones.[1]

EARLY PALEOINDIAN PERIOD (10,000–8500 B.C.)[2]

Migratory people of the Clovis culture entered Mississippi about 10,000 B.C.[3] The best archaeological evidence for these early Mississippians is their formidable stone spear points (called Clovis after their initial discovery near Clovis, New Mexico). Clovis points are found throughout the United States; the earliest examples discovered in Mississippi average 2.5 inches in length, with some specimens as long as 6 inches.[4] Two of the Clovis points' most distinctive characteristics are their bifacial fluted design and the display of flintknapping skill evident in their manufacture.[5] Based upon the low number of Clovis points found in Mississippi—less than 150—archaeologists have concluded that the human populations were quite small.[6] A number of early Clovis points found in the state were made of flint or chert from sources in northern Alabama and middle Tennessee,[7] leading Mississippi archaeologist Samuel O. McGahey to suggest that Clovis-wielding Paleoindians may have arrived in Mississippi from the Tennessee River valley.[8] McGahey and other archaeologists acknowledge the possible presence of pre-Clovis people in the Southeast; however, no pre-Clovis sites are known in Mississippi, and the sites and artifacts in other states purporting to represent these early populations have met with only limited acceptance.[9]

The Clovis hunter-gatherers ranged over a Mississippi landscape that was in transition from an Ice Age boreal forest to woodlands more closely resembling those of today. Around 10,000 B.C. the mixed conifers and northern hardwoods of the previous climate regime were giving way to oak/hickory/southern pine timber in the uplands and cypress/gum stands in lowlands along river valleys.[10] According to pollen studies, the northern Mississippi uplands during the period ca. 10,000–8000 B.C. supported a forest that was predominantly cool-adapted beech, with hornbeam, oak, hickory, elm, and ash. By 8000–6400 B.C. hickories and oaks were dominant in this area.[11]

At this time, the Mississippi River was still in its braided stream configuration, seen as an intertwining network of diverging and converging watercourses interspersed with gravel bars, following a general southward course down through the Yazoo Basin, somewhat east of its present bed.[12] Two large braided stream surfaces coinciding with the Paleoindian period have been identified in this area: one in the west-central part of the Yazoo Basin, between the Sunflower and Mississippi rivers, and the other along the base of the Loess Hills in the Tallahatchie River drainage. South of Vicksburg, the Mississippi River made its way to the Gulf of Mexico by way of the Atchafalaya Basin.[13]

In the western United States, Clovis points have been found in direct association with the remains of late Pleistocene megafauna such as mammoth and mastodon;[14] however, no such sites are known in Mississippi.[15] To date the only states in the eastern United States with confirmed megafauna/Paleoindian interaction are Arkansas, Missouri, Ohio, Tennessee, and Florida.[16] The "Natchez Pelvis," a human bone unearthed near Natchez in the early 1800s in close proximity to fossils of ground sloth, mastodon, and other late Pleistocene animals, was once thought to date to this time period: however, recent radiocarbon results date the bone to the Middle Archaic period (see below).[17] Just when the mammoth, mastodon, and other megafauna species disappeared from Mississippi is not known. These animals were likely gone from the state by ca. 10,000 B.C.[18]

To date no archaeological sites relating to early Paleoindian subsistence have been discovered in Mississippi or in surrounding states. The presence of oak forests over much of Mississippi during this period makes it seem likely that Clovis hunters found plenty of deer and smaller mammals to hunt. It is also probable that these early hunters were experimenting with wild plant foods. In the absence of any consistent data, archaeologists continue to debate the settlement strategy of Clovis people in the Southeast. Likely scenarios include small hunter-gatherer bands ranging out from semipermanent base camps versus more nomadic, wider-ranging units favoring temporary camps.[19] In addition to spear points, the tool kits of the Clovis Paleoindians included a variety of stone implements suitable for working with bone and wood, such as end-scrapers, side-scrapers, and gravers. Based upon the limited archaeological data produced thus far, it seems that early Paleoindians in Mississippi favored the Loess Hills, perhaps using these uplands as a base from which to exploit the adjacent Mississippi River floodplain. Clovis points have also been recovered from sites in the upper Tombigbee valley, from southeastern Mississippi, and from exposed braided stream surfaces in the Yazoo Basin.[20]

LATE PALEOINDIAN AND EARLY ARCHAIC PERIODS (8500–6000 B.C.)

Beginning with the introduction of the fluted Cumberland point, a variant of Clovis, the periods known as Late Paleoindian and the succeeding Early Archaic are characterized by a proliferation of regional point types, more use of local stone sources, and an increased number of archaeological sites, probably pointing to an expanding population.[21] Other regional Clovis variants include the Beaver Lake, Quad, Coldwater, Hinds, and Arkabutla point types.[22] McGahey believes that the Late Paleoindian and Early Archaic periods represent a continuum in Mississippi in terms of stone-working technology, perhaps best documented at the Hester site in Monroe County in the northeastern section of the state.[23]

The earliest consistent use of the Hester site was by the people who made the spear point type known as Dalton (ca. 8500–7900 B.C.). Dalton points, found throughout the state, average 1.75 inches in length and range up to 3 inches in length.[24] Whereas the distribution of Clovis points is nationwide, Dalton is a midwestern/southeastern point type that has been found in the area from Missouri to Florida.[25] The Dalton's serrated edges indicate that it probably functioned as a hafted knife as well as a spear point. The innovation of heat-treating chert for projectile point manufacture was introduced during the Dalton era, making less-suitable local varieties of stone easier to flake.[26] Mississippi archaeologist Samuel O. Brookes, who directed the excavations at the Hester site, determined that the Dalton people probably used the location as a "hunting-butchering station," presumably to process deer kills, although no animal bones were recovered from the site.[27] Based upon investigations in Mississippi and surrounding states, archaeologists have concluded that the Dalton people probably lived in small bands or extended families that exploited familiar territories while moving between a series of temporary campsites.[28] In addition to serrated spear point/knives, the Dalton component at Hester contained an impressive array of stone tools for working with wood and bone, including abraders, burins, end- and side-scrapers, gravers, spokeshaves, and utilized flakes.[29] Following the Dalton occupation, Hester was used more intensively—possibly as a base camp—for a succession of Early Archaic groups, which manufactured regional point types such as Big Sandy, Greenbrier, Decatur, Pine Tree, and Hardin/Lost Lake, as well as adzes that suggest a further emphasis on woodworking.[30]

Fragments of hickory nuts, walnuts, and hackberries were recovered from all of the occupational components at Hester, including Dalton, demonstrating that people camping there were exploiting the local hardwood forest. Other botanical fragments from Hester and neighboring sites include acorn and wild plum.[31] Several pitted stones (sometimes referred to as "nutting stones") found at Hester may have been used to process these nuts and fruits.[32] According to McGahey, holes in the ground that may have functioned as storage containers first appear in some of these Early Archaic sites.[33] Although no animal bones have been found at Hester and other Early Archaic sites in Mississippi due to poor preservation conditions, bone recovered from the Stanfield-Worley bluff shelter in nearby Colbert County, Alabama, indicates that Early Archaic hunters focused on white-tailed deer and a variety of smaller animals.[34]

Like the Paleoindians who preceded them, Early Archaic groups probably moved about in bands comprised of between 50 and 150 people that may have been linked to larger groups numbering between 500 and 1,500. Periodic contact with the larger group, perhaps at a seasonal location, could have allowed the exchange of information and provided mating possibilities. (These inferences about Early Archaic life are loosely based on ethnographic analogy, due to insufficient archaeological data.)[35] Sites associated with the Late Paleoindian and Early Archaic periods indicate widespread settlement in Mississippi, with concentrations in the Yazoo Basin, Loess Hills, and the drainages of the Pearl, Pascagoula, and Tombigbee rivers.[36]

According to geologist Roger T. Saucier, the Mississippi River made the transition from a braided stream to a meandering river sometime between 7900 and 7800 B.C. With the change to a meandering water course, the Mississippi River began its characteristic pattern of periodically shifting its channel, resulting in the formation of characteristic oxbow cutoff lakes. This process set in motion the sequence in which cutoff lakes evolve into backswamp, creating a rich habitat for wildlife.[37] During the period from ca. 7000 to 6000 B.C., the river's main channel hugged the Loess Hills on the eastern side of the Yazoo Basin between the present cities of Greenwood and Vicksburg. South of Vicksburg, the Mississippi River angled away from the Loess Hills toward the west and followed a course down through the Bayou Teche drainage, somewhat west of the present Atchafalaya River, passing just east of Lafayette, Louisiana, and entering the Gulf in the vicinity of Vermillion Bay.[38] On the eastern side of the state, the Tombigbee River and its tributaries flowed through more rugged, upland terrain that restricted meandering and the development of floodplain habitat.

MIDDLE ARCHAIC PERIOD (6000–3000 B.C.)

Post–Ice Age warming climaxed with the onset of a ca. 3000-year period of warmer and drier weather conditions, with seasonal temperatures in the Southeast somewhat more extreme than those of today. This warmer period, which scientists have identified as the Hypsithermal or Altithermal, coincides with the Middle Archaic archaeological period.[39] As would be

expected, environmental changes accompanied the drier weather conditions, with southern pine replacing oak-hickory forests in some upland areas. Reduced rainfall lowered lake levels and slowed stream flow. There is
also some indication of heightened El Niño activity during the Hypsithermal,
which would have occasionally caused erratic weather episodes and flooding.
Archaeologists generally view this period as having been a time of stress on
populations that had become adapted to the previous, more favorable post-
glacial conditions. Middle Archaic archaeological site distribution indicates
that people may have moved out of the uplands down into the river valleys
and coastal areas, where there was evidently competition for food resources.
Although probably not indicative of any widespread violence, spear points
have occasionally been found imbedded in human skeletal material from this
period.[40]

In addition to changes in weather and patterns of human adaptation, the
Middle Archaic period saw a decline in the artistry of projectile point manufacture. In contrast to the workmanship of the Early Archaic makers, whose
spear points, like the preceding Clovis and Dalton points, were perhaps made
to a higher standard than the hunting task demanded, the Middle Archaic
people made do with less sophisticated weapons.[41] McGahey suggests that
the decline in projectile point workmanship at this time may be linked to an
increasing emphasis on fishing and the gathering of wild plant foods.[42] Even
with this diversification of subsistence, regional varieties of projectile point
types continued to appear, with considerable variation over time in both size
and the treatment of the base or hafted end. Flaked stone tools also exhibit
evidence of frequent recycling that resulted in their continued use for varied
purposes. The trend toward cruder flaked tools during this period is offset
by the artistic sophistication shown in the grinding, polishing, and drilling
of stone such as red jasper, quartzite, limonite, and fine-grained sandstone.
Indeed, Mississippi seems to have been at the forefront in this prehistoric
lapidary technology. Ground stone implements include functional tools like
axes and more ritualistic items such as effigy beads.[43]

The stone tool culture of the Middle Archaic is well documented at the
Denton site in Quitman County, excavated by Mississippi archaeologist John
M. Connaway in 1969 with assistance from McGahey and Brookes. Like so
many other habitation sites in the Mississippi River floodplain, the Denton
site is located on a natural levee of an abandoned meander channel. The natural levees that formed beside the active channels of rivers and streams were
the highest elevations in the Yazoo Basin. These levees, or "ridges" as they are
sometimes called, were built up as the river periodically overtopped its banks,

depositing part of its sediment load.[44] The sandier and more fertile soils are found on the natural levees, while the off-levee, backswamp or bottomland areas are composed of more clayey soils.[45] Although the natural levees beside the Mississippi River's active channel offered the highest ground in the floodplain, the prehistoric residents of the Yazoo Basin knew better than to establish their home sites on these ridges; the Mississippi River's ever-shifting channel would have made bank-side living too precarious. Instead, the people sought out the levees of recently abandoned channels, which offered suitable high ground next to the quieter bayous and lakes that occupied the Mississippi River's old bed.[46]

Radiocarbon dates for the Denton site place its occupation around 3300 B.C. In addition to Middle Archaic projectile points and a wide variety of flaked tools, such as adzes, choppers, scrapers, and drills, the Denton site contained ground- and pecked-stone axes and metates (mortar and pestle tools for processing seeds and other plant material). There was also an array of ground and polished objects of questionable function, which have been identified by archaeologists for descriptive purposes as gorgets and bannerstones. Perhaps most interesting are the ground and drilled zoomorphic (animal-shaped) effigy beads, many with sleek, streamlined shapes that seem to vaguely resemble insects, mammals, or birds. The beads were made from a variety of exotic stones, including jasper, quartzite, trachyte, felsite, and hematite. Significantly, approximately 70 percent of all of the recorded zoomorphic beads of this type have been found in Mississippi. Raw material for stone beads was available in many areas, and manufacturing of these items took place in northwestern and southwestern Mississippi and in northeastern Louisiana.[47]

Although no animal bone was recovered there, the Denton site yielded some evidence of plant foods, including hickory, walnut, acorn, butternut, and persimmon.[48] Findings at other Middle Archaic sites around the Southeast indicate that people were hunting deer and smaller animals, beginning to make use of gourds and wild squash, and collecting the seeds of native plants such as chenopodium.[49] The presence at Denton of archaeological features possibly representing storage pits and house posts suggests a semipermanent occupation.[50]

Shell midden mounds found along many rivers and streams in Mississippi and other states in the region are another indication of a more sedentary lifestyle during this period.[51] Seasonal exploitation of freshwater shellfish to augment hunting and gathering began around 6000 B.C.[52] According to Mississippi archaeologist Evan Peacock, the shallow stream conditions during the period of warm, dry conditions provided a good habitat for mussels and made it relatively easy for people to gather them.[53]

In addition to shell mounds, earthen mounds first appear during the Middle Archaic period, indicating a growing emphasis on ceremonialism and strong ties to particular places for spiritual reasons. To date the oldest ceremonial earthworks identified in the eastern United States are found in Louisiana: Watson Brake, a complex comprised of eleven mounds near Monroe (ca. 4000–3500 B.C.); Monte Sano Mound near Baton Rouge (ca. 4000 B.C.); Hornsby Mound in St. Helena Parish (ca. 3000 B.C.); and two mounds on the Louisiana State University campus (ca. 3000–2500 B.C.).[54] To date the Paxton Mound in Lincoln County (ca. 3000 B.C.) is the only securely documented Middle Archaic mound in Mississippi.[55] Although mound construction requires considerable communal effort and organization, archaeologists are not ready to ascribe to these early mound builders the social complexity and stratified ranking of later mound-building societies. The Middle Archaic mound builders are considered to have been egalitarian groups who, like their predecessors, followed a migratory lifestyle, perhaps returning to the mound sites on a seasonal basis.[56] As will be seen in the Late Archaic period, the stone-working technology exemplified by the Denton site and the nascent mound building would soon coalesce into a sophisticated, preagricultural civilization with a substantial presence in Mississippi, as well as a long-distance trade network stretching from the Great Lakes to the Gulf of Mexico.

LATE ARCHAIC PERIOD (3000–800 B.C.)[57]

With the waning of the Hypsithermal and a shift toward somewhat cooler and wetter weather, the state's wetlands expanded, increasing the native people's opportunities to obtain fish, swamp-adapted game, and waterfowl.[58] Shellfish use also increased, and just to the north of Mississippi a cultural phenomenon known as the Shell Mound Archaic, in which mollusk shells were mounded in places to thicknesses of forty feet, developed during the Late Archaic period along the Tennessee River drainage. Many of these shell mounds contain packed-clay house floors, hearths, and posthole features, indicating that shelters were periodically erected on the shell heaps. Archaeologists speculate that the residents of these shelters abandoned them during the winter when flooding threatened the area and reoccupied them in the spring.[59] Shell Mound Archaic mounds also served a ceremonial purpose as burial sites for people and dogs. Archaeologist Cheryl Claassen has suggested that perhaps the people collected shellfish as fill material for mound building, using the mollusks they contained as an incidental food source. Shell mound sites contain ample evidence that the people consumed food from a variety of sources, including deer, hickory nuts, fish, and turtle.[60]

Around 2500 B.C. people on the Gulf Coast began exploiting saltwater mollusks in the game-rich estuaries like that of the Pearl River.[61] The sea level, which had risen steadily since the end of the Ice Age, stabilized around this time at close to the present level, making coastal living feasible.[62] Two important archaeological sites that reflect the early utilization of the Pearl River estuary are the Cedarland and Claiborne sites in Hancock County. The Cedarland site, which contained an oyster midden associated with Late Archaic artifacts, was apparently occupied first, beginning sometime between 2500 and 2000 B.C. The site was abandoned around 2000 B.C., at approximately the same time that the Claiborne site, some fifty-five yards to the south, was first inhabited. In contrast to Cedarland, Claiborne's shell midden contained both oysters and clams along with numerous artifacts linking the site to the burgeoning Poverty Point culture.[63]

At its peak, between 1500 and 1000 B.C., the Poverty Point culture developed a vast trade network in exotic stone and other materials derived from sources throughout the middle part of the present-day United States.[64] Trade goods included copper, novaculite, hematite, magnetite, quartz crystal, steatite, and various other fine-grained cherts, flints, sandstone, and quartzite. People used canoes to transport most of these materials on streams and rivers to distribution centers in the Lower Mississippi Valley.[65] The great Poverty Point site itself, situated in northeastern Louisiana on Maçon Bayou near the town of Epps, appears to have been the preeminent center of all of this trade activity; however, the Jaketown site north of Belzoni in the Yazoo Basin and the aforementioned Claiborne site at the mouth of the Pearl River also served as important trading centers.

Poverty Point sites can be recognized, in part, by the presence of several diagnostic artifacts. Clarence H. Webb, who defined the Poverty Point culture, lists the "primary" diagnostics as: tubular pipes, stone vessels, crudely made greenstone hoes or celts, jasper beads, clay figurines, microflints, hematite or magnetite plummets, and the fired-clay cooking balls known as Poverty Point objects.[66] Poverty Point objects are roughly the size of chicken eggs and come in many different shapes and decorative treatments. Archaeological investigations at numerous sites from this period show that the cooking balls lined earth ovens and radiated heat for baking. The culture's lapidary industry is reminiscent of the high level of artistry at the Denton site.[67] Archaeological sites indicate that the exotic goods flowing around the Poverty Point trade network were used by the general populace living near the big distribution centers instead of being hoarded by elite leaders or chiefs.[68]

Archaeologists continue to debate the nature of the social system that orchestrated this elaborate exchange system and left behind such monumental earthworks. A chiefdom-level society, similar to those of the much later Mississippi period, may have influenced the accomplishments of the Poverty Point culture, or perhaps the social structure was more egalitarian, like that assumed for the preceding Archaic populations.[69] Opinions also differ on the use and occupation of the culture's presumed hub, the Poverty Point site. Some view the site as the scene of periodic gatherings resembling seasonal trade fairs, while others see it as a town with year-round occupation.[70]

Similar questions surround the Jaketown site, a major Poverty Point regional center in the Yazoo Basin. Jaketown is situated on the west side of Wasp Lake, which occupies a meander cutoff of the Yazoo River.[71] The site once contained as many as twelve mounds, although most of these earthworks have been leveled by farming and highway construction.[72] The renowned Lower Mississippi Valley archaeologists James B. Griffin, Philip Phillips, and James A. Ford worked at Jaketown during the 1940s and discovered that the site contained the "entire ceramic chronology from Tchula to Mississippian," a more or less continuous occupation span of over 2,000 years. Louisiana archaeologist William G. Haag excavated at Jaketown in 1950 and confirmed the presence of a Poverty Point component below the site's ceramic sequence. A year later, Ford, Phillips, and Haag spent five months excavating at Jaketown. Their work focused on the site's Poverty Point occupation and turned up seven of Webb's eight primary Poverty Point diagnostics, missing only clay figurines. Based upon excavations at Jaketown in 2008 and 2009 by Lee J. Arco of Washington University, the site's Poverty Point occupation lasted from about 2150 to 1250 B.C., predating the earliest occupation of the Poverty Point site. Arco located two additional Poverty Point period mounds at Jaketown and noted evidence for a crevasse or flood that may have contributed to the mound center's abandonment.[73]

Numerous other sites within the Poverty Point sphere are scattered through the Yazoo Basin along the drainages of the Sunflower and Yazoo rivers, notably the Norman, Slate, and Teoc Creek sites.[74] Samuel Brookes has emphasized that, out of a multitude of Poverty Point era sites in Mississippi, only the Jaketown and Claiborne sites seem to have been participating fully in the Poverty Point trade network, based upon the array of artifacts recovered. Brookes also points out that no one knows what the Poverty Point people were shipping out of the Lower Mississippi Valley in return for the tons of exotic stone and other materials being received. The source locations of these exotic materials have yet to offer any clues. The conclusion thus far is that the commodity being exported must have been perishable items of some kind.[75]

Despite the lack of information about the inner workings of Poverty Point social organization and trade, some archaeological sites have yielded data on subsistence. At the Copes site, about eight miles south of the Poverty Point site, Mississippi archaeologist H. Edwin Jackson found evidence of a broad-based subsistence strategy utilizing mammals, birds, reptiles, amphibians, and fish. Jackson found that the local abundance of fish had much to do with the people's ability to adopt a relatively sedentary lifestyle. Plant food remains from Copes include acorns, pecans, squash, persimmon seeds, honey locust seeds, wild beans, goosefoot, and sumpweed.[76] Although no animal bone was recovered at the Teoc Creek site in the Yazoo Basin, plant food remains there consist of hickory nuts, walnuts, persimmon seeds, and acorns.[77]

The domestication of some North American plants that began in the Middle Archaic continued in the Late Archaic; however, there is little evidence for intensive experimentation with wild plants in Mississippi. To the north in present-day Tennessee and Kentucky, archaeological sites indicate manipulation of a group of native plants known by archaeologists as the "starchy seed complex." These are sunflower, marsh elder, goosefoot, maygrass, and amaranth, all probably valued for their storable seeds. Other annual seed plants such as chenopodium and sumpweed were also the focus of Late Archaic domestication efforts in some areas of the Southeast.[78]

The increasingly sedentary lifestyle of the Late Archaic seems to have placed a value on the use of containers for storage and transport. Squash and gourds, two of the earliest wild plants to be domesticated, may have been valued as much for their potential as containers as for their importance as food.[79] Evidence for cane baskets in the Late Archaic is seen in basket-impressed clay objects from Teoc Creek, Poverty Point, and other sites of the period.[80] Judging from their frequent occurrence within the Poverty Point trading sphere, bowls carved from steatite and sandstone were obviously valued highly. Hundreds of fragments and occasionally whole stone vessels are found at Poverty Point sites, while the Claiborne site held a cache of ten stone bowls.[81]

With this increasing emphasis on cooking and storage, the people of the Southeast were understandably receptive to the technology of clay pottery that appeared during the Late Archaic period. The technique for making clay pottery may have first reached the Atlantic Coastal Plain from the Caribbean Islands between about 3000 and 2500 B.C.[82] From there, communities along the Gulf Coast and inland river valleys apparently spread this important new technology westward. Fiber-tempered pottery,[83] classified as Wheeler, is documented in many of Mississippi's Poverty Point sites, including Jaketown, Teoc Creek, Norman, and Claiborne.[84] Likewise, Wheeler is found in sites in Mississippi's Tombigbee River valley at around 1300–1200 B.C.[85] In the Woodland period, pottery use became universal among the Indians of Mississippi, and the succession of archaeological cultures spanning the final 3,000 years of the state's prehistory are no longer identified only by their stone tools, but by the paste, temper, vessel shapes, and decoration of their pottery as well.

EARLY WOODLAND PERIOD (800–200 B.C.)[86]

As pottery came into widespread use in the Early Woodland period, different styles of manufacture emerged in Mississippi and surrounding states, eventually replacing the fiber-tempered ware of the Late Archaic. These new ceramic wares vary in terms of decorative treatment and tempering.[87] In the Tombigbee River valley, the Alexander/Miller I pottery group is characterized by sand-tempering. Pots were decorated by pinching the wet clay, stamping or marking the surface with shallow punctures (called "punctations") made with fingernails or implements of bone or shell, and by incising linear curved and rectangular patterns. Other decorative elements include bumps or protrusions made by punching the inside wall of the pot. Wedge-shaped feet were sometimes added to elevate the base.[88] Toward the end of the Early Woodland period, potters in the Tombigbee Valley began using fabric-impressed decorations on their sand-tempered ware.[89]

The pottery culture known as Tchefuncte is associated with much of the Lower Mississippi Valley, including the Yazoo Basin, the Louisiana Coastal Delta, and Mississippi's coastal plain. Tchefuncte pottery is usually described as being poorly fired, showing minimal preparation of the clay. Tempering is apparently absent in some examples, while others are tempered with grog (pulverized dried and fired clay). Vessels are sometimes plain, but were often decorated with incising, punctations, bone and shell stamp marks, and decorative protrusions punched from inside the pot. Some pots are red-filmed (a reddish color painted on the raw pot using a diluted clay-based pigment), and feet were sometimes added to the base.[90] In the northern Yazoo Basin, Alexander/Tchefuncte decorative elements are called Tchula.[91] The Cormorant/Withers pottery group in the northern Yazoo Basin is distinguished by fabric- and cord-impressed decorative treatment. The vessels are grog-tempered with varying amounts of sand.[92] All three pottery types are sometimes found together in Mississippi sites, especially in the Yazoo Basin and along the Gulf Coast. In southeast Mississippi, the type known as Bayou La Batre, characterized by grit tempering and scallop shell stamping, can occur with Alexander and Tchefuncte vessels.[93] There is some indication that, when sand was obtainable, it was chosen for tempering over grog.[94]

The people who made Tchefuncte pottery are assumed to be the descendants of the Poverty Point people.[95] The Tchefuncte culture occupies approximately the same territory as Poverty Point, and many Tchefuncte sites contain clay cooking balls and other Poverty Point diagnostics, indicating a connection between the two traditions.[96] Evidence for long-distance trade, however, is lacking in the wake of the now defunct Poverty Point exchange network.[97] Early Woodland period archaeological sites in the Lower Mississippi Valley show a preference for settlements close to slow-moving streams, bottomland, and coastal marshes, with upland hunting camps in the adjacent Loess Hills.[98] In southeast Mississippi, archaeologist Richard Marshall's survey of lower Archusa Creek, a tributary of the Chickasawhay River, indicates a mobile population using temporary camps from which to hunt and gather wild plant foods.[99] By the beginning of the Woodland period, the Mississippi River had moved into its modern bed, skirting the Yazoo Basin on the west and hugging the Loess Hills from Vicksburg past Natchez to the Tunica Hills. Although occupying a single channel (with several distributaries), the Mississippi River continued to actively twist and turn within its meander belt, creating numerous cutoffs and backswamp environment.[100]

The animal bones from Tchefuncte sites reflect this swamp adaptation, which appears to be a continuation of Poverty Point subsistence strategy with a heavy reliance on fish and turtle. Deer was apparently the most targeted mammal. In the coastal areas, saltwater mollusks were an important staple. Food plant remains from Tchefuncte sites indicate the use of acorns, hickory nuts, plums, grapes, persimmons, squash, and bottle gourd.[101] Although domestication efforts continued apace in other areas of the Southeast, scant evidence exists for Early Woodland native seed plant gardening in the Lower Mississippi Valley.[102] In northeast Mississippi, intensive federal and state archaeological work surrounding the construction of the Natchez Trace

Parkway and the Tennessee-Tombigbee Waterway has provided settlement evidence of a range of site types, from small, temporary camps to mound groups.[103] Here, too, is some evidence for use of domestic seed plants. People also concentrated on deer, smaller mammals, fish, and reptiles, while gathering hickory nuts, persimmons, grapes, and other wild plants.[104]

Ample discretionary time for spiritual and ceremonial activities is indicated by mound-building activity that became much more ambitious and widespread in the Woodland period. The majority of the mounds built in Mississippi during the Early Woodland period were conical burial mounds, with most of the mound-building activity taking place in the northern part of the state, from the Yazoo Basin across to the Tombigbee River. At the Batesville Mounds in Panola County, Mississippi archaeologist Jay K. Johnson has documented platform or flat-topped mound construction that began late in the Early Woodland period, signaling a significant departure from the round-topped burial mound tradition. Johnson suggests that the earthen platform may have been used periodically for communal feasting, based upon concentrations of fire-cracked rock indicative of fires and food preparation.[105]

In the transition from the Archaic to the Woodland, important information about social stratification can be drawn from funerary practices. During the Archaic period, people disposed of their dead in a variety of ways, including primary burials (body interred before decomposition), secondary burials (body decomposed elsewhere and disarticulated remains placed in a final grave), and cremations. Primary burials were interred with the body extended or flexed (fetal position). In Mississippi and the surrounding region, human burials prior to the Woodland period are sometimes accompanied by a few grave offerings, indicative of some form of funerary ritual; however, these sparse grave goods do not suggest that one person may have enjoyed higher status than anyone else.[106] Grave offerings in Early Woodland communal burial mounds and cemeteries in Mississippi are also meager, indicating a continuation of the Archaic egalitarian social organization.[107] In contrast, the Early Woodland Adena culture of eastern Kentucky operated a trade network specializing in exotic materials that served as grave offerings, signaling both the beginnings of social hierarchy and a concern for heightening the ritual activities surrounding disposal of the dead. Although Mississippi was outside the Adena sphere of influence, the succeeding Hopewell/Marksville culture, with its obsession with mortuary ceremonialism, drove developments in Mississippi during the Middle Woodland period.[108]

MIDDLE WOODLAND PERIOD (200 B.C.–A.D. 500)

"Marksville" is the term Lower Mississippi Valley archaeologists apply to the local variant of the cultural expression known as Hopewell in the Ohio River valley. Like the earlier Poverty Point exchange network, Marksville/Hopewell exchange moved primarily in canoes around the interconnected river systems of the Mississippi Valley.[109] Trade items included exotic raw materials and finished objects such as copper pan pipes and ear ornaments, human and animal shapes fashioned from copper and mica, flint blades, ground-stone axes, marine shell, quartz crystal, grizzly bear teeth, and obsidian. As mentioned above, these commodities became grave offerings accompanying the burials of high-status individuals.[110] The most elaborate Middle Woodland burial site in the region, the Helena Crossing mounds in Arkansas, just across the Mississippi River from Coahoma County, included log crypts within mounds containing items made from seashells, flint blades, copper ear ornaments and pan pipes, and wolf teeth. The mound tombs contained adults and children.[111] The burial process also involved the use of charnel houses, huts for warehousing and processing human remains prior to burial. Evidence for these structures comes from a number of Middle Woodland sites, including the Bynum and Pharr mounds on the Natchez Trace Parkway in northeastern Mississippi.[112]

Elite individuals receiving special funerary treatment during the Middle Woodland may have been comparable to the big-men and big-women documented in a number of modern-day societies. Big-men and big-women gain influence and power through their own charisma and entrepreneurial abilities. In some cases, this acquired status can temporarily elevate the big-person's lineage to encompass relatives. Unlike the inherited status seen in later Mississippi period chiefdoms, the big-person's power cannot normally be transmitted to his or her offspring.[113] In discussing the historic tribes in later chapters, we will see how big-man leaders were effective in forging alliances between tribes and with Europeans. Middle Woodland mound sites vary considerably in size and extent, indicating that chiefs of the period occasionally inspired loyalty among larger numbers than just their own lineage.

Although most archaeologists working in Mississippi recognize Hopewell influence in Middle Woodland sites across the state, debate continues over the extent of that influence versus homegrown developments.[114] In the Lower Mississippi Valley, the Hopewell exchange system is represented by the Marksville culture, named for the large mound group near Marksville, Louisiana. Situated beside an old channel of the Red River, the Marksville site contains seven mounds, both conical and platform, and circular earthen embankments. Marksville pottery is distinguished by new motifs representing contorted bird images that resemble birds of prey. The somewhat tubby-looking pots bear deeply incised lines, with stamped patterns and intricate cross-hatching near the rim.[115]

Around A.D. 200 in Mississippi's Yazoo Basin, the pottery groups known as Issaquena and Plainware became more prevalent than Marksville ceramics. Issaquena pottery is hard and durable, resulting from sophisticated preparation of the clay and an improved firing technique. These pots often lack the Marksville cross-hatching and bird motifs, and are decorated with punctations and fingernail impressions. Issaquena conical mounds and habitation sites are found in the southern Yazoo Basin and across the Mississippi River in the Tensas Basin of northeastern Louisiana. As its name implies, the Plainware Middle Woodland pottery group is characterized by undecorated vessels. This culture straddled the Mississippi River, taking in northwestern Mississippi and much of eastern Arkansas.[116]

In north-central and northeastern Mississippi, the Hopewell expression accompanies the Miller cultural sequence, with sand-tempered pottery decorated with fabric impressions and later cord impressions. The Pinson Mounds site in western Tennessee is the largest Middle Woodland mound group in the region. Along with the aforementioned Bynum and Pharr mound sites, substantial contemporary burial mound groups include the Ingomar and Miller sites. In extreme northeastern Mississippi, the Copena burial mound culture with its stamped instead of cord-impressed pottery was a localized, contemporary Hopewellian manifestation. As with other Middle Woodland cultures, platform mounds accompany conical burial mounds at a number of sites.[117]

Evan Peacock has noted an increase in the number of archaeological sites in the east-central part of the state during the Middle Woodland, especially in the North Central Hills physiographic zone that would later become the Choctaw homeland. Like the Choctaws, Middle Woodland people tended to settle on the ridge tops and terraces close to streams. According to Peacock, the region saw a marked decline in settlements by the beginning of the Mississippi period, possibly due to the concentration of populations around neighboring chiefdoms.[118] In southeast Mississippi, the McRae Mound in Clarke County produced materials associated with the Hopewell culture, including quartz crystals and a panpipe made of three wooden tubes covered with thin sheets of copper and bound together with cord.[119] Along the lower Tombigbee River, Mobile Bay, and the adjacent Gulf Coast, the Santa Rosa culture is recognized as a local Hopewellian expression with sand-tempered, stamped pottery; conical burial mounds; and much of the popular burial merchandise of the period.[120]

Besides conical and platform mounds, Middle Woodland mound building also produced numerous circular or semicircular earthworks, both in the Hopewell heartland of Ohio and in the Lower Mississippi Valley. First considered to be defensive structures and later assumed to be ceremonial in purpose, the archaeological evidence for their use is still not clear. These earthworks, referred to as enclosures, are found at several mound sites in the area, including Marksville and Pinson Mounds. In Mississippi's southern Yazoo Basin, three well-known semicircular enclosures—Spanish Fort, Little Spanish Fort, and the Leist site—are found within a few miles of each other in the vicinity of the Delta National Forest, approximately twenty miles southwest of Yazoo City. Obviously, the "fort" names derive from initial interpretations of these earthworks as being connected with warfare; however, the structures do not appear to be strategically placed to defend anything. To these should be added the Jackson Landing–Mulatto Bayou earthwork in Hancock County, near the mouth of the Pearl River. Mississippi's earthwork enclosures vary from 3 to 9 feet in height and extend from 1,500 to 3,500 feet in length. Recent studies of several earthen enclosures in the Lower Mississippi Valley have led to speculation that they were constructed and used by several groups linked by kinship or politics.[121]

Except for a burial mound investigated in Claiborne County, Marksville presence is poorly documented for the Natchez Bluffs in the southwestern part of the state.[122] Marksville living sites in the Yazoo Basin are found in both the bottomlands and adjacent uplands, while the later Issaquena settlements are primarily grouped in the southern part of the basin. Some of the Issaquena sites are large enough to be interpreted as hamlets or villages, indicating a rise in population. A maximum use settlement pattern is also seen in north Mississippi and the Tombigbee River valley, where a variety of physiographic zones are clustered. Along the Gulf Coast, communities appear to have been dividing their time between large shellfishing camps and inland stream valleys.[123]

Wild plant foods continued to be favored in the Mississippi region over domesticated native plants being grown in cultivated fields elsewhere in the Southeast. Sites provide evidence for the continued use of a wide variety of nuts, fruits, and seeds, including acorns, hickory nuts, walnuts, pecans, persimmon, wild beans, palmetto, raspberries, grape, and wild seed plants. As with previous cultures, hunting and fishing augmented gathering, with deer providing a seemingly endless source of protein, not to mention the importance of the animal's hide and antlers.[124] Stone tools perfected in the Archaic, such as scrapers, choppers, drills, and nutting/grinding stones, remained essential in the Middle Woodland, as did flint and chert spear points and knives. Point forms diminished somewhat in size and continued to vary in terms of the design of the stem or hafted end. The Middle Woodland weapons are crude and often asymmetrical in appearance, but no doubt were quite effective on deer and other game.[125] These spear or dart points were about to become obsolete, however, and hunting in the Southeast would soon make a quantitative leap—the bow and arrow was coming to Mississippi.

LATE WOODLAND PERIOD (A.D. 500–1200)

The arrival of the bow and arrow in Mississippi is marked in the archaeological record by a decrease in projectile point size from slightly over two inches in average length for Middle Woodland dart or spear points down to around one inch in length for arrow points.[126] Although it is not known how quickly hunters made the transition to the new weapon, all of the Late Woodland cultural groups in Mississippi (and throughout the Southeast) eventually adopted the new technology. The discovery of arrow wounds and points lodged in the skeletons of Late Woodland people in the central Tombigbee Valley and northern Yazoo Basin indicates that the bow and arrow was not just used for hunting game. Similar findings across the Southeast have led archaeologists to suggest that the new weapon may have contributed to conflict and aggression. These confrontations were probably more on the order of small-scale raids rather than open warfare, but the violence may have also signaled growing competition for resources.[127]

As with earlier archaeological periods, the transition to the Late Woodland is marked by noticeable changes in pottery-making, with new decorations, temper, and vessel shapes. In the Lower Mississippi Valley, Late Woodland ceramic evolution passed through two stages. The early stage is shared by the Baytown and Troyville cultures. Baytown is recognized generally north of Vicksburg in the Yazoo Basin, while Troyville is found generally south of Vicksburg. Below Baton Rouge, a variant of Troyville is called Coastal Troyville. Potters in the region continued to improve on clay preparation and firing to produce harder wares, and often used a combination of decorative techniques including incising, stamping, punctations, cord marking, brushing, and painting.[128]

On the Gulf Coast, the Coastal Troyville pottery group extended from an undefined western boundary around the mouth of the Sabine River eastward across the Mississippi River Delta to the Mobile Bay area, which marked the western extent of the Weeden Island culture. Weeden Island was a wide-spread coastal pottery group that evolved out of the preceding Santa Rosa culture and persisted until around A.D. 1200. Tate Hammock is the name of the Weeden Island cultural variant in the Mobile Bay area. Late Woodland pottery from the coastal region was skillfully made and includes distinctive zoomorphic and anthropomorphic (human-shaped) vessel shapes.[129] North of Mobile Bay in the Tombigbee River valley and northeastern Mississippi, the Miller III plain and cord-marked pottery is distinguished from Miller II by a change from sand to grog tempering. Throughout most of Mississippi the pottery group known as Mulberry Creek Cord Marked is viewed as a marker for the Late Woodland.[130]

As mentioned earlier, northeastern Mississippi has benefited from extensive archaeological work, including surveys (systematic examinations of surface areas for signs of archaeological sites) along the Tombigbee River and many of its tributaries. The survey data provide a picture of continuity of site distribution in the region through the succession of Miller I, II, and III cultures, with long-term use of some sites.[131] Miller III subsistence strategy continued to rely on deer, small mammals, and wild plant foods, and expanded to focus more on shellfish than had the Miller I and II populations. Significantly, evidence of the beginnings of maize or corn agriculture in the region first appears in Miller III times.[132] To the south, coastal populations continued to harvest saltwater shellfish to augment their exploitation of mammals and fish from the inland forests and streams.[133]

Corn (*Zea mays*) is the result of the domestication of the wild grass *teosinte* on western Mexico's Pacific slopes around 5000 B.C. By 2700 B.C. people were farming corn in the Tehuacan Valley, and within 1,000 years the crop was spread throughout Mexico.[134] Several varieties of corn passed along exchange routes from Mexico into North America, eventually reaching communities in the Mississippi River valley. Tropical flint corn, a fast-growing variety that produced edible ears in ten to twelve weeks, arrived in the Southeast around 200 B.C. Sometimes referred to as "little corn" or "early corn," tropical flint produced ears that were about five inches long. Eastern or northern flint corn (also known as Maize de Ocho), which matured in about fourteen weeks, found its way to the Southeast by A.D. 800–1000. Eastern flint, known as "great corn" or "late corn," produced stalks around ten feet high. Somewhat later, at least by the late seventeenth century, Mississippi Indians were farming a third variety called dent corn, named for a crease in each kernel. The flint corns had hard kernels colored white, yellow, red, and blue, while dent corn had softer white kernels. Native communities in Mississippi in the seventeenth and eighteenth centuries raised all three varieties, exploiting the characteristics of each to enjoy multiple harvests within a single growing season.[135]

Middle Woodland mound-building activity appears to have diminished in the Yazoo Basin and northeastern Mississippi during the Late Woodland period. To some extent, pit burials in these areas may have replaced burial mounds. Along the coast, Weeden Island/Tate Hammock sand mounds have largely been destroyed by modern residential and commercial development.[136] In the southern Yazoo Basin, Baytown culture mound sites are rare, while habitation sites are plentiful, mainly clustered along the Yazoo and Sunflower rivers and their tributaries. Judging from shell middens at numerous sites, the exploitation of mussels was a major activity that peaked around A.D. 600. After that time, site distribution in the region seems to have decreased, and shellfish use declined. In addition to shellfishing, fish and wild plant foods continued to be important to Baytown subsistence.[137]

In contrast to Baytown and Miller III groups, burial mound construction carried on in the Troyville culture, mainly in Louisiana's Tensas Basin.[138] The Troyville site itself, located at the town of Jonesville (formerly Troyville), Louisiana, at the confluence of three rivers, was spectacular and not at all typical of the culture that bears its name. The site once included from nine to thirteen mounds, some of which were platforms, and an extensive earthen embankment. The so-called Great Mound was eighty feet high, composed of a two-tiered earthen platform surmounted by a thirty-five-feet-tall conical mound. Sadly, the Troyville site was obliterated during the development of the town for which it was named. In 1931 what was left of the Great Mound was pulled down and used to construct the highway approach to a bridge across the Black River.[139]

Archaeologists date the end of the Troyville and Baytown cultures at around A.D. 700 and mark the beginning of a cultural expression known as Coles Creek; however, Baytown culture persisted in the northern Yazoo Basin until the Mississippi period. Geographically, Coles Creek took in the area encompassed by Troyville and the southern Yazoo Basin portion of the Baytown culture. In eastern Arkansas, the Baytown culture developed into a Coles Creek variant known as Plum Bayou.[140] Coles Creek ceramics are typically well-made grog-tempered bowls and beakers with decorative elements that include parallel incised lines encircling the rim, punctations, stamping, and cross-hatching.[141] In addition to its development to new pottery types, Coles Creek culture is also characterized by a new concept in mound construction: flat-topped mounds shaped like truncated pyramids, surmounted by sacred buildings, facing ceremonial plazas. Evidence indicates that elite individuals lived in more or less permanent dwellings atop these mounds. As will be seen, this type of mound complex would become an integral part of the succeeding Mississippian culture. The origins of Coles Creek ceremonial mounds and plazas are a continuing source of archaeological debate. Some scholars see a parallel with an already established temple-plaza configuration used by pre-Columbian civilizations in parts of Mexico and Central America, while others argue for an indigenous development out of the earlier platform mound tradition.[142]

The Coles Creek culture was the first population to establish mound centers and attendant settlements in the Natchez Bluffs. Two important Coles Creek mound groups in this region are the Smith Creek site in Wilkinson County and the Feltus site in Jefferson County. These and other Coles Creek sites were placed at the edge of the hills near where tributary streams emptied into the Mississippi River.[143] Coles Creek settlement seems to have been variable, with some communities grouped close to the developing mound centers while others followed a more dispersed pattern, leaving only a few houses near the mounds, presumably for people who were entrusted with the maintenance of the site and its elite occupants.[144] People in the Yazoo Basin continued the tradition of their predecessors in living on the natural levees of abandoned river channels.[145] On the Gulf Coast, the Graveline platform mound on Pascagoula Bay represents a Coles Creek period ceremonial center, with ceramic influences from both the Mississippi Valley and the Florida panhandle.[146]

Numerous Coles Creek mound sites were later expanded into enormous Mississippian ceremonial centers. Two of the best known are Winterville in Washington County and Lake George in Yazoo County, which have been designated National Historic Landmarks. Winterville's first occupation was a Coles Creek village associated with a small mound group.[147] The Coles Creek mound complex at Lake George was in many ways typical of Late Woodland ceremonial centers in the region, with two to four mounds facing an open plaza. Coles Creek mounds, most of which were less than twenty feet in height, were modest in size compared to what would come later. A significant characteristic of Coles Creek culture is its introverted, parochial nature; scant evidence exists for prolonged contact with outside cultures or long-distance trade of the kind pursued by Poverty Point and Marksville populations.[148]

Focusing on deer and smaller mammals, fish, and wild seed plants and fruits, Late Woodland cultures in Mississippi showed little change in subsistence strategy from their predecessors. Coastal populations continued to exploit saltwater shellfish species, and, as mentioned, Miller III and Baytown groups took an increased (though temporary) interest in gathering freshwater mussels.[149] Archaeological evidence indicates that Mississippi's Woodland period inhabitants of some sites (for example, Feltus site, Jefferson County) made use of domesticated native gourds and native seed plants that other groups in the Southeast had incorporated into their seasonal routine. Likewise, the state's populations were some of the last in the region to augment their hunting and gathering pursuits with the laborious and time-consuming business of corn agriculture. For Mississippi's Late Woodland people, the motivation to make this important lifestyle change was coming from powerful chiefdoms that were forming in neighboring areas, setting in motion the final era of southeastern prehistory, the Mississippi period.[150]

MISSISSIPPI PERIOD (A.D. 1200–1700)

The dramatic emergence around A.D. 1000 of the Cahokia chiefdom in the American Bottom region of southwestern Illinois, near the confluence of the Missouri, Mississippi, and Illinois rivers, marked the beginnings of the influential Mississippian culture. In addition to its focus on corn agriculture, Mississippian culture is usually identified with a combination of other traits, including large-scale mound building, a leadership structure based on social ranking (indicated by burials with differential grave offerings), houses that were rectangular in floor plan with wall posts set in trenches (as opposed to setting posts in individual holes), jar-shaped pottery vessels, triangular-shaped and stemmed arrow points, and the use of burned mussel shell for tempering pottery, all bound up in a compelling spiritual world represented by iconography about ancestor veneration, fertility, war, and death.[151] Cahokia, which reached its zenith around A.D. 1200, encompassed a 300-acre ceremonial complex that included over 100 mounds. The site is dominated by Monk's Mound, North America's largest prehistoric earthwork, which is over 100 feet high with a base covering sixteen acres.[152]

As the Cahokia chiefdom declined in the thirteenth century, other Mississippian societies were on the rise, fueled by an increasing focus on corn agriculture. For the eastern Mississippi region, the next influential development was the chiefdom that rose to power at the Moundville site on the Black Warrior River in present-day west-central Alabama. Between A.D. 1200 and 1300 the people of the Moundville chiefdom constructed more than thirty mounds spread over 185 acres, with the site's largest mound (Mound B) reaching approximately fifty-five feet in height. The growing importance of corn in the diet of the Moundville population is demonstrated by studies of the carbon- and nitrogen-stable-isotope ratios in human bone collagen. These studies indicate that corn accounted for 65 percent of the Moundville group's caloric intake by about A.D. 1250, with gathering, hunting, and fishing providing for the rest the people's diet.[153] The ethnohistorian Patricia Galloway has pointed out that the adoption of corn agriculture involved more than just the cultivation of the crop—in itself a substantial commitment entailing the arduous removal of forest and tedious planting and tending–but the people also had to learn how to prepare corn for consumption and how to store it for future use.[154]

By A.D. 1200 numerous Mississippian-style ceremonial mound centers were appearing in Mississippi. In the northeastern part of the state, the Owl Creek and Lyon's Bluff sites (in Chickasaw and Oktibbeha counties, respectively) were the scene of early Mississippi period mound construction, though these sites were quite modest in size compared to the contemporary Moundville ceremonial center. Owl Creek, the largest of the two, contains five flat-topped mounds arranged around a central plaza. An important feature of Mississippian mound centers is the presence of one dominant mound, which clearly received more mound-building attention than other mounds at the site. Mound 1, the dominant mound at Owl Creek, is just under ten feet tall. The next highest mound is approximately five feet high, with the heights of the remaining mounds between one and three feet. As with almost all mound centers, erosion and plowing have diminished the earthworks over time.[155]

Mississippi archaeologist Janet Rafferty has termed the Owl Creek mounds a "vacant" ceremonial center, meaning that little evidence of habitation contemporary with the Mississippi period use of the site was found near the mounds. The people who built and used the Owl Creek ceremonial center apparently lived and farmed elsewhere. This distinction is important when Owl Creek is compared to the Moundville ceremonial center, just 100 miles to the southeast. At approximately the same time that the Owl Creek mounds were in use, the people of Moundville had enclosed their ceremonial center—an area of around 185 acres—within a massive palisade wall. Archaeological evidence indicates that the entire Moundville populace, estimated to be around 900 to 1,000 people, had moved inside the fortress to live in the shadow of their mounds.[156] Clearly the Owl Creek population was not experiencing the same warfare pressures that affected Moundville, perhaps because of less competition from Owl Creek's neighbors for farmland.

Moundville's close proximity to Mississippi's Tombigbee River valley made it an influential presence in the region, and Moundville connections have been noted at the Lyon's Bluff mound site; however, the extent of Moundville's impact on populations in northeastern Mississippi is uncertain.[157] On the other side of the state, in the Yazoo Basin and Natchez Bluffs, the pervasive Mississippian force emanated from Cahokia and other large chiefdoms up-river in the Middle Mississippi Valley. Like Owl Creek, Mississippi period mound centers in the lower Yazoo Basin and Natchez Bluffs tended to be sparsely populated, occupied largely by high-ranking officials and their attendants, while the main populace lived on farmsteads in dispersed settlements. In contrast, some of the Mississippi period mound centers in the northern Yazoo Basin show evidence of associated village settlements.[158] Corn agriculture flourished in the rich soils of the Mississippi River floodplain and adjacent Loess Hills and was more than adequately supplemented by the age-old gathering, hunting, and fishing. At Winterville and Lake George in the Yazoo Basin, intensive mound building transformed modest Coles Creek sites into premier Mississippian ceremonial centers rivaling Moundville. Indeed, the Carson mound group in Coahoma County once contained at least eighty-five mounds.[159]

Winterville is situated on a natural levee of the Mississippi River, which had been abandoned by the active channel in the familiar pattern of channel meandering and cutoff described earlier.[160] By the time of mound construction activities at Winterville, the old river channel was occupied by a small bayou that strategically linked the ceremonial center via Williams Bayou to Deer Creek, a major distributary or outflow of the Mississippi River and an important north-south conduit in the western Yazoo Basin.[161] Lower Mississippi Survey archeologist Jeffrey P. Brain excavated at Winterville in 1967 and found that the site originally had twenty-three mounds and two ceremonial plazas, with the dominant mound being Mound A, at a height of about fifty feet.[162] Based upon his work, Brain determined that most of the mound-building activity occurred between A.D. 1200 and 1350. Near the end of the fourteenth century, a great fire swept over Winterville, which Brain believes marked the beginning of the end of the mound center. Use of the mounds continued with little additional earth-moving until sometime in the early sixteenth century.[163] In 2005 the University of Southern Mississippi (USM) began a series of archaeological field school excavations at Winterville under the direction of H. Edwin Jackson. Preliminary findings include a large sample of animal bones and plant remains that will provide important pre-historic environmental data and dietary information. The USM archaeologists are also uncovering features that may relate to native houses and other structures in the plazas between the mounds.[164]

Some fifty miles to the southeast of Winterville is the other major mound center in the Yazoo Basin, the Lake George site. In its heyday Lake George commanded the confluence of the Yazoo and Sunflower rivers, and was accessible from Deer Creek via Rolling Fork Creek. The Yazoo River provided Lake George with a crucial connection to the Mississippi River. The site may have originally contained as many as thirty mounds; however, farming and erosion had reduced their number to twenty-five by the 1970s. After preliminary archaeological testing at the site in 1949, Stephen Williams and Jeffrey P. Brain directed excavations at Lake George during three summer field seasons in 1958, 1959, and 1960. Radiocarbon dates and ceramic sequences indicate a long period of occupation at Lake George, beginning around A.D. 500 and continuing for about 1,000 years. The dominant mound, Mound A, is approximately fifty-five feet high. Like Winterville, the Lake George mound center was built on a natural levee remnant and had two ceremonial plazas. The complex fronted on the Yazoo River cutoff and was ringed by an artificial canal resembling a medieval moat. The dirt from the canal excavation had been used to form an embankment around the edge of the site. Archaeological evidence indicates that the embankment may have been surmounted by a wooden palisade, a defensive feature absent from most other Lower Mississippi Valley ceremonial centers, but common farther north in the Middle Mississippi Valley.[165] An alternative explanation for the "moat" is that it might have served as an access canal for people traveling to the ceremonial center in wooden dugout canoes.

As with preceding ceramic-using cultures, the Mississippian culture is tracked archaeologically by its pottery—in this case, pottery tempered with burned and crushed mussel shell. Shell-tempered pottery was first developed sometime between A.D. 700 and 1000 in the boot heel of southeastern Missouri, in the St. Francis River bottomland, and on the adjacent Ozark Plateau.[166] The use of shell tempering spread down the Mississippi Valley and eventually reached the southern end of the Yazoo Basin, thus defining the geographic reach of the Mississippian culture. Below the Yazoo Basin in the Natchez Bluffs and across the Mississippi River in Louisiana's Tensas Basin, the prevailing Mississippi period ceramic culture is called Plaquemine and is derived from the earlier Coles Creek pottery. Plaquemine pottery is distinguished from Mississippian by its heterogeneous tempering paste containing a mixture of burned plant material, sand, grog, and occasional bits of crushed shell. Undecorated Mississippian ware is usually called Mississippian Plain, while undecorated Plaquemine ware is usually classified as Addis Plain. Decorated types and varieties abound. Some of the major Mississippian decorated types include Barton Incised, Grace Brushed, Leland Incised, Parkin Punctated, and Winterville Incised. Common Plaquemine decorated types include Fatherland Incised, Plaquemine Brushed, and Maddox Engraved. Some of the types, such as the Mississippian Leland Incised and Plaquemine Fatherland Incised, are nearly identical except for the presence/absence of shell tempering.[167]

One of the largest Plaquemine ceremonial mound centers is the Anna site in Adams County. Located about eleven miles north of the city of Natchez, Anna contains eight mounds grouped on a bluff-top prominence that overlooked what was the active channel of the Mississippi River in the thirteenth century.[168] Archaeologists Ian W. Brown and Richard S. Fuller conducted limited excavations at Anna in the summer of 1997 with a team of students from the University of Alabama. Brown and his colleagues, who were primarily interested in uncovering evidence of structures, worked on the summit of Mound 3 and near the base of Mound 4. Specific dates of construction and occupation for Anna remain elusive; Brown conservatively estimates the mound site's span of occupation from A.D. 1200 to 1682.[169] Mound 3, Anna's dominant mound, is 52 feet high, with its western flank seated at the very edge of the 150-foot-high bluff. Surmounted by their imposing religious buildings, the Anna mound group could not have failed to impress river travelers.

Only about eight miles to the southeast of Anna, the Plaquemine people constructed what is perhaps their crowning mound-building achievement: Emerald Mound. Although the archaeology at the site indicates that the earthwork was completed in three construction stages, Emerald was undoubtedly the result of a single visionary plan. In a remarkable feat of engineering, the people first modified a natural hill at the crest of the highest ridge in the area to create a broad, casket-shaped platform covering over seven acres. The casket's head and shoulders are at the western end of the earthwork, and the whole earthwork is laid out square with the cardinal directions. On the broad platform surface, two mounds were placed at either end of the earthwork's long axis, with six more mounds sited symmetrically along the north and south edges to enclose an expansive plaza. The dominant mound at the western end of the platform is close to sixty feet above the surrounding flat. Jeffrey P. Brain has suggested that Emerald was built as a replica of Anna, with its eight mounds grouped on an artificial bluff. By implication, the construction and use of Emerald is considered to be later than Anna, with overlap in the use of the two ceremonial centers. While Anna loomed over the Mississippi River, Emerald was strategically placed astride the Natchez Trace, an ancient trail connecting the Natchez area with the southern Appalachian Mountains to the northeast.[170]

In addition to these four major mound centers, over fifty other Mississippi period mound centers with dominant mounds at least fifteen feet high are recorded in the Yazoo Basin and Natchez Bluffs. Of these, more than a dozen have dominant mounds at least thirty feet high.[171] While most of the archaeological attention has focused on the high-profile mound sites, many of the much smaller habitation sites of the people who built the mounds have also been recorded. Unfortunately, these small sites are often discovered in the course of construction or land-leveling, and many are destroyed before they can be adequately investigated. This has been the case with a number of habitation sites in the northern Yazoo Basin; however, salvage archaeology has permitted some information to be recovered. Most of the Mississippi period houses—often referred to as "farmsteads"—are found to have had a rectangular floor plan, with the wall posts set in trenches. Often the wall trenches are not joined at the corners, indicating corner doorways and ventilation gaps. Isolated farmsteads as well as villages with up to 100 houses have been found, sometimes in conjunction with small ceremonial mounds. Where burial remains have been found, examples include individual interments beneath house floors and multigrave cemeteries. These farmsteads typically include refuse and storage pits. The Clover Hill site in Coahoma County, a small village site, contained fragments of corn, beans, and persimmon seeds. Evidence indicates that these Mississippi period structures vary somewhat in size, with a typical floor plan of about twenty by twenty-five feet, and were built with posts and cane matting and covered with clay.[172] Archaeology at the Wilsford site in Coahoma County uncovered evidence of a distinctive elevated platform house utilizing wall trenches and over 100 interior support posts. The Wilsford house is one of only two structures of this type known from the region and may have served as a domicile or perhaps as a ceremonial building.[173] In the Natchez Bluffs, archaeologist Ian W. Brown has identified several types of Mississippi period architectural patterns incorporating both circular and rectangular floor plans. Circular floor plan houses include both wall trenches and individually set posts. The circular patterns seem to have been carried over from the Coles Creek period and cease to be used after about A.D. 1350. The rectangular wall trench pattern is the most common for the Mississippi period, although rectangular floor plan houses have been noted with individually set posts and a combination of wall trenches and individually set posts.[174]

Some of the most remarkable and unlikely artifacts to survive from this time period are cypress dugout canoes. The earliest Lower Mississippi Valley example is a nearly complete cypress dugout recovered from the Homochitto River in Franklin County, Mississippi, measuring fourteen feet in length and radiocarbon dated to the period A.D. 1325–1605.[175] This canoe has a sleek, shallow-draft design that must have been typical of thousands of such vessels produced and used in the Lower Mississippi Valley. The Homochitto River empties into the Mississippi River some fifty miles south of Natchez and would have been an important prehistoric waterway into the Natchez Bluffs.[176] Three other cypress dugouts, discovered in lakes and streams in central and eastern Mississippi, are radiocarbon dated to the seventeenth century. These vessels range in length from fourteen to twenty-three feet.[177]

During the winter of 1973–1974, flooding along the Homochitto revealed another unexpected survival from the Mississippi period; this time the river's shifting channel uncovered a fishweir. The weir, or trap, consisted of pine stakes driven down into the stream bed and interwoven with cane mats. The entire structure, named the Sturdivant Fishweir after the property owner, was about seventy-five feet in length and formed an effective V-shaped funnel. To use the weir, a team of waders walking downstream herded fish into the weir's mouth, with catchers working at the narrow end of the funnel to grab fish and toss them to people waiting on the stream bank. Radiocarbon dates taken from the pine stakes indicate that the Sturdivant Fishweir was constructed about A.D. 1549–1619.[178] In 1990 a second prehistoric fishweir on the Homochitto River came to light a short distance upstream from the Sturdivant Fishweir. Named the Brown Fishweir after the owners, the structure has been radiocarbon dated to A.D. 1046–1449.[179] Like the dugout canoes, the remarkable survival of the Homochitto River fishweirs is due to their having been completely encased in river channel sand and clay.[180]

The Mississippian cultural variant on the Gulf Coast is known as the Pensacola culture, best represented by the Bottle Creek mound site located in the Mobile-Tensaw delta, just south of the confluence of the Tombigbee and Alabama rivers and just to the north of Mobile Bay. The site contains eighteen mounds, with the dominant mound, Mound A, being approximately forty-five feet tall. Bottle Creek was occupied between A.D. 1250 and 1550. Like their Mississippian and Plaquemine counterparts to the north and west, the people who constructed the Bottle Creek mounds grew corn, which they supplemented by gathering freshwater and estuarine clams and oysters, fishing, exploiting native seed and fruit plants, and hunting mammals and birds.[181] Interestingly, the site's plant remains include yaupon holly, the source of the notorious "Black Drink." The Black Drink, documented by early European travelers in the Southeast, was used for stimulation and purging by some historic tribes.[182] Analysis of Bottle Creek ceramics indicates contact with the Mississippian culture at Moundville and with the Plaquemine culture in the Lower Mississippi Valley.[183] Ian Brown has suggested an overland connection between Bottle Creek and the Natchez area across the intervening Pearl River valley.[184] Although urban development on the Gulf Coast has probably obliterated countless archaeological sites, some Mississippi period mound centers have been identified, such as the Deer Island site on Biloxi Bay and the Singing River site on Pascagoula Bay. Archaeologists John H. Blitz and C. Baxter Mann have suggested that coastal populations using these ceremonial centers relied less on corn agriculture than inland Mississippi period societies, where river flooding continuously replenished the soil. Based upon colonial observations, people living in villages up the Jourdan, Wolf, Biloxi, Tchoutacabouffa, Pascagoula, and Escatawpa rivers may have followed an annual cycle in which they planted their corn in the spring before moving down to the coastal estuaries to catch fish and gather shellfish during the summer. Blitz and Mann also point out that coastal populations appear to have increased during the Woodland and Mississippi periods, a trend that quickly reversed with the arrival of Europeans.[185]

The emergence of Mississippi period ceremonial mound centers signals the rise of powerful chiefdom societies in the Southeast. Chiefdoms are characterized by a hierarchy of kinship lineages within a social group. The supreme chief in the highest-ranked lineage is often considered by the people of the chiefdom to be related to a recognized deity, which legitimized his or her power. Redistribution of food by the ranking lineage to the people helped to hold the chiefdom together. Corn agriculture played an important role in the rise of chiefdoms by providing a delicious and nourishing food crop that was suitable for long-term storage. Tribute of surplus corn to the ruling chief by the populace filled large granaries controlled by the elite, which could be emptied and redistributed to lesser centers and villages during ceremonial events or in times of need.[186] Tribute and redistribution might involve activities other than the exchange of tangible goods, such as labor for mound construction on the part of the people and the performance of religious rites and ceremonies on the part of the chief.[187] Archaeologists and ethnologists recognize different levels of chiefdoms depending upon how many tiers of chiefs are involved. "Simple" chiefdoms had several towns or lineages under the control of one chief, while "complex" chiefdoms had a paramount chief with political control over several simple chiefdoms, creating a provincial hegemony.[188] An important characteristic of southeastern chiefdoms was their inherent instability—they had a tendency to develop, collapse, and re-form in cycles. Patricia Galloway has pointed out that soil exhaustion from corn agriculture posed a threat to expanding Mississippi period populations. As the fertility of its available farming space declined, chiefdoms could unravel.[189]

The rise of the Mississippi period chiefdoms is linked to the matrilineal kinship system, in which descent was traced through the female line.[190] This type of kinship system is well documented for the Natchez Indians' society in the early eighteenth century.[191] Chiefdoms are descent-based societies, and matrilineal descent leaves no question as to an individual's parentage. Under the system of matrilineal descent, residence was "matrilocal," in that extended families of females lived together on farmsteads or in villages, and men married into these families. Children took the name and social status of their mothers. A chiefdom society was strengthened and supported by matrilineal descent, which had the effect of adding men to a social group's labor force to clear land for farming.[192] Women's roles in tribal leadership most likely increased during this period. Although men probably occupied most of the positions of leadership within the chiefdom, women determined who would hold the rank of chief. Because at least one female paramount chief is documented in the Southeast during the sixteenth century, we can assume that females probably held this position in other Mississippi period societies.[193]

Chiefdom leadership was closely tied to the society's religious belief system. Archaeology has revealed scattered clues to the spiritual beliefs of the Mississippi period mound builders, and several religious movements or cults have been identified structured around themes such as warfare, fertility, and ancestor worship.[194] Some of these concerns are reflected in the enigmatic symbolism of the Southeastern Ceremonial Complex (sometimes called the Southern Cult and more recently the Mississippian Ideological Interaction Sphere). Possibly rooted in the art and spiritualism of the Hopewell/Marksville culture, the Southeastern Ceremonial Complex arose along with the Mississippian culture between A.D. 900 and 1400 and is characterized by extensive trade in ceremonial artifacts, particularly engraved seashells. The engravings depict a variety of cryptic symbols and fantastic creatures like winged serpents and bird-men. Archaeologists recognize in the iconography a connection with similar symbolism in Mesoamerica, although it is uncertain whether the connection was by direct face-to-face contact or the result of indirect contact along trade routes. Nevertheless, the widespread distribution of these iconic symbols indicates an understanding of the meaning behind the images by people at sites such as Moundville, the Spiro mounds in eastern Oklahoma, and the Etowah mounds in northwestern Georgia. Based upon low numbers of Southeastern Ceremonial Complex artifacts in Mississippi, archaeologists suggest that the movement never gained the strength here that it did in other locations.[195]

Possible causes for the collapse of the Mississippian chiefdoms in the American Bottom and surrounding Middle Mississippi Valley lie embedded within the entangled political, economic, and environmental forces affecting the chiefdoms of the region. To begin with, the Mississippian reign in the Mississippi Valley north of Memphis was plagued by chronic warfare, a state of affairs to which the chiefdoms of the Lower Mississippi Valley and other areas of Mississippi seemed immune. Assuming that much of the interchiefdom conflict was due to competition over farmland, the available space for cultivation in the Yazoo Basin and Natchez Bluffs may have been sufficient to support expanding mound builder populations. Also, the tendency of chiefdoms to cycle in and out of existence may have played a role in the disappearance of the Middle Mississippi Valley chiefdoms, with the downfall of a major chiefdom having had a domino effect on neighboring chiefdoms through the loss of a trading partner or a military ally.[196]

The tendency of corn to sap nutrients from the soil no doubt exacerbated the situation where available farmland was constrained. Although the practice of planting beans along with corn helped to replace the nitrogen that corn removes from the soil, there is some evidence that increased concentration on corn negated this balance. The increasing dependence on corn during the Mississippi period left those populations with limited access to suitable farmland in a vulnerable situation.[197] As the historian Paul Kelton has pointed out, the conversion to corn agriculture eventually drew many southeastern chiefdoms into a debilitating spiral in which overpopulated communities began to suffer from water-borne pathogens associated with human waste and unsanitary living conditions. Such a situation would have been particularly acute in groups forced by warfare to crowd into palisaded towns for extended periods of time. The archaeology seems to bear this out, with skeletal samples from the late Mississippi period exhibiting a lower life expectancy than earlier groups.[198]

Too heavy a reliance on corn agriculture also exposed the Mississippians to hard times when the worldwide weather phenomenon known as the "Little Ice Age" commenced during the fourteenth century. Although the drop in temperature was nowhere near as severe as the event for which it is named, the Little Ice Age brought colder, longer winters that would have made the annual corn harvest increasingly difficult to sustain, especially for the northerly Mississippian settlements.[199] It is during this same time period that archaeological evidence indicates population drift from the Middle Mississippi Valley southward.[200]

On the eastern side of Mississippi, Moundville had ceased to be a strong force in the region by 1500, and settlements throughout the Tombigbee River valley, though continuing to farm corn, gave up mound building and most of the other Mississippian trappings.[201] Moundville's decline coincided with the appearance of an archaeological culture characterized by the use of ceramic burial urns for child burials. Mainly confined to the Tombigbee and Alabama river valleys, the burial urn culture represents the remnants of the Moundville chiefdom, which later formed a part of the historic Choctaw confederation.[202]

On the Gulf Coast, the people of the Pensacola culture, a Mississippian cultural variant, continued to enlarge their mounds at Bottle Creek and other sites on into the 1500s.[203] In the Yazoo Basin, the Mississippian centers at sites such as Winterville and Lake George were winding down by the beginning of the sixteenth century, while the people of the Plaquemine culture farther to the south in the Natchez Bluffs seem to have prospered, as evidenced by their construction of Emerald Mound. The causes and effects of these demographic changes brought about by the waning Mississippian chiefdoms are poorly understood and, to a great extent, obscured by the impending contact with the world beyond the Americas. Jeffrey P. Brain has noted in the archaeology of the Lower Mississippi Valley indications of a shift in population settlement away from the Mississippi River during the fifteenth century. In the Natchez Bluffs, this trend is dramatically illustrated by the placement of Emerald Mound approximately eight miles inland from the Mississippi River.[204]

Regardless of how the economic and environmental factors might have impacted the native people of Mississippi at the beginning of the sixteenth century, they could scarcely have dreamed how their world would soon be affected by events playing out thousands of miles away across the Atlantic Ocean. In May 1492 Christopher Columbus was making final preparations to set sail to the west from the bustling Mediterranean seaport of Palos, Spain, and as the fifteenth century drew to a close, the formidable Spanish army expelled the Moors from the Iberian Peninsula. Now Spain's military prowess was about to be loosed upon the unsuspecting inhabitants of the Americas. In Mississippi, some of the Indian children born in the year of Columbus's epic voyage would live to see the unimaginable: the armored knights and horses of Hernando De Soto's army.

Chapter 2.

1540–1684

EARLY EUROPEAN CONTACT

The interval between Columbus's voyage and the founding of French Louisiana, a span of 190 years, has become known among archaeologists and historians as the Protohistoric period. During this period, Mississippi's American Indians had only sporadic contact with the Europeans—principally Spanish—probing this hemisphere in search of opportunities for wealth and empire. The Protohistoric period ended with the commencement of permanent European occupation following La Salle's 1682 Mississippi River expedition.

The Protohistoric period was a time of profound change for the native people in Mississippi and throughout the Southeast. Over the course of these two centuries, mound building ceased, and radical demographic disruption occurred, especially in the Lower Mississippi Valley. As discussed at the end of Chapter 1, the chiefdoms along the Mississippi River were in a state of flux before 1492, due in part to the natural tendency of these societies to go through cycles of growth and fragmentation. Environmental factors coupled with overuse of available farmland drove some of the people from northern chiefdoms southward into the Yazoo Basin, where the large chiefdoms represented by Winterville, Lake George, and other late prehistoric mound centers were beginning to decline in the early sixteenth century. Perhaps in response to the arrival of people from farther north, some of the Yazoo Basin societies were shifting their settlements away from the Mississippi River. To the south in the Natchez Bluffs, the Emerald/Anna chiefdom near Natchez seems to have been a viable force in the region until sometime in the late 1500s. In eastern Mississippi, the declining chiefdoms of the Tombigbee region were coalescing into egalitarian confederations that were better adapted to cope with the chaotic times at hand. Likewise, the Gulf Coast communities persisted into the Protohistoric period as the Pensacola culture discussed in chapter 1.[1]

Except for intermittent Spanish contact with native groups along the Gulf Coast and the passage of the Hernando De Soto expedition between 1540 and

1543, there are no surviving eyewitness accounts of the state's native people during this critical transitional period until the coming of the French in the late seventeenth century. The journals and records of La Salle's party reveal the stark aftermath of the demographic changes wrought over the previous 200 years. The ostentatious mound centers were all abandoned, their caretaker populations seemingly vanished. In their place were only a few relatively small tribal groups that would offer little resistance to European colonization.[2] The specifics of this transformation, in terms of tracking the changes in particular native groups, remain largely outside the reach of archaeologists, ethnologists, and historians. Because of these limitations, the question of exactly what happened during the Protohistoric period is open to speculation and lively debate. In general, most scholars agree that the transformation was a combination of environmental and social processes that were already in motion before Columbus sailed and the staggering consequences of European contact.[3]

THE SPANISH INVASION

The native people of Florida may have been the first southeastern Indians to come in direct contact with Europeans during encounters such as Juan Ponce de León's landing on Florida's western coast in 1513. Soon, other Spanish ships were reconnoitering the Gulf Coast from Florida to Mexico, offering Mississippi's coastal residents their first opportunity to glimpse the tall sailing vessels as they cruised within sight of shore. One of these early reconnaissance forays was that of Alonso Álvarez de Pineda, which sailed along the Gulf Coast in 1519. If Pineda's sailors had any contact with the native people on shore, their experiences apparently went unrecorded.[4]

Throughout the 1520s Spanish expeditions continued to probe Florida's coast and the southern Atlantic seaboard. Ponce de León returned to Florida in 1521 to attempt to establish a colony; however, the effort failed, largely due to disease among his party, which no doubt spread to neighboring Indians. Francisco Gordillo, Lucas Vásquez de Ayllón, and others prowled the Atlantic coasts of Florida and South Carolina raiding seaside villages for Indian slaves to sell in the Caribbean. Perhaps typical of these forays was Vásquez de Ayllón's 1526 visit to the mouth of the Santee River on the South Carolina coast, which brought an unspecified disease to the local Indians there.[5]

Early contact between Mississippi Indians and Europeans may have occurred when the remnants of Panfilo de Narváez's ill-fated 1527 Florida expedition rafted along Mississippi's Gulf Coast en route to Spanish settlements in Mexico. Suffering from the lack of food and water, with some of the men ailing from unspecified sickness, the party apparently went ashore in several places, which led to inevitable confrontations with local natives. One of the survivors of the Panfilo de Narváez expedition, Cabeza de Vaca, left a description of the journey, which unfortunately reveals little information about the people living along the Mississippi Gulf Coast. Patricia Galloway has suggested that these coastal people were associated with the Pensacola archaeological culture described in chapter 1. Galloway points out that Cabeza de Vaca's narrative is at least clear on one issue—the Indians mistrusted Narváez's men and made every effort to kill them or drive them away, indicating that these coastal residents had probably been treated badly by previous Spanish visitors.[6] A little over a decade later, the inhabitants of Mississippi's interior would discover why the coastal residents looked upon the Spaniards with such hostility.

The chronicles of Hernando De Soto's march across the Southeast in the mid-1500s provide a brief window on the Protohistoric world that, otherwise, is known mainly through archaeology. De Soto and his party of around 650 soldiers and civilian adventurers, accompanied by hundreds of hogs and horses, landed on the west coast of Florida in May 1539 and traversed the Southeast in search of native states with mineral riches like those recently conquered by the Spanish in Mexico and Peru. The native people of the interior Southeast could hardly have found themselves facing a more brutal invader. A veteran of harsh campaigns to subjugate the people of Panama, Nicaragua, Honduras, and Peru, De Soto had amassed a fortune in silver and gold, much of which he had gained through the Indian slave trade.[7]

The footmen and cavalry marching with De Soto epitomized sixteenth-century military power, which far overshadowed the most effective fighting capability found in the Americas. The Spanish possessed fighting and campaigning skills honed by relentless wars to drive the Moors from the Iberian Peninsula. The reconquest of Spain was all the more ruthless because the church and state viewed it as a "just war," that is, a campaign against infidels. For Spaniards intent on gaining wealth in the New World, the just war concept made it all too easy to classify the southeastern Indians as infidels, which validated the rape, torture, execution, and subjugation that characterized the sixteenth-century conquest of the Americas.[8] The most important weapon in the European arsenal turned out to be the horse, or rather, skilled cavalry. Indian footmen were easy game for mounted soldiers because they lacked the special training necessary for foot soldiers to be able to defend themselves against a cavalry charge, tactics that were common knowledge among their counterparts in Europe. As De Soto discovered and used often to his advantage, the invaders' military supremacy tempted tribal chiefs to seek the Spaniards' help in pursuing petty disputes with neighboring tribes or villages, thereby introducing a new level of mayhem to intertribal conflicts.

By the time De Soto reached Mississippi in late 1540, he and his army had covered close to 1,500 miles without discovering the mineral riches they sought. Although the expedition's goals included colonization, De Soto realized to his disappointment that the native polities he encountered in the Southeast were unsuitable for Spain's *encomienda* (royal land grant) system of governing conquered native societies. With *encomienda*, Spanish noblemen had taken control of Aztec and Inca states where productive bureaucracies already existed to manage corps of laborers working at mining operations and large-scale agriculture. Subjugating both the native managers and their laborers, the Spaniards commandeered the bureaucracies and the states' wealth. Among southeastern Indian societies, a traditional *encomienda* was not feasible because there was no professional bureaucracy or labor force. The extended family was the primary production unit, providing the food necessary to feed its own members along with a modest surplus to help support the chief.[9]

De Soto's army sustained itself on the long campaign by taking advantage of the cornfields and communal granaries they found at the ceremonial centers of the chiefdoms they encountered along their route. A successful strategy that the army used repeatedly was to follow the natives' trails from outlying villages to the chiefdom's main center. Along the way, they sacked the storage granaries, which the hungry soldiers often found stocked with corn, beans, dried plums, chestnuts, and walnuts. The Spaniards routinely burned villages and killed any warriors who opposed them. They also enslaved as many people as was necessary to carry their armor and baggage, and used captured women as concubines. A favored tactic was to hold chiefs as hostages, thereby ensuring the cooperation of the people.[10]

To communicate with the native groups the expedition encountered, De Soto relied heavily on Juan Ortiz, a survivor of the Narváez expedition who had lived for ten years with a tribe near Tampa Bay and learned to speak a local language. Bilingual speakers captured along the route made up an ever-lengthening chain of interpreters that ended with Ortiz, who provided the Spanish translation. In reading accounts of the De Soto expedition, it is important to understand that conversations between the Spaniards and Indians were time-consuming and prone to misunderstanding.[11] As the expedition's reputation for violence and deceit spread among the tribes, the Spaniards encountered ever more hostile native militia. The combat was often desperate, but the military advantage offered by the seasoned warhorses and De Soto's savage attack dogs always provided the winning edge.[12]

At the Indian town of Mabila, probably located on the Alabama River in western Alabama, warriors led by the legendary Chief Tascaluza managed to catch De Soto and some of his men in a surprise attack, killing twenty-two Spaniards and wounding over 100 more. The Indian death toll in this desperate action was much higher. Estimates of the number of Indians killed (provided by the Spaniards themselves) range from 2,500 to 3,000, although Galloway has suggested these figures might be exaggerated.[13] Mabila was also costly to De Soto's men in terms of valuable horses killed and wounded, and clothing, equipment, and other belongings lost. In the aftermath of the Mabila fight, De Soto's demoralized invasion force nearly mutinied in favor of a retreat to the Gulf Coast, where there was a good possibility of rescue by Spanish ships. Unwilling to admit to failure and invite certain ruin, De Soto somehow managed to rally his men, leading the army away from Mabila along a northwesterly route toward northeast Mississippi.

De Soto's line of march crossed the valley of the Black Warrior River in the general vicinity of the Moundville ceremonial center, now abandoned or in decline.[14] Here the army passed through the province of a chief named Pafalaya (also Apafalaya), where the soldiers replenished their supply of corn by emptying the granaries of a village named Talicpacana (also Taliepataua). When Pafalaya came to meet the Spaniards, De Soto made him a hostage to serve as a guide and interpreter. The people of Pafalaya's province offered no resistance to De Soto. Galloway has suggested that these people, being aware of what happened at Mabila, simply wanted to avoid a confrontation.[15]

News of the struggle at Mabila must have traveled ahead of De Soto, because when the army reached the Tombigbee River, an opposition force glared at them from the western bank. These were the Chicazas, ancestors of Mississippi's historic Chickasaw tribe. When De Soto dispatched one of his Indian hostages across the river to parlay, the Chicazas' reply was impossible to misconstrue—they immediately killed the unfortunate envoy. Despite their numbers and the violent warning, the Chicazas retreated a safe distance away when De Soto and his men finally crossed the river. In the usual fashion, the army's scouts followed the Indians' footpaths and quickly located the town the Spaniards came to call Chicaza, a small village of around twenty houses, which its occupants had abandoned. To their relief, the army found an abundance of corn in nearby fields and set up camp at Chicaza to wait out the winter and recover from the Mabila battle. To date archaeologists have not located Chicaza; De Soto historians have narrowed the possibilities down to Clay, Lowndes, Oktibbeha, and Noxubee counties, and the search for the actual site continues.[16]

The Little Ice Age of prehistoric times remained in effect throughout the sixteenth century, and by Christmastime the expedition was beset by heavy snow and bitter cold. The Chicaza warriors continually harassed the De Soto encampment, until it became obvious that the invaders were not about to depart. The two sides then entered into an uneasy truce that occasionally dissolved into clashes. The Spaniards plundered all of the Indian homes and granaries that lay within the reach of the cavalry, forcing the Chicazas to risk their lives in trying to steal the expedition's hogs and supplies. During the winter, in what may have been a desperate plan to divide the invaders' forces and ambush them, the Chicaza chief persuaded De Soto to bring part of his army and join with him to attack a neighboring village called Saquechuma, probably the same group as the eighteenth-century Chakchiuma tribe. The Saquechumas apparently got wind of the assault (or perhaps they were in on the ambush) and abandoned their village. If the Chicazas did indeed hope to turn on De Soto's men, their plan failed because the Spaniards suspected a trap and kept on their guard.[17]

In the spring the army made ready to leave Chicaza, and, in a final insult to the chief and his people, De Soto demanded 200 slaves to carry the expedition's baggage. No doubt believing that the invaders would soon come to capture the bearers they required, the Chicazas resolved to strike first. In the predawn hours of March 8, 1541, the Indians approached silently in four companies and surrounded the Spaniards' encampment. The attack was well planned. Warriors infiltrated the village and set fire to the thatch-roofed houses, confusing the soldiers with a cacophony of war hoops and drumming. Fierce as it was, the Chicaza attack failed to rout the Spaniards; however, many of De Soto's men received wounds, of which twelve soldiers later died, and over fifty horses and around 400 hogs burned to death. The fires also destroyed much of the army's weaponry, armor, saddles, and clothing. After the attack subsided, the invaders left the smoking ruins of Chicaza and occupied a nearby village in a more defensible location. Seven days later, the Chicazas staged a second predawn attack, but the soldiers were more vigilant, and the Indians were repulsed.[18]

On April 26 the army moved out, with foraging cavalry units dispatched to locate provisions for the march. Failing to acquire new bearers, the Spaniards were obliged to make do with the surviving baggage-carriers who had

Figure 3. Probable corridor of De Soto's route across Mississippi (shaded area) and approximate locations of native groups in 1539–1543. (Based upon Hudson, *Knights of Spain*, Maps 7 and 8; Morgan, *The Mississippi De Soto Trail*, Map 7)

accompanied the army from Mabila. A day's march brought De Soto and his men to an abandoned village of the Alibamos (Alibamus), a group with probable (but uncertain) connections to the well-documented Alabama tribe of the eighteenth century.[19] The Spaniards' reputation preceded them, and the Alibamos had stripped their village of its food stores before leaving. The next day De Soto's scouts came upon a well-built stockade manned by Alibamo warriors. The fort seemed unusual to the Spaniards because there was no sign of an associated village or women and children. The anonymous chronicler known as the "Gentleman of Elvas" left a vivid description of the scene:

> On top of [the stockade] were many armed men daubed over with red ochre and with their bodies, legs, and arms painted black, white, yellow, and red, in the manner of stripes which made them look as though they were in breeches and doublet. Some had feather plumes on their heads and others horns, with their faces black and eyes ringed round in red in order to look more ferocious.[20]

The Alibamo men taunted the Spaniards and plainly indicated that they wanted to fight. As Charles Hudson has pointed out, De Soto might have simply skirted the stockade and its defenders and continued on his march. Instead, he attacked and by doing so played into the hands of the Alibamos. The Indians designed the stockade so that when the attackers broke through the outer wall, the defenders retreated to a second palisade and continued to shoot their arrows at point blank range. When the Spaniards finally pushed past the interior barricade, the Alibamos escaped out the back of the stockade across temporary bridges over a steep-sided creek. When De Soto's cavalry rushed to pursue the fleeing Indians, the horsemen found that they had no way to get across the high-banked creek. The Spaniards ended up with fifteen dead and many more wounded from the Alibamos' arrows in what turned out to have been a needless confrontation. Only three Indians died in the action, and the attackers found no food stored inside the fort.

For the Alibamos' part, the stockade ruse appears to have been a well-planned and perfectly timed trap into which the Spaniards had obligingly fallen. Of course, there is no way to know what machinations lay behind the Alibamos' actions, but it seems likely that, as De Soto made ready to leave Chicaza, the Alibamos knew which route the army would follow and committed considerable time and resources toward the construction of their stockade. The Indians also took care to remove their women and children from the vicinity and figured out how to nullify De Soto's deadly cavalry. Finally, in the intricacy and extent of their body paint, it is obvious that the Alibamo warriors anticipated by several hours the arrival of the invaders.[21]

Preparing their wounded for travel as best they could, De Soto and his army departed, having spent four months with the Chicazas. The Spanish sojourn in northeast Mississippi undoubtedly placed severe hardship on the Chicazas due to the army's confiscation of the tribe's fall corn harvest and the looting of most of the granaries in the area. The narratives provide little information about the Chicazas, Alibamos, and neighboring groups because the tribal leaders managed to shield their women and children and most of their settlements from the invaders. The narratives do reveal that the Chicaza people lived in small, dispersed towns or villages. Like their counterparts across the Southeast, they grew corn. Scholars continue to debate whether the Chicazas represented a chiefdom. Whatever their level of social organization, the Chicazas and Alibamos clearly benefited from shrewd leadership. They planned and executed successful military operations against the Spaniards, kept their own loss of life to a minimum, and managed to prevent the enslavement of their people.[22]

The expedition, dangerously low on food supplies and carrying badly wounded men, moved out in a westerly or northwesterly direction, probably on the advice of Chicaza informants who no doubt were anxious to see the last of the invaders. Although the exact route remains a mystery, the army moved over Pontotoc Ridge and traveled through an uninhabited forest broken up by numerous westward-flowing streams. Without corn granaries to loot, the Spaniards were desperate for food when the expedition crossed the Loess Hills and entered the Lower Mississippi Valley after an arduous nine-day march. Reconstructions of De Soto's march across Mississippi have the army reaching the Mississippi River somewhere between Memphis and Rena Lara in southern Coahoma County (Figure 3).[23] The hungry soldiers stormed the first Indian town they came upon, taking the inhabitants completely by surprise. The town was part of a chiefdom known as Quizquiz.[24]

The soldiers found the town undefended, with the fighting-age men away tending their cornfields. One of the De Soto narratives (Garcilaso) mentions the presence of a mound at this town.[25] The soldiers rounded up all of the women as hostages, including the mother of a chief. With the town under their control, the Spaniards lost no time looting the granaries and confiscating whatever native belongings were available to patch or replace their tattered clothing. The chief of Quizquiz, communicating with De Soto through messengers, managed to secure the release of the women. The next day the men of Quizquiz assembled out of crossbow range, armed with their bows and arrows, and sent messengers to talk with the invaders. The envoys flattered De Soto by explaining how a legend predicted that one day white men would appear and subjugate them. They also reassured De Soto that their chief would come soon to pay his respects. In the next few days, De Soto's scouts found more towns and granaries a little farther west, and the Spaniards soon came to realize they had arrived at the banks of a river comparable in size to the Danube.[26]

The Quizquiz chief never came, and his people ignored De Soto's demands for canoes to carry the Spanish entourage across the Mississippi River, which the Spaniards called *el río grande*. Establishing their camp in a former corn-field, work details set about cutting wood for boats to ferry the army to the Arkansas side of the river. As always, the Spanish commanders dispatched heavily armed squads to raid the granaries of Quizquiz's towns.[27] Although the Spaniards realized that they had encountered a sophisticated society in-habited by "lords" and "vassals," De Soto had, in fact, intruded upon a multi-tiered chiefdom. Quizquiz was closely allied with Aquixo, a similar-size chief-dom across the river. Both Quizquiz and Aquixo were under the hegemony of Pacaha, a third chiefdom a short distance upriver.[28]

The magnitude of the chiefdom into which De Soto had wandered revealed itself soon after the Spaniards began building boats. A day after envoys de-livered a formal notice to De Soto that he would receive a visit from the local chiefs, some 200 war canoes emerged from around an upstream bend. The canoes, wooden dugouts made from enormous cypress logs, were decorated with white and colored feathers. In the larger vessels, a row of archers stood in a line down the center, flanked on either side by seated paddlers. The archers wore bright red paint with elaborate feathered headdresses. Shields made from tightly woven cane protected the paddlers. Chiefs sat under awnings in the sterns of some of the bigger canoes, and banners fluttered in the wind. Moving in concert, the formidable armada drew close to shore, and smaller canoes issued forth to deliver gifts of fish and plum bread to the Spaniards. Seeing an opportunity to take a high-ranking hostage, De Soto tried to coax the chief in the lead canoe to come ashore, but the Indians were wary of the Spanish crossbowmen brandishing their weapons. As the chief gave the order to withdraw, the crossbowmen loosed a volley at point blank range, killing several of the warriors. What happened next impressed even the militaristic Spaniards. According to the Gentleman from Elvas: "[The armada] withdrew in splendid order; no one abandoned his paddle even though the one near him fell."[29]

With the Spaniards' lethal aggression now apparent, the warrior boatmen returned daily to taunt the invaders (keeping out of crossbow range) and monitor the progress of the boats under construction. Similarly, thousands of warriors assembled on the west bank to attempt to intimidate the army. Despite the show of force, De Soto and his men crossed the Mississippi River in mid-June of 1541.[30] The expedition had spent approximately one month at Quizquiz. Although the Spaniards had had little contact with the people of the chiefdom, the army's theft of the Indians' stores of corn and other foods no doubt placed a severe hardship on the local population. Perhaps just as detrimental was the people's realization of the powerlessness of their chiefs and warriors to impede the progress of the alien invaders.

Unlike the Chicazas and Alibamos, who can be connected with some confidence to the historic Chickasaw and Alabama tribes, the descendants of Quizquiz have proven more difficult to pin down. Archaeologist Jeffrey P. Brain has linked Quizquiz to the historic Tunica tribe, who were living on the lower Yazoo River in the early eighteenth century. In his book *Tunica Archaeology*, Brain cites similarities in pottery between the historic Tunicas and archaeological sites representing late prehistoric occupations in northwest Mississippi, and references an oral tradition among the Chickasaws and Choctaws placing the Tunicas in this same area. According to Brain's argument, the ancestral Tunicas entered northwest Mississippi from Arkansas sometime not long before De Soto's appearance.[31] Arkansas archaeologist Marvin Jeter offers an alternative interpretation of Quizquiz genealogy, suggesting that Quizquiz might have been a Natchezan group. Jeter makes reference to the similarity of the word "Quizquiz" to other named chiefdoms encountered by De Soto that have been tentatively identified with the Natchez language. These include the chiefdom of Quigualtam, which I will discuss in a moment.[32] Despite the existence of several mound sites in northwest Mississippi that may have been in use at the time of De Soto's expedition, archaeologists have failed to identify the location of Quizquiz.[33]

After a yearlong march around present-day Arkansas, where the Spaniards clashed repeatedly with the natives and withstood another bitterly cold winter, De Soto returned to the Mississippi River in the spring of 1542. Near the mouth of the Arkansas River, south of the Aquixo/Quizquiz chiefdom, the Spaniards occupied the town of Guachoya after the inhabitants had fled with whatever food and belongings they could carry. While at Guachoya, De Soto learned about a prominent chiefdom called Quigualtam, which lay across the Mississippi River and three days journey downstream. There was even some hint from Guachoya informants (who wanted to be rid of the Spaniards) that Quigualtam might possess the mineral wealth the expedition had long sought. With his army weakened by the three-year campaign and his own health diminishing, De Soto resolved to incorporate Quigualtam into a grandiose plan to resuscitate the expedition. He would send a picked group of his best soldiers down the Mississippi River to the Gulf of Mexico in search of Spanish settlements from which to replenish the expedition's supplies. In the meantime, the rest of the army would take over Quigualtam's principal town and wait there to be reprovisioned.[34]

To set the plan into motion, an Indian courier went from Guachoya to Chief Quigualtam and told him that De Soto, the son of the sun, demanded his obedience. The courier instructed the chief to come and visit De Soto with gifts of the most valuable objects in his territory. Of course, the Spaniards were in hopes that Chief Quigualtam would bring silver or gold. When the courier returned and the chief's reply was interpreted for De Soto, the general was enraged. In a display of arrogance to rival even De Soto's, Chief Quigualtam challenged the Spaniard to dry up the Mississippi River as proof of being the son of the sun. The chief also refused to come to De Soto, but, rather, made a counter demand that the general must come to Quigualtam, where his warriors would be waiting for either war or peace.[35]

Had the army encountered Quigualtam earlier in the campaign, De Soto would certainly have delighted in subjugating this haughty chief, but now the general was dying, and his men had no desire to invade another chiefdom. Following De Soto's death, his successor, Luis Moscoso de Alvarado, led the army in a disastrous overland march following a southwesterly trail to attempt to reach Spanish settlements in Mexico. The Spaniards had to turn back when the expedition entered a region, probably southeastern Texas, where there were no corn granaries and the native people lived by hunting and gathering.[36] Trekking back to the Mississippi River, Moscoso and his soldiers and the horde of camp followers spent the winter of 1542–1543 at the chiefdom of Aminoya, on the west bank of the Mississippi River some seventy-five miles north of Guachoya. The Spaniards took over Aminoya's main settlement and commandeered the people's stores of corn and dried fruit, heedless of the hardships they were causing the native inhabitants. During the winter months, the soldiers set about building boats for the journey down the Mississippi River and along the Gulf Coast to Mexico.[37]

The failed De Soto expedition, with Moscoso in command, embarked from Aminoya with about 350 soldiers in seven boats on July 2, 1543. The army's remaining horses stood in canoes lashed to the boats. Because there were only enough boats to transport the soldiers and a few essential native servants, the Spaniards abandoned about 500 Indian slaves who had served the expedition in its overland campaign, including many women and children.[38] The next day, Moscoso's boats encountered Chief Quigualtam's warrior boatmen, triggering a floating mêlée lasting around forty-eight hours in which the native fleet chased the Spaniards over 150 miles down the Mississippi River. The De Soto chronicles tell us that the Quigualtam fleet was comprised of between 50 and 100 giant dugouts similar to those of the Pacaha encountered upriver.[39]

As the Mississippi's current carried them all southward, the native oarsmen kept pace by singing rhythmic songs and calling out the name "Quigualtam." Quigualtam's formidable fleet refrained from encircling the Spaniards' boats and putting an end to their flight. Instead, the war canoes took turns cruising alongside Moscoso's terrified men to call out insults to the Spaniards and pelt them with volleys of arrows launched from rows of standing archers. The soldiers survived by huddling behind the gunwales and shielding themselves as best they could with cane mats taken from Aminoya. Quigualtam's forces finally gave up the chase around ten o'clock on the morning of July 6, probably somewhere south of the present-day city of Natchez. Farther downstream, other riverside villages sent out a few canoes to harass weary Spaniards as they passed.[40]

The Quigualtam episode is unique in the De Soto chronicles. Had the expedition held to its overland mode of travel instead of taking to the Mississippi River in boats, the world might never have known about the phenomenal warrior boatmen. The battle tactics employed by Quigualtam's warriors suggest considerable training and indicate that river-oriented chiefdoms incorporated long-standing traditions that prepared men for the precision handling of 100-foot-long war canoes. The men who operated Quigualtam's colossal war canoes were militia and not professional soldiers. Because every man had been raised from childhood to be intimately familiar with both the river and their dugout canoes, the Quigualtam warriors were as accustomed to their boats as the Spaniards were to their warhorses. Although we cannot know precisely how the Quigualtam navy was organized, I have suggested elsewhere that perhaps towns within the chiefdom sponsored their own boats.[41]

As mentioned above, Quigualtam is usually considered to have been a Natchezan chiefdom, ancestral to some degree to the historic Natchez Indians of southwest Mississippi. Geographically, the stretch of the Mississippi River under Quigualtam's control extended well into the area of the prehistoric Plaquemine culture, which is closely linked with the historic Natchez tribe. Along with geography, there is some tentative linguistic evidence for classifying Quigualtam as Natchezan, based upon comparisons of words recorded by Natchez-language speakers in the 1930s with the names of chiefdoms documented by the De Soto expedition.[42]

Like their Quizquiz neighbors to the north, the people of Quigualtam were fortunate to have had little direct contact with the Spaniards, and because the army never went to Quigualtam's main town, its location remains a mystery. The De Soto narratives indicate that the province of Quigualtam was located on the east side of the Mississippi River; however, determining a more precise location has become part of a larger debate over reconstructing De Soto's route. Two conflicting interpretations have emerged, both of which place Quigualtam in Mississippi, but at proposed locations over 100 miles apart. In Charles Hudson's much-publicized reconstruction of De Soto's route, Moscoso's flotilla embarked from a point in southeast Arkansas several miles north of the mouth of the Arkansas River, which would seem to place Quigualtam somewhere in the Yazoo Basin.[43] On the other hand, Jeffrey Brain believes Moscoso entered the Mississippi River much farther to the south, in northeast Louisiana, and locates Quigualtam in the Natchez Bluffs.[44] Within these two regions, four late prehistoric mound sites are certainly impressive enough to have been Quigualtam's headquarters: Winterville and Lake George in the Lower Yazoo Basin, and Anna and Emerald in the Natchez Bluffs.[45] Other mound sites in the region with occupations around De Soto's time include the Transylvania and Fitzhugh mound sites on the west side of the Mississippi River in the Tensas River Basin, and the Law, Magee, and Silver City mound sites in the Yazoo Basin. In the northern part of the Natchez Bluffs, the Haynes Bluff, Glass, and Yokena mound sites contain dominant mounds of thirty feet or more in height. If none of these secondary centers was Quigualtam's headquarters, then perhaps the people who built these mound centers were part of his chiefdom.[46]

After De Soto, no Europeans are known to have traveled in the Lower Mississippi Valley for well over a century; however, Spanish interest in the region continued. In 1559 Tristán de Luna y Arellano sailed to Pensacola Bay and Mobile Bay, and sent expeditions among the tribes living up the valleys of the Alabama, Coosa, and Tombigbee rivers. Luna hoped to build on intelligence gathered by the De Soto expedition and lay the groundwork for establishing a port and colony in the Pensacola/Mobile Bay area. Although Luna's expeditions did not enter Mississippi, the observations made by his men reflect on the general condition of the region. The Spaniards found populous native settlements along the coast and in the Mobile-Tensaw delta. Guided by Indian women captured by De Soto who had been held as slaves in Mexico, and by several men who had participated in the De Soto expedition, Luna's exploratory forces found a string of villages as they probed northward up the river valleys. The native people were justifiably wary of the Spaniards and took care to hide their food and women, placing a hardship on soldiers awaiting sporadic supply ships from Mexico. Low morale led to mutiny among Luna's men, and the expedition ended in 1561.[47] Following Luna's departure, Spanish ships continued to pass along Mississippi's Gulf Coast, but few if any sailors were inclined to venture ashore. For the next 121 years, Mississippi's Indians avoided direct European contact; however, the interval gave the people little respite. Chiefdoms that had stood for centuries disappeared. Indeed, among the most elusive answers sought by southeastern archaeologists today are the details about what happened to the mound-building populations in the Lower Mississippi River valley during that dark interval.

The demographic changes that occurred during the Protohistoric have led some historians to characterize the period as a time of holocaust brought about by the introduction of European (and later African and Asian) diseases into the Americas. For foreign viruses and bacteria, the American Indian populations were what epidemiologists call "virgin soil."[48] Early European contact inadvertently exposed American Indians to infection from a host of pathogens, including smallpox, measles, influenza, bubonic plague, diphtheria, typhus, cholera, scarlet fever, and whooping cough.[49] Of these, smallpox was the most deadly. With an incubation and communicability period of one to two weeks, infected individuals lived long enough to carry the virus from village to village, enabling it to spread throughout a population. The virus can also live for months in dried form on clothes or baggage and thus be transported a considerable distance from the source of the contagion. Among American Indian groups whose systems had never encountered smallpox and therefore had no natural immunity, the disease could extinguish an entire community. Once the pathogen took hold, there would be few people left standing to care for the sick and dying, or to bury the dead. In futile desperation, people would have turned to the medicinal plants upon which they had relied for generations. Likewise, efforts by religious leaders to explain and stem the dying would have been in vain. For preliterate societies like the southeastern Indians, which relied upon the oral transmission of cultural information across generations, a smallpox epidemic could erase a tribe's identity.[50]

Sixteenth-century Spanish contact launched several devastating smallpox epidemics throughout Latin America beginning in 1519, and scholars are sharply divided over whether one or more of these epidemics spread out of Mexico or the Caribbean into the southeastern United States during the Protohistoric period.[51] The De Soto chronicles give every indication that the populations the expedition encountered in Mississippi during the 1540s were as yet unaffected by European diseases. Although the impact of De Soto's army brought hardship and destabilization to the native societies unlucky enough to be in its path, it is unlikely that De Soto's soldiers harbored lethal diseases by the time they reached Mississippi. Patricia Galloway has pointed out that any deadly pathogens the army might have carried when it came ashore in Florida would have played out in the course of De Soto's yearlong trek through the southeastern interior before reaching Mississippi. The Luna expedition reports seem to bear this out. Luna's documents describe what appear to have been healthy populations near Mississippi's coast and eastern border in 1560, not far from De Soto's route through Mabila.[52]

Instead of carrying deadly viruses like smallpox to the southeastern Indians, the historian Paul Kelton has suggested that the De Soto expedition and other Spanish forays in the region may have spread malaria, a less-lethal but still debilitating illness. Kelton points out that preexisting environmental conditions, including the presence of the anopheles mosquito, needed only the plasmodium parasite carried by the Spanish to bring malaria to the Southeast. Although malaria would not have caused severe depopulation, its presence would have weakened native societies, perhaps contributing to the collapse of some chiefdoms. Malaria, if it did indeed spread through the Southeast in the sixteenth century, would have diminished the native peoples' resistance to the array of contagions that would come with continued European contact.[53]

Along with malaria, De Soto's wandering host of soldiers, slaves, pigs, horses, and dogs were capable of exposing Mississippi's native people to milder but potentially dangerous forms of sickness associated with indigenous water-borne illnesses bred in the filth generated by such a multitude. There is also some suspicion that the large herd of hogs traveling with the expedition harbored influenza and could have inflicted trichinosis and other maladies on natives with whom they came in contact.[54] Having shared microbes with their domesticated animals for centuries, Europeans possessed a protective tolerance for viruses that routinely jumped between animals and humans. On the other hand, American Indians had relatively few domestic animals—the dog being the only domesticated animal in the prehistoric Southeast. Some have argued that, had the American Indians lived with a similar array of animals, they might have built up a level of tolerance that would have reduced their susceptibility.[55]

Aside from disease, an important factor in the region's Protohistoric demographic upheaval was the trauma associated with the passage of the De Soto expedition. This catastrophic event undoubtedly interrupted the rise-and-fall cycling characteristic of chiefdoms. Along with the loss of life by violent confrontation, the appearance of the Spanish army impacted the native societies on spiritual and economic levels. The people were suddenly forced to incorporate the formidable European fighters into their understanding of the world, much to the detriment of their own leadership. Chiefs who were unable to defeat De Soto or successfully bargain with him would have stood to lose the confidence of their people. Belief systems that legitimized chiefdoms became undermined during this period, and overt acts of communal tribute such as mound building ceased. Egalitarian societies would have fared better in this regard. With big-man chiefs, leadership change was more commonplace and caused less impact than a leadership change in a hierarchical chiefdom.[56]

Economic catastrophe followed from the Spanish army's theft of food stores wherever they went. By the time the army reached Mississippi, it would have numbered around 1,000 people, including soldiers and Indian slaves, not to mention hundreds of hungry hogs and the army's herd of precious warhorses. To feed such a host, De Soto and his men depended almost entirely upon the native towns' fields and granaries. No documentation exists to tell us how the people of Chicaza and Quizquiz coped with this disaster; however, we can infer what might have happened from the condition of the people of Aminoya, who were reduced to starvation when the Spaniards seized their corn stores.[57] In this regard, Quigualtam was spared, and indeed Chief Quigualtam can only have gained stature in the eyes of his people through his resounding victory over the Spanish invaders.

As discussed above, the Luna expedition seems to have found healthy native populations in Alabama only twenty years after De Soto's army marched through the region; however, Luna's party sailed directly to the Gulf Coast from ports in Mexico and the Caribbean that were frequently contaminated with smallpox and other contagions. There was unspecified sickness aboard Luna's ship when he arrived, and the expedition's supply ships from Mexico could have introduced contagions. As Galloway has pointed out, Luna's party had sustained contact with the native people of western Alabama, spending several months at some native villages.[58] Although Luna's extended presence created an opportunity for a smallpox outbreak, it is questionable whether the contagion would spread very far beyond the initial point of European contact. According to Paul Kelton, the presence of buffer zones between many native polities, such as the one crossed by De Soto between the Chicazas and Quizquiz, would have made it difficult for smallpox to spread over great distances. Kelton argues that regionwide epidemics among southeastern native groups did not occur until English and French colonial communities established trading networks that linked tribes to persistent sources of European diseases in the 1690s.[59]

Luna's reports are the last surviving eyewitness accounts of native people in the region for over a century. During this period, powerful mound-building chiefdoms like Quigualtam and Quizquiz fell apart, and their former constituents pieced together new lives without the luxuries or burdens of social ranking and elite lineages. Likewise, the flourishing coastal communities that Luna saw melted away, perhaps into the interior where coalitions were forming that would emerge as the historic Choctaw confederacy. Although the picture is far from complete, archaeology has been able to outline some of the broad demographic changes that occurred during the Protohistoric period. In the Yazoo Basin and Natchez Bluffs, archaeologists have documented a reduction in the size and number of archaeological sites during the Protohistoric period along with evidence of abandonment of long-established sites.[60] To some, fewer and smaller archaeological sites hint at depopulation by European-introduced epidemics; however, others argue that these demographic changes, if they are not due to sampling bias, could instead be attributed to other causes, including chiefdom cycling and environmental factors. More direct archaeological evidence has been hard to marshal because quick-killing diseases like smallpox would not leave obvious marks on the bones of victims, and archaeologists have not found mass graves that might suggest the aftermath of a sixteenth- or early-seventeenth-century epidemic.[61]

ARRIVAL OF THE FRENCH

In the late 1600s expeditions out of New France (Canada) descended the Mississippi River and passed through the former territories of Pacaha, Quizquiz, Aquixo, Aminoya, Guachoya, and Quigualtam. In place of the populous chiefdoms and flamboyant canoe armadas that had confronted De Soto, the French found just a few relatively small native settlements comprised of the remnants of local sixteenth-century chiefdoms, such as the Natchez, along with relative newcomers to the region, such as the Quapaw. Many of the people in the Lower Mississippi Valley lived in villages at some distance from the Mississippi River. Even the Natchez, whose core group remained in its prehistoric location, situated their villages several miles inland from the Mississippi River. It was as if the river that once nurtured mound-building chiefdoms had become a potential source of danger in the eyes of the native inhabitants. French probing along the Gulf Coast at the end of the seventeenth century found this once populous region sparsely inhabited as well. As discussed in the next chapter, the French were obliged to look deep into the interior to find Mississippi's largest native populations.[62]

In 1673 Father Jacques Marquette and Louis Joliet led the first French expedition to explore the Mississippi River south of the Illinois country, traveling as far as the Quapaw villages near the mouth of the Arkansas River. This group, also known as the Acansa or Arkansas, occupied four villages named Tongigua, Tourima, Ukakhpakhati, and Uzutiuhi. The Tongigua village was initially on the Mississippi side of the river, although these people later joined the Tourima on the west bank. At the Quapaws, the expedition learned of Tanikoua (possibly Tunica) and Akoroa (possibly Koroa) villages farther up the Arkansas River valley, but did not attempt to contact them. The Quapaws, identified as a Dhegiha Siouan group from the upper Ohio River valley, may have arrived at their Mississippi River location around 1660. Historians and archaeologists believe that the Quapaws were one of several Siouan-speaking groups displaced by the aggressive Five Nations Iroquois, an armed confederacy motivated by commerce with the Dutch in the Northeast. Among the Quapaws' possessions, Marquette and Joliet noted English trade goods, a sign that the commerce of the Carolina English had reached the Mississippi River by that time.[63]

The La Salle party followed nine years behind Marquette and Joliet. After stopping at the Quapaw villages during the second week of March 1682, the expedition entered the unexplored territory downstream. Near the site of present-day Memphis, Tennessee (an area later known as Chickasaw Bluffs), La Salle's party encountered two Chickasaw men from a hunting group. One of the men opted to join the French and Indian party for a few days, and La Salle learned of the general location of the main Chickasaw villages (present-day Tupelo area), but made no effort to reach them. At the Quapaw villages, La Salle and his men participated in a calumet ceremony.[64] Put simply, smoking the calumet created a fictive kinship relationship between strangers, from which further negotiations for trade or allegiance could proceed. Although Europeans and American Indians appreciated the diplomatic value of the calumet ceremony, history reveals that the two cultures viewed the ritual in different ways. To the French, the calumet ceremony was often tantamount to a treaty that was permanently binding upon all participants, even extending to members of both sides who were not present at the time. In contrast, the Mississippi tribes usually saw the calumet ceremony as a temporary pact affecting only those who were present, and frequent repetition of the ritual was necessary to provide reassurance of continuing goodwill.[65]

Quapaw guides accompanied La Salle farther downriver and made him aware of the Tunica settlement up the Yazoo River, although the expedition leader chose not to seek it out. Six days' journey below the Quapaws, the La Salle party reached the Taensas village situated beside an oxbow lake on the west side of the river. The Taensas provisioned the French with corn, dried fruits, and salt, and frightened the Indians traveling with La Salle with stories of cannibals living to the south.[66] Reaching the Natchez river landing on March 26, La Salle and a few of his men visited the Grand Village ceremonial center, where they spent three days as guests of the Great Sun. The Frenchmen received hospitable treatment from their hosts, and they probably experienced another calumet ceremony.[67] Importantly, La Salle did not venture out to any of the settlement districts, and the settlement district chiefs did not come to the Grand Village and welcome the French. Conspicuous by their absence, the settlement district chiefs may have already come under the influence of the English, whose allies in the region would have warned them against the French.[68]

In contrast to the coolness of the Natchez village chiefs, a Koroa chief made the effort to travel from his tribe's settlement some eighteen to thirty miles downriver and meet La Salle at the Grand Village. After leaving the Natchez, the expedition moved downstream to the main Koroa village on a bluff close to the Mississippi River, where they remained two days and received a calumet ceremony.[69] Whatever diplomatic gains La Salle made among the Natchez and Koroas were set back a few days later when the expedition had a violent confrontation with a group called the Quinipissas, near the site of present-day New Orleans. The La Salle narratives indicate that the Quinipissas instigated the incident, and members of La Salle's group killed and scalped several Quinipissa men. The Quinipissas appealed to the Koroas and Natchez to avenge them, and a large, hostile contingent of warriors awaited the La Salle party at the Koroa villages on the expedition's return trip upriver. Fortunately for the Frenchmen, the Koroa chief was able to restrain the warriors until the expedition could paddle upstream and out of the Natchez/Koroa territory.[70]

During his journey La Salle learned that several of the tribes in the region were warring, an indication that the Carolina Indian slave trade may have reached the Mississippi River by that time. Hostilities existed between the Quapaws and at least two groups, the Chickasaws and Tunicas. Likewise, the Houmas and a group called Chigilousa had recently raided a village not far from the Quinipissa settlement. In his journal, Nicolas de La Salle described the scene: "We saw close by [the village] a great number of vultures and crows. We went to the village and saw only human carcasses and ruined lodges. There were a few standing lodges, but these were full of dead bodies. The canoes were all broken to pieces. They appeared to have been chopped with very sharp hatchets."[71] The mention of "very sharp hatchets" may be a reference to the iron trade hatchets traded among the tribes by the English and the French.[72] Given the circumstances, the Quinipissas' confrontational behavior toward the Frenchmen is understandable. Nicolas de La Salle's journal also documents slave transactions by La Salle and his party. La Salle purchased a Mosopelea boy from the Quapaws (Mosopelea is another name for the Siouan-speaking Ofo group), and his lieutenant Henri de Tonti traded for a Koroa boy from the Taensas. Unlike the English version of the Indian slave trade, these exchanges by the French were casual and without violence. As we will see in chapter 3, the French never developed the business of the Indian slave trade to the extent of the Carolina English.[73]

Even though the members of the Marquette/Joliet and La Salle expeditions were probably the first Europeans since De Soto to meet the Mississippi Valley Indians face-to-face, the Mississippi tribes had long felt the effects of European presence in the region. European and North African plants noted by La Salle's party include domesticated apple, peach, watermelon, plum, pear, and pomegranate. These plants could have reached the region from Spanish missions in Florida and northern Mexico during the late 1500s.[74] By the 1680s guns, iron knives and hatchets, and glass beads from Illinois country French and the Carolina English were finding their way into the hands of the Lower Mississippi Valley tribes. At the Taensa villages, which were probably typical of the region, La Salle's men saw guns, copper and brass objects, and even a Spanish sword. The French also noted copper springs of possible English origin at the Koroa village.[75]

Unquestionably, the demographic changes that swept over the whole region during the final century of the Protohistoric period are in some way attributable to European contact, but exactly what took place in the interim between De Soto and La Salle remains a mystery. In coming chapters, I examine postchiefdom refugees such as the Tunicas, who found migration necessary for survival. Likewise, small remnant groups gravitated toward the more powerful tribes such as the Chickasaws, Natchez, and Choctaws. Even as the region was reshaping itself, the Southeast's first documented smallpox epidemic was moving toward Mississippi. Ironically, the disease did not stem from one of the many Spanish-induced epidemics in Mexico and Florida, but came overland from the eastern seaboard, carried by the harbingers of the Indian slave trade.

Chapter 3

1685–1715

THE ERA OF THE INDIAN SLAVE TRADE

For more than thirty years the native people in the Mississippi region lived with the specter of the Indian slave trade. It was a time when bands of Indian slave catchers, sometimes led by English agents and sometimes numbering in the hundreds, ranged across the Tombigbee River valley to the Mississippi River and beyond, and from the Tennessee River down to the Gulf Coast. Driving this chronic violence was the burgeoning Atlantic market economy that connected the southeastern Indians through the Carolina English to a trade network linking merchants in Europe and West Africa with their counterparts in the Americas. Native people across the Southeast coveted the things the market offered, such as guns, gunpowder, ammunition, blankets, iron hatchets, knives, pots and pans, and glass beads, and bought them with two forms of currency: deerskins and Indian slaves. While the slave trade lasted, human captives always purchased more trade goods than deerskins. Although values for both commodities varied widely according to demand, a French musket was worth fourteen deerskins in 1713, at the height of the slave trade.[1] In contrast, Carolinian Thomas Nairne noted in 1708 that one slave could be traded for a gun, ammunition, a horse, a hatchet, and clothes.[2] A French report that same year claimed that the English at Charleston were paying up to sixteen trade muskets per Indian slave. This may be an exaggeration, but the historian Alan Gallay notes that the English could afford to pay seven or eight guns per slave and still make a profit.[3]

The Chickasaws were one of the first of the Mississippi tribes targeted by the Indian slave trade as raiding parties fanned out westward from Carolina in search of victims. Indirect English contact may have come as early as the 1670s with raids on their villages by slave-catching parties from tribes farther east. The Chickasaws responded by forming their own slave-catching bands. They were encouraged in this pursuit by Carolina traders such as Thomas Welch and Anthony Dodsworth, who offered guns and ammunition, along with other European articles.[4] Much has been made of the early supplying of guns to the Chickasaws and the advantage this gave them against their neighbors, but Alan Gallay has pointed out that the primitive smoothbore muskets of the late seventeenth century were less effective than the bow and arrow.[5] The real advantage the Chickasaws and other slave raiders had was predatory planning incorporating the weight of superior numbers and the crucial element of surprise. Fear spread quickly among the people of the region because the slave raids represented a new form of aggression. Victims were not simply being carried away to the attackers' villages; they were removed beyond the forests of the Southeast, never to be seen again. Although individuals or small groups were the most likely targets, large slave-raiding parties occasionally swooped down on entire villages.[6] Thomas Nairne's laconic description of a Chickasaw slave raid belies the terror and violence of the event: "If [the target is] a Village to be surprised, [the Chickasaws] place themselves in [the] form of a half moon, march towards it, when the Chief Officer gives the signal with his whistle, every man Claps his hand to his mouth, gives the War Whoop, and then catch as catch can."[7]

Importantly, the slave raids also provided a means by which young men could gain honor and a war name. Whether the raiding party met with success depended heavily on the supernatural. Nairne mentions the singing of carefully guarded songs and the use of amulets—small deerskin bags containing medicinal roots, dried animal parts, and locks of hair taken from previous captives. The amulets required special handling and ritual to remain powerful. Before the attack, a warrior hung items from his amulet around his neck, and, after the raid, a man honored his amulet by hanging it temporarily about the neck of his captive. Chickasaw women accompanied men on slave raids and sang loudly during the attack, no doubt adding to the terror of the fracas.[8]

The Chickasaw towns lay some 550 miles from Charleston, and transporting guns and the other accoutrements of trade by bearers and packhorses over that distance required a substantial commitment of time and effort on the part of the English traders. The two-and-a-half-month trek was also dangerous, since the traders and their coveted goods passed through the formidable Creek confederacy and came close to the Choctaws' eastern villages (Figure 4). From Charleston, the road west led through New Savannah on the Savannah River (at present-day Augusta, Georgia) and forked at the Ogeechee River into two trails known as the Upper and Lower paths. The Lower Path led to the Lower Creek village of Coweta on the Chattahoochee River (in the vicinity of present-day Columbus, Georgia) and linked traders to the Lower Creek towns strung out along the river to the south. The Upper

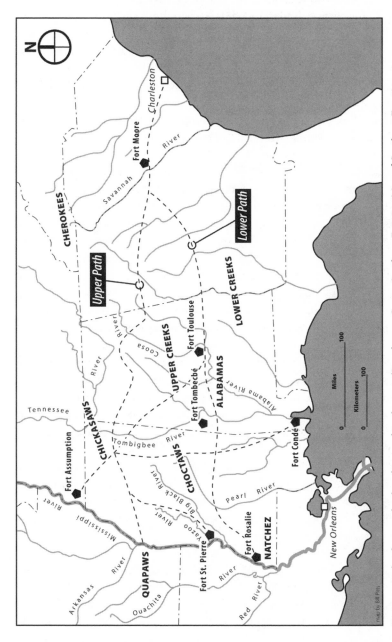

Figure 4. Paths, forts, and tribes discussed in the text. (Based upon Crane, *Southern Frontier*, Map of Southern Frontier, 1670–1732; Galloway, *Choctaw Genesis*, Figure 2.2.; Kelton, *Epidemics and Enslavement*, 142; Le Maire [map 1716], *Carte nouvelle de la Lousiane*; Swanton, *Early History of the Creek Indians*, Plate 5)

Path, the route to the Chickasaws, crossed the Chattahoochee River about fifty miles upstream from Coweta at the Chattahoochee trading village and led to the Upper Creek villages on the Tallapoosa River (northeast of present-day Montgomery, Alabama). Passing through the Upper Creek tribes along the Coosa River, the Upper Path turned west again for the final 100-mile leg to the Chickasaws.[9] During the years of the Indian slave trade, profits kept the packhorse trains going to the Chickasaws. Later, the incentive for the English to keep this tenuous trading relationship open shifted to military strategy when the Chickasaws held the front line of Carolina's western defense against French incursion.

The Indian slave trade in the Southeast sprang from similar European-instigated turmoil among the tribes of the eastern Great Lakes area. The need to replenish native populations ravaged by waves of European diseases first introduced in the 1630s led the Iroquois confederacy to conduct so-called mourning wars to capture people from neighboring tribes. Already connected to Dutch, English, and French markets by the beaver skin trade, the Iroquois soon began to sell their human captives.[10] Unable to compete with the Iroquois in the beaver skin trade and probably wary of slave catchers, a group known as the Westos left the southern shore of Lake Erie and migrated south to the Savannah River around 1670. Initially in league with slave traders in Virginia, the Westos were in on the ground floor of the Carolina Indian slave trade. They formed partnerships with Carolina traders and soon began terrorizing weaker tribes in the region. As the Carolina appetite for slaves burgeoned with markets developing in the Caribbean sugarcane plantations, the Westos ranged farther and farther west to find victims, setting in motion a chain of violence that eventually led to the Chickasaws.[11] At the close of the seventeenth century, the slave trade encompassed the entire Southeast. In 1698 the traders Welch and Dodsworth traveled from Carolina to the Mississippi River recruiting slaving partners among the tribes. Besides the Chickasaws, slaving societies active at that time included the Abihkas, Alabamas, Tallapoosas, Apalachicolas, Cussetas, and Cowetas.[12]

SMALLPOX

According to historian Paul Kelton, the chain of person-to-person interaction across the Southeast created by the Indian slave trade helped to spread the devastating smallpox epidemic of 1696–1700.[13] The chances of a disastrous epidemic in the Southeast increased substantially with the arrival in Virginia of shipments of African slaves beginning in 1676, coupled with the burgeoning English population in the colony. Children are especially vulnerable to smallpox, and the American-born children of Britons and Africans lacked prior exposure to smallpox, giving the disease a secure foothold.[14] However, for smallpox to spread beyond its initial infected community, the disease had to breach the empty buffer zones that had previously separated native settlement areas across the Southeast. In fact, Kelton notes that this was one of the results of the Indian slave trade, as slave-catching bands moved back and forth across former buffer zones and herded coffles of unfortunate captives through villages toward the markets in Carolina.[15]

Even though the southeastern Indians were highly susceptible, smallpox did not spread uniformly through the Indian population. Groups living close to colonial towns or in places frequented by travelers were more susceptible than people in more isolated locations, making the Mississippi River and Gulf Coast tribes much more exposed than the interior groups such as the Chickasaws and Choctaws. Likewise, those living in dispersed villages as opposed to more nucleated settlements probably fared better. For example, the Natchez seem to have avoided the brunt of the 1696 smallpox epidemic, perhaps in part because the Natchez lived in widely dispersed settlement districts where family farms were distanced from each other. In addition, the tribe's settlement districts were all situated several miles away from the Mississippi River.[16] Kelton has also argued that slave-catching groups enjoyed more subsistence opportunities and healthier living conditions than groups on the receiving end of the attacks, who were forced to crowd together for long periods inside walled villages for protection.[17]

EARLY FRENCH MISSIONARIES

The paths leading west from Charleston were not the only conduits for the spread of European diseases. La Salle's 1682 voyage opened the Lower Mississippi River valley to visitors from New France and the newly settled Illinois country. In 1686 and 1690 Tonti retraced part of his journey with La Salle, and other voyageurs probably visited the Mississippi region during this time.[18] The first missionaries to descend the Mississippi River and contact the tribes were members of the Society of Foreign Missions, called Seminarians. In the fall of 1698 Tonti ferried three Seminarian priests—Antoine Davion, Jean François Buisson de Saint-Cosme, and François Joliet de Montigny— down the river to selected tribal groups. J.-B. La Source, a lay adult and possibly a servant of one of the priests, traveled with the group.[19] They found the Tunicas and other tribes in the region beset by the horrors of a lethal sickness, possibly the smallpox epidemic that originated in Virginia and Carolina in 1696. La Source wrote simply that the Tunicas were "dying in great numbers."[20]

Before they reached the Natchez, the missionaries heard of the death of a Natchez chief, accompanied by funeral sacrifices. In June 1699 De Montigny, who had been named vicar-general of the Louisiana mission, presented himself to the Natchez and made some critical observations. The vicar had already spent several months among the Taensas, and he found that the Natchez and Taensas spoke the same language. He also noted that other tribes in the region referred to the Natchez as "Challaouelles." Around the time of De Montigny's visit with the Natchez, the vicar noted the death and funeral of another Natchez chief, with thirty sacrificial victims. De Montigny said that the Natchez were "warring . . . with almost all the nations that are on the Mississippi," an indication that the Natchez were becoming actively involved in slave raiding.[21] By 1704 the Seminarian missionary Henry Roulleaux de La Vente confirmed that the Natchez were active slave catchers.[22] Father Davion settled with the Tunicas on the lower Yazoo River, beginning a residency with the tribe that continued intermittently over a twenty-year period.[23] Although Saint-Cosme began a residence with the Tamaroas in the Illinois country, he later moved downstream to reside with the Natchez after De Montigny's departure in 1700.[24]

IBERVILLE'S ARRIVAL AT THE GULF COAST

The coming of the French to the Mississippi Gulf Coast during the height of the English-led slave raids gave the small tribes of the area some hope of protection. The dramatic arrival of Pierre LeMoyne d'Iberville's tall ships signaled the presence of a different type of European, and a powerful one at that. Shortly after making his first contact with Mississippi Indians in February 1699, Iberville brought some of them aboard his vessels for a demonstration of firepower. The frigates *Badine* and *Marin*, each with thirty cannons, must have made a strong impression.[25]

During this initial visit, Iberville and his brother, Jean-Baptiste LeMoyne de Bienville, met with representatives of the Bayogoulas, Mougoulachas, Annochys (an alternative spelling of Biloxi), and Moctobys.[26] The Bayogoulas and Mougoulachas, who happened to be on a hunting trip in the vicinity, occupied a single village on the Mississippi River with the Quinipissas (recall La Salle's contact with them).[27] The Biloxi and Moctoby villages were nearby on the lower Pascagoula River. These Indians mentioned a group called Chozeta, a possible reference to the Choctaws, although anthropologist and linguist James Mooney suggested that they may have been a separate Siouan-speaking group.[28] The Pascagoula tribe lived near the Biloxis and Moctobys, but Iberville did not mention them as being present in this initial diplomatic encounter.[29]

Iberville was a keen observer of native etiquette and left a good description of the Bayogoulas' greeting ritual in his journal:

> the chief or captain of the Bayogoula came to the seashore to show me friendliness and courtesy in their fashion, which is, being near you, to come to a stop, pass their hands over their faces and breasts, and then pass their hands over yours, after which they raise them to the sky, rubbing them together again and embracing again. I did the same thing, having watched it done to the others.[30]

The French commander's careful notes about the fine points of Mississippi diplomacy helped him and his men to learn the appropriate sounds and gestures that would give them a friendly entree into other Indian groups they would meet in the region. Two calumet ceremonies with the Bayogoulas followed the greeting ritual, and Iberville optimistically wrote in his journal that he had established alliances with the Bayogoulas and eleven other tribes: Mougoulacha, Ouascha, Toutymascha, Yagueneschyto, Bylocchy (Biloxi), Moctoby, Ouma (Houma), Pascoboula (Pascagoula), Thecloël, Bayacchyto, and Amylcou.[31] Since Iberville's journal makes it clear that the only Indians present that day were Bayogoulas, Mougoulachas, Biloxis, and Moctobys, the other tribes named must have been considered their allies. A group called the Capinans may have also been present that day or at least represented among the tribal allies. Little is known about the Capinans aside from their poorly documented affiliation with the Pascagoulas. They may have been the same ethnic group as the Moctobys.[32] The Ouascha (Washa or Chawasha), Toutymascha (Chitimacha), and Yagueneschyto (Yakni-Chito) were three small tribes located at the time across the Mississippi River on Bayou Lafourche.[33] As we will see, Thecloël, a variation on De Montigney's Challaouelles, was an alternate name for the Natchez. Iberville's journal entry is the only known reference to the aforementioned Bayacchytos and Amylcous, two groups noted in his journal only as living "east of the [Mississippi] river."[34]

In 1699 or 1700 André-Joseph Pénicaut, a carpenter traveling with Iberville, visited the Pascagoula village that was located three days' travel by boat up the Pascagoula River from Pascagoula Bay.[35] The name Pascagoula translates to "bread people" in Western Muskogean languages; we have no information about this group's own language or the name that they called themselves.[36] Pénicaut's narrative does not mention the villages of the Biloxi and Moctoby/ Capinan. It being summertime, the Frenchmen found the people wearing little clothing; men and boys "went naked as one's hand," and women wore only a small skirt of Spanish moss. A "grand chief" greeted Pénicaut's group and provided them with a feast of buffalo, deer, and bear meat, along with peaches, plums, watermelons, pumpkins, and bread, plus the ubiquitous corn dish known as *sagamité*, a rich hominy stew fortified with boiled meat, beans, nuts, pumpkin, and any other available ingredients. Pénicaut noticed people using bowls of wood and clay, and described the houses as being circular in floor plan, with wooden walls plastered with mud. The roofs were covered with tree bark and palmetto leaves. A drum and *chichicois* (gourd shakers or rattles) provided music for evening dances. The Frenchmen slept in the chief's house on cane beds covered with buffalo skins. Pénicaut also inspected the village's fields of corn and beans, and noted that women and men worked together to plant and tend the crops using wooden sticks to work the ground.[37]

Pénicaut's typically idyllic description of the Pascagoula village belies the ever-present danger of disease and slave raids. In February 1699 Iberville found the partially decomposed remains of over sixty people on an island he named "Massacre Island" (later renamed Dauphine Island, located at the entrance to Mobile Bay). The tribal identity of this group is unknown. Their presence on the island may have been a desperate effort to avoid slave catchers, only to succumb to smallpox or some other lethal pathogen. To add to the dangers already stalking the people on the Mississippi Gulf Coast in 1699, Iberville's own ships brought the plague from Santo Domingo.[38]

On his second voyage to the Gulf Coast in 1700, Iberville ascended the Pascagoula River to a village site formerly occupied by the Biloxis (several miles downriver from the Pascagoula village described by Pénicaut). The French commander found the village abandoned and attributed the disappearance of the residents to disease, which is quite likely; however, the scene as he described it also invokes images of a slave raid and a terrified population ultimately overwhelmed by superior forces:

> *It did not appear to me that in this village there were more than thirty to forty huts, built oblong and roofed with tree bark, as we make ours.*

They were all of one story, about 8 feet high, made of mud daub. Only three are left; the others were burned. The village was enclosed with pales 8 feet high and about 18 inches thick. There still remain three square lookout boxes, each side being 10 feet wide; they are raised 8 feet high, on posts; the sides were made of clay daub mixed with grass, 8 inches thick, well covered. There were several loopholes for them to shoot their arrows through. It appears to me that there was a lookout box at each angle, and one in the middle of the [walls]. It was strong enough for them to defend themselves against enemies that have nothing more than arrows.[39]

New information about the small tribes of the interior Lower Mississippi River valley came to light when Iberville traveled up the Mississippi River in the spring of 1699. His expedition went as far north as the Houma village located at the place that came to be known as the "Portage of the Cross." In Iberville's time, the Mississippi River made a wide meander loop toward the west at this location. The eastern end of the meander formed a relatively narrow neck, about six miles wide, across which travelers could carry their canoes and cargo and reenter the river, thus avoiding approximately thirty miles of paddling around the meander loop. A bayou flowed from north to south across the neck through a small oxbow lake, making it possible during much of the year to paddle canoes across the portage. The location was adjacent to the mouth of the Red River, which entered the western end of the meander loop.[40]

The main Houma village was located on the east side of the Mississippi River atop the loess bluff that overlooked the meander neck. As mentioned in chapter 2, when La Salle passed through here in 1682 he was aware of the Houmas but did not stop to meet them.[41] The village was set back some 300 yards from the edge of the bluff and comprised around 140 houses that encircled a village square. Iberville noticed scattered cornfields on neighboring hills and slopes. Upon his arrival, the Houmas treated the French commander and his men to a marathon calumet ceremony with exchange of presents, feasting, and dancing that lasted from mid-morning until around midnight. The male and female dancers wore only breechclouts and were heavily tattooed and painted.[42]

Another description of the Houma village comes from the Jesuit missionary Jacques Gravier, who was there several months after Iberville. By that time other missionaries had erected a chapel and cross near the Houma temple building. Gravier observed that the temple contained the tribe's sacred fire and woodcarvings of human and animal figures. The missionary also viewed the bones of a powerful female chief who had died the previous year. Although Gravier did not record her name, she apparently gained her position of leadership through her bravery in warfare. At the time, the Houmas and Bayogoulas were involved in a cycle of revenge-motivated hostilities. Both tribes were also harassed by English/Chickasaw slave raids, and anyone who left the confines of the village risked being captured. Gravier wrote that the Houma women cried when their men departed on hunting expeditions and were jubilant when they returned safely. Of course, crowding together for protection exposed the people to unsanitary conditions and water-borne diseases. Both Iberville and Gravier reported that dysentery was rampant among the Houmas throughout 1700. Searching for a cause, the missionary attributed the affliction to the people's custom of bathing in streams during cold weather. Ominously, Gravier wrote that the tribe's medicine men were powerless to stop the dying.[43]

During his 1699 stop at the Houma village, Iberville had the good fortune to interview a Taensa with extensive knowledge of the geography and tribes farther up the Mississippi River. French reconnaissance later verified the accuracy of much of what Iberville heard that day. Importantly, the Taensa informant helped Iberville draw a map of the region showing his own tribe's villages and those of several other tribes, including the Theloel (Natchez), Koroas, Yazoos, Tunicas, Ofos, Tious, Taposas, Chakchiumas, and Ibitoupas.[44] The Taensa placed the Koroas on the west side of the Mississippi River, north of his own villages, and subsequent narratives confirm a Koroa presence in that area. In 1700 Bienville heard about a Koroa village on the Ouachita River in the upper Tensas Basin, where they were active in the salt trade between Caddoan tribes to the west and the Mississippi tribes. Other French narratives from around that same time document another Koroa settlement east of the Mississippi River, on the lower Yazoo River in the extended settlement that included the Yazoo, Ofo, and Tunica villages. The Taensa made no mention of the Koroa villages near the Natchez that the La Salle expedition visited just seventeen years earlier (see chapter 2), and the fate of these villages remains a mystery. The ethnohistorian John R. Swanton has pointed out that were it not for La Salle's chroniclers, we would never know that this branch of the Koroas ever existed. Like so many other small tribes of the region, the Koroas' origins are uncertain. They may be the Akoroa on the 1674 Joliet map, shown as one of several villages on the lower Arkansas River, and some scholars have suggested that the Koroas were De Soto's "Coligua," found near present-day Batesville in northeastern Arkansas.[45]

The Taensa informant also located the Yazoos on the west side of the Mississippi River; however, subsequent contact with them placed them about ten miles up the Yazoo River on the bluffs along the south bank. It was Tonti who named the Yazoo River after the Yazoos, and Swanton speculated that they might have been settled on this river longer than their neighbors. The Yazoo language included the "r" sound and thus may have been related to Tunican.[46] Despite the Yazoos' longevity, their neighbors, the Tunicas, are better known, thanks in part to Father Davion's long residence with them.[47] The Tunicas' origins are obscure and open to speculation. They have been tenuously linked with at least two groups encountered by the De Soto expedition—the people called the Tanico in central Arkansas and the mound-building chiefdom known as Quizquiz in northwestern Mississippi, discussed in chapter 2.[48] Chickasaw and Choctaw traditions refer to the area near Friars Point, Mississippi, as "Tunica Old Fields," which lends support to the Tunica-Quizquiz connection.[49]

As discussed in the introduction, several colonial listings of tribes settled on the lower Yazoo River, beginning with that of Iberville's Taensa informant, name the Ouispés and Ofos (or Ofogoulas) as separate groups.[50] In the late seventeenth century the Tious (Tioux, Thysia, Tougoula, Thoucoue) lived near the Tunicas, Yazoos, Ofos, and Koroas on the lower Yazoo River. Their language was closely related to the language spoken by the Tunicas, and some sources indicate that the two groups may have spoken the same language. Around 1700 they migrated down the Mississippi River to escape English/Chickasaw slave raids. Some of the Tious settled with the Bayogoulas, and another group may have relocated on the Pearl River. The most well known contingent joined the Natchez confederacy and remained part of the pro-French faction there until around 1727. Their supposed complicity with the Natchez in the 1729 uprising earned them harassment from pro-French tribes such as the Quapaws.[51]

The Taensa told Iberville about three other tribes living on the Yazoo River—Taposas, Chakchiumas, and Ibitoupas. The largest of these groups was the Chakchiumas, with an estimated sixty to seventy families in 1699. In the early eighteenth century they lived at the junction of the Yazoo and Yalobusha rivers, at present-day Greenwood, Mississippi. In 1702 Tonti found a Chakchiuma village near the Chickasaw villages in southern Lee County or northern Monroe County; however, this group apparently left this location shortly thereafter and joined the Chakchiuma village on the Yalobusha. Tonti also noted a place the Choctaws called "Chakchiuma Old Fields" in the vicinity of Sucarnoochee Creek in present-day Kemper County.[52] As discussed in chapter 2, the Chakchiumas are one of three Mississippi tribes (with the Alabamas and Chickasaws) to be named in the chronicles of the De Soto expedition (variously as the Sacchuma, Saquechuma, and Saktchihuma). Some scholars have suggested a possible relationship between the Chakchiumas and Houmas, noting that Chakchiuma translates to "red crawfish" in Choctaw and the Houmas, whose name means "red" in Choctaw, venerated the red crawfish as their war emblem.[53] The Chakchiumas also figure in the origin stories of both the Choctaws and Chickasaws.[54] Although no clear documentation exists about their language, their links with the Chickasaws and Choctaws indicate that the Chakchiumas were probably Western Muskogean speakers.[55]

The other two groups on the upper Yazoo River in Iberville's time were the Ibitoupas and Taposas. The Taposa village was placed about twenty-five miles north of the Chakchiumas (probably in Tallahatchie County), although they apparently joined the Chakchiumas at times for protection from Quapaw and Chickasaw slave raids. By the 1720s the Taposas numbered around twenty-five families.[56] The Ibitoupas may have lived in the vicinity of present-day Tchula in Holmes County around 1700; however, narratives from the early 1720s place them north of the Chakchiumas near present-day Tippo (the town is named after them). At that time, the group only comprised six families.[57] A fourth group, the Choulas (Choctaw for "foxes"), are documented by Jean-Baptiste Bénard La Harpe in 1722 in the vicinity of present-day Tchula, which is named after them. The Choulas may have been a faction of the Ibitoupas.[58]

THE NATCHEZ

Upon Iberville's arrival at the Gulf Coast, the Bayogoulas informed him of an allied group on the Mississippi River called the Theloels.[59] At the Houma village, a Taensas man provided more information about this nation, noting that the Theloel people were in nine villages three days' journey upriver.[60] When Iberville's party returned to the Mississippi River valley in the spring of 1700, the commander wanted to solidify the tribal alliances established the previous year. The Theloels, who later became better known as the Natchez, were an important diplomatic objective. Traveling upriver by canoe, Iberville's expedition reached the Theloels' landing on March 11. Employing the greeting ritual he had learned from the Bayogoulas, Iberville received a friendly welcome and an introduction to the chief. The commander's journal entry for that occasion provides the earliest description of the Grand Village mound center:

We repaired to [the chief's] cabin, which is raised to a height of 10 feet on earth brought thither, and is 25 feet wide and 45 long. Near by are eight cabins. Before that of the chief's is the temple mound, which forms a round, a little oval, and bounds an open space about 250 paces wide and 300 long. A stream passes near, from which they draw their water.[61]

The chief gave Iberville a letter from the missionary De Montigny, who had been among the Natchez just three days earlier. Although Iberville noted that the chief, an elderly man, was suffering from dysentery, neither he nor De Montigny reported finding smallpox among the Natchez, indicating that the tribe may have somehow avoided the epidemic that devastated so many other groups. Iberville also noted that the Natchez had recently been the target of Chickasaw slave raids.[62]

The earliest record of the names of the Natchez confederacy's settlement districts comes from Iberville's Taensa informant, who listed nine settlements: Natchés, Pochougoula, Ousagoucoula, Cogoucoula, Yatanocha, Ymacacha, Thoucoue, Tougoula, and Achougoucoula. The Taensa also stated that "these villages together make only one nation, which is named Theloel."[63] As later narratives make clear, the "village" called Natchés was not a separate settlement district, but was instead the place the French came to call the "Grand Village," a ceremonial mound center located adjacent to a settlement district that later writers called the "Flour" settlement. In time, the name Theloel was lost, and Natchés, with its French variation "Natchez," became the common title for the tribe.[64] Early colonial accounts vary with regard to the number of settlements making up the Natchez confederation; however, by the time that the French established Fort Rosalie at the Natchez in 1716, the narratives consistently speak of only five settlement districts: Flour, Tiou, Grigra, White Apple, and Jenzenaque (Figure 5). The districts were set well inland from the Mississippi River, along St. Catherine Creek, Coles Creek, and their tributaries. Within the settlement districts, the people lived on dispersed family farms.[65]

The Flour, White Apple, and Jenzenaque settlements were mainly comprised of Natchezan remnants of the prehistoric Emerald/Anna chiefdom.[66] The Tious and Grigras were probable Tunican-speaking groups living with the Natchez for protection against slavers. In the early 1980s archaeologists investigated the remains of a sixth colonial-period Natchez settlement district located to the north of the Jenzenaque area, near the mouth of Coles Creek. This settlement, called the Fairchilds Creek/Coles Creek area, is not named in the French colonial narratives, and the ethnicity of the people who lived

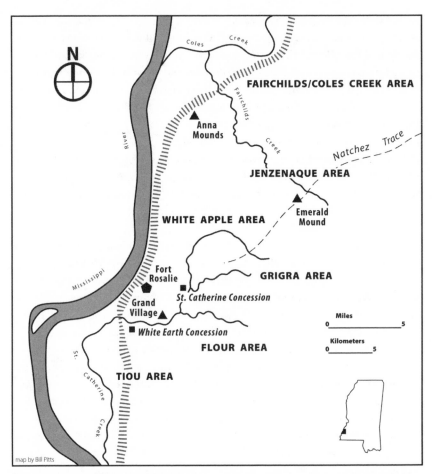

Figure 5. The Natchez area with archaeological sites, Indian settlement districts, and French colonial installations. (Based upon Brown, *Natchez Indian Archaeology*, Figure 3; Broutin [map 1723], *Carte des environs du fort Rosalie aux Natchez*)

there is uncertain; the predominance of shell-tempered pottery may indicate the presence of yet another northern refugee group attached to the Natchez. Patricia Galloway has noted the possibility that another ethnic group, a portion of the Chitimacha tribe, may have been living with the Natchez around the turn of the eighteenth century.[67]

For the most part, the French arriving at the Natchez settlements via the Mississippi River interacted with the chiefs at the Grand Village and the people of the nearby Flour and Tiou settlement districts. Accounts of French visits to the White Apple, Jenzenaque, and Griga settlements are conspicuously absent from the colonial narratives. These three northerly settlement districts, distant from the Mississippi River and arrayed around the Natchez Trace, interacted with the Carolina English and their Indian allies in the region, principally the Chickasaws. This precarious dual relationship with the French and English is how the Natchez adapted to life in the shadow of the two competing European superpowers.[68]

During the colonial period, the ceremonial mound center known as the Grand Village served as the main point of contact for the French. The Great Sun, the hereditary Natchez chief whom the French viewed as the monarch of the tribe, had his residence there along with a few tribal officials, including the Great Sun's younger brother, known by his office title of Tattooed Serpent. Today, the Grand Village is a National Historic Landmark administered by the Mississippi Department of Archives and History. The site is located on the west bank of St. Catherine Creek, a tributary of the Mississippi River, and contains three ceremonial mounds designated A, B, and C, from north to south. Mound A, known as the Abandoned Mound, was apparently not in use during the French colonial period. The Great Sun lived in a house on Mound B, while Mound C supported the tribe's temple building, arguably the Natchez Indians' most sacred place. Ignace Broutin's 1723 map of the Natchez area seems to depict other mounds at the site; however, the French narratives only mention Mounds B and C. Despite the French use of the term "village" for the site, only a few people had permanent residences there. Colonial observers counted three to eight houses in addition to the structures on the mounds, and archaeological investigations have found evidence of only five off-mound building locations.[69]

Excavations by the Mississippi Department of Archives and History in 1930 and 1962 document the construction and use of Mounds B and C. Radiocarbon dates indicate that mound building started around A.D. 1200, and the Natchez had ceased all mound construction activities by the time of first French contact in the late 1600s. Moreau B. C. Chambers led the 1930 excavations with the help of a Works Progress Administration (WPA) labor force, concentrating on Mounds B and C. Robert S. Neitzel supervised the 1962 work, further investigating the two mounds studied by Chambers. Neitzel returned to the site in 1972 to examine the plaza areas between the mounds. This work revealed that the Natchez built two successive buildings on the premound surface beneath Mound B. Subsequent Mound B construction took place in four stages, beginning with a low earthen platform on which two successive buildings stood. Over an undetermined length of time, the builders raised the mound's height three more times, with structures placed atop each building stage. The structures were all single-room dwellings of square or rectangular floor plan. Unfortunately, erosion destroyed most of the remains of the mound's final structure, the house of the Great Sun who was a friend of the colonial French. The floor plans of Mound B's prehistoric structures measure about forty by fifty feet, making them somewhat larger than the site's off-mound houses.[70]

Mound C also had four building stages, with some evidence of premound occupation beneath the first construction stage. The mound incorporated a sloping earthen ramp on its north end, extending from the summit down to the historic plaza. Chambers and Neitzel found the remains of twenty-six burials in Mound C, along with a substantial portion of the archaeological footprint of the historic temple building. This sacred structure is well documented thanks to the wealth of French eyewitness descriptions. The French accounts agree substantially among themselves and with the building's floor plan as revealed through archaeology, and they add the invaluable details that are only present in firsthand observations. The temple building was composed of two rooms, an anteroom or portico measuring about twenty by thirty feet, and a larger room measuring about thirty feet deep and forty feet wide, which contained the tribe's eternal fire and its most sacred objects. According to the eyewitness accounts, the building's main room was dark, lit only by the dim glow of the sacred fire. None of the Frenchmen who entered the temple were the least bit impressed with what they saw, but spoke of smoke-blackened walls and furnishings, tables covered with cane mats and animal skins, baskets or boxes containing the bones of past chiefs, pottery, and humanlike figures fashioned from wood and stone. One writer (Gravier) mentioned stone crystals, and another (Pénicaut) saw a figure of a rattlesnake and strings of pearl beads. Most writers agree that several men served as temple guardians, keeping constant vigil over the building and carefully maintaining the tribe's sacred fire. French observers also noted the presence of two or three large bird effigies mounted atop posts above the roof of the temple. The meaning behind these bird figures is unknown, although at least two other Mississippi Valley temples, those of the Taensa and Bayogoula, were known to have had similar features.[71]

The Natchez built their houses using mud and clay mixed with grass, which they plastered on a pole and cane lathe framework to make permanent walled structures that were usually square or rectangular in floor plan. Vertical wall poles bent together and tied formed a dome-shaped roof, over which the builders placed a covering of thatched grass and corn stalks. French colonial observers also noted that the Natchez covered their houses inside and out with woven cane mats to provide insulation and help shed rainwater.[72] Archaeological investigations of Natchez house sites reveal the use of different construction techniques. Some houses utilized wall trenches—shallow ditches into which vertical wall posts were set; however, other archaeological floor plans show wall posts seated in individual holes. Houses typically included a centrally located hearth and a corner doorway. Experiments with hearth fires inside a reconstructed Natchez house demonstrate that the fire draws air in through the corner door, while the smoke rises into the ceiling dome and passes out through the grass thatch.[73]

Le Page Du Pratz, who lived in the Natchez area from 1720 to 1728, reported that the grass used by the Natchez to cover their house roofs was four to five feet in length. This was the native long prairie grass, probably big bluestem (*Andropogon gerardi*), which is now gone from the Natchez region. French colonial accounts confirm that large expanses of open prairie dominated the Natchez area in the early eighteenth century. This grassland environment was not an accident of nature; the Indians maintained the prairie with controlled grass fires that prevented saplings from taking hold and converting the land to forest. Du Pratz observed that the Natchez burned the tall grass each fall to facilitate travel and hunting, and noted that the prairie land was more easily prepared for agriculture than forested land.[74]

French narratives describe the clothing of the Natchez as minimal during the summer months, with men wearing only a breechclout (also breechcloth or loincloth, a cloth passed between the legs and looped over a belt to hang down in front and back) and women a skirt. Traditionally, they made their clothes and moccasins from tanned deerskins. Women sometimes wore skirts made from the woven fiber of mulberry tree bark and from feathers. In winter, men wore deerskin shirts, and both sexes donned buffalo skin robes in extremely cold weather. Both men and women painted their faces using colors derived from natural sources, including plants and clays. Both sexes also wore tattooed images such as circles, snakes, and other designs over much of their bodies. The Natchez custom of head flattening attracted the colonists' attention, and most writers mentioned something about it. To achieve the desired look, a mother bound a piece of hard ceramic or wood against her child's forehead every night. Gradually, the skull above the eyes flattened and retained the abnormal shape. Most Europeans thought the practice was simply for beautification, but head flattening may have also had a deeper social or religious significance. Men and boys wore their hair in a "pudding bowl" cut, with bangs hanging across the forehead. A small area on the top of the head was shaved or plucked, leaving a patch of hair in the center to which feathers were sometimes attached. Colonial illustrations often show men with a braid of hair hanging down the side of the head, reaching to the shoulder. Girls and women generally wore their hair straight, usually long and hanging down the back.[75]

As French explorers and colonists became more familiar with the Natchez, they noticed aspects of the tribe's society that reminded them of their own society back in Europe, and the irony of the "Sun" coincidence was especially significant. The French viewed the Great Sun as a counterpart to their own Sun King, Louis XIV, a misperception of the chief's power that would have important consequences. Colonial observers saw the Great Sun in his ceremonial role, presiding over tribal feasts and other social and religious events, leading to the conclusion that the chief had despotic authority over the settlement district chiefs.[76] As mentioned above, the French writers who are responsible for the wealth of documentation about the Grand Village apparently never ventured out to the outlying settlement districts (except during the 1723 French raids on these settlements—see below), where they might have observed council meetings and noticed the political power of the district chiefs. If the Great Sun's elite status was a carryover from the Mississippi period chiefdoms such as Quigualtam, by the late seventeenth century the circumstances surrounding European presence in the region had relegated his role to that of a figurehead. Indeed, the history of the tribe makes it clear that the settlement district chiefs were autonomous and free to act outside the Great Sun's authority.[77]

Because the French colored their perception of Natchez society with terms drawn from their own experience back in Europe, it is perhaps not surprising that they related the tribe's ranked social organization to the class system with which they were familiar. The French viewed the social rank to which the Great Sun belonged as nobility and spoke of the lower social rank as commoners, giving the Natchez the appearance of having a European-like social order. Du Pratz, who was enamored with the Natchez, seized on this distinction to proclaim the tribe "more civilized" than other groups in the region.[78]

Unlike European classes, however, the French observed that the Natchez social ranks were exogamous, that is, members of one rank took their marriage partners from the other rank. Various French texts also mention two other social categories—Suns, the group with the highest social status, and Honored, a social distinction below nobles and above commoners. In the early twentieth century John R. Swanton presented an interpretation of the Natchez social system with the nobility being comprised of three distinct classes: Suns, Nobles, and Honored. Although Swanton's interpretation seemed to explain what the colonial French had described, his description of three social classes taking marriage partners from the single commoner rank presented an asymmetry that puzzled subsequent researchers. When analyzed mathematically using the tribe's matrilineal descent rules, the three noble classes would deplete the commoner rank within a few generations, resulting in a noble rank without a source for marriage partners. The "Natchez Paradox," as Swanton's interpretation came to be known, was resolved after closer scrutiny of the Suns and Honored categories, as they are described in the French colonial narratives. The Suns were in fact not a class but a royal family or elite lineage within the nobility. Likewise, the Honored was a men's society within the commoner rank. These two corrections to Swanton's interpretation restored the necessary symmetry resulting in two social ranks.[79]

More recently, Patricia Galloway and Jason B. Jackson further clarified the picture with their identification of the Natchez social ranks as exogamous moieties.[80] "Moiety," the French term for "half," refers to the division of the tribal group into two parts, with one moiety usually viewed by the people as being senior or having an elder brother relationship with the other moiety, hence the French perception of nobility and commoners. Moieties are also documented among the Choctaws, Creeks, Chickasaws, and other groups in the region, although their roles and the social rules governing them are complex and tend to differ from tribe to tribe. The Natchez moieties seem to have been competitive in nature, while also providing certain social and ceremonial services, in addition to supplying marriage partners for each other.

THE SMALL TRIBES IN THE MOBILE BAY AREA

After establishing diplomatic relations with the lower Mississippi River tribes, Iberville and Bienville moved the colony's base of operations in 1702 from Fort Maurepas near present-day Biloxi Bay to Fort Louis (later moved and renamed Fort Condé), located on Mobile Bay. There they found the region's native population in a state of flux. Slave-raiding parties from the Alabamas, Abihkas, Tallapoosas, and others hammered the small tribal settlements along the lower Tombigbee River and in the Mobile-Tensaw delta.[81] Some of these small tribes were probably remnants of the late prehistoric Bottle Creek society (see chapter 1), and most historians agree that the early-eighteenth-century Mobile tribe derived from the sixteenth-century Mabila (Mavilla, Mavila, Mauvila) group, against whom De Soto and his army fought a desperate battle in 1540.[82] By 1702 some of these groups had left the area, having fled to friendly villages in the Choctaw confederacy if they were not lost to slave catchers.

Those that remained, including the Mobiles, Tohomés, and Naniabas, saw the incoming French as a potential ally against the slave raids. The Mobile villages were on the Mobile River a few miles south of the junction of the Tombigbee and Alabama rivers. The Naniabas, also sometimes called the Little Tohomés and Gens des Fourches (People of the Fork), were above the Mobiles at the junction of the two rivers. The Tohomés were a few miles farther to the north on the lower Tombigbee River.[83] The ethnohistorian George Lankford has noted that these groups occupied seasonal camps near their cornfields in the lowlands along the rivers, while maintaining permanent villages in the adjacent bluffs. The area north of the junction of the Tombigbee and Alabama rivers, in present-day Clarke County, Alabama, contains salt springs that the Mobiles, Tohomés, and Naniabas exploited to trade with their neighbors, particularly the Choctaws. These three tribes seem to have been closely associated; in 1704 Pénicaut witnessed a "festival" in which all three participated. Along with feasting and dancing, Pénicaut reported the severe beating of a number of children, ostensibly to toughen them for warfare.[84]

FRENCH CONTACT WITH THE CHOCTAWS AND CHICKASAWS

By the turn of the eighteenth century Chickasaw slave raids on Choctaw villages had fostered a bitter enmity between these two nations. The earliest English-led slave raids on Choctaw villages are undocumented, although these attacks had been ongoing for several years when Choctaw chiefs began requesting guns and ammunition from the French on the Mississippi Gulf Coast in late 1701. Despite its formidable size, the Choctaw confederacy's dispersed villages were difficult to defend against surprise attacks by large raiding parties. As the slave raids by groups of Chickasaws, Chakchiumas, Abihkas, Alabamas, and others escalated during the early years of the eighteenth century, hundreds of Choctaws perished, while slave catchers herded hundreds more, mostly women and children, along the arduous 500-mile-long path to the markets in Charleston and Port Royal.[85]

The intertribal tension in the region was palpable when Tonti undertook a diplomatic mission to the Choctaws and Chickasaws at Iberville's behest in February and March 1702. Tonti and his party of Frenchmen, with Tohomé, Mobilian, and Choctaw guides, traveled northwest from Iberville's Mobile

Bay outpost and skirted the eastern edge of the Choctaws' territory, generally following the western side of the Tombigbee River. The group passed through two Choctaw villages, and Tonti noted that individual households were widely dispersed. He learned of a third Choctaw village to the northeast that was so hard-pressed by Chickasaw, Alabama, and Abihka slave raiders that its people could no longer plant and tend their fields in safety. Although the Choctaws and Chickasaws seem to have suspended some of their hostilities to allow the little diplomatic party to move between the two tribes, Tonti's guides had to use evasive action to avoid running into a combined Chickasaw-Chakchiuma slave-raiding force of some 400 gunmen led by Englishmen in native dress.[86]

Following through on his mission, Tonti persuaded seven chiefs—three Chickasaws and four Choctaws—to return with him to Mobile Bay to meet with Iberville and receive presents. Using Bienville as his translator, Iberville vilified the English and berated the Chickasaws for allowing themselves to be manipulated. (The chiefs had undoubtedly heard a similar harangue about the French from their English contacts.) After lecturing the chiefs on the advantages offered by allegiance to the French, Iberville threatened to arm several tribes, including the Natchez and Illinois, and send them to attack the Chickasaws if they continued their slave raids. To establish a lasting peace, the French commander offered to unite the Chickasaws and Choctaws around a trading post that he would establish between their two nations. In the end, the chiefs returned home laden with French presents that included guns, bullets, powder, knives, axes, kettles, and glass beads.[87] With the Mobile meeting, which changed nothing as far as these two tribes' relationships with the English and with each other were concerned, the Mississippi Indians' game of playing off one group of colonial Europeans against the other for presents and trade had officially begun.

THE PEOPLE ON THE LAND

When Tonti arrived at the Chickasaw villages in early 1702, a surprise awaited him:

> *[The Chickasaws] made us sit on some mats near the [chief's] cabin. The chief was seated there and an Englishman that I had trouble recognizing for one. He was seated holding a gun in his hand and a saber at his side. He had on a rather dirty blue shirt, no pants, stockings, or shoes, a scarlet wool blanket and some discs at his neck like a savage.[88]*

This anonymous Englishman was one of two Carolinians among the Chickasaws that winter accompanying a party of about 400 warriors in slave raids against the Choctaws. The man appeared to be completely at ease with his hosts and had obviously been living with them for some time. In addition to Chickasaw, he spoke Shawnee. Tonti, on the other hand, had considerable difficulty communicating with the Chickasaws until he found a member of the tribe who spoke Illinois, a language with which the Frenchman had some experience. The Chickasaws no doubt took note of the fact that their English friend and the Frenchmen spoke different languages, and that animosity existed between the two groups. (Tonti wrote to Iberville that he had "regarded [the Englishman] with nothing but anger" upon meeting him.)[89]

Tonti had trouble identifying the man as an Englishman because his dress was similar to that of the Chickasaw warriors—a combination of European and Indian apparel. When Tonti wrote that the Englishman was not wearing pants, the Frenchman probably meant that his adversary wore a traditional breechclout. Trade shirts or shirts made from trade cloth were common, and men often wore deerskin boots that reached the thighs. While elderly men generally wore their hair long and straight, fighting-age men opted for more intimidating hairstyles, such as the "Mohawk" look—with hair shaved or plucked from the sides of the head and a tall roach or crest down the center stiffened with bear grease. Male ornamentation included tattoos (done with garfish teeth and pitch pine ink), nose rings, and earrings. During times of aggression, face paint signified clan membership, and eagle and swan feathers, worn about the head and shoulders, denoted warriors. Eighteenth-century accounts of Chickasaw women's clothing and appearance also document a blending of traditional materials and European trade items. Women covered themselves from the waist down with red and blue trade cloth, and in cooler weather wore a jacket or robe of cloth or animal skin. Jewelry for women included bead necklaces, wristbands, armbands, and ear pendants. Women oiled their hair with bear grease. Younger women usually tied up their hair, except in times of mourning, while older women wore their hair loose and straight.[90] Like the Natchez, the Chickasaws followed the custom of head flattening, reshaping their male and female infants' foreheads by applying pressure with bags of sand or a padded board. The shaping process continued into childhood and gave adults a distinctive broad-faced appearance. The social acceptance of head flattening apparently declined during the eighteenth century, and the practice eventually ceased.[91]

The Choctaws also practiced head flattening and, like the Chickasaws, eventually abandoned the practice. The members of the various component

groups of the Choctaw confederacy displayed ethnic identity and family affiliation in their personal appearance with distinguishing tattoos, ornaments,
dress, and other accoutrements. In the early eighteenth century Choctaw
men and women characteristically wore their hair long and straight, although
some observers noted in the 1770s that some of the younger Choctaw men
were beginning "to imitate the Chickasaw fashion." This probably refers to the
"Mohawk" look described above.[92] Choctaw women traditionally wove bison
hair to make shirts, robes, and blankets, and bison skin robes worn with the
hair turned inward were preferred during very cold weather. Traditional apparel also included deerskin shirts and feather robes and blankets, with feathers attached to a net made from woven grass; however, European trade rapidly replaced these traditional materials with blankets of French Limbourgh and
English Stroud, colorful shirts, and jackets. Choctaw men wore the ubiquitous breechclout, increasingly made from imported fabric, sometimes adding
deerskin leggings. Deerskin and bearskin moccasins remained the preferred
footwear throughout most of the eighteenth century. Bernard Romans, who
traveled among the Choctaws in the 1770s, observed some men who dressed
as women. Ornaments made of silver and brass, glass trade beads, and other
materials worn as necklaces and ear pendants had spiritual connotations,
as did feathers, which conferred to the wearer the powers of the birds from
which they came.[93]

In addition to speaking closely related Western Muskogean languages, the
Chickasaws and Choctaws share similar origin stories. Stories associated with
both groups speak of two different tribal beginnings: migration from an unspecified land west of the Mississippi River and emergence from beneath a
mound. Both of these themes appear in combined form as early as the 1720s,
when someone related the story of the Choctaws' beginnings to Le Page du
Pratz: "According to the tradition of the [Choctaws] this nation passed so rapidly from one land to another and arrived so suddenly in the country which it
occupies that, when I asked them from whence the Chat-kas came, to express
the suddenness of their appearance they replied that they had come out from
under the earth."[94]

In some versions of the migration story, the ancestral group in the west
included the Chickasaws, Choctaws, and Chakchiumas. Both the Chickasaws
and Choctaws considered the Chakchiumas as their senior or elder relatives,
indicating a feeling of relatedness between these groups similar to the "brother" relationship documented between the Choctaws and Alabamas and between the Natchez and Chitimachas. The Chickasaw and Choctaw migration
stories share the element of the sacred pole, which leaders staked upright in

the campground at the end of each day's journey. The following morning the people found the pole leaning to the east, pointing the direction in which they were to travel, eventually leading the people to their historic homeland. The Chickasaw stories often include a faithful dog that served as a guardian and guide.[95]

The Chickasaw version of the emergence legend tells of the people coming out of a cave beneath a mound called Nanne Hamgeh that was associated with the Natchez. One nineteenth-century source places this mound on the Big Black River in southwestern Mississippi, while Swanton tentatively located Nanne Hamgeh on the east side of the Mississippi River near the mouth of the Arkansas River.[96] In their emergence stories, the Choctaws came from beneath the prehistoric Nanih Waiya mound in southern Winston County. The early-twentieth-century archaeologist Calvin S. Brown described the Nanih Waiya mound as being rectangular-shaped, measuring 218 feet in length and 140 feet in width, with a height of 22–25 feet. Some 800 yards from the main mound, Brown noted the presence of a section of earthen wall or rampart about 2.5–4.0 feet high and around 300 feet in length. A local farmer told Brown that at least three other sections of the wall existed. About 250 yards northeast of the main mound, Brown found a smaller, conical mound 7–8 feet in height and noted that all of the site's earthworks were being reduced by cultivation. Choctaw tribal archaeologist Kenneth H. Carlton reported recently that the main mound, part of the conical mound, and part of the earthwork remain relatively intact. Confusingly, a natural geological feature known as the Nanih Waiya "cave mound" is located about one mile to the east of the Nanih Waiya mound site in northeastern Neshoba County. Some versions of the Choctaw origin story place the emergence at the cave mound, which has a small cave entrance on its east side near the banks of Nanawaya Creek. Both Nanih Waiya sites are now under Mississippi Band of Choctaw ownership.[97] The existence of conflicting origin stories for these two tribal groups may be attributable to their multiethnic background.[98]

But what does modern archaeology and ethnohistoric research say about the origins of these tribes? In her landmark 1995 book *Choctaw Genesis: 1500–1700*, the ethnohistorian Patricia Galloway made a strong argument for a late-seventeenth-century coalescing of several different ethnic groups, brought about by the decline of nearby Mississippi period chiefdoms and the arrival of Europeans. According to Galloway, Choctaw ancestors include mound-builder populations from the Black Warrior River in western Alabama (perhaps the Pafalaya chiefdom encountered by De Soto—see chapter 2), the Mobile-Tensaw delta, the Tombigbee River, and the lower Pearl River in southwest

Mississippi, the last apparently an offshoot of the Natchezan group. These immigrants moved into a largely uninhabited region in east-central Mississippi, where they joined forces with a Muskogean-speaking population moving south from the Black Prairie. This last group may have been associated with the construction of the Nanih Waiya mound center discussed above. During the eighteenth century, the Choctaw confederacy continued to take in groups displaced by European encroachment.[99]

As discussed in chapter 2, De Soto encountered the Chickasaws living somewhere in the vicinity of Clay, Lowndes, Oktibbeha, and Noxubee counties. Archaeologist James R. Atkinson suggests that the historic Chickasaws were descended from Mississippi period chiefdoms settled on the lower river terraces and bottomlands along the Tombigbee River and its tributaries. These prehistoric populations constructed the Owl Creek ceremonial mound center and several smaller mound sites in northeastern Mississippi. The ancestral Chickasaws probably moved onto the Black Prairie during the Mississippi period, although their time of arrival is uncertain.[100] The archaeology also shows that the Chickasaws left this area shortly after their confrontation with De Soto and moved about seventy miles to the north, eventually settling at the junction of the Natchez Trace (sometimes called the "Chickasaw Trace") and the trail to Carolina.[101]

As Tonti passed through the Choctaw and Chickasaw villages, he would have likely seen houses with both circular and rectangular floor plans. Most of the structures had vertical poles, domed roofs, and mud- or clay-plastered walls, with roofs covered by bark or thatch. The information on the Choctaws is scanty, but they may have had summer and winter houses as is documented for the Chickasaws. Chickasaw winter houses were either rectangular or circular in floor plan, with walls of vertical poles interwoven with branches and cane, covered with mud and clay. Roofs were made of thatched prairie grass and bark. Summer houses were usually rectangular in floor plan and of somewhat lighter pole and mud construction than winter houses, with roofs of layered bark. Corn granaries would have been ubiquitous in all settlements, usually raised several feet off the ground to discourage varmints from entering. Choctaw and Chickasaw families maintained small gardens of corn, beans, and squash near their houses, and some families tended larger communal fields at some distance away.[102]

Although the Choctaw confederacy experienced a population decline from an estimated 28,000 people in 1685 to around 14,000 in 1790, the Choctaws still consistently outnumbered by four to one the next largest tribal groups in Mississippi, the Natchez and Chickasaws.[103] During much of the eighteenth century, the confederacy comprised between forty and fifty towns or villages.[104] Figure 6 shows the approximate locations of some of the Choctaw villages mentioned in the text. Although the map is somewhat helpful in understanding the tribe's history, it is important to avoid the map's illusion that Choctaw society remained static during the eighteenth and early nineteenth centuries. Over time, villages merged, divided, and changed their locations. In a few cases, conflicts resulted in the destruction of villages. Likewise, settlement patterns and cultural practices were rapidly evolving in response to European encroachment. The English trader James Adair described the Choctaw settlement pattern in the mid-eighteenth century as being shaped by defensive requirements:

> *The barrier towns, which are next to the Muskohge [Creek] and Chikkasah countries, are compactly settled for social defense, according to the general method of other savage nations; but the rest, both in the center, and toward the Mississippi, are only scattered plantations, as best suits a separate easy way of living. A stranger might be in the middle of one of their populous extensive towns, without seeing half a dozen of their houses, in the direct course of his path.[105]*

By the beginning of the eighteenth century, the various ethnic components of the Choctaw confederacy had formed into divisions or districts that influenced Choctaw politics throughout the remainder of the colonial period. Although the French perceived from two to four divisions at various times, colonial narratives seem to point to three main divisions: Western, Eastern, and Sixtowns (Figure 6), each occupying a separate river drainage system. The Black Prairie Muskogeans dominated the Western Division grouped along the upper Pearl River and its tributaries. This district came to be known as Okla falaya (Long People). Immigrants from the Black Warrior and Tombigbee settlements made up the Eastern Division, called Okla tannap (People of the Opposite Side), situated along the Sucarnooche River and its feeder streams. The Eastern Division included the Concha villages, a separate ethnic group, on Ponta Creek and its tributaries. The southern division, known as Okla hannali (People of Sixtowns), was strung out along the Chickasawhay River and its tributaries, including Chunky, Okatibee, and Tallahatta creeks. These southern villages were home to the Natchezan Pearl River group and people from the Mobile-Tensaw River region. These two regions had been linked prehistorically by a trail from the Natchez area running eastward across the lower Pearl River to Mobile Bay.[106]

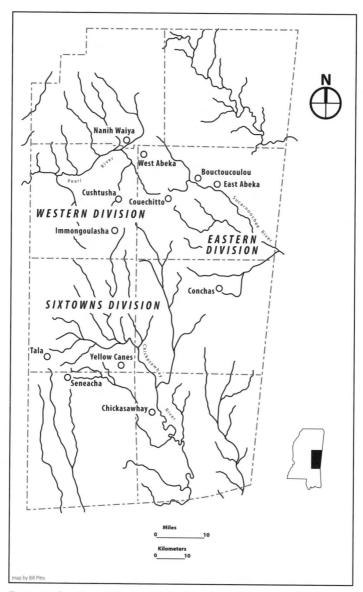

Figure 6. The Choctaw homeland showing the approximate tribal divisions and some of the villages discussed in the text. Mississippi counties shown are (clockwise from upper left): Winston, Noxubee, Kemper, Lauderdale, Clarke, Jasper, Newton, and Neshoba. (Based upon Blitz, *An Archaeological Study of the Mississippi Choctaw Indians,* Maps 3 and 6; map by Clara Sue Kidwell reproduced in O'Brien, *Pre-removal Choctaw History,* x; Galloway and Kidwell, "Choctaw in the East," Figure 1)

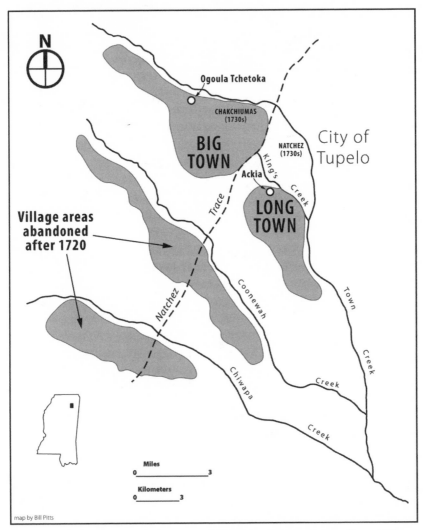

Figure 7. Area of Chickasaw villages near present-day Tupelo, Mississippi. (Based upon Atkinson, *Splendid Land, Splendid People*, Figures 4–6; Ethridge, *From Chicaza to Chickasaw*, Figure 9)

The earliest documentation of Chickasaw settlements in the Tupelo area appears on a map of the Mississippi Valley by Vicenzo Coronelli dating to 1684, which lists eight villages or towns: Fabatchaous, Malata, Archebophoni, Totchinaske, Chichafalara, Ontcha Patafa, Pakaha, and Chikoulika.[107] Coronelli's information apparently came from the 1682 La Salle expedition.

When La Salle encountered a Chickasaw hunting party near present-day Memphis, the hunters indicated to the Frenchmen that their villages were several days' journey to the east.[108]

During the colonial period, the Chickasaw villages occupied a series of prairie ridges along Kings Creek, Coonewah Creek, and Chiwapa Creek, three streams flowing generally northwest to southeast into Town Creek, a tributary of the Tombigbee River (Figure 7). Listings of Chickasaw villages or towns compiled at different times during the eighteenth century vary considerably, due in part to inconsistencies in rendering Chickasaw village names into French and English.[109] The lists also document the disappearance and appearance of several villages over time, reflecting the instability experienced by the tribe during a century in which they suffered from almost constant warfare.

One of the most important sources on the eighteenth-century Chickasaws is James Adair, an English trader who lived with the tribe intermittently over a period of about thirty years. Adair gives the names of seven Chickasaw villages in 1720, immediately prior to the onset of war with the Choctaws: Yaneka, Shatara, Chookheereso, Hykehah, Tuskawillao, Phalachecho, and Chookka Pharáah.[110] These villages covered large settlement areas, which became more and more compact as warfare pressure increased. For example, the village of Yaneka, located on the broad ridge along the south side of Chiwapa Creek, lay exposed to Choctaw advances from the southwest. The Chickasaws abandoned this village in the 1720s as the tribe's settlements pulled back toward the north to take advantage of the natural protection offered by swamps along the Chiwapa and Coonewah drainages.

Alexander De Batz's 1737 map of the Chickasaw settlements documents the assimilation of Natchez and Chakchiuma groups and shows the approximate locations of eleven villages clustered on Kings Creek (Figure 7).[111] The village locations on the De Batz map are grouped into two divisions, about 2.5 miles apart. The northern division was known variously as the large prairie, Chuckalissa, Big Town, and Old Town, while the southern division was known as the small prairie, Chukafalaya, Long House, and Long Town. When Bernard Romans visited the Chickasaws in 1771, the small prairie settlements had merged with the large prairie group on the north side of Kings Creek to form one extended town. Romans recorded the component village names as Melattaw, Chatelaw, Chukafalaya, Hikihaw, Chucalissa, Tuckahaw, and Ashuck hooma.[112]

MATRILINEAL SOCIETIES

As with the Natchez, matrilineal kinship formed the fabric of Choctaw and Chickasaw social organization, yet important differences colored each of these societies. With the Choctaws, descent traced through the female line determined each individual's membership in a family group, iksa or clan, and moiety. Within the family group, matrilocal residence (a man moving to the woman's home upon marriage) would be expected to accompany a matrilineal kinship system; however, the ethnohistorian Greg O'Brien points out the lack of documentary evidence on Choctaw residence practices. He suggests that the Choctaws may have followed residence practices similar to those of the Creeks, where the wives of higher-status males moved to the houses of their husbands, while lower-status males moved to the houses of their wives. Polygamy was not widespread, and usually involved a man marrying sisters.[113]

Families belonged to iksas, an intermediate kinship association between family groups and moieties. Scholars sometimes use the term "iksa" interchangeably with "clan," although totemic clans may not have existed among the Choctaws prior to their incorporation into the tribe from outside groups. By the time that Swanton and others began to collect information about iksas, the term's precise meaning had blurred, and informants sometimes applied the word indifferently to families, clans, and moieties. Choctaw iksas were probably ranked, and each community recognized the leaders of iksas residing there. According to information gathered by Swanton, the Choctaws had from six to eight iksas (three or four within each moiety), and the number of iksas likely fluctuated over time. Most scholars agree that iksas were exogamous, and, from a settlement standpoint, Choctaw villages were probably comprised of families belonging to several different iksas.[114]

The two Choctaw moieties, Inholahta ("Beloved People") and Imoklasha ("Their People Are There" or "Divided People"), are also poorly understood today. Like iksas, the two moieties were ranked, with Inholahta being the "elder" and Imoklasha the "younger." Galloway has identified the Inholahta moiety as the white moiety or moiety of peace, and the Imoklasha moiety as the red or war moiety. The associations of white with peace and red with war should not be taken in a literal sense; the duality held a deeper meaning that affected the Choctaw worldview. The peace/war dichotomy is a common element in southeastern Indian culture, with peace represented by the color white and war by the color red. Although the terms "peace" and "war" are unambiguous opposites in the English language, the ethnohistorian/folklorist George

E. Lankford has cautioned that, from the viewpoint of southeastern Indians, these two terms and the colors representing them conveyed a complex set of meanings. To quote Lankford, "'Red' and 'white' are thought to capture a dualistic vision of reality that was applied to individuals, clans, towns, political structures, and the cosmos."[115] Importantly, one scholar (O'Brien) suggests that what some perceive as moieties among the Choctaws are instead two ethnic groups representing the indigenous Black Prairie people (Imoklasha) and the emigrant society from the collapsed Moundville chiefdom of western Alabama (Inholahta). While some scholars view the Imoklasha and Inholahta as exogamous groups, O'Brien suggests that the two groups may have been endogamous (restricted to marrying someone from the same moiety) with exogamy maintained between iksas. A single letter from the Jesuit missionary Michel Baudouin, who was in residence at the southern town of Chickasawhay between 1729 and 1748, indicates that whole Choctaw villages were comprised of either Imoklasha or Inholahta. As with some of the other Mississippi tribes, the Choctaws recognized "brother" relationships among neighboring groups, with the Alabamas seen as elder to the Inholahta, the Chickasaws elder to the Imoklasha, and the Creeks elder to both Choctaw groups; however, each tribe's perception of these relationships seems to have been different.[116]

Our knowledge of Choctaw leadership, especially as it functioned in the eighteenth century, also suffers from a lack of information. Swanton recognized four levels of status for men in village leadership: chiefs, Hatak holitopa (honored or beloved men), Tashka (warriors), and those who had not yet attained warrior status. This system provided a way in which men could advance according to their charisma and prowess in war.[117] An anonymous 1730s French narrative indicates that boys began preparing to become warriors by participating in a painful initiation rite:

The ceremony is that the one who undergoes it suffers two hundred blows of a neck-band, which is a piece of hide five or six fathoms long, of the breadth of a finger, doubled many times, with which the warriors strike him full arm blows in turn on his back and on his belly, in order to make him understand that a warrior must endure everything patiently, even when he is taken by the enemy, and sing while they make him suffer and die. He must suffer the blows while singing, for if he should weep he will never be received and would pass as a woman, and unworthy of being admitted into the body of warriors.[118]

As with the Chickasaws and other southeastern groups, Choctaw men rose to the rank of warrior and received a war name when they killed an enemy in battle. Of the numerous war names supplied to Swanton by a Choctaw informant, many incorporate variations on the Choctaw verb *"abi"* (to kill), and several incorporate variations on the Choctaw word *"humma,"* the term for the color red, denoting war.[119] Perhaps because all of the sources on Choctaw names were men, we have little information about traditions surrounding Choctaw women's names. One of Swanton's informants remembered the names Nompashtika and Nompatisholi, both signifying "speaker," as names given to women married to tribal leaders. Sources indicate that the wife of a dead chief could speak in her husband's place in council meetings.[120]

Larger villages had a head chief and war chief, plus an array of up to six subordinate offices with titles such as Tascamingoutchy (assistant chief) and Tichou-mingo (chief in charge of ceremonies). There seems to be no information on how the heads of iksas residing in the villages fit into the hierarchy of village chiefs. Ambitious village chiefs could attain recognition as chief of one of the three tribal divisions, although the office of division chief may have only existed during periods of diplomatic necessity. Even though Choctaw chiefs could attain high status, their power was limited to their persuasive abilities, placing heavy emphasis on a chief's oratory skills in council meetings. In commenting on the many dualities in Choctaw culture—moieties, red and white, peace and war, male and female roles—Galloway has noted that paired peace and war chiefs often formed an effective governance team in negotiations with Europeans.[121]

In a presumptuous move to streamline French-Choctaw diplomatic relations, Bienville created the office of "Great Chief" of the entire confederacy, conferring the title on Chicacha Oulacta, a chief of the Couechitto village. Bienville's strategy was to empower the Great Chief by giving him lavish presents, which Chicacha Oulacta could then distribute to his supporting chiefs to build a pro-French coalition. Chicacha Oulacta had garnered Bienville's favor by ousting English traders from the villages of Couechitto and Cushtusha, and by killing the chief who had invited the Englishmen into the Choctaw towns. Although Chicacha Oulacta willingly played the role of the head of the confederacy, most of the Choctaw chiefs failed to accept the Great Chief's authority.[122] Father Baudouin, the Jesuit missionary to the Choctaws, tells us that Chicacha Oulacta took Bienville's appointment seriously enough to hand the title of Great Chief down to his own maternal nephew; however, Baudouin also makes it clear about how the confederacy's other chiefs viewed the artificial office: "As regards the authority of the Great Chief of the Choctaws it is not one of the most absolute and his power is far from being despotic in his nation. All the villages are so many little republics in which each one does as he likes."[123]

Despite their lack of success in establishing a single office through which to control the Choctaw confederacy, the French nevertheless found it expedient to reward supportive village leaders by naming them "medal chiefs." Medal chiefs received an official-looking parchment document called a "commission" and a medal to wear about the neck. The earliest medals were of porcelain, but soon silversmiths in France were making engraved medals especially for presentation to medal chiefs. To the dismay of French colonial leaders, handing out medals and commissions to Choctaw chiefs was no guarantee that those chiefs would favor the French over the English, who later distributed their own medals.[124]

Among the Chickasaws, descent traced through the female line determined an individual's membership in a house group, clan, and moiety. House groups were comprised of related females and their husbands (from other house groups), children, and unmarried brothers. House groups were ranked according to status and were organized into similarly ranked iksas or clans. Each clan in turn belonged to one of the tribe's two moieties. Clans were exogamous (restricted to marrying outside the clan) while moieties were generally endogamous (restricted to marrying someone from the same moiety), although Swanton documented instances in which certain clans could marry into either moiety. The names of the two Chickasaw moieties have been documented variously as Panther and Spanish, Imosaktca ("their hickory chopping") and Intcukwalipa ("their worn-out place"), and Tcukilissa and Tcukafalaha (two Chickasaw towns alternately spelled Chucalissa and Chukafalaya). Swanton considered the relationship of Chickasaw moieties to town names to be significant and suggested that because Chickasaw moieties were endogamous, towns may have been comprised largely of members of a single moiety. Swanton's Chickasaw informant designated Tcukilissa as the peace moiety and Tcukafalaha the moiety of war.[125]

During the colonial period, Chickasaw villages were autonomous and operated independently with regard to alliances and trade. Each village recognized hereditary "peace chiefs," who descended from elite lineages; however, the advent of European trade and French-English enmity empowered village "war chiefs," who rose to positions of authority by their leadership qualities.[126] Three Chickasaw leaders named by Nairne—Chincoboy Micho, Oboystabee, and "the war king"—obtained their positions of leadership "by the greatness of their Actions."[127] Peace chiefs, associated with the color white, argued against warfare and bloodshed and served as a brake against a rush to confrontation. Nairne noted at least one instance when the lure of the Indian slave trade caused a Chickasaw peace chief named Fattalamee to switch from white to red: "[Fattalamee] finding that the warriors had the best of time of it, that slave Catching was much more profitable than formall haranguing, he then turned Warrior too, and proved as good a man hunter as the best of them."[128]

With no power to enforce their positions, peace chiefs and war chiefs led by persuasion. Even though villages were free to act independently, whether in support of a peace chief or war chief, decisions concerning warfare were normally made only after careful consideration of a council comprised of white and red chiefs along with the heads of village clans. Village councils observed a strict order of seating and proceeded with formal speeches and debate.[129] Nairne also documented the Chickasaw tradition of Fane Mingo, or Squirrel King. A warrior who had attained a level of recognition and honor could be selected by a family (not his own) to be the family's protector, and thus take the title of Fane Mingo. Nairne's informant (possibly Thomas Welch) indicated that the ceremony installing a Fane Mingo lasted four days, and families could apparently choose a protector from another tribe, which would no doubt help promote peace between the two groups.[130]

QUEEN ANNE'S WAR: 1702–1713

Iberville's diplomatic efforts among the Choctaws and Chickasaws in 1702 took on added significance with the outbreak of Queen Anne's War (the War of Spanish Succession), the first of several major European conflicts to involve Mississippi's Indian tribes. Colonial representatives of the war's two main adversaries, the French and English, quickly recognized the military importance of the Choctaws and Chickasaws. Although the Choctaws could potentially field a larger warrior force, the Chickasaws had demonstrated their capacity for aggression in the slave trade. Besides controlling the intersection of the Upper Path and the Natchez Trace, the Chickasaws held partial control of the Mississippi River from their hunting camps at Chickasaw Bluffs. Iberville, acting as governor of Louisiana, saw the southeastern tribes as potential military units to be moved about strategically like game pieces to outflank the English in Carolina. A part of his scheme was to establish peaceful relations between the Chickasaws and Choctaws in order to make them both allies of the French, something Tonti's awkward 1702 mission had failed to accomplish. Another method of establishing a rapport with Indian groups, which had already proven successful for the French in Canada, was to place teenage boys with the important tribes to learn their languages. These boys, typically cabin boys from French ships, also functioned occasionally as spies. The Chickasaws received a boy named St. Michel, who remained with them for about one year, until the French heard from an unnamed Choctaw chief that the boy had been killed by his hosts. To prove that the rumor was false, the Chickasaws returned St. Michel safely to the French.[131] The French also used Catholic missionaries to good diplomatic advantage, the best example being the Seminarian Antoine Davion's twenty-year mission with the Tunicas, which helped to keep that tribe a staunch ally in wars against the Natchez.[132]

As the historian Verner Crane pointed out, Iberville's touted vision of the Choctaws, Chickasaws, and French living and trading peacefully among each other masked a much more sinister scenario. With the outbreak of Queen Anne's War, Iberville proposed a coordinated land and sea invasion of Carolina by a joint French and Spanish army augmented with Spanish-allied Florida Indians. After the destruction of the English in Carolina, Iberville would recruit the Creek confederacy to join his newly pacified Chickasaws and Choctaws and even bring in the Sioux and Illinois from the upper Mississippi River. This host of some 6,000 to 8,000 Indians, naturally with French and Canadians in overall command, would sweep north along the eastern seaboard rolling up one English settlement after another all the way through New York. The grandiose plot may have looked tempting on paper, but Iberville overestimated his ability to manipulate the tribes. By the time that the French did manage an unsuccessful naval attack on Charleston in late 1706, Iberville had already succumbed to malaria while fighting the English in the Caribbean.[133]

In Iberville's absence from Louisiana during the war, Bienville assumed command of the colony. Instead of trying to launch the kind of military offensive his brother envisioned, Bienville found himself struggling simply to hold France's place on the Gulf Coast. When warriors from the Alabamas brazenly killed several Frenchmen approaching their villages to trade, Bienville responded with a scalps-for-guns strategy, issuing muskets in exchange for Alabama scalps. Despite the increasing number of guns in Choctaw villages, Alabama and Chickasaw slave raids continued to beleaguer the confederacy.[134] The French presence at Mobile Bay did little to deter the slave raids, and the port became a conduit to the Caribbean Islands and the many European diseases rampant at places like Santo Domingo. In 1704 yellow fever struck the native population around Mobile Bay, and that same year the French ship

Pélican brought the plague.[135] These diseases further reduced the area's native population; however, other groups soon were migrating to Mobile Bay in order to escape English-led Shawnee and Apalachicola slave raids farther east. The raids on small tribes near the Spanish missions west of the Apalachicola River began in the 1680s and intensified with the outbreak of Queen Anne's War. In the winter of 1703–1704, Colonel James Moore's force of about fifty Englishmen and around 1,000 Creeks scattered the Apalachees during a sweeping slave raid on the mission tribes. After Moore's invasion, numerous refugee groups from the Apalachicola River area, including the Apalachees, Tawasas, Pensacolas, Chacatos (Chatots), and Yamasees, sought French protection and places to settle on Mobile Bay.[136]

In attempting to form military alliances to offset the English/Chickasaw threat, Bienville and his minions desperately tried to identify their Indian counterparts among the Choctaw confederation of ethnically diverse, autonomous villages. The Choctaws' ad hoc coalition and shifting factionalism served as a constant source of frustration for the French and English. For example, a group of Choctaw families receiving English trade goods visited the Chickasaw villages in February 1705, where their hosts captured them and sold them as slaves to the English. This occurred at about the same time that other Chickasaws were seeking to establish peace with the Choctaws and French. Such behavior naturally induced angry Choctaw factions to arm themselves with French weapons and retaliate against any Chickasaws within striking range.[137]

In the fall of 1705 the Chickasaws participated in a large slave raid against the Choctaw villages. Reports on the number of attackers vary wildly from 4,000 down to a more likely 300-man raiding party, apparently led by several Englishmen, including the aforementioned Thomas Welch. Members of various other Carolina-allied Indian groups probably augmented the Chickasaw force. The raiders killed an unknown number of Choctaw men, burned cornfields, and supposedly captured around 300 women and children for the slave market at Charleston.[138] Although only a portion of the Chickasaw group participated in this attack and others like it, slave raids such as this one fueled a cycle of vengeance that haunted the tribe throughout the eighteenth century.[139]

ACTIVITIES IN THE LOWER MISSISSIPPI VALLEY

To the west, in the Lower Mississippi Valley, years of epidemics and slave raids drove factions of some of the small tribes to take desperate chances. Such was probably the case in the late summer of 1702, when members of the Koroa tribe murdered the Seminarian missionary Nicolas Foucault and two other Frenchmen. The incident happened on the Mississippi River near the mouth of the Yazoo River.[140] Some French reports indicate English complicity in the attack, which happened to coincide with the beginning of Queen Anne's War, although the Koroas' motivation was more likely to have been thievery or vengeance. At Bienville's urging, Quapaw and Illinois war parties destroyed a Koroa village on the Ouachita River in northeast Louisiana. Remnants of this group apparently joined the Koroa settlement near the Yazoos and Tunicas on the Yazoo River.[141] In 1704 the Koroa chiefs prevented a French and Indian assault on their Yazoo River village by executing the men responsible for the attack on the missionary and his companions.[142]

In late 1706 members of the Chitimacha tribe murdered Saint-Cosme, the Seminarian missionary with the Natchez. The attack took place while the missionary and some of his companions were camped beside the Mississippi River, out of reach of Natchez protection. If the reasons behind Father Foucault's death are obscure, there is little question as to the motivation behind the Chitimachas' attack. Louis Juchereau de Saint-Denis, Iberville's relative by marriage, had been leading parties of Colapissas and Natchitoches in attacks on Chitimacha villages along Bayou Lafourche, killing the men and carrying off the women and children to sell as slaves in the Mobile settlement. Saint-Cosme and his small party simply gave the Chitimachas an opportunity for revenge. Bienville, however, viewed Saint-Cosme's murder as an unprovoked crime and declared war on the Chitimachas, sanctioning other tribes to raid the Chitimachas relentlessly for more slaves. This persecution continued until 1718, when the Chitimachas succeeded in making peace with the French.[143] Patricia Galloway has noted that some Chitimachas may have joined the Natchez confederacy as refugees from French persecution, pointing out that the Chitimachas considered themselves brothers of the Natchez.[144]

The Colapissa tribe (sometimes called Acolapissa) was another small group in the region with a possible connection to the Natchez.[145] In 1699 the Colapissas lived in six or seven villages, located on the lower Pearl River about twelve miles from the river's mouth. At that time, a small group called the Tangipahoas lived with them for protection. Colonial sources indicate that the Colapissas may have done some slave catching themselves, but, more often, they found themselves targets of more powerful raiding parties.[146] The missionary Paul Du Ru noted in 1700 that English-led Chickasaw bands were attacking the Colapissas, now consolidated into two villages with an estimated population of 500.[147] In 1702 Iberville estimated that they comprised around 250 families. From the 1680s into the early eighteenth century, colonial narratives place them variously on the lower Mississippi River, the lower Pearl River, and beside Lake Pontchartrain. For a time in the early eighteenth century, the Colapissas permitted part of the Natchitoches, a Caddoan Red River tribe, to settle with them. Pénicaut noted that the Colapissas "prick almost their entire bodies with needles and rub the pricks with willow ash crushed quite fine, which causes no inflammation of the punctures. The arms and faces of the Colapissas women and girls are tattooed in this way, which disfigures them hideously." Since the Natchitoches wore no tattoos, the two groups were easily distinguished.[148] Drawing closer and closer to the French for protection, many Colapissas eventually found employment as guides and suppliers of meat and corn for the colonists in New Orleans.[149]

In 1706 the Taensas and Tunicas abandoned their settlements on the lower Yazoo River and migrated southward. Both tribes were weakened by diseases and weary of the constant threat of enslavement. Compelled to leave behind their cornfields and granaries, survival dictated that these refugee groups displace established tribes since the option of clearing and planting new fields was untenable. The Taensas seized the village of the Bayogoulas on the west side of the Mississippi River several miles north of the Bayou Lafourche outflow and drove out its inhabitants. Defeated and homeless, the Bayogoulas in turn became refugees, eventually settling farther downriver near the French Fort Mississippi. The Tunicas commandeered the village of the Houmas at their lucrative Portage of the Cross settlement. Some reports indicate that the Tunicas took the Houma village by force, although Pénicaut wrote that the Houmas had already abandoned the site in favor of resettlement on Bayou St. John near Lake Pontchartrain. The Houmas and Bayogoulas later united under the name of the former.[150]

After the departure of the Tunicas, the small tribes remaining on the lower Yazoo River came increasingly under English influence. The Yazoos themselves were already becoming active in the Indian slave trade, and in the spring of 1708 they hosted an assemblage of several Mississippi River tribes to council with the English slave trader Thomas Welch. A 1716 map by François LeMaire shows Welch's probable route to the Yazoo village, labeled as the "Chemin des anglais" (road of the English). The trail passes through the

Chickasaw and Chakchiuma villages and follows the west bank of the Yazoo River down to the Yazoos. At the Yazoo council, Welch reportedly offered to relocate some of these tribes to Muscle Shoals on the Tennessee River, where an English trading post would buy their deerskins and slaves. Apparently, none of the chiefs accepted Welch's proposition.[151]

Welch's attendance at the Yazoo village council was part of an ambitious scheme by fellow Carolinian Thomas Nairne. The author of Carolina's Indian policy and the colony's first Indian agent, Nairne's job was policing abuse of the Indians by traders, but in 1707 he had grand intrigue on his mind. Like Iberville, Nairne envisioned mobilizing Indian armies, in this case, to march against the French at Mobile to expand what he called the "English American Empire."[152] Queen Anne's War had interrupted supplies to Louisiana and brought distress to the colony, not the least of which was Bienville's inability to continue the generous distribution of presents to the Indians.[153] With the French lacking, the Mississippi tribes looked to the English for support and welcomed Nairne to their villages, but his Indian army never materialized.

THE END OF THE INDIAN SLAVE TRADE

At the conclusion of Queen Anne's War in 1713, a large party of Choctaws traveled to Mobile to sing the calumet to Louisiana's new governor, Antoine de Cadillac, sieur de La Mothe, who had supplanted Bienville as governor of the Louisiana colony.[154] Despite this demonstration of Choctaw loyalty, French-Choctaw relations remained strained by the colony's lack of sufficient trade merchandise and the diplomatic confusion associated with the transition of leadership from Bienville to La Mothe and then to his successor, Sieur de Lépinay.[155] At the same time, English merchants working among the Chickasaws, Creeks, and Alabamas eagerly displayed their wares in Choctaw villages. In a brazen attempt to capture the Choctaws' trade and allegiance, the Welshman Price Hughes entered the Choctaw confederacy in April 1714 with a packhorse train loaded with English goods. At his back was a force of several hundred Chickasaws, Abihkas, Alabamas, and Talapoosas, to assist Hughes in coercing the Choctaws to abandon the French. In the end, some twenty-eight Choctaw villages chose to do business with the English, while at least two and possibly three Choctaw villages doggedly remained loyal to the French. According to La Harpe, the holdout communities came under siege from Hughes's mercenaries. In defiance, the people in these besieged villages pulled up stakes and moved to the vicinity of Fort Condé at Mobile for protection. Bienville later forced the Choctaws to readmit these communities after the Yamasee War and the subsequent collapse of English trade in the region.[156]

Not to be gainsaid, Hughes was at the Natchez villages in early 1715, where Pénicaut happened to encounter the Welshman buying captive Indians from a raiding party comprised of Natchez, Yazoos, and Chickasaws. More than simply dealing in Indian slaves, Hughes was negotiating with the Natchez to establish 500 Welsh families there on the bluffs overlooking the Mississippi River. Although the French had placed a deerskin trading post close to the Grand Village the previous year, Hughes informed Pénicaut that the Natchez were now allies of the English. The Welshman was subsequently captured by Bienville and released, just in time to meet death at the hands of the Tohomés, a victim of the repercussions from the distant Yamasee War.[157]

In searching for the causes behind the Yamasee War of 1715 and the abrupt collapse of the Indian slave trade, the historian Alan Gallay cites decades of abuse at the hands of unscrupulous traders, insurmountable debt brought on by the for-credit basis of the trade, settler encroachment, and, not unexpectedly, fear of enslavement on the part of suspicious slave catchers.[158] The early-eighteenth-century epidemics of smallpox and other diseases further reduced the pool of potential captives.[159] The first to rebel was the Yamasee confederacy, a coalition of native groups in the Carolina region who had been displaced by earlier Westo raids.[160] When the Yamasees began attacking Carolina traders in April 1715, Thomas Nairne was one of the first victims. Captured at a Yamasee village while trying to stop the rebellion through diplomacy, he was tortured by burning for three days before he died. Word of the attacks spread rapidly to other Indian villages, where warriors joined in the revolt by killing the traders in their midst. The deaths of several Englishmen at the Chickasaw villages have been attributed to visiting Creeks; however, if the Chickasaws were not directly involved in these killings, they apparently made no effort to intervene. One of the casualties at the Chickasaws was Bienville's nephew Sieur de St. Hélène, who was in the wrong place at the wrong time and was mistaken for an Englishman.[161] As Gallay points out, the Indians who turned against their English traders must have felt confident that they could establish new trade relationships with the French and Spanish.[162]

Chapter 4.

1716–1762

THE DEERSKIN TRADE AND
CLIENT WARFARE

By ridding the Southeast of the Carolina traders, the Yamasee War opened a window of opportunity for commerce and alliances that neither of England's colonial rivals managed to exploit. Although the Spanish at Pensacola made tenuous alliances with the nearby Lower Creek villages, Spain's declining imperial capabilities prevented the Florida colony from establishing a wider trade network.[1] For the French, the timing was bad. The French Crown's decision to lease its Louisiana holding to a private enterprise, first to the financier Antoine Crozat and then to John Law's Company of the West, resulted in a debilitating turnover in leadership at Mobile during the years immediately following the collapse of the Indian slave trade.[2] Meanwhile, a new and somewhat wiser corps of English traders came on the scene, rapidly regaining the confidence of the Creeks and Chickasaws by purchasing deerskins and liberally distributing presents to tribal leaders.[3]

The southeastern deerskin trade had operated from the earliest days of commerce between Indians and European colonists, moving along the same trading paths with the more lucrative Indian slave trade. English sailing ships delivered about 50,000 deerskins to European ports every year between 1699 and 1715, with the harvest topping 100,000 skins during some years. By the 1720s French Louisiana was exporting similar amounts of deerskins for the overseas market.[4] At the consumer end of this lengthy exchange network, deerskins provided the raw material for a variety of products, including parchment, saddles, book covers, and breeches.[5]

This remarkable chain of exchange far surpassed the Indian slave trade in both distance and complexity of partnerships. The deerskin trade also transformed thousands of Indian families into cottage industries focused on the business of hunting, skinning, and tanning hides.[6] Although deerskins proved the most valuable currency after the collapse of the slave trade, Indians augmented their income with a steady but minor trade in other animal skins, including bear, fox, bobcat, skunk, otter, and raccoon.[7] As several scholars have noted, when Europeans arrived in the Southeast, deerskins were already a valued item among the native groups. Early travelers like Iberville noted that finely dressed deerskins, in addition to their utilitarian value, functioned in ceremonial and diplomatic contexts. Importantly, the exchange of deerskins between tribes symbolized bonds of friendship.[8]

After 1715 English colonial administrators attempted to take tighter control over the trade with the Indians. Both the English and French colonial governments established prices (to be paid in trade goods) for deerskins; however, the market was too far-flung, too informal, and involved too many middlemen to allow that kind of top-down control. A host of factors affected the going rate for skins, including escalating client warfare, which prevented warriors from hunting, stiff competition, and shortfalls in trade goods.[9] The for-credit nature of the deerskin trade also caused problems for colonial regulators due to the four- to five-month delay between dispersal of payment and collection of merchandise. Typically, traders arrived at Indian villages in the winter and distributed trade materials to the hunters. The following spring, the hunters presented their tanned deer hides to the traders.[10] The credit system also provided unscrupulous traders plenty of opportunity to defraud their clients.

Despite the long distance between the Mississippi tribes and the Carolina markets, the English usually managed to outcompete the French in the deerskin trade.[11] Archaeologist Jay Johnson has pointed out that the English took a "corporate" approach to trade through individual entrepreneurs licensed by the Carolina authorities that easily outstripped the more cumbersome "bureaucratic" approach of the French, who channeled trade and the distribution of presents through the office of the governor.[12] Also, the English seem to have consistently offered better prices for deerskins than did the French.[13]

Harnessing this backwoods deerskin market was one of the items on Antoine Crozat's agenda when he took control of Louisiana at the close of Queen Anne's War. In 1714 Crozat's colonial administrators established outposts with the Alabama and Natchez tribes. The Alabama post, called Fort Toulouse, was near the Alabamas' main village, where the Lower Path crossed the Alabama River (near present-day Montgomery). In addition to bringing the Alabamas under more direct French influence, Fort Toulouse served as an advance outpost to capture the regional deerskin trade and guard against English incursions that might threaten Fort Condé.[14] Unlike Fort Toulouse, Crozat did not intend for the Natchez post to serve a military function; the

French viewed the Natchez as allies and lucrative trading partners. In Crozat's Louisiana scheme, the Natchez area would eventually need a French fort and garrison to accompany a future colonial settlement there, but other potential locations for forts were of a higher priority.[15] All of that changed when the Natchez began killing Frenchmen on the Mississippi River in late 1715.

THE NATCHEZ COLONY

Following the Yamasee War, numerous raiding parties that were accustomed to the excitement and profit of slave catching suddenly found themselves cut off from their source of English trade guns and other merchandise. It is fair to say that some of these ruffian bands probably turned to marauding as an alternative to slave raiding. The Natchez chief whom the French called Le Barbu (The Bearded) may have been leading one of these rogue outfits when he and his force of about 150 men received the blame for the murder of four Frenchmen on the Mississippi River in late 1715.[16] Bienville used the incident as an opportunity to attribute the violence to his rival La Mothe, alleging that La Mothe had enraged the Natchez by refusing to smoke the calumet with them.[17] However, Bienville's calumet story is dubious since it portrays the attack on the Frenchmen as the act of a single unified polity when, as discussed in chapter 3, the Natchez group was a confederacy of at least five settlement districts, each led by autonomous chiefs. The Bearded was chief of the Jenzenaque settlement district. Even though he was the maternal uncle of the Great Sun and the Tattooed Serpent, these chiefs had not sanctioned The Bearded's actions.[18] La Mothe's side of the story is not published, but there is some indication that the murdered Frenchmen may have even provoked the attack.[19] Regardless of the motivation behind the violence, the incident triggered the first Natchez war and led directly to the establishment of a French fort at the Natchez settlements.

In response to the hostilities, Bienville set out with a small force of forty-nine men from Mobile with orders to subdue the Natchez and establish a fort to maintain control over the area. The erstwhile governor of Louisiana was optimistic, to say the least, since the French believed that the Natchez could field 800 warriors. Stopping at the Tunica villages opposite the mouth of the Red River, Bienville learned that the Natchez had killed and robbed another Frenchman traveling downriver. To protect themselves from a surprise attack, the little army set up camp on an island in the Mississippi River somewhere between the Tunica villages and the Natchez river landing. From a group of voyageurs whom the Natchez had captured and released, Bienville learned of a recent council of Natchez chiefs in which several leaders had argued in favor of seeking peaceful relations with the French. Never above playing his opponents false, Bienville took advantage of the tribe's apparent desire to move toward friendly relations. Using the calumet ceremony as a ruse, he lured eight Natchez chiefs to his island and imprisoned them in a makeshift jail.[20]

Among Bienville's captives were the Great Sun, the Tattooed Serpent, a chief called the "Little Sun," and The Bearded.[21] Using the captured chiefs as hostages, Bienville ordered the Little Sun to return to his people and bring back the heads of the guilty individuals, a task that placed the chief in the difficult position of having to execute his fellow tribesmen in order to save his brothers and the other captured chiefs. In the end, the Little Sun only complied in part with Bienville's demands, providing the heads of two of the murderers and that of a third man who was innocent, but related to one of the killers. Bienville also demanded the execution of a White Apple settlement district chief named Oyelape, but the Little Sun assured Bienville that this chief had absconded. Given the tribe's strong prohibition against causing the violent death of a chief, it is not surprising that Oyelape escaped execution.[22]

Here it is important to point out how the French and Natchez viewed the pursuit of justice. The Natchez and other southeastern Indians viewed acts of aggression as crimes between groups rather than individuals. In this way of thinking, any member of the offender's group (for example, family or tribe), not just the guilty individual, could be the target for revenge. For this reason, the Natchez had cause to worry about the safety of their chiefs in Bienville's custody, because the chiefs stood to die for the murders committed by their tribesmen. On the other hand, Bienville's concept of *lex talionis* (law of retaliation) meant that he was solely interested in punishing the guilty individuals. Furthermore, Bienville's demands that a member of the Natchez behead a fellow tribesman placed the executioner in a quandary; the murder could potentially instigate a cycle of vengeance between the two men's families. Patricia Galloway has noted that, among the Choctaws, an individual could kill a close relative and remain exempt from vengeance by kinsmen. If this principle held true with the Natchez, it may explain how the Natchez carried out the executions of their own tribal members. That the Little Sun followed through on Bienville's demand, or at least part of it, is an indication of the extent to which the chief feared for the lives of his fellow chiefs. For his part, Bienville had built his reputation by coercing Indians to kill other Indians, usually pitting tribes friendly to the French against those allied with the English. In 1706 he had instituted a scalps-for-guns policy that incited Indians to kill and scalp members of tribes that were unfriendly toward the French.[23]

The springtime rise in the Mississippi River's water level flooded Bienville's island and eventually forced the French to return to the Tunica villages and higher ground. Before leaving, Bienville ordered the execution of two of the chiefs, including The Bearded, and released the other chiefs. (Oyelape remained at large under a death sentence.) Meanwhile, a detail of soldiers commanded by Jacques Barbaza de Pailloux, one of Bienville's officers, assisted by a labor force of the Natchez, followed through on the French Council of the Navy's directive and constructed Fort Rosalie on a prominent spot atop a bluff overlooking the river. The fort was named for the Duchess of Pontchartrain, wife of the king's minister of the navy, Jérome Phélypeaux de Maurepas, count de Pontchartrain. On August 25, 1716, the Natchez held a calumet ceremony for Bienville at the new fort, joined by representatives from the Ofo and Yazoo tribes. Given the temporary slowdown in English trade following the Yamasee War, the Natchez probably welcomed the access to French commerce that the fort and reopened trading post made possible; however, the tribe continued to follow its risky strategy of dual relationships with the two colonial adversaries.[24]

The distance between the new Natchez outpost and French headquarters at Mobile made the provisioning of the soldiers at Fort Rosalie difficult to sustain. Inevitable delays in the shipments of food and other supplies forced Bienville's men to trade with the Natchez for corn, fish, and deer meat. In time, a growing number of Natchez found a lucrative niche in providing services for the soldiers and later for the increasing population of civilian residents. The usual manner of colonial exchange called for the French to provide the Indians with trade items in advance for food and deerskins, a system that tended to keep the Natchez in chronic debt. As more and more French colonists entered into trading arrangements with the Natchez, the exchange system and its built-in indebtedness became a source of friction between the two sides. The intermingling of French and Natchez was further complicated as soldiers abandoned the fort's barracks for cabin life with Natchez women.[25]

Fort Rosalie might have remained a half-forgotten outpost were it not for the takeover in 1717 of Crozat's Louisiana concession by John Law's Company of the West. Law, who was already involved in banking in France, sold shares in the Louisiana venture to wealthy speculators across Europe, touting the profits to be made with the fur trade and mining ventures. By 1718 hundreds of adventurers (including Le Page du Pratz) representing a multitude of newly formed companies were arriving at Mobile and the recently founded town of

New Orleans. The Natchez outpost found a place in Law's scheme as a suitable location for raising tobacco and wheat. Arriving at the Natchez landing in January 1720, Du Pratz described the four-year-old French settlement:

> *At last we arrived . . . and we put on shore at a landing place, which is at the foot of a hill two hundred feet high, upon the top of which Fort Rosalie is built, surrounded only with palisades. About the middle of the hill stands the magazine, nigh to houses of the inhabitants, who are settled there, because the ascent is not so steep at that place; and it is for the same reason that the magazine is built there. When you are upon the top of the hill, you discover the whole country, which is an extensive beautiful plain, with several little hills interspersed here and there, upon which the inhabitants have built and made their settlements.*[26]

The newcomers the company enticed to Louisiana swarmed up the Mississippi River heedless of the frontier etiquette employed by La Salle, Tonti, Iberville, Bienville, Pénicaut, and other early travelers to grease interactions with the tribes. Fresh from villages and cities in continental Europe, the people arriving at the Natchez settlements had no understanding or insight into the culture of the native people in whose midst they had come to reside. The company's introduction of Africans to the Natchez colony only intensified the potentially volatile fusion of three radically different ethnic groups, each often bewildered by the behavior of the others.

The French colony at the Natchez settlements spread out from Fort Rosalie to the south and east into the broad St. Catherine Creek valley. Having no reason to fear the presence of the Natchez, the company's agents blithely staked out tracts of land miles from the fort. Elsewhere in Louisiana, speculators made their arrangements with company representatives for the possession of lands on which to farm; however, at the Natchez colony, Du Pratz and others purchased land directly from the Indians.[27] Regrettably, no details have come to light about the nature of these transactions to tell us whether the French bought property from individuals, families, or chiefs. Patricia Galloway and Jason Jackson have suggested that the Natchez viewed the French use of the land as a usufruct, while the colonists saw the land purchases as a transfer of ownership.[28]

Du Pratz purchased property for two large plantations, or concessions as they were called, one for the Company of the West, called "White Earth" (or *Terra Blanche*), and the other, called "St. Catherine," for Marc-Antoine Hubert, who held the position of *commissaire-ordonnateur* for the Louisiana colony.[29] The two concessions were located on St. Catherine Creek equidistant upstream and downstream from the Grand Village (Figure 5). As will be seen, Hubert's St. Catherine concession was uncomfortably close to the Jenzenaque, White Apple, and Grigra settlement districts and became the target of occasional harassment as relationships between the French and the Natchez began to deteriorate.

Not long after his arrival at the Natchez settlements, Hubert secured a pardon for Oyelape, the chief who had managed to escape Bienville's death sentence four years earlier. Perhaps indicative of the pardoned chief's status among his tribesmen, Pénicaut reports that the Natchez held celebrations in all of the settlement districts, not just in the chief's home district of White Apple.[30] Although Hubert's gesture of goodwill gave a temporary boost to French-Natchez relations, other developments caused an ever-widening rift between the two groups. In 1720 the French instigated a war between the Choctaws and Chickasaws (discussed below), backing the former in order to prevent an alliance between the two strongest tribes in the region. The Natchez refused to bow to pressure from their French neighbors to attack the Chickasaws, with whom they had enjoyed long-standing friendly relations.[31] Anti-French sentiment also came from the Carolina English, who had reestablished trade with the Chickasaws.[32] Closer to home, French immigrants were oblivious to their insensitivity toward their Natchez hosts, and whatever diplomatic gains Hubert may have made were lost when Hubert's successors at the St. Catherine concession mistreated members of the nearby White Apple settlement district.[33]

The inevitable flare-up came in the fall of 1722, when an argument over a debt of corn ended with a Natchez man dead at the hands of several French soldiers. A five-day uprising ensued, in which White Apple men armed with muskets harassed the St. Catherine concession and burned a number of French houses, including Du Pratz's cabin. The hostilities ended through the efforts of the Tattooed Serpent, who directed negotiations between the French and Old Hair, the ranking White Apple chief. Fighting erupted again within a year, this time between the St. Catherine concession and the neighboring White Apple district, purportedly because of Natchez attacks on the concession's livestock. Colonists' complaints brought Bienville upriver with an army of French soldiers and Canadian voyageurs, accompanied by Tunica, Yazoo, and Choctaw mercenaries. At the Natchez colony, a mob of civilian vigilantes (led by Du Pratz) joined Bienville's force, and the whole rabble spent two days marauding through the White Apple, Jenzenaque, and Grigra settlements, burning houses and granaries. Bienville ordered all Natchez men from these settlements killed and scalped. Any women deemed unsuitable for labor or concubinage received the same treatment. Even though most of the residents of these areas went into hiding, the French and Indian raiders killed or captured some sixty Natchez men, women, and children. The casualties included the Little Sun, who died defending the Jenzenaque district.[34]

Repeating his harsh retribution after the 1716 clash, Bienville forced the Natchez to deliver to him the heads of several tribesmen, along with the head of a free African man who had been living with the Natchez, apparently because Bienville feared he might teach the Indians about French military tactics. One of the executed Natchez men was Chief Old Hair.[35] In his brutal campaign against the three northeastern settlements, Bienville did irreparable damage to French-Natchez relations. During the next five years, as the tribe's elderly pro-French leadership dwindled and disappeared, the Natchez quietly turned against the unsuspecting French settlement at their doorstep.

1720s CHOCTAW-CHICKASAW WAR

When the Louisiana colony's administration came under the Company of the West, Bienville, whose authority had been diminished under Crozat, was promoted to governor-general. Immediately, he began inciting the Choctaws to attack the Chickasaws, implementing a policy shaped by his fear that these two powerful groups might join forces. He reasoned that if united and drawn into the influence of the English through presents and trade, a Choctaw-Chickasaw coalition would pose a serious threat to French Louisiana. Although undocumented, some of Bienville's enmity toward the Chickasaws may have stemmed from the tribe's failure to prevent the execution of his brother, St. Hélène. In a 1723 letter to the company (now reorganized under the name Company of the Indies), Bienville's intentions are plain: "Without risking a single Frenchman . . . I have . . . put these barbarians into play against each other, [which is] the sole and only way to establish any security in the colony because they will destroy themselves by their own efforts eventually."[36]

Bienville also tried to coerce the Alabamas and Upper Creeks into making war on the Chickasaws.[37] While not wanting to alienate the French, these two groups took a neutral position with regard to the Chickasaws in order to keep their trade options open with both Louisiana and Carolina. The Choctaws, on the other hand, had decades of Chickasaw slave raids to avenge and were much more open to Bienville's encouragement.[38]

By early 1721 French colonial officials were claiming that the Chickasaws had unilaterally declared war on the French.³⁹ This seems unlikely; however, the claim allowed Bienville to justify his decision to encourage further Choctaw attacks on the Chickasaws by offering a powerful incentive—he would exchange a musket and bullets for every Chickasaw scalp. For comparison, a French musket was currently worth twenty deerskins, a whole winter's work for a man and his family. Likewise, Choctaws could receive 80 livres worth of trade goods for every captured Chickasaw woman or child.⁴⁰ Understandably, violence spiked, and north Mississippi became a war zone. When a Chickasaw party reportedly killed two Frenchmen on the Mississippi River in the spring of 1722, Bienville called on the Choctaws to avenge the killings. In the fall of that year a large contingent of Choctaws destroyed three Chickasaw villages along with their cornfields.⁴¹

The war with the Chickasaws helped the Choctaws to satisfy the need to avenge their family members' deaths at the hands of slave raiders, and, perhaps more important, the conflict provided opportunities for men to gain political power through their exploits in combat. One Choctaw warrior whose career Bienville's war helped to launch was Red Shoe of the Couechitto village. Also known in the colonial narratives as Soulouche Oumastabé and Imataha Chitto, Red Shoe was an ambitious and cunning warrior who advanced up through the ranks, distinguishing himself in fights against the Chickasaws and Natchez.⁴² Like many of his contemporaries among the Mississippi tribes, Red Shoe was ready and willing to throw his allegiance behind France or England, depending upon which course best suited his purposes. As mentioned in the introduction, "Red Shoe" was a title of office and not a personal name, and other Choctaw and Chickasaw leaders were also called Red Shoe; however, it was Red Shoe of Couechitto who gave the name its prominent place in Mississippi history.⁴³

Along with giving rise to warriors like Red Shoe, it was through Bienville's 1720s Choctaw-Chickasaw war that the Choctaw confederacy realized its considerable military potential. In contrast to their earlier role as targets for raiding parties, the Choctaws found the advantage in going on the offensive, destroying three Chickasaw villages in the fall of 1722. The following year the Chickasaws began to appeal for peace, and in late 1724 the Choctaws agreed to accept the Chickasaws' calumets. The French were opposed to a cessation of hostilities, but they could not reasonably continue to demand that the Choctaws do their fighting for them without losing face.⁴⁴

Learning of repeated Choctaw attacks on the Chickasaw villages, Carolina officials extended an invitation to the Chickasaws to move east to the relative safety of the Savannah River region. Despite the pressure from the Choctaws, only one group of about forty families moved east in 1723, eventually settling near Fort Moore, across the river from present-day Augusta, Georgia. The leader of this refugee group held the aforementioned title of Squirrel King, or Fane Mingo. Beginning around 1717 other groups of Chickasaws had already left the Mississippi settlements and migrated eastward to settle on the Savannah River. These migrants hoped to secure better trading opportunities with the Carolina English, who in turn needed the Chickasaws as a defensive shield on their western border. Like the earlier Chickasaw emigrants, Squirrel King and his warriors found a niche serving as mercenaries for the Carolina and Georgia assemblies in ongoing hostilities with the Lower Creek towns. The eastern Chickasaws, as Squirrel King's band came to be called, resisted colonial efforts to establish a permanent settlement where they might be more effectively controlled, preferring instead to maintain their independence by ranging back and forth across the Savannah River.[45]

CHARLEVOIX'S VOYAGE

While the Choctaws and Chickasaws fought each other during the winter of 1721–1722, the Jesuit historian and journalist Pierre-François-Xavier de Charlevoix made a historic journey down the Mississippi River. The priest's journal provides a glimpse of some of the small tribes in the Mississippi Valley that were often overlooked in the French narratives of the day. Reaching the Quapaw villages in early December 1721, Charlevoix's party stopped at the village called Ouyapes, which had been recently decimated by smallpox. The priest described an appalling sight: "The Burying Place appears like a Forest of Poles and Posts newly set up, and on which there hangs all Manner of Things: There is every Thing which the Savages use. I had set up my Tent pretty near the Village, and all the Night I heard weeping."[46]

Nearby, Charlevoix noted the presence of a Company of the Indies magazine or trade warehouse tended by a clerk. Probably because of the smallpox epidemic, the Quapaws had abandoned their Mississippi River villages and established new settlements on the lower Arkansas River, above the mouth of the White River.[47]

Continuing downriver, Charlevoix and his party entered the mouth of the Yazoo River. Some ten miles upriver, they found a small French settlement on the bluff along the south side of the river, clustered around the newly constructed Fort St. Pierre and a company trade warehouse. The Yazoos, Koroas, and Ofos lived together in an extended village on the same side of the river about three miles from the fort. The priest estimated the total number of Indian men at about 200. The native people were suffering from dysentery, which Charlevoix thought was caused by the "extremely unwholesome" air and the reddish-colored waters of the Yazoo River. The Yazoos and Koroas had a long-standing reputation as allies of the Chickasaws and English, so the French population around Fort St. Pierre had to remain wary, yet at the same time, they depended upon their neighbors to supply them with food and other support services. The Company of the Indies had recently granted the Yazoo concession to a group of investors back in France, who entrusted the development of a tobacco plantation to a man named M. de la Tour. Charlevoix thought the Yazoo country was a poor choice, especially when compared to the French holdings he saw later at the Natchez settlements. M. de la Tour apparently shared the priest's assessment; a little over a year later, the plantation manager pulled up stakes and relocated in the Natchez area.[48]

A contemporary of Charlevoix, the French soldier Jean-François Benjamin Dumont de Montigny (who also wrote about the Natchez) spent some time at Fort St. Pierre in the early 1720s and described aspects of the Yazoos' spiritual belief system and funerary behavior. Dumont was always skeptical of the Indian sorcerers or medicine men, but admitted astonishment when a Yazoo sorcerer brought about rain during a severe drought in 1723. Commenting on Yazoo and Chakchiuma burial practices, Dumont wrote that funerals of the chiefs included hanging the deceased person's head (presumably the skull following decomposition) on a post carved with symbols like those that the chief had worn in paint or perhaps as tattoos. For those other than chiefs, Dumont noted that interment took place immediately following death, without an intermediate scaffold phase of decomposition. Before they covered the body with earth, relatives threw lit torches into the grave, and mourners visited the spot daily for six months after the burial. Of the tribe's spiritual beliefs, a Yazoo man told l'Abbé Juif, chaplain at Fort St. Pierre, of a benevolent spirit called Minguo-Chitou (great chief) and a bad spirit called Minguo-pouscoulou (child chief). The Yazoos called upon the latter to spare them from storms, sickness, and other maladies.[49]

During 1974–1977 archaeologists from Harvard's Peabody Museum joined forces with Mississippi Department of Archives and History archaeologists to search for the remains of Fort St. Pierre and the village sites of the Yazoos, Koroas, Ofos, and pre-1706 Tunicas. The archaeologists located the fort site some ten miles northeast of Vicksburg on the loess bluff adjacent to the Yazoo River. Although part of the fort's remains had been lost to erosion, archaeologists recorded features in the ground representing two buildings, portions of a palisade wall, a dry moat, and part of one of the bastions. In his analysis of the archaeological investigations at Fort St. Pierre, archaeologist Ian W. Brown noted that the fort had deteriorated during its decade of use without receiving repairs, an indication that the structure's defensive role diminished over time.[50] Several archaeological sites in the Fort St. Pierre vicinity probably represent historic Indian settlements, and archaeologist Jeffrey P. Brain identified the Haynes Bluff mound site as the probable location of the Yazoo village. Haynes Bluff is 2.5 miles northeast of Fort St. Pierre, and the site contains four mounds. Mound construction took place in the late prehistoric period between A.D. 1200 and 1600. By the time that Europeans first reached the area, mound building had ceased. There are no colonial accounts of the Tunicas or Yazoos using the mounds for ceremonies, and these historic tribes were probably unrelated to the people who constructed the Haynes Bluff mound center.[51]

After visiting the thriving French settlement at the Natchez colony, Charlevoix continued southward to the Tunica settlements at the Portage of the Cross. At the main Tunica village, he took note of the Tunica houses, describing them as "partly square . . . and partly round," resembling those of the Natchez (square or rectangular floor plan with a rounded, domed roof), arranged around a large central square. Two smaller Tunica villages lay nearby, one near the northern end of the portage and another on the west side of the Mississippi River several miles downstream from the mouth of the Red River. The Tunica chief met Charlevoix and his party wearing French clothes, and the priest reported seeing several chests full of trade goods and other valuables in the chief's cabin. In fact, the Tunicas had acquired a reputation as traders by exploiting their location at the junction of the Red and Mississippi rivers. Also at this location, the Atchafalaya River, an outflow or distributary of the Mississippi River, formed an interconnecting series of bayous leading to Atchafalaya Bay and the Gulf of Mexico. Trading with the Red River tribes and with the French at Natchitoches and the Spanish at Los Adaes, the Tunicas acquired horses and other items that they sold to the French at New Orleans.[52]

The impressive collection of eighteenth-century European trade goods known as the "Tunica Treasure," discovered in the late 1960s, is evidence of the Tunicas' success as traders during the tribe's approximately sixty-year residence at the Portage of the Cross. The so-called treasure came from a Tunica burial site called Trudeau, on the east side of the Mississippi River near the mouth of Tunica Bayou, adjacent to the Louisiana state penitentiary known as

Angola Prison. A Harvard archaeological team investigated Trudeau and two other archaeological sites associated with the eighteenth-century Tunica tribe between 1972 and 1981; however, the site of the main Tunica village described by Charlevoix and others remains undiscovered.[53]

Some fifteen river-miles below the Tunicas, Charlevoix began encountering small French settlements representing concessions sold by the Company of the Indies. He also noted an abandoned Bayogoula village site on the west side of the Mississippi River, which had been the scene of a recent smallpox outbreak. A French concession occupied the old village grounds hoping to produce silk, tobacco, and indigo for export. Charlevoix thought that smallpox killed all of the Bayogoulas, unaware that remnants of the tribe were living with the Houmas. About six miles below the outflow into Bayou Lafourche, Charlevoix's party passed two Houma villages on the east bank, a small one near the riverside and a larger one about three-quarters of a mile inland. The priest also found an abandoned Colapissa village eighteen miles below the Houmas. The Colapissas had established a new village farther downstream on the east bank close to New Orleans, which Charlevoix described as "the finest [Indian settlement] in all Louisiana." He estimated the tribe's number of warriors at "not above two hundred" and noted their reputation for bravery. Later in his narrative, Charlevoix mentioned that the Biloxis, or a portion of their group, had moved to the lower Pearl River and settled on the site of the 1699 Colapissa villages. Clearly, village sites were seldom permanent for the small tribes during the colonial period. If anything, Charlevoix's journal entries reveal a traumatized native population, stunned by waves of epidemics and coping as best they could with the mounting pressures of European encroachment.[54]

RITUAL AND CEREMONY

Charlevoix spent Christmas 1721 at the Natchez post. In his journal, he recounts a visit to the Grand Village on a day when everyone was away attending a festival. The priest took the opportunity to prowl around the deserted mound center and even entered the temple building, but was disappointed in what he saw there: "Ornaments I saw none, nor any thing indeed which could inform me that this was a temple."[55] Like many other Frenchmen, Charlevoix was fascinated by Pénicaut's account of a female chief's funeral held at the Grand Village in 1704, which involved human sacrifices. In 1725 Du Pratz witnessed the Tattooed Serpent's funeral, again documenting sacrifices. In addition to providing insight into the spiritual beliefs of the Natchez, archaeologists have repeatedly used the French narratives describing these two events to interpret the activities at prehistoric ceremonial mound sites. Though not identical, the details of the two funerals, over twenty years apart, are quite similar. In both funerals, the deceased lay in state for four to five days while participants danced and rehearsed the formal procedures they would follow on the day of interment. The persons selected for human sacrifice were the spouses and people who had performed certain services for the deceased in life. Their sacrifice allowed the dead chief to take his or her entourage along into the next life. In almost all cases, those scheduled for execution were members of the opposite moiety. The single exception seems to have been a noble woman who volunteered to die with the Tattooed Serpent in 1725.

The Great Sun injected an element of drama into the 1725 funeral by threatening to extinguish the tribe's sacred fires and commit suicide out of grief over his younger brother's passing. According to Dumont,[56] the French garrison at Fort Rosalie became quite alarmed at this development, fearing that such a rash move could cause the tribe to collapse into chaos and possibly spark violence. The availability of French brandy exacerbated the situation, which culminated in a struggle between the Great Sun, some Natchez chiefs, and a few Frenchmen. To everyone's relief, the inebriated chief was safely disarmed.[57]

At the 1704 funeral, the bodies of twelve children aged three and younger were brought to the ceremony to join those who were scheduled to be executed. Similarly, the 1725 funeral included the body of one child. The French informants indicate that the parents strangled their children for the funeral ceremony so that the children's spirits could join the chief's entourage in the next life. As a reward for this sacrifice, the fathers of the dead children joined the Honored men's society. One of the benefits of receiving Honored status was exemption from any future consideration as a funerary sacrificial victim.[58] Indeed, the willingness of the sacrificial victims to accept their fate varied considerably. For example, the second (and younger) wife of the Tattooed Serpent apparently required some coercion on the part of tribal officials before she submitted to sacrifice. Likewise, other potential sacrificial victims sought protection from the French until the obsequies had run their course.

The most scandalous of the shirkers was a Natchez man named Etté-actal (also known in other accounts as Taotal, Tactal, and Wideawake), whose story came out as part of the Tattooed Serpent's funeral narrative. It seems Etté-actal had some time earlier fled the Natchez area to avoid execution at the funeral of his wife, a member of the nobility. Since that escape, he had lived with the French in New Orleans, serving Governor Bienville as a scout and hunter, where he no doubt felt safe from further sacrificial danger. At the time of the Tattooed Serpent's death, however, Bienville had returned to France, leaving Etté-actal without protection from reprisal by his dead wife's family. The French stood by while warriors captured him and dragged him to the Tattooed Serpent's funeral. The Tattooed Serpent's widow informed Etté-actal that he could make up for avoiding execution at his wife's funeral by joining the sacrificial victims preparing to accompany her dead husband. Pleading loudly that he wished to remain among the living for a while longer, Etté-actal somehow convinced two elderly women to be sacrificed in his stead. In a final irony, Etté-actal joined the warriors selected to strangle the victims and so killed one of the women who had taken his place, an act that earned him Honored status and immunity from any future sacrificial obligations.[59]

Both the 1704 and 1725 Natchez funerals culminated with a solemn procession to the temple. The funeral march began at the house of the deceased chief, located close to the mounds. Many people assembled around the fringes of the open space to mourn the dead chief, some of whom expressed their sorrow by cutting their hair short. The color red appears to have been an important component in the ceremony, and red paint and red-dyed feathers adorned the bodies of the dead chiefs and ceremonial officials. To achieve this effect the Natchez favored vermilion paint (mercuric sulfide), a highly coveted trade item supplied by the French. The Flour chief, as master of ceremonies, led the procession, followed by senior chiefs and the litter carried by warriors bearing the body of the deceased. The sacrificial victims, their hair and faces painted red, followed behind the litter bearers. Close by stood the parents of the dead children. As the procession moved along, the parents tossed the bodies of their children in the path of the litter bearers, who trampled them under foot. The procession followed a winding route across the plaza, circling back several times to retrace the line of march. As part of the ceremony, the houses of the deceased chiefs were burned, and the chiefs' bodies, along with several sacrificial victims, were interred at the Grand Village in the temple mound near the sacred building (recall that archaeologists found the remains of twenty-six individuals in Mound C). Family members carried other victims away for burial near their homes.[60]

The French accounts of the funerals of the two Natchez chiefs are unique in North American history. After 1725 outsiders never again witnessed this extraordinary ceremony. Indeed, the nuisance of French intervention in the

Tattooed Serpent's funeral probably led the Natchez to hold the funeral ceremony for the Great Sun in secret when he died in 1728. In an essay on cultural survival among Louisiana tribes, Hiram F. Gregory Jr. has noted the tendency of American Indian groups to move ceremonial activities to clandestine locations, away from interference by the non-Indian population, as a strategy for maintaining a tribe's cultural integrity.[61] Finally, were these funeral ceremonies vestiges from the tribe's prehistoric past, when the ancestors of the Natchez were part of the powerful chiefdom that built Emerald Mound? Of course, there is no way to be sure; however, some archaeologists have remarked on the persistence of ritual and myth in American Indian cultures.[62]

These funerals of chiefs attracted much attention, but similar descriptions of funerals for lower-rank Natchez individuals are lacking. Accounts of Chickasaw and Choctaw mortuary behavior show considerable variation in burial practices among the Mississippi tribes. Describing Chickasaw funeral practices, Nairne noted that "an opposite family to [the deceased]"—probably members of a designated clan in the opposite moiety—assumed responsibility for preparing the body and carrying out the interment. After washing the deceased, applying face paint, and rubbing his hair with bear oil, attendants seated him on animal skins outside of his house, propped up with his belongings and facing into the doorway. Attendants prepared a special chair painted white "to put [the deceased] in mind of peace." In a Chickasaw funeral witnessed by the English trader James Adair, attendants carried the deceased around his house three times before interment. Both Nairne and Adair note that the corpse was buried beneath the floor of his house. Adair wrote that in order to achieve purification, those who had handled the corpse isolated themselves from the rest of the group for three days and cleansed themselves by ingesting the emetic plant called button snakeroot.[63] If the deceased was a warrior, attendants erected a "mourning" pole nearby, which they painted red and hung with the dead man's weapons and other accoutrements. If another tribe was responsible for the warrior's death and a member of that tribe captured, the captive was tied to the same mourning pole for torture and execution.[64]

With regard to Choctaw mortuary practices, Galloway has noted the "fevered fascination" with which scholars have scrutinized the tribe's elaborate handling of its dead. Although some details vary over time and are probably attributable to ethnic differences and changes wrought by acculturation, the basic elements of the Choctaws' distinctive mortuary procedures remained more-or-less consistent to the end of the eighteenth century. Early narratives document the preparation of an individual for mortuary processing before the occurrence of death, and some sources reveal the practice of euthanasia when a native doctor deemed the patient beyond recovery. In the first phase of the funeral process, the corpse lay for several months in a covered enclosure atop a scaffold within a few yards of the home of the deceased. Items needed for the transformation into the afterlife accompanied the body, including weapons and a change of clothing for men or cooking ware and a blanket for women. After several months a mortuary specialist called a "bone-picker" separated the decomposed flesh from the bones and presided over a ceremonial feast involving the family of the deceased. The flesh was either burned or buried. At least one source identifies the bone-picker as a female, while most of the narratives state that men performed this task. Several sources say that the bone-picker had long fingernails for dislodging the rotted flesh, although Adair says a knife was used. The cleaned bones went into a basket or box placed in a bone house maintained by the family or iksa. In the final funerary phase, the containers of bones were removed from the bone house and either interred in a cemetery or stacked and covered with earth to form a low conical mound. Inevitably, the onslaught of acculturation in the early nineteenth century brought changes in the Choctaws' mortuary traditions, and the use of scaffolds, bone-pickers, and bone houses ceased.[65]

THE NATCHEZ REBELLION

The Tattooed Serpent and the Great Sun were the leaders of the pro-French faction among the Natchez. After their deaths, the confederacy silently shifted its allegiance to the English, and a time bomb began ticking. It was during this volatile period that the directors of the Company of the Indies made the fateful decision to reduce the garrison strength at the forts guarding its Louisiana concessions. Despite having guaranteed the concessionaires adequate military protection for their plantations, the company cut the troop strength in the Louisiana colony by 50 percent during the 1720s in order to maximize profits. To make up for the decrease in soldiers at distant outposts, company directors negotiated an agreement with the Jesuits to place missionaries with the tribes at some of these locations. The company expected the missionaries to attach their parishioners to the French and function as spies in order to head off diplomatic problems that might endanger the concessions. As part of this initiative, Jesuit fathers Jean-François Souel and Paul du Poisson departed New Orleans in 1727 to take up missions at the Yazoos and Quapaws, respectively.[66]

When these missionaries ascended the Mississippi River, the region was quickly evolving toward chaos; both men were destined for martyrdom in the 1729 Natchez and Yazoo massacres. However, like the vast majority of new colonists in the Lower Mississippi Valley, Souel and Du Poisson took the seemingly docile native population for granted. At the main Tunica village, the chief asked the missionaries about Father Davion, who had left the tribe some seven years earlier, and expressed sadness at the news of his death. Farther upriver, Father Souel disembarked at the Yazoo post, which must have seemed a desolate place to the young missionaries. Du Poisson's own journey ended thirteen days later at the Quapaw villages, which were all situated along the south side of the lower Arkansas River, about twenty-seven river-miles from its mouth. He estimated the total population of the Quapaws at 1,200. On the north side of the river, opposite the Quapaws, was a small community of French people, many of whom were sick and destitute.[67]

In contrast to the French settlement at the Quapaws, the colony at the Natchez settlements was thriving, with at least seventeen concessions or plantations raising tobacco, indigo, and cotton. Although the Company of the Indies collapsed briefly in 1720 due to overzealous speculation, it had re-formed by 1723 under more prudent management, and the French population at the Natchez colony burgeoned to around 400. Responding to incessant pleas for laborers, company ships brought hundreds of African slaves to Louisiana during the late 1720s, and the number of Africans in the Natchez settlements increased to around 280. Although the civilian population was growing, the Fort Rosalie garrison numbered only thirty men. The fort itself had deteriorated through lack of maintenance, and, as mentioned above, most of the soldiers were quartered elsewhere in their own cabins. Despite the optimism on the Natchez concessions, morale in the little garrison was low due to the confrontational nature of the post's highest-ranking officer, Commander Chépart. Ignoring warnings about the Natchez's growing discontent with the French presence, the commander used his position to seek control of one of the settlement districts for the establishment of his own plantation. According to Du Pratz and Dumont, Chépart was particularly interested in the White Apple settlement district, which by this time probably included elements of the Jenzenaque and Grigra populations, and is certain to have been a center of strong anti-French sentiment.[68]

Given the circumstances surrounding the Natchez colony, the disaster that befell the French on November 28, 1729, seems to have been inevitable. Seeking retribution for Bienville's atrocities in the 1723 conflict, the Natchez killed 229 French colonists and an unknown number of Africans. Among the

dead were Chépart and most of his command, along with most of the concessionaires. Also killed were Du Codère, commandant of Fort St. Pierre; Jean-
Daniel Kolly, one of the owners of the St. Catherine concession; and Father
Du Poisson, all of whom were unlucky enough to be visiting the colony at the
time of the massacre. Echoing Bienville's methods, the Natchez scalped and
beheaded the white males. Some women and children were also killed while
others were rounded up for ransom or enslavement. There is some evidence
to suggest that a number of the Africans at the local concessions joined the
Natchez in the massacre, making the revolt in part a slave rebellion. A few
Africans and around twenty white men managed to escape downriver and
raise the alarm in New Orleans.[69]

A party of Yazoo warriors happened to be present at the Natchez settlements on the day of the massacre, having accompanied Du Codère on a visit
to the Natchez fort. Although the Yazoos failed to protect Du Codère, they
apparently did not join the Natchez in the killing (they are even credited with
helping an escaping Frenchman). Instead, the Yazoo men returned to their
village, where the tribe and their neighbors, the Koroas, resolved to emulate
the Natchez victory with the destruction of the Fort St. Pierre settlement.
Reports indicate that Father Souel was the first casualty, killed while visiting the Indian villages. The following morning the Yazoos and Koroas fell
on the unsuspecting French, who were not aware of what had taken place at
the Natchez colony. The warriors easily overwhelmed Chevalier des Roches,
commanding in Du Codère's absence, and his seventeen-man garrison. Of
the French civilians, five women and four children survived, spared by Koroa
women who defied their warrior husbands. Although the Yazoos and Koroas
intended to sell these survivors as slaves, some were eventually rescued by
Indians friendly to the French.[70]

Before news of the Natchez uprising had reached Mobile, the post commander, Diron D'Artaguette, dispatched a chief and small party of warriors
from the Cushtusha village to carry a message to Chépart. These men arrived
at the Natchez villages shortly after the massacre and received a friendly welcome from a chief. Prudently destroying Diron's note, the Cushtusha men
listened to the Natchez chief's anti-French harangue and accepted a share
in the loot, including a nine- or ten-year-old French boy, an African man,
three horses, and some articles of French clothing; however, the Natchez
stopped short of giving away any of the prized guns and ammunition they
had confiscated. Before the Choctaws' departure, the Natchez chief presented
the Cushtusha chief with a red fan, the acceptance of which amounted to a
pledge to attack the French. To refuse the fan would have been suicidal, so the

Cushtusha chief waited until his party was safely away from the Natchez area before disposing of it. On their return trip, the Choctaws met their country-men rushing to attack the Natchez on behalf of the French.[71]

When word of the disaster reached Governor Etienne Perier in New Orleans, Perier sent Pierre-Charles Le Sueur to the Choctaws to enlist their help in subduing the Natchez. Le Sueur convinced numerous Choctaw chiefs and warriors to join the French in attacking the Natchez and the Yazoos. Based upon the journal of Joseph de Lusser, who visited some of the Choctaw villages in early 1730, the Choctaw force that went to attack the Natchez was comprised mostly of men from the villages of Chickasawhay, Cushtusha, Couechitto, Concha, Yowani, Yellow Canes, Tala, Nacchoubanouanya, Caffetalayas, and Boucfouca. With the exception of Concha, these villages represent the Western and Sixtowns divisions.[72] Fielding an army of around 700 warriors, the Choctaws were the dominant power at the siege of the Natchez forts in January and February 1730. To underscore this fact, the Concha chief Alibamon Mingo negotiated the transfer of the French and African hostages held by the Natchez into Choctaw custody.[73] Refusing to simply hand the hard-won hostages over to the French, the Choctaws forced the humiliated colonial soldiers to barter for them. From the Choctaws' point of view, they had not only come to the aid of the French but also had ac-cepted the obligation to avenge the French people killed in the Natchez mas-sacre. When the French appeared to renege on making adequate payment for this service, the Choctaws took offense and used the hostages as bargaining chips.[74]

The following year Governor Perier, assisted by his brother, Antoine-Alexis Perrier de Salvert, led a force of French soldiers, militia, and Indians up the Black and Tensas rivers to the southern toe of Maçon Ridge near present-day Sicily Island, Louisiana, where the Natchez had established a village and fort. During a five-day siege that began on January 20, 1731, Perier used Bienville's tactic of pretending a desire to parlay in order to lure three Natchez chiefs out of the fort and into French custody. The three chiefs were the young Great Sun, the chief known as Saint-Cosme (named for the missionary),[75] and the Flour chief, one of the leaders of the Natchez revolt. Despite the presence of French guards, the Flour chief was able to escape, taking a number of Natchez warriors and their families with him. The following day, the remainder of the Natchez, about 400 people—including Tattooed Arm, the mother of the last Great Sun—came out of the fort and surrendered to Perier. Despite having assured the Natchez of protection, Perier imprisoned the captives in New Orleans, where many of them died or were sold as slaves. In May 1731 the

French sold 160 Natchez into slavery on the island of Santo Domingo, including the chief Saint-Cosme.

Upon questioning the Natchez prisoners, Perier learned that around 200 Natchez, Yazoos, and Koroas were not in the fort at the time of the siege, some of these people having left the area immediately to seek safety among the Chickasaws.[76] Defiantly, the Flour chief and fighters loyal to him carried on guerrilla warfare against the French, attacking groups of soldiers traveling on the Mississippi River and harassing the small garrison occupying the rebuilt Fort Rosalie. Feigning a desire to establish friendly relations, the Flour chief and about 150 warriors caught the Tunicas off guard in June 1731 and killed a number of them, including their chief, in retribution for the Tunicas' part in Bienville's 1723 war. Later that summer, with his force dwindling through attrition, the Flour chief died in a failed attempt to capture the French fort at Natchitoches. A small group of Natchez refugees, including some of the Africans who had joined the rebellion, settled briefly with the Ouachitas. It is perhaps not surprising that at least one small Natchez group continued to live in hiding for a time near the tribe's old settlement districts, where they risked being killed or captured by Ofo and Choctaw mercenaries. The leader of this group was a man known as "the little chief of the Corn."[77]

The Ofos, whose village lay close to those of the Yazoos and Koroas, declined to join their neighbors in the massacre at Fort St. Pierre and instead fled to the Tunicas and declared their allegiance to the French. One of the French women rescued from the Yazoo post reported that the Ofos had sided with the insurgency and captured a French missionary; however, this is probably a garbled reference to the Yazoo and Koroa attack on Jesuit Father Stephen Doutreleau. The ambush took place near the mouth of the Yazoo River in early January 1730 as the missionary and a party of Canadians descended the Mississippi River en route to New Orleans. Doutreleau and two of the men accompanying him managed to escape and make their way downriver. At the Tunica villages, they met the small French army on its way to attack the Natchez.[78]

In the wake of the 1729 Natchez rebellion, scalps-for-guns incentives, opportunities for young men to gain warrior status, and the pursuit of unrequited vengeance fueled relentless warfare among the Mississippi tribes that lasted until the demise of the Louisiana colony in 1763. The pro-French Quapaws, Tunicas, Chakchiumas, and Ibitoupas clashed with the pro-English Koroas, Yazoos, and Tious. Combined Choctaw and Chakchiuma raiding parties hammered the Yazoos in 1730 and 1731, forcing the tribe's few surviving members to seek refuge with the Chickasaws.[79] At Bienville's urging,

Chakchiuma and Ibitoupa warriors gamely struck at the Chickasaw villages, drawing retaliatory raids from numerically superior forces of Chickasaws, Natchez, and Yazoos.[80] Quapaw assaults on the Tious led the French to report that the latter group had been wiped out in 1730; however, later colonial maps may indicate that the small tribe survived.[81]

FRENCH-CHICKASAW WARS

Overlooking their own mistakes in dealing with the Natchez, French colonial officials were quick to blame the Chickasaws and the English for fomenting the rebellion, and indeed it is doubtful that the Natchez would have cut themselves off from French trade without firm assurances of sustenance from the English.[82] As the Natchez war played out, the migration of a large number of the Natchez refugees to the Chickasaws seemed to support French claims of conspiracy. Governor Perier, following a familiar policy of sending Indians to do the fighting for the French, called on his Canadian counterpart, Marquis de Beauharnois, to order Iroquois and Huron parties to attack the Chickasaws. Perier also sought to mobilize the Choctaws to resume harassing their old enemies, but the tribe was divided in its desire to fight the Chickasaws on behalf of the French.[83] The hesitance on the part of the Choctaws stemmed in part from their disapproval of the performance of French soldiers during the Natchez war and the reluctance of French officials to pay for hostages taken from the Natchez.[84] It is also likely that some of the Choctaws wanted to continue selling deerskins to English traders operating in the Chickasaw villages.

Why a large contingent of Natchez chose to retreat to the Chickasaws is open to speculation. Having cut their ties with the French, the Natchez needed help from the closest and most powerful English ally, and at least some of the Chickasaws wanted the Natchez badly enough to go to their aid and escort them through Choctaw territory to the Chickasaw villages.[85] James Atkinson has pointed out, however, that the Chickasaws were by no means unanimous in the decision to provide refuge for the Natchez. A significant faction of the tribe, headed by the peace chief Ymahatabe, strongly opposed the influx of Natchez refugees on grounds that such a move would lead to war with the French. On the other hand, two war chiefs, Oulactatasca and Quouatchitabe, welcomed the Natchez and defied subsequent French requests to surrender them.[86] One French report characterized Oulactatasca as the "most rebellious" of the Chickasaw headmen.[87] The seriousness of the rift between the two Chickasaw factions became apparent when Ymahatabe visited the Choctaw village of Couechitto in early 1731 to request permission for four Chickasaw villages to relocate to Choctaw territory. The four dissenting villages were reported as Achoukouma, Taskaouila, Tchitchatala, and Falatchao, all part of the northern large prairie settlement. Although the Great Chief of the Choctaws approved the immigration, French-instigated Choctaw attacks on the Chickasaws had already begun, forcing the dissenting villages to remain where they were.[88]

Red Shoe led some of these Choctaw sorties against the Chickasaws.[89] Over the next few years Red Shoe and other Choctaw raiders harassed the Chickasaws and destroyed their cornfields, while French-allied mercenaries from tribes in the Illinois River, Ohio River, and Great Lakes regions applied pressure from the north. These attacks incited the Chickasaws to fight back with raids against the Illinois and other tribes that attacked them. During one of their Illinois country raids, a group of Chickasaws attacked a small party of Frenchmen on the Mississippi River, killing two and capturing three others. Parties of Chickasaws, Natchez, and Yazoos also attacked nearby groups such as the Chackchiumas, who endeavored to remain neutral in the war.[90]

Despite the mounting incentive to fight and avenge those killed in raids, a faction within the Chickasaw tribe repeatedly appealed to the Choctaws and to the French for peace. Between 1730 and 1735 Chickasaw peace delegations carried calumets to the Choctaws, Perier, and later Bienville, all without success. The desire for relief from frequent attacks on their villages and hunting parties appears to have been the main motivation behind the Chickasaw entreaties; however, English traders whose packhorse trains en route to the Chickasaws were suffering from Choctaw attacks also wanted an end to hostilities. Furthermore, the war prevented English traders from establishing a stable trade with the Choctaws. For their part, the French were adamant that peace was only possible when the Chickasaws surrendered the Natchez, whose new village lay on the eastern edge of the large prairie settlement.[91]

Given the questionable strength of Louisiana's military force following the Natchez war, some colonial officials thought that the decision to declare war against the Chickasaws was ill advised. By 1734 it was becoming apparent that the French strategy of relying solely on Choctaw mercenaries to fight the war against the Chickasaws was not working. Despite the standing offer of guns for scalps and reminders about the Chickasaw slave raids of the past, Choctaw forays against the Chickasaws were sporadic and usually targeted individuals or small groups out hunting or tending their fields. The real military objectives were the hilltop forts of the Chickasaws and Natchez, and taking them would require an army.[92]

In early 1736 Bienville, who had returned to Louisiana in 1733 to begin his third stint as governor, began piecing together an ambitious campaign designed to accomplish this goal. He himself would lead an army departing from Fort Condé to rendezvous with a Choctaw force and approach the Chickasaw villages from the south. At the same time, Pierre D'Artaguette (Diron's brother) would lead a French and Indian force down the Mississippi River from the Illinois country to Chickasaw Bluffs and from there proceed overland to approach the Chickasaws from the northwest. For the French, the primary objective was the destruction of the Natchez village. The northern Indians accompanying D'Artaguette and the Choctaws sought a confrontation with the Chickasaws, motivated in part by desire for revenge stemming from Chickasaw attacks on their own villages.[93]

The remote location of the Chickasaw villages made the venture an expensive undertaking, which the French justified by the prospect of the final destruction of the Natchez. Bienville also wanted to prevent the establishment of peaceful relations between the Chickasaws and Choctaws, something that might allow the English to pull both tribes into their trade network. As a further hedge against English encroachment into the eastern Choctaw villages, Bienville's Chickasaw campaign plans included the establishment of Fort Tombecbé on the Tombigbee River (near present-day Epes, Alabama).[94]

The vanguard of D'Artaguette's force comprised of soldiers, militia, and Indian mercenaries reached Chickasaw Bluffs on March 4, with two other French-led Indian contingents expected to arrive shortly. En route to the Chickasaws, he received a message from Bienville reporting that delays were hampering the departure of the southern force from Fort Condé. Lacking sufficient provisions to sustain his army while waiting for Bienville, D'Artaguette decided to go ahead and proceed to his objective.[95] At the Chickasaw villages, the people were aware of the French invasion and prepared their defenses. At least five forts and numerous fortified cabins were ready to repel attackers, and warriors remained on alert to rush reinforcements from one village to another. The Chickasaw village of Ogoula Tchetoka stood on the western flank of the large prairie, in present-day northwestern Tupelo near U.S. Highway 78, and it was this settlement that D'Artaguette's force first sighted on March 25.[96] From the viewpoint of the French, Ogoula Tchetoka appeared to be a relatively easy target at some distance from the next closest villages, so D'Artaguette resolved to capture it and use it as a base until Bienville's arrival.

As the French and Indian force approached the village, a Chickasaw chief came forward with calumets, seeking to establish peaceful negotiations. Unwilling to avoid a fight, Indians marching with the French shot and killed the chief, and the Chickasaws prepared to defend their town. Once the French drew within musket range, Chickasaw gunmen firing from outlying fortified houses slowed D'Artaguette's approach long enough for reinforcements from other villages, including Natchez warriors, to join the battle. With more and more firepower brought to bear on the exposed attackers, the French advance fell apart and withdrew. Retreat quickly turned into a rout, forcing the fleeing French to abandon their wounded along with their provisions and ammunition. Reveling in their victory, the Chickasaws burned their captives, which included a wounded D'Artaguette and the Jesuit missionary Father Senat.[97]

After various delays, Bienville and his force set out from Mobile in May, unaware of D'Artaguette's fate. The French army moving up the Tombigbee River numbered about 600 men, including French and Swiss troops drawn from the posts at New Orleans, Mobile, Natchez, Natchitoches, and Belize (at the mouth of the Mississippi River), a militia comprised of settlers and voyageurs along with African slaves commanded by free blacks. Upon reaching the site selected for Fort Tombecbé, Bienville counseled with a number of Choctaw chiefs, and the army later rendezvoused with around 600 Choctaw warriors during the final overland march to the Chickasaw villages. At around ten o'clock on the morning of May 26, Bienville's force halted within sight of the small prairie settlements. Eager to strike at their enemy, groups of Choctaws broke away from the main force to fight on their own. Bienville was determined to attack the Natchez village first, but it lay over three miles away to the north, across the King's Creek drainage. Unwilling to back away from the small prairie towns and go in search of the Natchez, the Choctaw chiefs overruled Bienville, and the army formed up before the small prairie village of Ackia, located on a knoll south of King's Creek, near the site of the present-day Tupelo Middle School. When a group of Chickasaws approached bearing a calumet, excited Choctaw fighters killed and scalped two of them. A confrontation was inevitable, and French drummers sounded the attack at around three o'clock in the afternoon. By this time, hundreds of reinforcements had arrived, and the Chickasaw defenders were well armed and waiting. As Bienville watched from below, his soldiers ascended the hill to approach the Ackia fort, where they immediately came under withering musket fire from a number of fortified positions. Unable to target the Chickasaw defenders and lacking cover, the attack floundered and then collapsed in retreat.[98] In the aftermath of the campaign, while trying to put the best light on his embarrassing failure, Bienville grudgingly gave some credit to the Chickasaw fighters: "We were expecting to deal with Indians who we knew were brave,"

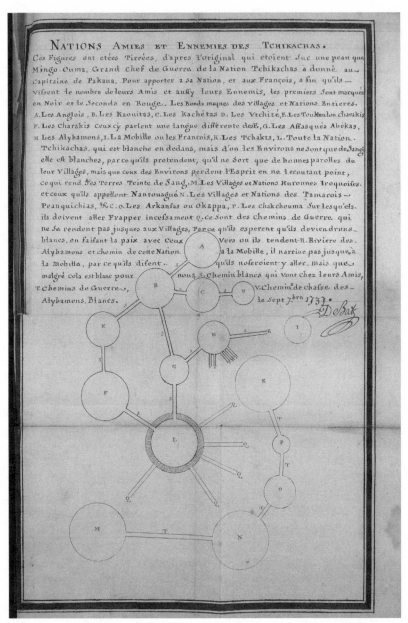

Figure 8. Nations Friends and Enemies of the Chickasaws. Alexander De Batz's copy of Mingo Ouma's deerskin map. (With permission from the Archives Nationales d'Outre-Mer, Aix en Provence, C13A 22FOL67)

and concluded that the hilltop forts would be impregnable without bringing French artillery to bear on them.[99]

Back in France, Maurepas, minister of the navy, was understandably displeased with the results of the Chickasaw campaign. Likewise, the reputation of the French colonial military plummeted among the tribes in the region as Red Shoe and other Choctaw leaders ridiculed the troops' inability to stand up to the Chickasaw gunmen. With no other honorable way to conclude the matter, planning for a second campaign commenced amid bickering and finger pointing by Bienville and other colonial administrators. This time, recruits from France and soldiers drawn from foreign regiments would augment Louisiana's colonial troops.[100]

While the French began preparations for another military offensive, groups of Chickasaw warriors made occasional raids on Choctaw villages and in May 1737 attacked the small French garrison at Fort Tombecbé. In retaliation, Bienville dispatched one of his officers, Sieur Délery, to lead Choctaw parties in raids to destroy the Chickasaws' cornfields. Because the Chickasaws kept to their forts, Délery's Choctaw forays resulted in few casualties; however, the loss of the corn meant serious hardships. In response to the Choctaw raids, the Chickasaws abandoned and burned their small prairie settlements, which were exposed to attack from the south, and temporarily consolidated their villages and forts in the large prairie, on the north side of the King's Creek drainage.[101]

A growing number of Chickasaws blamed the presence of the Natchez for these attacks, joining the peace chief Ymahatabe and other tribesmen who had opposed the merger from the beginning. In response to this pressure, a number of Natchez families left the Chickasaws and moved eastward to seek the protection of the Upper Creeks and Cherokees. Likewise, a party of Chickasaws, possibly accompanied by some of the Natchez, left their home villages and resettled close to the Upper Creek towns on the Coosa River, founding the village of Ooeasah just north of the Abihka villages. Ooeasah later became known to the English as the "Breed Camp"; the name comes from the term "half-breed," a reference to the children resulting from the intermarriage of English traders with Chickasaw women. The settlement became an important staging area for English traders en route to and from the Chickasaws. During the decades of war with the Choctaws, Breed Camp warriors served as escorts for the Carolina traders and their packhorse trains carrying guns and ammunition along the dangerous Upper Path between the Upper Creeks and Chickasaws.[102]

Despite intermittent fighting between factions of Chickasaws and Choctaws in the run-up to Bienville's second Chickasaw campaign, elements of both sides also expressed a desire for peace. A 1737 Chickasaw appeal for peace survives in a French copy of an extraordinary map originally painted on a deerskin by Chickasaw war chief Mingo Ouma (Figure 8). In addition to its geographical content, Mingo Ouma's map illustrates the chief's perception of his allies and enemies. Counted as allies were the Cherokees, Tougaloo Cherokees, Cowetas, Kashitas, Yuchis, Okfuskee Abihkas, Alabamas, and English. Unbroken paths lead out from the white (peaceful) core of the Chickasaw circle to connect with these allies, while incomplete paths originating outside the red (violent) cortex around the Chickasaw circle extend hopefully toward the northern tribes of Hurons, Iroquois, Nantouagues, Tamaroas, and Piankashaws, and the southern tribes of Quapaws, Chakchiumas, and Choctaws. The map expresses the Chickasaws' desperation after relentless harassment by these powerful adversaries. Mingo Ouma also drew an incomplete white path that extends from the Chickasaws through the neutral Alabamas toward the French and the Mobile Indians at Fort Condé. According to De Batz, who produced the copy of Mingo Ouma's map, the Chickasaw chief made two of these deerskin maps, one for the Alabamas and one for the French, neither of which survives.[103]

The craving for access to English trade goods, which came through the storehouses at the Chickasaw villages, motivated Red Shoe and other Choctaws to try and mediate a peace treaty. These efforts ultimately failed, in part because Chickasaw factions continued to mount raids against the Choctaws and the French.[104] More important, by early 1738 the king of France had already set the second Chickasaw war in motion by dispatching from the harbors at Brest and Rochefort four frigates and two merchant ships loaded with troops, cannons, ammunition, and supplies.[105] In New Orleans, Bienville struggled to organize a military strike that was clearly beyond his abilities. Once again, the distance to the enemy weighed heavily in the Chickasaws' favor. This time, Bienville decided to ascend the Mississippi River to make his attack, counting on remote contractors to drive herds of oxen and horses from Natchitoches and the Illinois country and rendezvous with the French force at the newly established Fort Assumption on Chickasaw Bluffs. From there, the teams and drivers would haul the crucial cannons and munitions over the 100-mile trail to the enemies' forts, following D'Artaguette's 1736 route. Under ideal circumstances, the campaign just might have worked. As it was, bad weather, unreliable contractors, inadequate planning, and sickness plagued the French at every turn.[106]

From November 1739 to February 1740 Bienville, his army, and cannons sat immobilized at Fort Assumption awaiting oxen and horses that never materialized. To make matters worse, chronic sickness laid most of his troops low, and supplies dwindled. In the end, Bienville gave up, realizing that he could not face the Chickasaw forts again without artillery. Disgruntled at yet another display of weakness on the part of the French, the northern Indians gathered at Fort Assumption marched to the Chickasaw villages accompanied by a French officer and a few soldiers. Joined by a contingent of Choctaws, the attackers briefly threatened the village of Ogoula Tchetoka, where D'Artaguette had met his end four years earlier. When none of the attacking force seemed willing to try and breach Ogoula Tchetoka's fortifications, both sides finally agreed to suspend hostilities. Peace chief Ymahatabe made two trips to Fort Assumption, where he concluded the terms of a treaty with a weary Bienville, who celebrated his sixtieth birthday in a tent atop Chickasaw Bluffs surrounded by his sickly troops and useless piles of munitions.[107]

The Chickasaws had little cause to celebrate their second victory. Their neighbors, the Choctaws, refused to recognize the arranged peace and redoubled their raids on the Chickasaw villages. Even though the defenders could protect themselves indefinitely behind the walls of their forts, they were helpless to stop the Choctaws from cutting down their corn and inflicting a new insult learned during the last campaign—the wanton slaughter of the Chickasaws' horses. Bienville's replacement, Pierre François Rigault de Cavagnal et Vaudreuil, saw no reason to veer from the policy of keeping the Chickasaws and Choctaws at war. Likewise, Governor Beauharnois in Canada continued to encourage mercenaries among the northern tribes to raid the Chickasaws frequently.[108] After Vaudreuil rejected Chickasaw peace overtures in 1745, the Chickasaws increasingly looked to the English for sustenance. Not surprisingly, the victories over the French were cause for celebration back in Carolina and helped the Chickasaws garner support for their role as the colony's western gatekeeper. By soundly defeating Bienville, the Chickasaws had proven their worth as England's first line of defense against French encroachment eastward out of Mississippi.[109]

The active participation of English traders in the 1736 and 1739–1740 wars expanded the strategic role of these backwoods merchants. Over the next twenty-five years, the colonial government in Charleston increasingly entrusted its far west diplomacy to these frontiersmen with their considerable knowledge of native languages, politics, and customs. One of these English trader/government agents was James Adair, who arrived at the Chickasaw villages in the late 1730s. Until the late 1760s, Adair spent much of his time there with a Chickasaw wife and their children. He proudly called himself an English Chickasaw, and his book, *The History of the American Indians*, originally published in London in 1775, is an essential primary reference on the tribe. While much of Adair's *History* is devoted to the author's thesis that American Indians derived from the biblical Hebrews, the book contains a wealth of ethnographic material.[110]

NATCHEZ REFUGEES

On Bienville's return to Louisiana in 1733, his ship stopped at Cape Français, Santo Domingo, where he chanced to speak with the Natchez chief Saint-Cosme, who admitted that the Natchez had acted alone in their rebellion instead of being part of a wider conspiracy:

> *I have seen here, my lord, the chiefs of the Natchez who are slaves, among others the man named St. Cosme, who had been made to hope that they would be able to return with me. They assured me that it was only their nation that had entered into the revolt and that the harsh treatment that had been given them had forced them to it and that they had decided upon it without taking council of the other nations, and if I am willing to believe them about it, my arrival in the colony will restore to it the tranquility that I had left there.[111]*

At the time of Bienville's first military campaign against the Chickasaws, the defenders included around 200 Natchez fighters and their families; however, some Natchez had already left the area and migrated well beyond the reach of Bienville and the Choctaws, settling along the Savannah River in South Carolina. The Natchez interest in the Savannah River area may have been due to the Chickasaw groups that relocated there.[112] By the 1740s the majority of the Natchez refugees had left the Chickasaws and drifted eastward, although one Natchez band was living with the Ouachita tribe in northeast Louisiana at this time.[113] The largest Natchez group, numbering around 150, settled near the Upper Creek Abihka villages along the Coosa River in present-day Talladega County, Alabama. The Natchez refugees, apparently accompanied by a group of Chickasaws, were scattered through several villages known as Shawano, Ooeasah, Abikudshi, and Notchee Town.[114] Another Natchez party settled with the Cherokees and established their own Notchee Town in the 1740s on the Hiwassee River in present-day North Carolina. The

Cherokees called the Natchez "Anítsi" and referred to the Natchez settlement as Gwalgwahi (Frog Place), perhaps in recognition of the important spiritual role played by Natchez descendants, since frogs are often attributed with supernatural powers by southeastern Indians. Indeed, the ethnologist James Mooney noted that the Natchez descendants came to be "regarded by the Cherokee as a race of wizards and conjurors," in reference to the niche they occupied as spiritual leaders and defenders of tradition.[115]

COMPETITION FOR DEERSKINS

In 1726 Bienville speculated that the Choctaws could supply the Company of the Indies with 15,000 deerskins per year.[116] The governor also acknowledged the tribe's military strength: "[The Choctaw confederacy is] the only nation with which [the French] must be considerate because it can cause us trouble." Accordingly, the French had to pay attention to the Choctaws' complaints about having to travel to Mobile and New Orleans to trade while the English offered to deliver the merchandise to their villages. Apprised of the situation, the company approved Diron D'Artaguette's proposal to establish trading posts with the Choctaws and Chickasaws. In response to the company's initiative, the Carolina traders aggressively increased the amount they were willing to pay for skins, initiating a price war that Diron found difficult to sustain.[117] For the Mississippi tribes, playing the English and French against one another was a dangerous game with tangible benefits during times like these.

When Perier took over as governor of the Louisiana colony in late 1726, he proposed doing away with Diron's monopoly in favor of opening the Choctaw trade to other French merchants, a move backed by the company to the detriment of Diron's business.[118] One of Diron's competitors among the Choctaws was the Jesuit priest Mathurin Le Petit, who established a mission in the southern village of Chickasawhay in 1727 as part of an agreement between the Jesuits and the Company of the Indies. Diron complained that Le Petit was trading knives for deerskins, an activity that may seem out of place for a missionary; however, the company was in favor of its missionaries being self-supporting, and Le Petit was merely bartering for food and supplies.[119] The Jesuit Michel Baudouin assumed Le Petit's Choctaw mission in 1729 and remained at Chickasawhay until 1748. Bienville considered Baudouin an authority on the Choctaws. More than once the priest proved himself a valuable political agent with his knowledge of the Choctaw language and his ability to move freely among the confederacy's villages gathering useful information.[120]

Even though the company saw benefits in emulating the English entrepreneurial business model, French officials stopped short of condoning mar-
riages between the traders and Indian women, a ploy used to much advantage
by English traders.[121] Back in 1708 Thomas Nairne had crowed about the advantages offered the English traders by the matrilineal kinship system:

> It is the easiest thing in the world, for an English Traveller to procure
> kindred among the Indians, It's but taking a mistress of such a name,
> and he has at once relations in each Village, from Charles Town to the
> Missisipi, and if in traveling he acquants them with what family he is in-
> corporated into, those of that name treat, and wait on him as their kins-
> man. There are some of our Countryman of such prudence and forecast,
> that in case one family should fail them, take care to make themselves
> akin to severall.[122]

Through their residences in tribal villages and extended personal contact
with their customers, English traders gained a secure base from which to op-
erate. House group membership also provided the traders with a measure
of protection; anyone who harmed them risked retribution by the trader's
wife's family members.[123] However, owing to their annual circuit between
Charleston and the Chickasaw villages, most Carolina traders were only in
residence with their Indian wives during the winter months. Following the
trading pattern established in the early 1700s, English merchants typically arrived at the Chickasaws in January leading packhorse trains of up to seventy
horses loaded with trade goods. In May the traders departed for Charleston
with their packhorses carrying deerskins.[124]

Alarmed at reports of the Choctaws seeking to do business with the
English traders, Governor Perier sent the officer Régis du Roullet into the
confederacy in 1729 on a fact-finding mission. In his meetings with village
leaders, the chiefs voiced complaints about the behavior of Diron's agents
and accused Diron of making them pay for merchandise that they should
have received as presents. Red Shoe complained about a rumor circulating
among the Choctaws indicating that Diron had called him a "woman," which
the warrior gave as his excuse for being friendly with the English. In an effort
to address the Choctaws' grievances, Perier and the company's administrative council revoked Diron's trade agreement in October 1729.[125] At the time,
Diron claimed that the Choctaws owed him 14,000 deerskins, but tribal leaders responded by saying they had received shoddy merchandise, and, furthermore, their service in the Natchez war canceled their debt. During the 1730s

and 1740s, the English continued to dominate the Mississippi deerskin trade, consistently providing better quality merchandise and a more favorable exchange rate than did the French.[126]

THE CHOCTAW CIVIL WAR

King George's War (the War of the Austrian Succession), beginning in 1744, manifested itself in Mississippi as an intensification of the ongoing competition between Carolina and Louisiana for Choctaw allegiance.[127] This larger conflict served as the backdrop for the bloody Choctaw civil war (1746–1750), which, according to Patricia Galloway, "must have been the most momentous happening in Choctaw history from the beginning of European contact until removal." Although the Choctaw civil war can be characterized as intratribal fighting between pro-English and pro-French factions, Galloway has shown that the conflict was rooted in the Choctaws' struggle to come to grips with the French view of *lex talionis*, or law of retaliation.[128]

By the early 1740s Red Shoe had become the most powerful chief in the Choctaw confederacy, with medals from both the French and the English as proof of his extraordinary ability to manipulate colonial officials and obtain presents.[129] When the war interrupted French supplies of trade merchandise to Louisiana, Red Shoe entered into negotiations with English traders based among the Chickasaws, including James Adair. Touting the promise of English presents and trade, Red Shoe was able to build a strong coalition among Choctaw villages by late 1745, especially in the Western and Sixtowns divisions.[130] The tension building up between Red Shoe's pro-English faction and the remaining pro-French faction surfaced in October 1745 when Choctaws killed two English traders on the path to the Chickasaw villages. Another incident occurred in March 1746 when three Chickasaws were killed in an attack on an English trader at the village of Bouctoucoulou in the Eastern Division.[131] These attacks threatened Red Shoe's negotiations with the English and obliged the chief to carry out a counterstrike as a show of good faith. Adair, who was a part of this intrigue, also reported an incident that affected Red Shoe personally, involving the reputed rape of one of the chief's wives by a French soldier.[132]

Whether provoked by one or all of these events, most sources agree that Red Shoe was behind the August 1746 killing of three French traders near the Western Division towns of West Abeka and Immongoulasha.[133] The following month Vaudreuil sent the officer Jadart de Beauchamp from Mobile to meet with Eastern Division chiefs and demand that they give the French satisfaction by executing three men from the pro-English Western faction. As leverage, French presents and trade would be withheld. The French colonial view of *lex talionis* called for the Choctaws to administer this punishment to their own people. Beauchamp was alarmed to discover that the consensus among the chiefs was that Red Shoe's faction was much too strong for them to attempt to carry out Vaudreuil's order. Besides, the Choctaws saw *lex talionis* quite differently and expected the French to exact their own vengeance. With this in mind, Alibamon Mingo stressed to Beauchamp that French retaliation should be directed at the Western faction and not at his Eastern villages.[134]

In the meantime Red Shoe sought to broaden his base by reaching out to the Alabamas and Abihkas, but both groups were reluctant to turn against the French. When Adair attempted to pass through the Abihkas' villages carrying the scalps of the three assassinated Frenchmen, he was forced to hand over the trophies, which the Abihkas then returned to the French.[135] The refusal of the Alabamas and Abihkas to join Red Shoe's coalition prompted Vaudreuil to change his demand and insist that the Eastern chiefs deliver up the head of Red Shoe himself.[136] Beauchamp gamely relayed this to a number of chiefs assembled at Chickasawhay, who responded that Red Shoe's assassination would be far too risky given the strength of the rebel chief's faction. The Concha chief Alibamon Mingo argued in favor of the French. Alibamon Mingo had initially supported Red Shoe, but now assumed leadership of the opposing Eastern Division. A chief of the Yanabé village, perhaps wondering if the French realized the full implication of their demand, told Beauchamp that he feared the prospect of a civil war.[137]

The tense situation entered a new and more volatile stage in June 1747, when an anonymous assassin killed Red Shoe in an ambush as the chief accompanied an English trade caravan from the Chickasaw villages into the Choctaw confederacy.[138] Contrary to French expectations, Red Shoe's faction remained intact after his death, and two Western Division chiefs, Mingo Ouma of Cushtusha and Pouchimataha of Caffetalaya, assumed dual leadership.[139] At first, Western faction retaliation avoided direct assaults on the Eastern Choctaws and focused instead on the French, with attacks on the Natchez post and settlements near Mobile.[140] Had the French responded to these insults with a counterattack against Cushtusha and Caffetalaya, they might have prevented the civil war; however, the garrisons at Fort Tombecbé and Mobile remained silent. In retaliation, a party from the Concha villages ambushed an English packhorse train, and a Western Choctaw chief was among those slain. Galloway points to this incident, which she notes might have been unintentional since Choctaws had avoided killing other Choctaws up to this time, as the spark that ignited the civil war.[141]

In retribution for the chief's death, Western faction Choctaws attacked the Concha villages, and, for the next three years, both French and English looked on in disbelief as Choctaw villages assaulted one another with escalating ferocity. To make matters infinitely worse, smallpox and measles epidemics swept through the Choctaw settlements in 1747 and probably killed as many people as were lost in the fighting.[142] Although most of the surrounding tribes stayed out of the war, about fifty Chakchiumas joined a party of Chickasaws at the village of Nushkobo and fought alongside the Red Shoe faction.[143]

Ultimately, the warring factions were limited by their access to European merchandise, most particularly guns and ammunition. In this instance, the French decided the outcome of the civil war by keeping Alibamon Mingo and his allied chiefs well supplied. To the dismay of the Red Shoe faction, the English supplies came too slowly, due in part to the distance involved. The English were also less inclined to give presents; the traders wanted deerskins in exchange for weapons, which the Choctaws were unable to supply while occupied with fighting. The conclusion of King George's War in 1748 further cooled English desires to prolong the Choctaw conflict with military supplies.[144]

In September and October 1750 the small garrison at Fort Tombecbé belatedly entered the fighting and captured the towns of Cushtusha and Caffetalaya to subdue the last major holdouts of the Red Shoe faction. In their fury, Eastern Division fighters had already burned the villages of Couechitto, Nushkobo, and West Abeca. French estimates of the number of Choctaw casualties vary. Vaudreuil guessed that the Red Shoe faction alone lost around 800 men, while his successor, Kerlérec, placed the total dead on both sides at around 600.[145] Peace was finally concluded with a calumet ceremony at Fort Tombecbé in November 1750. Since the pro-French faction had emerged victorious, Vaudreuil dictated the terms of the treaty, under which the reunited Choctaw divisions agreed to abide by four main conditions: refrain from killing Frenchmen, stop bringing Englishmen into Choctaw villages, renew attacks on the Chickasaws, and dismantle their fortifications and release all prisoners.[146]

In spite of the relative abundance of documentation on the Choctaw civil war from both French and English sources, much about the conflict remains uncertain. Although the two opposing factions clearly represented political and economic interests, some evidence suggests that kinship affiliation also played a part in the war. In late 1746 Vaudreuil wrote that the Choctaw factions involved "the principal castes of this nation,"[147] an apparent reference to the kinship-based iksas and moieties discussed earlier. Galloway has pointed out that in the cases where we know the moiety affiliation of faction leaders, it appears that Imoklasha (Red Shoe's moiety) aligned with the pro-English faction, while Inholahta (Alibamon Mingo's moiety) represented the pro-French faction.[148] As discussed in the first part of this chapter, Greg O'Brien argues that the moieties should be viewed as separate ethnic groups,[149] which if correct would make the Choctaw civil war appear to be less of an internecine struggle. As for how the loyalties sorted out in terms of geography, the six Sixtowns villages fought with the Western Division, while the Chickasawhay and Concha villages aligned with the Eastern Division. Couechitto and Nushkobo, located closest to the Eastern Division, were strong centers of support for the Red Shoe faction.[150] Surprisingly, the factionalism that characterized the Choctaw confederacy during the civil war seems to have evaporated after the Tombecbé treaty. Although the treaty was obviously designed to distance the Choctaws from the English and bind them more closely to the French, documentation from the 1750s indicates that the chiefs immediately returned to their pre–civil war strategy of seeking presents and trade from any available European source.[151]

CLIENT WARFARE INTENSIFIES

At the conclusion of the Choctaw civil war, the French once again used presents and scalp bounties to encourage Choctaw and Quapaw raids against the Chickasaws. Although much of the fighting involved small raiding parties, a force of over 1,000 Choctaws accompanied by a few French soldiers descended upon the Chickasaw villages in September 1752 and destroyed the ripening corn crop. Fighting also broke out on other fronts as some Chickasaws joined Creek warriors in attacking the Cherokees. Through it all, the English traders doggedly kept the Chickasaws equipped with guns and ammunition, which the latter used to make retaliatory strikes against the French.[152]

The French tradition of giving presents to favored Choctaw chiefs began with Bienville, and subsequent governors continued his practice of using the occasion to praise those chiefs who had been loyal while chiding others for disloyalty. For the Choctaw chiefs, the presents were an obligatory commitment of friendship on the part of their French "father" and receiving them validated their personal power. Going further, Patricia Galloway has argued that French and English colonial leaders from patrilineal societies sought obedience from the Indians by casting themselves in the role of father. For their part, the Indians understood this role-playing according to their matrilineal framework in which the father belongs to a separate lineage from his children. In the matrilineal societies of the Mississippi tribes, the father was not an authoritarian figure, but instead treated his children with kindness and generosity. It was the maternal uncles, adult males with the same name as their nieces and nephews, who assumed parental-like authority over their sisters' children.[153] Although Bienville's successors had plenty of occasions to curse the expense and inconvenience, they all recognized the necessity of keeping the tradition of annual presents. Governor Kerlérec wore the mantle of father to the Choctaws with suffering in the fall of 1754:

> *In going [from New Orleans to Mobile to distribute the annual presents to the Choctaws and Alabamas] I experienced the longest and most unpleasant voyage; the sojourn that I made [at Mobile] was no less afflicting. This is easy to imagine if one is acquainted with all the troublesomeness of the Indians, especially in a number of more than two thousand as they came together, who one by one, wishing to address speeches to their father, left me not ten minutes from sunrise until after midnight, and even then I had much difficulty in sending them away. That, my lord, is the life I led for sixty-two days; my health even broke down, and I experienced there a most serious illness from which I am barely recovered.[154]*

The English rarely distributed presents to the Chickasaws since Carolina's traders expected deerskins for the merchandise they hauled from such a distance. The English trader John Buckles was in the Chickasaw villages in 1754 and estimated that the population totaled 1,275, of which he considered about 340 to be "able gun men." The trader also noted that several Chickasaw families succumbed to the pressure from the Choctaw attacks and migrated eastward to the relative safety of the Breed Camp and the Chickasaw settlement on the Savannah River. Buckles's mission to the Chickasaws was in response to the tribe's urgent plea to Carolina's governor Glen for help in holding off the French and their allied tribes. The trader's cargo, carried on packhorses from Charleston, included seventy-five guns, 600 pounds of powder, 1,200 bullets, and 4,000 gunflints. Buckles also reported that not all of the Choctaws approaching the Chickasaw villages were there to fight; some Choctaws representing factions friendly to the English came to the Chickasaws to carry on trade.[155]

The munitions that Buckles supplied to the Chickasaws allowed them to carry out a surprise attack on the French post at Natchez in July 1754, where they captured several women of the Ofo tribe that had resided there since the Natchez war. That same summer, on the upper Ohio River near present-day Pittsburgh, British soldiers clashed with the French in a series of confrontations leading into the French and Indian War (known in Europe as the Seven Years War). The commencement of war was virtually unnoticed in Mississippi as nearly continuous fighting between the Choctaws and Chickasaws escalated through the 1750s. In late 1755 large French and Choctaw forces attacked the Chickasaws repeatedly and burned one of the villages.[156]

Fighting between the Chickasaws and several French-allied tribes peaked in 1756–1757 before the English navy began shutting down French supply ships bound for Louisiana. Without presents and trade goods, Louisiana colonial officials once again found it increasingly difficult to purchase mercenary services among the Choctaws and other nominally pro-French tribes. On the English side, traders managed to keep the Chickasaws supplied with guns and ammunition, along with other necessities like blankets and clothes. The guns going to the Chickasaws may have included the newly developed rifled barrel models, which were superior to the old smoothbores and gave the shooter an accurate range of up to 200 yards. By necessity, these packhorse trains on the Upper Path went heavily guarded, with up to 100 gunmen as escorts to ward off Choctaw attacks. The traders' risks paid off during the late 1750s when Chickasaw raiding parties assisted the English by harassing the newly built French Fort Massiac, situated on the Ohio River, just below the mouth of the Tennessee River.[157]

The back-and-forth raiding between the Choctaws and Chickasaws simply continued the complex relationship they had established thirty years earlier in which warfare was intermittently suspended for trade.[158] Hardship and danger were omnipresent, and no living Choctaw or Chickasaw could remember any other way of life. Both groups had adapted under pressure to the complex political and economic roles forced upon them by the powers that be in Louisiana and Carolina. The key to that adaptation lay in the dangerous game of playing one colonial power off against the other.[159] Now a war was raging across Europe that would radically alter the game and the roles associated with it.

Chapter 5

1763–1800

CULTURAL SURVIVAL AND EMIGRATION

Fighting elsewhere in the French and Indian War overshadowed the intermittent violence in Mississippi, and battles won and lost in Canada and the Caribbean Islands determined the future of the Mississippi tribes. The terms of the 1763 Treaty of Paris divided French Louisiana between England and Spain, with the land east of the Mississippi River falling to the English while the Spanish received title to New Orleans and the land west of the river. In November 1763 the Choctaws and Chickasaws confronted the new reality at treaty conferences in Augusta, Georgia, and Mobile. In the changed political landscape, the Chickasaws lost their strategic importance to the English. As the historian Colin Calloway has pointed out, the tribes that the English formerly viewed as allies became subjects now that the French were out of the picture.[1] In late 1763 English soldiers occupied Mobile without a fight. On November 14, 1763, English major Robert Farmar and French director general Jean Jacques Blaise d'Abbadie counseled a group of Choctaw chiefs gathered at Fort Condé to accept the partition of the Louisiana colony: "As you are free men who must have learned to think since you have been associating with white men, the two Great Chiefs whom you see present here for the English and the French assure you today that for your repose and that of your old men, of your wives, and of your children you must conform inviolably to this arrangement."[2]

Despite this paternalistic bravado, Farmar, who had charge of the Mobile area, was well aware of the Choctaws' strength. The confederacy could field the largest fighting force in the region, and Farmar feared that its chiefs might react violently upon hearing that they had lost a war in which they had barely even fought. There was good reason to be apprehensive; six months earlier a host of pro-French tribes in the country north of the Ohio River led by the Ottawa chief named Pontiac had attacked British garrisons occupying former French outposts. To keep the Choctaws happy, Farmar went beyond his authority and promised the chiefs that the English would supply them with everything they were accustomed to receiving from the French.[3] This included awarding annual presents to the numerous Choctaw chiefs and headmen, a diplomatic expense that the commander called the "vile custom the French have introduced."[4]

Given the option of swearing an oath to England and remaining in West Florida, numerous French inhabitants chose to stay, including over 100 residents of the Mobile area. Under the English, Fort Condé became Fort Charlotte, and by the end of 1763 English soldiers occupied Fort Tombecbé.[5] In the Lower Mississippi Valley, the occupation of the old French fort at Natchez became a priority, as did the establishment of a new post at the confluence of the Mississippi River and the small distributary stream known as the Iberville River (present-day Bayou Manchac, just south of Baton Rouge). Called Fort Bute, this new installation would serve as a trading post and provide the English with a military presence in the area.[6] Fort Bute had another strategic purpose since the Iberville River now formed part of the international boundary between British West Florida and the New Orleans area. Although the distributary was only navigable during periods of high water on the Mississippi River, the Iberville passage linked the Mississippi River with the Mississippi Gulf Coast via the Amite River and Lakes Maurepas and Pontchartrain. West Florida governor George Johnstone and his officers in the Mississippi region saw this watercourse as a way to bypass the coming Spanish occupation of New Orleans, which could sever English boat traffic between the Lower Mississippi Valley and the Gulf Coast.[7] Despite considerable effort spent clearing the Iberville River of rafted trees, the stream never became a viable passageway for the English.[8]

When the rebellious pro-French tribes led by Chief Pontiac prevented the English from occupying Fort Chartres in the Illinois country, Governor Johnstone ordered a company of the Twenty-second Regiment of Foot, stationed then in West Florida, to ascend the Mississippi River and take control of the outpost. Major Arthur Loftus commanded the expedition, which left New Orleans on February 27, 1764, with between 320 and 360 officers and men plus around thirty women and twenty children. Struggling upstream against a strong current and coping with continuous rains, the flotilla made slow progress. Troop morale was low, and Loftus's journal notes at least twenty-eight desertions. On March 4 the expedition reached a Houma village located sixty-nine river-miles north of New Orleans. Here, Loftus received word that a number of hostile Indians were waiting upstream to attack his convoy. Like Pontiac's fighters, these warriors were members of longtime pro-French tribal groups. Over the next two weeks, as the English force approached the landmark known as Roche á Davion, or Davion's Rock, named for the late Seminarian missionary (present-day Fort Adams, Wilkinson County), friendly Indians relayed more warnings about an ambush. The anticipated strike came on March 20 when shooters concealed on both riverbanks fired upon the expedition's lead boats. With six men dead and four more wounded, Loftus ordered the boats about, and the expedition made an ignominious retreat back to New Orleans. Loftus wrote that his attackers were Houmas, Tunicas, Chitimachas, and Ofos. Other sources indicate that the hostile group may have also included members of the Avoyel and Choctaw tribes. Estimates of the number of Indian fighters ranged from 30 to Loftus's report of 200. As might be expected, the major received criticism for giving up so easily, and English prestige on the frontier suffered accordingly. For the Indians' part, their triumph only briefly stalled the English advance. The English finally reached Fort Chartres via the Ohio River in 1765, and the Natchez post came under English control the following year.[9]

1765 MOBILE TREATY CONFERENCE

To secure their position and encourage colonists to settle in the new province of West Florida, the English sought land cessions and pledges of peace from the Creeks and Choctaws. In late May 1765 the Creeks ceded their land around Pensacola, including part of present-day south Alabama. Two months later, chiefs and headmen from the Chickasaw and Choctaw villages gathered before English officials at Mobile. For the Chickasaw delegation, led by the war chief Paya Mattaha, the Mobile conference was merely a formal reaffirmation of diplomatic relations with the English. The West Florida officials were much more interested in meeting with the Choctaws and in obtaining a land cession first discussed two years earlier at the Augusta talks. Specifically, Governor Johnstone and District Superintendent John Stuart desired a large tract of land above Mobile Bay, bounded on the west and east by the Chickasawhay and Tombigbee rivers, respectively. An elderly Alibamon Mingo headed the group of Choctaw chiefs. For the most part, Alibamon Mingo had remained pro-French during the client wars. Because of his reputation, the new regime at Mobile considered him a potential threat even though the chief must have been well into his sixties at the time.[10]

Although the Choctaw chiefs respectfully deferred to Alibamon Mingo, the land in question fell under the jurisdiction of the southern Sixtowns

Division, represented at the conference by the chiefs Tomatly Mingo of Seneacha and Nassuba Mingo of Chickasawhay.[11] As has been mentioned elsewhere, the American Indians' view of land ownership was different from that of the Europeans. The Choctaws, at least in the early treaties set before them, saw the cessions as formal grants of permission for use of the land, not as a transfer of ownership. Tomatly Mingo also informed his English counterparts that the Choctaw land cession would not include the villages of the Naniabas, Tohomés, and Mobilians on the lower Tombigbee River. Although these small tribes were not part of the Choctaw confederacy, Johnstone and Stuart may have assumed that they were in the Sixtowns Division.[12]

For the Choctaws, the subject of presents was a more important item on the conference agenda. Two years had passed since the last annual distribution of presents by the French, and the chiefs now looked to their English "father" to make good on Farmar's promise.[13] Tomatly Mingo declared that he was formerly "a Frenchman" but was now firmly on the side of the English, adding: "If I am [the son of the English], they must act the part of a father in supplying my wants by proper presents and also by furnishing a plentiful trade." Despite the Choctaws' desire for commerce, many felt a growing resentment toward the English traders who were now moving freely among the Choctaw villages. Along with a request for a trade storehouse at Fort Tombecbé, Tomatly Mingo warned Johnstone and Stuart that the traders were insulting their warriors and making indecent advances toward their wives, activities that might lead to "very great disturbances."[14]

LIQUOR FOR DEERSKINS

When Alibamon Mingo addressed the English officials at the 1765 Mobile conference, he echoed the complaints from other Choctaw and Chickasaw chiefs about the bad behavior of the traders. In addressing this problem, Governor Johnstone rightly blamed much of the discontent on the effects of the alcohol the traders swapped for deerskins. This was nothing new; from the earliest contact days, the Mississippi tribes faced increasing exposure to French brandy and English rum.[15] Although the English colonial administration attempted to license and control the traders, their efforts proved ineffectual, with as many as 100 traders circulating among the Chickasaws by 1765.[16] During the same period, traders from Carolina and Georgia were becoming fixtures in the Choctaw villages. A few were reputable and held licenses, but many others drifted through the confederacy with scales weighted in their favor and a keg or two of rum to put their customers at a decided disadvantage. Prior to the Treaty of Paris, the French were unable to police the sale of brandy and wine to the tribes at frontier posts such as Fort Tombecbé; however, French liquor was usually in short supply, and the distance back to Charleston prevented English liquor from reaching the Mississippi tribes in any appreciable quantity.[17] After 1763, the source of supply changed from Charleston to Mobile, practically on the Choctaws' doorstep.[18] As it became increasingly available, English rum quickly joined guns and blankets as a sought-after commodity in frontier trade. The Choctaw chief Poucha Ouma of the Concha villages put this plainly to Governor Johnstone: "You must not be surprised at my asking [for] rum, in return, for the [cession] lands, rum is a liquor we are fond of, and that you have so I will beg for rum and must have some, it is the English drink."[19]

On the Savannah River, proximity to white settlements and plenty of liquor had already seriously weakened Squirrel King's band of eastern Chickasaws. During the 1750s English settlers crowded into the region, and Squirrel King's people were subject to the usual depredations that came with unscrupulous traders. Since the Georgia and South Carolina authorities no longer needed Squirrel King's warriors as mercenaries, the chief's authority declined accordingly. When incoming settlers finally took over their land after the Treaty of Paris, these eastern Chickasaws found temporary residence in the villages of their old enemies the Lower Creeks, and eventually many of them rejoined the tribe in their Mississippi homeland.[20]

POST-1763 DIASPORA

Alcohol addiction also plagued the small tribes, many of whom lived close to the New Orleans and Mobile settlements for protection and employment. Colonial narratives document deaths and debilitation from alcohol consumption among the Alabamas, Tunicas, Houmas, and Apalachees, and we can assume that the rest of the small tribes had problems as well. As mentioned above, both the French and English realized the folly of supplying the Indians with liquor, but neither side took any effective measures to address the issue.[21] Reduced by alcohol, warfare, and epidemics, the small tribes attached to French settlements faced exile west of the Mississippi River following the Treaty of Paris and the subsequent breakup of Louisiana. From this point in history, the paths of Mississippi's small tribes become difficult to trace due to the splintering and fusing of groups seeking to survive in a new political realm. By the 1760s the Houmas had become a ragged confederacy composed of remnants of their own tribe plus families of Colapissas, Bayagoulas, Quinipissas, Mougoulachas, Tangipahoas, and Biloxis. Abandoning their villages near the Mississippi River, they moved down Bayou Lafourche and eventually settled in present-day Terrebonne and Lafourche parishes. Around the coastal estuaries southwest of New Orleans, the Houmas turned from farming corn and beans to focus on hunting, fishing, and trapping.[22]

When Spanish administrators assumed control of their portion of the Louisiana colony, they welcomed the pro-French tribes as a means of defense against the possibility of English incursion. A large number of refugees came from the New Orleans, Mobile Bay, and Fort Toulouse areas, including bands of Alabamas, Apalachees, Chacatos, Koasatis, and Taensas. Bands of Choctaws, Biloxis, Pascagoulas, Capinans, and Ofos eventually joined the exodus so that the westward migration happened piecemeal, stretching out over the course of more than a decade. A 1778 map by George Gauld shows Pascagoula, Biloxi, Tunica, Ofo, Alabama, and Houma villages still on the Mississippi River at that time, indicating reluctance on the part of these tribes to quit their homeland completely, despite the growing English presence in the region. At the urging of Spanish authorities, however, most of these people eventually left the Mississippi River and settled on small land allotments along the Red River in present-day Rapides and Avoyelles parishes. The Avoyel tribe had been living in this area since Iberville's time and suffered from the encroachment of so many disparate groups.[23]

In addition to the Choctaws who settled on the Red River allotments, a large number of Choctaws crossed the Mississippi River and established villages along the Ouachita River in northeast Louisiana (present-day La Salle, Morehouse, Union, and Ouachita parishes). These Choctaws ran into opposition from the Caddo tribes, who considered the Ouachita River part of their territory and resented the newcomers' invasion.[24] Disputes over space also plagued the Red River settlements, and the cramped living conditions helped to spread smallpox and measles among the villages. In desperation, some of the families drifted farther west and northwest into what is now Texas and Oklahoma.[25]

During the last decades of the eighteenth century, the tribal histories reflect the inevitable fusion of immigrant nations in what Hiram F. Gregory has called a "polyglot mixture." The Avoyels and the Ofos were eventually absorbed into the Tunicas. The Capinans became part of the Pascagoulas, some of whom later joined the Biloxis and Alabamas. Members of the Biloxis merged with the Choctaws and Tunicas, while others moved on to Texas and Oklahoma. In the nineteenth and twentieth centuries, four of the former Mississippi tribes coalesced into three tribal groups that are now associated with Louisiana: Tunica-Biloxi, Jena Band of Choctaw, and Houma. Likewise, the Alabamas fused with their longtime allies the Koasatis as the Alabama-Coushatta tribe of eastern Texas.[26]

For the most part, the small tribes that remained in Mississippi after the Treaty of Paris favored the English and their allies the Chickasaws and pro-English factions within the Choctaw confederacy. The Chakchiumas, probably combined with the Taposas and Ibitoupas, were scattered among the Chickasaws and Choctaws by the 1760s.[27] Patricia Galloway has noted the presence of an Eastern Division Choctaw town named Ibitoupougoula (Ibitoupa people), suggesting a connection with the Ibitoupas. Likewise, Galloway points out the two Choctaw towns named East Yazoo and West Yazoo, but any link these settlements might have to the Yazoo tribe remains a mystery. As mentioned above, the remnants of the Yazoos probably joined the Chickasaws following attacks by pro-French tribes in the wake of the Natchez Rebellion.[28] The last reports on the whereabouts of the Tious placed them on the Big Black River in the mid-1700s; however, Mississippi archaeologist Jack D. Elliott Jr. found references to place-names in early-nineteenth-century letters, indicating that a Tiou group may have lived for a time on the Pearl River near the Natchez Trace in present-day Madison, Hinds, and Rankin counties.[29]

THE DISPERSAL OF THE NATCHEZ

After the Treaty of Paris, West Florida administrator John Stuart proposed that the Natchez settlements among the Cherokees and Creeks be reconstituted and induced to move back to their former homeland, where they could serve as watchdogs for the English along the Mississippi River.[30] For whatever reason, Stuart's scheme never reached fruition, and the Natchez refugees became well integrated into their host tribes. Scattered references to the Cherokees and Creeks in the latter half of the eighteenth century mention prominent Natchez headmen and chiefs, including the Creek/Natchez chiefs Notchee King, Dog Warrior, and Co-tau-lau.[31] Also notable among the descendants of the Natchez who settled with the Abihka Creeks is the mixed-blood historian George Stiggins, who was raised among the Natchez/

Creeks and wrote a history of the Creek confederacy.[32] Stiggins was the son of Joseph Stiggins, an English trader, and Nancy Grey, niece of the Natchez chief Chinnabe, a leader of the Natchez refugee group that settled with the Abihkas.[33]

Remarkably, at least a few Natchez seem to have persevered in their home area until the region passed into English control. In a memoir by Colonel Anthony Hutchins, a retired British army officer who settled in the Natchez area in 1772, a man who identified himself as a Natchez led the colonel to a place the Indian called "White Apple Village," some twelve miles south of Fort Rosalie on Second Creek. By the time that Hutchins arrived in the Natchez area, the Treaty of Paris had made it safe for the first time in over thirty years for the Natchez to reveal their identity in their old homeland. As previously discussed, the White Apple settlement of the 1720s was located on St. Catherine Creek northeast of Fort Rosalie; however, examples from Chickasaw accounts indicate that, as the people who occupied a particular village moved to a new location, they often took their village name with them.[34] A third "White Apple" place-name is associated with a small community about twenty miles southeast of Fort Rosalie, in northwestern Franklin County. Although at this point we can only speculate, the possibility exists that a small band of Natchez chose to risk capture and remain in the Natchez area. A concern for safety may have necessitated them to move periodically, resulting in at least three places known as "White Apple." If so, then the group may have been a remnant of the renegade White Apple settlement district.[35]

Another Natchez community, possibly derived from the early settlement on the Savannah River, became part of the Catawba confederacy in 1734. A violent confrontation with their Catawba hosts in 1744 forced this Natchez group to take up residence with the Cherokees.[36] Part of this Natchez community apparently remained in South Carolina, joining the Kussoe on the Edisto River near Charleston. As was the fate of all of the southeastern tribes, the Kussoe-Natchez endured a series of progressively unfavorable treaties designed to strip them of their land; however, the group persevered long enough to have what little real estate they had managed to hold surveyed, giving them legal title. Today, the group persists as the Kussoe-Natchez.[37] For the Natchez descendants attached to Creek and Cherokee groups, their subsequent fate became fused with that of their hosts.

CHOCTAW-CREEK WAR: 1766–1775

The emergence of Mobile as an English supply depot put the Creeks and Choctaws in direct competition for merchandise. A certain amount of friction had always existed between the two confederacies, and now British West Florida officials found reasons to use that friction to orchestrate a war. Just as the French had once feared an English-Choctaw-Chickasaw alliance, some English officials worried that the Spanish could threaten West Florida by harnessing a Choctaw-Creek coalition. As Greg O'Brien has pointed out, young warriors from both groups had been harassing British settlers and traders, causing Choctaw and Creek chiefs to admit to their British contacts that they were having trouble controlling their warriors. Thus the British would benefit from a Choctaw-Creek war by focusing the attention of the tribes' young men away from the white settlements. The hostilities would also empower the chiefs, who stood to enhance their status by leading war parties. Significantly, the fighting would provide young Choctaw and Creek men with the opportunity to earn their war names.[38]

As it happened, the hoped-for war was relatively easy to kindle. In January 1766 a warrior turned up missing from the Upper Creek (Abihka) town of WeKay (Wokukay), and a rumor spread that some Choctaws had killed him. Two months later, a party of Creeks attacked a group of Choctaws near the Tombecbé fort, killing one of them. Overnight, with encouragement to their warriors from certain chiefs, the Choctaw-Creek War was a reality; however, the British soon realized that the conflict would not be the bloodbath they might have envisioned. The ever-present traders enticed many Choctaws and Creeks into using their guns and ammunition for deer hunting instead of fighting. Importantly, O'Brien has noted that killing a deer, although less prestigious than killing a man, still gave a young man the right to add the word "killer" ("*abi*" or "*abé*") to the end of his name. Even though the violence may not have been intense, British settlers suffered occasional casualties; however, many of these confrontations arose out of arguments over debts and white encroachment beyond the Creek cession land. Because the British were never overgenerous with presents, warriors occasionally looted storehouses and helped themselves to the king's merchandise.[39] Although the Chickasaws briefly joined the Choctaws in fighting the Creeks, they managed to remain neutral and at peace through most of the conflict.[40] Both the Choctaws and Creeks were well aware of Governor Johnstone's efforts to orchestrate a war between them, which later made it difficult for the English to marshal these tribes to fight the American rebels.[41]

NEW ELEMENTS MERGE WITH OLD TRADITIONS

Scattered references document the perseverance of traditional ceremonial and social activities among Mississippi tribes throughout the eighteenth century, notwithstanding the chronic intertribal violence. Importantly, around the time of the French and Indian War the Choctaws and Chickasaws adopted the European-style clothing for dances and ceremonial occasions that these tribal groups still wear today for important events. The "new traditional" dress for women includes long-sleeved, ankle-length dresses with aprons decorated in beadwork, appliqué, and ruffles. Men wear black trousers and colorful long-sleeved shirts augmented with appliqué and ribbons. Wide, flat-brimmed, dark felt hats also became part of men's formal dress at this time.[42] Dancers and musicians also adopted European bells and drums of African and European design to use alongside traditional clay-pot and wooden drums, gourd and turtle shell rattles, and wooden flutes. Despite these changes, the people maintained a large repertoire of traditional songs for social and religious occasions. Music historian Victoria Lindsay Levine noted that many of the old Choctaw and Chickasaw songs became "recontextualized" to relate to the people's interaction with Europeans, Africans, and other displaced tribal groups.[43]

During the eighteenth century, the most important ceremonial activities accompanied the first corn harvest, sometimes called the Green Corn Ceremony or Busk. Perhaps best documented among the Creek confederacy, the ceremony combined the ripening of the year's first corn crop with the renewal of the tribe's sacred fire. The use of purifying emetics, namely the Black Drink and button snakeroot, was an important part of the ceremony. Among some southeastern groups, the event culminated in the sacrificial burning of ears of corn in a fire kindled by a tribal elder designated as fire-maker, after which women carried the sacred flame to their home hearths. Adair's description of the Green Corn Ceremony among the Chickasaws seems to be the only reference to the tribe's observance of this festival during the eighteenth century. Nairne, who knew the Chickasaws some thirty years before Adair's time, reported tribal dancing as part of a green corn feast, although he noted that the Chickasaw ceremony was not the same as that of the Creeks. Swanton believed that the Chickasaws adopted the tradition from the Creeks.[44] The Choctaws also celebrated the first corn harvest with three days of feasting and social dancing.[45] Likewise, French observers during the 1720s recorded much about the Natchez harvest celebration, usually held in

July. After several days of feasting, the Natchez event culminated in all-night dancing by torchlight.[46]

Corn harvest ceremonies and other annual events were also occasions for ball games. Stickball, related to lacrosse, was the principal team sport of the southeastern Indians, and colonial Europeans found variations of the game throughout the Great Plains, Great Lakes region, Ohio Valley, and the Northeast.[47] The earliest mention of the game in the Lower Mississippi Valley comes from the Jesuit missionary Paul Du Ru, who accompanied Iberville's 1700 exploratory expedition. Du Ru watched a group of Houma women competing in the tribe's village at the Portage of the Cross:

The women . . . separate into two parties between two large posts in the square. Somebody throws a little ball in the center, and the one who seizes it first tries her best to run around the post on her side three times, but she is prevented by the women of the opposite party who seize her if they can. When she can no longer resist them, she throws the ball to her people who make a similar effort to run around the post. Sometimes the ball falls into the hands of the other side, which then tries the same maneuver. The games are very long and ordinarily when they are over the women plunge into the water to refresh themselves. Sometimes the men play this game also.[48]

As Du Ru noted, the sport appealed to both men and women, and the game, also known as racket (or by its Creole name, *raquette*), had many variations, even within the Southeast. Most observers mention two goals, but sometimes teams used just one goal, or pole, and some groups (as seems to have been the case with the Houma women) played without sticks. Despite several references to the hands-only version of the game, the use of two hickory sticks by each player seems to have been more common in the Southeast, while the northern tribes typically used just one stick. The sticks were two-and-a-half to three feet in length, with the end carved thin enough to bend the tip back to the shaft and form a small pocket secured with deer hide thongs. The pocket webbing was made of strips of deer or raccoon skin, and the ball was usually a piece of deerskin filled with deer or squirrel hair and stitched with sinew. Rules varied about players touching the ball with their hands. In many cases, players could catch and throw with their hands, but could not use their hands to pick up the ball. Choctaw and Chickasaw men's games used two goals, composed of either single posts or two poles with cross bars. Instead of trying to score a point by driving toward the opponent's goal, players tried to carry the ball to their own goal. There were no sidelines or out-of-bounds. Playing fields varied greatly in length; one eighteenth-century Chickasaw field was reportedly 500 yards long. Matches often pitted the best players of two villages against each other, generating considerable excitement and wagering on the outcome. Stickball games may have occasionally helped settle disputes between villages, but the violence of the contests sometimes resulted in injuries or deaths that spawned bitter feuds. Players wore only breechclouts and decorated their bodies with paint, feathers, and animal tails. Women's games often followed the men's play. In the 1720s the Natchez played the game without sticks, and opposing teams wore red and white feathers, which may have represented the tribe's two moieties. French observers noted that the Natchez located their playing field away from their Grand Village ceremonial center, and the two goals were the temporary cabins of the Great Sun and his brother, the Tattooed Serpent.[49]

Reminiscent of the lucky numbers and good luck charms of modern athletes, success in stickball matches depended heavily upon intervention from the spirit world. During the night dancing before a Choctaw stickball game, Adair observed women chanting to implore the spirits to favor their husbands' team, and on the morning of the game he watched the players assemble to hear their leaders' "religious invocations" seeking victory. Dancing and singing typically lasted throughout the night before a game. The Choctaws used a series of ball game songs aimed at inspiring the players, calling for supernatural assistance, and jinxing the opposition. While most of the celebrants feasted, the players took care to avoid food while ingesting emetics to purify themselves for the coming contest. Other purification rituals included bathing prior to the game, scratching the arms and chest to draw blood, food taboos, and abstinence from sex. Failure in the game usually implied a team's failure to prepare properly. Although Father Du Ru believed that the Houma women swam after their match to "refresh themselves," purification through bathing was also necessary after a game. As important as its players was a team's medicine man or conjurer. Indeed, a big stickball game sometimes became a showdown between two powerful medicine men. Although the extent to which stickball figured into tribal belief systems is not known, the game is woven into mythologies, and stories of games between animals are as widespread as the game itself.[50]

Father Du Ru also watched the Houmas playing another game, the two-man athletic contest that later became widely known as "chunkey." This sport, a variant of the hoop and pole game played all over North America, was ubiquitous among the southeastern Indians. Chunkey players used a small, carefully ground, wheel-shaped stone made especially for this game, and two spearlike poles some eight to fifteen feet in length. According to Adair, chunkey stones "belonged to the town where they were used" and were "kept with the strictest religious care, from one generation to another." Bernard Romans, who watched Choctaws playing chunkey in the 1770s, described the playing field as an "alley of about two hundred feet in length, where a very smooth clay ground is laid, which when dry is very hard." The game began when one player rolled the chunkey stone down the alley and both players sprinted after it. Players threw their poles trying to anticipate where the stone would come to rest, with the player whose pole came closest scoring a point.[51] Like stickball, chunkey inspired prolific wagering, as attested by Benjamin Dumont, who observed the Natchez playing the game: "The savages have another kind of game in which they exercise themselves, not merely for amusement, but also to gain each other's property, to the point of ruining themselves . . . wagering on the game their powder, their guns, their skins, their Limbourg [cloth], in a word, all that they may have."[52]

Although chunkey playing declined after removal, stickball and the harvest celebrations continued among Choctaw and Chickasaw communities in Mississippi, Louisiana, and Oklahoma. Maintenance of the Green Corn rituals helped to sustain late-nineteenth-century conservative movements such as the Four Mothers and Keetoowah societies. Natchez descendants were active in these societies and shared the Medicine Springs ceremonial ground near Gore, Oklahoma, with Creek and Cherokee groups. Square grounds flanked by open-sided structures called arbors, elements of the Green Corn festival, also became a component of the campground meetings encouraged by the missionaries.[53] As they had in the eighteenth century, the corn harvest celebrations continued to provide a social backdrop for stickball after removal, despite the upheaval caused by the forced emigration of the tribes. Some of artist George Catlin's dramatic paintings from the Indian Territory during the 1830s attest to the persistence of the sport. Several of Catlin's canvases depict a tumultuous Choctaw stickball match with hundreds of players.[54]

THE REVOLUTIONARY WAR

Hostilities between the Choctaws and Creeks dragged on for ten years before the outbreak of the American Revolution prompted the British to restore peace and seek the help of the two groups. For their part, the Choctaws held no feelings of loyalty for the British; their "service" in the Revolutionary War was on a strictly mercenary basis. In 1777 Choctaws agreed to help patrol the Mississippi River under British supervision, a job that quickly became boring to men used to an active lifestyle. Despite the protests from their white supervisors, the Choctaws returned to their home villages in February 1778 and in so doing missed James Willing's notorious Mississippi Valley raid harassing English loyalists. The Choctaws received the blame for being away from their post, although Willing's foray proved to be more of an embarrassment than a threat to the British. At the time, however, British officials feared that Natchez might come under subsequent attack and sought a Choctaw force to go and protect the town. The influential chief Franchimastabé of the Western Division village of West Yazoo responded to the call and, with around 155 warriors, duly occupied Fort Panmure, the run-down fortification on the site of the old French Fort Rosalie. An Englishman named Farquhar Bethune was in overall command, and the expedition included some sixty-four British militiamen. The monthlong occupation was without incident; however, the fierce-looking Choctaw warriors no doubt convinced many Natchez residents to keep any pro-American feelings to themselves for the time being.[55]

The Mississippi theater of the Revolutionary War only began to become active when Spain declared war on England in 1779. Without a significant British force to confront them, the Spanish quickly captured Baton Rouge and Natchez, and Mobile was in Spanish hands by March 1780. The war now divided the loyalties of the Choctaw divisions, with the Sixtowns leaning toward the Spanish while the Western and Eastern divisions felt closer politically to the British. Probably with an eye toward a future trade relationship, representatives from the Sixtowns carried the calumet to the Spanish commander at Mobile. Although the British managed to raise an army of over 1,600 Choctaws, Chickasaws, and Creeks to help defend Pensacola, most of these warriors had left by the time the Spanish captured the town in 1781.[56]

The alliance between the American colonies and France placed most of the Chickasaws squarely on the side of the English during the Revolutionary War. The Scottish trader James Colbert took command of a Chickasaw militia force assigned to patrol the Mississippi River and the lower Ohio River, leading the Americans to counter by constructing Fort Jefferson near the confluence of the two rivers. Angered at the placement of an enemy fort within their hunting territory, the Chickasaws attacked the outpost repeatedly until its garrison fled. Despite the British capitulation at Yorktown in 1781, Colbert and his mixed-blood sons remained defiant, temporarily providing refuge to British loyalists from the Natchez district. Leading a diverse band of mixed-blood

Chickasaws, Africans, and loyalists, the Colberts brazenly attacked the Spanish fort at the old French settlement at Arkansas Post before the elder Colbert's death in 1783 brought an end to the raids.[57]

THE UNITED STATES

The historian Daniel Usner has noted that by the 1780s, non-Indian colonials outnumbered Indians in the Mississippi region. Usner's population estimates for the Choctaws and Chickasaws are 13,400 and 2,300, respectively. Since 1700 both groups had lost 4,000 to 5,000 members through contact attrition and migrations (groups of Choctaws moving to the west and groups of Chickasaws moving east). In contrast, Usner's estimates for the growing non-Indian population are 13,000 whites, 16,000 enslaved blacks, and around 1,000 free blacks. The white residents included around 500 traders ensconced in Indian villages, most of whom did business with the English firm of Panton, Leslie & Company. Although the Spanish had opposed the English during the late war, Spanish officials had no qualms about relying upon the English trading company to establish their Indian trade.[58] From the perspective of many Choctaws and Chickasaws, Spain promised to be an effective trading partner, as did the states of North Carolina, South Carolina, and Georgia. The dark horse regarding trade potential was the new federal government, the victorious Americans whom the Choctaws initially called "Virginians."[59]

Treaty conferences hosted by the Spanish, the state of Georgia, and the United States in 1784 and 1785 provided opportunities for Choctaw and Chickasaw chiefs to receive presents and establish new trade relationships. The Western Division Choctaw chief Franchimastabé and the Chickasaw chief Ugulayacabe (also known as Wolf's Friend) headed delegations to the conference hosted by Spanish governor Estevan Miró in Mobile in June 1784. While Franchimastabé met with the Spanish, another Choctaw delegation held concurrent trade talks with Georgia officials at the Savannah River.[60] For both tribes, the chance to hold a formal meeting with the Americans finally came in late December 1785 at the Hopewell Treaty Conference in South Carolina. Chief Taboca, who, like Franchimastabé, resided in the Western Division, led the Choctaws' Hopewell delegation. Greg O'Brien's analysis of the negotiations at Hopewell and the transcript of the chiefs' speeches by General Joseph Martin, one of the three U.S. treaty commissioners, make it clear that the Choctaws viewed themselves as a "nation" on equal footing with the Americans. In contrast, the transcript of the treaty itself indicates that the

Americans looked upon the Choctaws as a part of the losing side in the War for Independence. Importantly, O'Brien reveals the extent to which ritual and ceremony figured in the Choctaws' approach to the diplomatic proceedings.[61]

Of the eleven articles in the Hopewell Treaty to which the Choctaws agreed on January 3, 1786, perhaps the most damaging was Article 3, which defined the boundaries of the Choctaws' lands and provided for the cession of "three parcels of land six miles square each" (11,520 acres) for the use of the U.S. government. By agreeing to the treaty's definition of their confederacy's boundaries, the Choctaws gave up an unknown amount of land around their borders that the tribe had formerly been accustomed to using as hunting grounds.[62] The Choctaw chiefs' speeches as translated by their interpreter and transcribed by Joseph Martin give the impression of the chiefs' acceptance of the treaty; however, later testimony from some of the Choctaw signatories raises questions about the conference. Chiefs later said that they did not understand the paper they were asked to sign and, as O'Brien suggests, perhaps regarded the act of signing to be the Americans' ritualistic counterpart to their calumet ceremony. Choctaw blame was also directed at their interpreter, John Pitchlynn, whose job it was to make the meaning of the articles clear to the chiefs. A more serious charge came from a chief named Yockonahoma, who said that the Americans gave the Choctaws liquor and made them sign the document while they were drunk.[63]

Soon after the Choctaws concluded their Hopewell treaty talks, the Americans entered into treaty negotiations with the Chickasaw chief Piomingo. The Chickasaw Hopewell Treaty, signed on January 10, 1786, included a cession of land for a U.S. trading post in the vicinity of present-day Iuka, Mississippi, and an estimate of the land controlled by the tribe. As with the Choctaws, this loosely worded boundary description probably cost the Chickasaws some of their hunting lands in subsequent treaty negotiations. Although unenforceable, the United States claimed exclusive control over trade in both the Choctaw and Chickasaw Hopewell treaties.[64] The Chickasaws' cooperation with the Americans drew attacks from a coalition of southeastern Indian groups seeking to coerce the Chickasaws into opposing American encroachment on the Ohio and Mississippi rivers. This coalition, headed by mixed-blood Creek leader Alexander McGillivray, received Spanish support and included factions drawn from the Creeks and Cherokees. Despite their pressure, McGillivray and his supporters were unsuccessful in forcing the Chickasaws to join their alliance.[65] In 1791 the Americans enlisted around fifty Chickasaw warriors to help put down an uprising by combined forces of Kickapoos, Shawnees, Miamis, Patawatomis, Chippewas, Delawares, and other tribes of the Wabash region, who were resisting the annexation of their land. The Wabash campaign gave the Chickasaw warriors an opportunity for revenge against some of the northern tribes that had raided them so relentlessly in the past.[66]

DECLINING DEERSKIN TRADE

Both Mississippi tribes were disappointed in the Americans' lack of interest in discussing trade at the Hopewell conference. Although the American government was slow in meeting the Indians' trading needs, hunters could turn to the traders residing in their villages, many of whom now worked for Panton, Leslie & Company. The field agents employed by Panton, Leslie & Company transacted business with the Chickasaws and Choctaws in much the same way as earlier French and English traders; that is, the agents gave the deer hunters their payment in advance, and the hunters later supplied the skins they owed. It continued to be a system fraught with opportunities for the company agents to cheat their illiterate clients, and the tribes ran up large debts that the United States would use against them in future treaty negotiations.[67]

As values of deerskins declined after the American Revolution, increasing numbers of Indian families bartered with more of the sideline commodities that had always augmented the deerskin trade, including beeswax, small animal skins, dugout canoes, tallow, corn, and medicinal herbs such as snakeroot. Choctaws and Chickasaws also sold cane baskets, hired on as laborers, and carried the mail. The buying and selling of hogs, horses, and cattle, which had been a way of life for some Indians since the 1720s, became more commonplace throughout the region toward the end of the eighteenth century. For many, cattle ranching became especially lucrative, and Choctaw and Chickasaw communities spread out to allow room for fenced pastureland. By the 1790s this transition to a frontier farming lifestyle increasingly included family cotton production made possible by the proliferation of Eli Whitney's gin.[68]

Along with the economic opportunities that accompanied the growing influx of American settlers into the area came the first efforts by individual states to possess the Mississippi region. By virtue of the 1763 Treaty of Paris, which some state officials argued superseded the 1783 Paris treaty, the states of Georgia and South Carolina extended their western boundaries all the way to the Mississippi River. These proposed boundaries ran counter to the federal government's assertion of authority over the western territory in order to make Indian treaties and establish new states.[69] South Carolina eventually capitulated under pressure from other states, but the Georgia state assembly brazenly asserted its right to the western land by creating Bourbon County in 1785. The new county comprised the Natchez District, and Georgia traders stepped up their merchandising among the Choctaws and Creeks in order to weaken the tribes' alliances with Spain and the United States. The ambitious Georgia assembly also created Houston County in present-day northern Alabama; however, the Spanish presence at Natchez and the close proximity of Houston County to the Creek confederacy discouraged plans for Georgia settlements in the West.[70]

The failure to establish the two counties did not prevent Georgia officials from seeking to capitalize on what they considered their state's land west of the Chattahoochee River. In 1789 the Georgia legislature passed an act opening the state's western lands to purchase by speculators, who eagerly formed a number of land companies, many of which incorporated the word "Yazoo" in their names. Although some of the companies made feeble attempts to establish settlements at Natchez and Muscle Shoals, opposition from Spain, the United States, and Indian groups ended the venture in late 1790. A few years later, rumors that Spain was about to abandon the Natchez District led to renewed interest in re-forming the Yazoo companies. In response, the Georgia legislature hastily passed a bill in 1795 authorizing land sales. Like previous attempts to usurp federal control, the scheme was doomed to fail, and the Georgia legislature repealed the bill known as the "Yazoo Fraud" in 1796.[71]

Spain responded to Georgia's encroachment by strengthening ties to the Choctaws, Chickasaws, and Cherokees. At a treaty conference in Natchez in May 1792, the Choctaws officially condoned Spain's Fort Nogales near the mouth of the Yazoo River and Fort Confederation (old Fort Tombecbé) on the Tombigbee River. A new Spanish post at Chickasaw Bluffs, called Fort San Fernando de las Barrancas, provided another trade outlet for Panton, Leslie & Company. The 1792 Choctaw treaty with Spain also reinforced Panton, Leslie & Company's position as the principal trader with the tribe. Since the 1763 Treaty of Paris, English traders had established residences with the Choctaws and married into elite Choctaw matrilineal kinship groups. By the 1790s these traders wielded considerable influence among Choctaw chiefs, especially with regard to diplomatic issues involving Spain and the United States. Even though many of the traders were licensed by Spain, they sometimes advised chiefs against Spanish directives in order to pursue their own agendas. Resident traders with the Choctaws in the late eighteenth century included Nathaniel and Edmond Folsom, Louis and Michael Leflore, and Isaac Pitchlynn, whose mixed-blood descendants became important Choctaw chiefs in the nineteenth century.[72]

In an effort to establish a coherent federal Indian policy, the U.S. Congress passed the Indian Trade and Intercourse Act of 1790. Increasingly, federal officials in the George Washington administration favored efforts to "civilize" the tribes, a sentiment that would later influence removal strategies. The 1795 Treaty of San Lorenzo, also known as "Pinckney's Treaty" after Thomas Pinckney, the U.S. treaty commissioner to Spain, shifted Spain's northern boundary South to the thirty-first parallel.[73] Despite the terms of the treaty, the Spanish optimistically continued to maintain garrisons at Fort St. Stephens (San Esteban), Nogales, and Natchez in case the United States proved unable to occupy the Mississippi region. Spain's reluctance to abandon the river settlements and the persistent Georgia land claims helped provide incentive for President John Adams and Congress to create the Mississippi Territory on April 7, 1798. Initially the territory took in the land between the Mississippi and Chattahoochee rivers, bounded on the south by the thirty-first parallel and on the north by a line from the mouth of the Yazoo River to the Chattahoochee River (32° 28' north latitude). These territorial boundaries encompassed portions of the lands occupied by the Choctaws, Chickasaws, Creeks, and Cherokees, creating conflicts of overlapping authority between the new territory and the United States with regard to Indian relations.[74]

The formation of the Mississippi Territory and Spain's diminishing influence in the region ended the Indians' century-long game of playing competing colonial powers against each other. Although the game had often been perilous, numerous chiefs and warriors among the Choctaws, Chickasaws, Natchez, and other Mississippi tribes had skillfully used the competition to enhance their own status and provide trade opportunities for their people. Now, as the eighteenth century drew to a close, the Choctaw and Chickasaw leaders again faced two competing entities—federal and territorial governments. But unlike the colonial regimes of the past, which were willing to bargain with the Indians for military assistance and deerskins, the tribes had little to offer these new entities. In fact, both federal and territorial officials viewed the Mississippi tribes as a brake on economic development. Soon, the Mississippi Territory would achieve statehood and close ranks with the federal government to marginalize and remove the state's native peoples.

Chapter 6.

1801–1837

TREATIES AND REMOVAL

In the fall of 1801 a delegation of Chickasaw chiefs and warriors led by King Chinubbee gathered at Chickasaw Bluffs (present-day Memphis, Tennessee) to negotiate a right-of-access treaty with the United States (Treaty of Chickasaw Bluffs, signed October 24, 1801). Fifteen years had passed since the first U.S. treaties with the Chickasaws and Choctaws at Hopewell, South Carolina. Now, President Thomas Jefferson needed the Chickasaws' assurance of safe passage for travelers and mail delivery between Nashville and the Natchez District. With the land west of the Mississippi River and the region below the thirty-first parallel under foreign control, Jefferson also needed a network of roads in order to move militia around to defend the country's southwestern border. Representing the interests of the United States in the treaty negotiations were General James Wilkinson, Colonel Benjamin Hawkins, and Andrew Pickens. Hawkins, of North Carolina, and Pickens, of South Carolina, were commissioners for the Hopewell treaties. Since 1796, Hawkins had served as the federal government's principal Indian agent, a post authorized by the Indian Trade and Intercourse Act of 1793. Wilkinson, who followed Anthony Wayne as commander of the U.S. Army, had a checkered career that included clandestine employment with the Spanish government in New Orleans.[1]

Chinubbee (also Chinmimbe Mingo, Chenumbe) succeeded his brother Taski Etoka (also Mingotushka, The Hare Lip King) as leader of the Chickasaws in the mid-1790s and at the time of the Treaty of Chickasaw Bluffs Chinubbee was probably in his late fifties. Besides George Colbert, who spoke for Chinubbee in the negotiations, five other Chickasaw chiefs at the treaty conference signed with Anglo-American names, indicating the growing influence of mixed bloods in the tribe. The commissioners made it clear that they were not seeking a land cession, but only wanted free passage through the Chickasaws' territory, stressing that the federal government would improve and maintain the roads to the tribe's benefit. Chinubbee agreed to allow the use of the roads, but refused permission for whites to establish wayside inns in Chickasaw country, informing the commissioners through Colbert that the Chickasaws themselves would look after the needs of travelers. In exchange for signing the Treaty of Chickasaw Bluffs, the chiefs received $700 worth of merchandise to distribute among their people.[2]

Less than two months later, Wilkinson, Hawkins, and Pickens conducted treaty negotiations with Choctaw chiefs at Fort Adams on the east side of the Mississippi River, some thirty-five miles below Natchez (Treaty of Fort Adams, signed December 17, 1801). Leading the Choctaw delegation was Chief Tuskona Hopoia (Tuskona Hoopoia, Tusconohopia), from the confederacy's Lower Towns Division (corresponding to the eighteenth-century Eastern Division). Chief Toota Homo (Tuskahoma) of the Sixtowns Division was second in rank among the Choctaw chiefs at the Fort Adams negotiations. Significantly, both Tuskona Hopoia and Toota Homo had signed the 1786 Hopewell Treaty. Oak Shumme (Oak Chummy) served as the ranking chief of the Upper Towns Division (corresponding to the Western Division).[3]

In contrast to the Chickasaw delegation of chiefs at Chickasaw Bluffs, only one mixed-blood Choctaw chief, Robert McClure, signed the Treaty of Fort Adams. (Although mixed-blood Choctaw and Chickasaw men usually had warrior names, these individuals tended to identify themselves in treaty signings by their Anglo-American names.) Besides requesting the use of wagon roads through Choctaw territory, President Jefferson's commissioners asked the Choctaws to cede approximately 2.6 million acres of land in the southwestern corner of the Mississippi Territory, an area roughly corresponding to the present-day counties of Warren, Claiborne, Jefferson, Adams, Franklin, Wilkinson, and Amite. Known as the Natchez District under English and Spanish dominion, this was the former territory of the Natchez, Koroas, Houmas, and Tunicas, among other groups. With the exodus of these tribes, the Choctaws claimed the area by default. Its cession did not deprive the Choctaws of any land historically occupied by their confederacy, and the influx of whites into this region made the district less attractive as hunting land. Despite the fact that the Choctaws did not lose any part of their ancestral homeland in the Treaty of Fort Adams, the chiefs considered the land cession a significant gesture of conciliation. In return, the Choctaws received $2,000 worth of merchandise plus three sets of blacksmith tools.[4]

William C. C. Claiborne, who succeeded Winthrop Sargent as territorial governor in 1801, wrote to Secretary of State James Madison from Natchez asking for clarification of the duties of his office regarding Indian affairs.

The new governor seemed bewildered upon receiving "many visits" from the Choctaws, although perhaps the chiefs of the confederacy's three divisions needed to establish separate diplomatic relations. "Governor Sargent," Claiborne wrote, "frequently complained of embarrassment with regard to the Indians," and Claiborne himself viewed Indians as savages in need of "humanization." To that end, he supported efforts to civilize the Mississippi tribes by teaching girls to spin and weave and apprenticing boys to wheelwrights and blacksmiths.[5]

Civilizing the tribes was also one of the goals of the federal agents assigned to Indian affairs. During Mississippi's early territorial period, federal Indian agents with the Chickasaws and Choctaws reported to their district superintendent, Benjamin Hawkins, and, by necessity, to the territorial governors, especially as problems arose between the tribes and increasing numbers of white settlers and traders. Hawkins appointed Samuel Mitchell as agent to both the Choctaws and Chickasaws in 1797. Two years later, John McKee, an appointee of the secretary of war, joined Mitchell as Choctaw agent, and the following year Mitchell left the Choctaw post to McKee and became the Chickasaw agent. As official representatives of the federal government, the Indian agents also served as spies, on the lookout for tribal interaction with representatives of foreign governments.[6]

For their part, the Choctaws and Chickasaws offered little resistance to the territorial and federal efforts to peddle "civilization." By the turn of the nineteenth century, many Choctaws and Chickasaws already resembled white settlers in outward appearance and lifestyle—wearing Anglo-American clothing, living in log cabins, using plows and wagons, herding cattle, growing cotton, and (for a few at least) owning African American slaves. Along with these cultural changes, Choctaw and Chickasaw populations were undergoing a significant demographic transformation. The mixed-blood offspring of English, Scottish, and French traders now comprised minorities among the tribes, creating a new social category that cut across moieties, iksas, and, with the Choctaws, the confederacy's three divisions. The Chickasaws had hosted traders since the early years of the eighteenth century, while resident traders only became commonplace in the Choctaw villages after 1763. The ethnohistorian Greg O'Brien has noted the predilection of traders to marry tribal women of elite status, putting their male offspring in line for leadership roles. O'Brien also notes that, to the Choctaws, people with Choctaw mothers were Choctaws, regardless of the ethnicity of the father. (The same statement holds true for the Chickasaws.) However, the sons and daughters of traders also received their father's surname and tended to use it to identify themselves in interactions with Anglo-Americans and Europeans. During the early nineteenth century, some mixed-blood families formed communities apart from full bloods, and differences in tribal politics often led to feelings of animosity between the two groups.[7]

Although many Chickasaw and Choctaw families were moving into ranching and cotton farming, the tribes still controlled vast tracts of hunting land. President Jefferson and other American leaders sought to convert these reserves to more efficient use as farmland for both the Indians and immigrant white families. Attracting white settlers to the western part of the Mississippi Territory was key to Jefferson's plan for defense of the region, which contrasted sharply with the tactics of the colonial French and English. Instead of arming the Chickasaws and Choctaws to serve as surrogate armies, Jefferson wanted the Indian land to establish a farmer militia comprised of men who would guard the country's border while defending their homes. The Choctaw land cession at the Treaty of Fort Adams marked the beginning of Jefferson's efforts to implement his strategy. In early 1802 the U.S. government's need for more Indian land took on a heightened sense of urgency when word spread about Spain's cession of Louisiana back to the French as part of the Treaty of San Ildefonso. After all, many Americans knew about Napoleon Bonaparte's military campaigns and could easily imagine a French army gathering in the Mississippi Valley.[8]

At the same time, fears of a strengthening Spanish-Choctaw alliance alarmed American settlers in the Tombigbee River valley, leading the federal government to take steps to secure its border on the north side of the thirty-first parallel above Mobile.[9] To achieve this, the boundaries of the Choctaw confederacy at strategic locations had to be determined. The close proximity of the southern Choctaw villages to the Spanish in Mobile prompted the Jefferson administration to reestablish boundaries in this region that were agreed upon in the Choctaws' 1765 treaty with the British at Mobile. To this end, Commissioner Wilkinson called for a treaty conference with the Choctaws at Fort Confederation in the summer of 1802. Understandably, the Choctaws were not amenable to more negotiations with the United States; however, Wilkinson argued somewhat disingenuously that, without knowing the precise boundaries, the territorial government could not prevent white settlers from encroaching on Choctaw land.[10]

As he had at Fort Adams, Tuskona Hopoia assumed the role of the senior Choctaw chief at the Fort Confederation discussions, which lasted over three months. The protocol observed by the chiefs in the order in which they signed the treaty (each with an "x") indicates that men who had signed

the Fort Adams treaty took precedence over the other chiefs from their division. Included in the list of chiefs is Poosha Mattahaw, better known as
Pushmataha, an important chief of the Sixtowns Division who would have
been about thirty-five years old at the time.[11] John Pitchlynn, the father of
the mixed-blood Choctaw chief Peter Pitchlynn, was one of four interpreters during the long negotiations at Fort Confederation. The son of trader
Isaac Pitchlynn, John was about ten or eleven years old when he and his
father arrived in the Choctaw confederacy around 1775 and settled in the
Eastern, or Lower Towns, Division. Among the witnesses to the treaty was
Silas Dinsmoor, who had replaced John McKee as Choctaw agent.[12] Under
the Treaty of Fort Confederation, the Choctaws authorized the survey of
a tract containing over 800,000 acres, bounded on the west and east, respectively, by the Chickasawhay and Tombigbee rivers, and on the south by
the boundary of Spanish West Florida (the thirty-first parallel). Since these
boundaries were already well established, the treaty negotiations focused on
the northern boundary. Eventually, the chiefs and Wilkinson agreed upon a
northern boundary line running eastward from near the confluence of the
Chickasawhay River and Bucatunna Creek (in present-day Wayne County,
Mississippi, about fifteen miles southeast of Waynesboro) to the Hach-a-
Tig-geby (Hatchetigbee, Hatcheettigebee) Bluff, near the confluence of the
Tombigbee River and Sinta Bogue Creek (in present-day Washington County,
Alabama). Although the Treaty of Fort Confederation was ostensibly limited
to establishing boundaries without a land cession, Choctaw tribal historian
Robert B. Ferguson maintained that the tribe lost some 50,000 acres in the
boundary delineations, which included an adjustment (in the United States'
favor) of the tribe's boundary with the Natchez District. The treaty negotiations concluded without any compensation for the Choctaws.[13]

Barely six months after the Treaty of Fort Confederation, Napoleon surprised the Spanish by selling Louisiana to the United States. In New Orleans
and Mobile, the Spanish commanders maintained that the old West Florida
province below the thirty-first parallel was not part of the Louisiana Purchase
and tightened control over the lower stretches of the Mississippi and
Mobile rivers, hampering shipments in and out of the Mississippi region.[14]
Reactions to word of the Louisiana Purchase varied among the Chickasaws
and Choctaws. In the Chickasaw villages, chiefs who had been uneasy while
the French were back in control of Louisiana were no doubt relieved to hear
the news.[15] When news of the Louisiana deal reached the Choctaws, Silas
Dinsmoor reported the reaction of the pro-Spanish faction to Governor
Claiborne: "The old Spanish chiefs who were so troublesome begin to hang

their heads and I suspect when the country is taken possession of that they will be perfectly obsequious."[16]

Spanish influence among the Choctaws depended heavily upon Panton, Leslie & Company traders working out of New Orleans, Mobile, and Pensacola; however, the federal government's Trade and Intercourse Act of 1802 banned Indian trade with foreign countries not licensed by the United States. With the death that same year of William Panton, the firm's principal owner, Panton's partner, John Forbes, sought to settle his firm's account with the Choctaws by trading the tribe's debt for land in the Mississippi Territory, something the United States could not condone.[17] The Jefferson administration used the situation to the United States' advantage by forcing the Choctaws either to cede the land surveyed under the Treaty of Fort Confederation or settle immediately their debt with Forbes. With no means of paying what they owed, the tribe's representatives found themselves once again facing Commissioner Wilkinson, this time at St. Stephens on the lower Tombigbee, a place the Choctaws called Hoe Buckintoopa. Chief Mingo Pooscoos, of the Lower Towns, who had signed fifth at Fort Adams and second behind Tuskona Hopoia at Fort Confederation, served as the principal Choctaw chief at the treaty conference. Tuskona Hopoia's absence at Hoe Buckintoopa may indicate that he had died or become too infirm to negotiate. Acting as second to Mingo Pooscoos was the Sixtowns chief Alatala Hooma (Latalahomah, Illatalla Homo), who had also signed the Fort Adams and Fort Confederation treaties. With them were six chiefs living in the cession land, making the Treaty of Hoe Buckintoopa (signed August 31, 1803) the first U.S. acquisition of land historically occupied by the Choctaws. In return for giving up approximately 853,700 acres, the Choctaws received "fifteen pieces of strouds (high quality blankets), three rifles, one hundred and fifty blankets, two hundred and fifty pounds of powder, two hundred and fifty pounds of lead, one bridle, one man's saddle, and one black silk handkerchief."[18]

One of the witnesses to the Treaty of Hoe Buckintoopa was Joseph Chambers, with the title of "United States factor." Chambers operated the U.S. government's new trading house, or factory, at St. Stephens (later moved north near Fort Confederation), which aimed to keep the Choctaws supplied with merchandise and weaken their dependence upon traders representing the Spanish. The Chickasaws received a similar government factory at Chickasaw Bluffs. Like the federal agents living with the tribes, government factors served as diplomats, and they kept Washington informed about tribal affairs. The Jefferson administration congratulated itself on providing the Indians with manufactured goods at reasonable prices; however, the new factories were too far from most of their intended customers, who were accustomed to having traders in their villages. Naturally, the pro-Spanish chiefs were vocal in their opposition to the U.S. factories, and Spanish-licensed traders continued to circulate among the tribes despite federal laws to the contrary.[19]

Aside from giving the Indians an alternative to foreign trade, the U.S. government factories may have had a more sinister purpose, according to historian Arthur H. DeRosier Jr., who notes that President Jefferson saw the Indian trade as a way to foster indebtedness among the tribes, which the government could use to leverage future land cessions.[20] Certainly, the Jefferson administration had seized upon the timely demand for payment from Panton, Leslie & Company to help persuade the Choctaws to sign the Treaty of Hoe Buckintoopa. As other trading companies and individual traders joined Panton, Leslie & Company in calling for a settlement of debts, the Jefferson administration developed a strategy in which the U.S. government would pay the tribes' debts in return for title to enormous tracts of Choctaw and Chickasaw land. Importantly, congressional authorization for the Louisiana Purchase and its division into territories provided Jefferson with a convenient place for the southeastern Indians to go after the appropriation of their land, and, for the first time, removal became an acceptable solution to the "Indian problem."[21]

The Chickasaws had thus far avoided making any substantial land cessions to the United States, but in the summer of 1805 they found themselves negotiating with U.S. commissioners General James Robertson and Silas Dinsmoor at the tribe's Big Town village. Robertson had served as the Chickasaws' first federal agent. As mentioned above, Dinsmoor was the federal agent to the Choctaws at the time.[22] King Chinubbee once again led the delegation of chiefs and warriors, which included at least six tribal leaders who had signed the 1801 treaty. The agreement, known as the Treaty of the Chickasaw Nation (signed July 23, 1805), focused on the tribe's debts to traders. Article 1 of the treaty gives the impression that the United States had come to the Chickasaws' rescue: "Whereas the Chickasaw nation of Indians have been for some time embarrassed by heavy debts due to their merchants and traders, and being destitute of funds to effect improvements in their country, they have agreed and do hereby agree to cede. . . ."[23]

Under the terms of the treaty, the Chickasaws ceded approximately 2.25 million acres of their hunting land in present-day western Kentucky, central Tennessee, and northern Alabama (Figure 9). In return, the federal government distributed $20,000 on the tribe's behalf to trading companies and

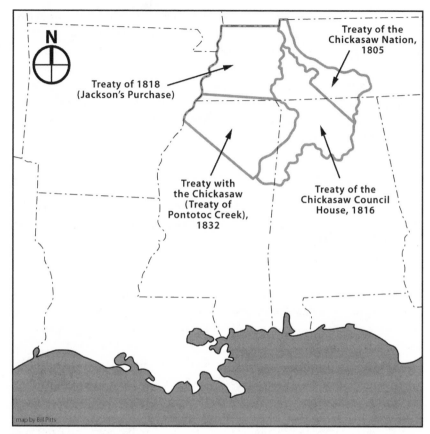

Figure 9. Chickasaw land cessions.

individuals. In all likelihood, these traders would have been content to continue doing business but were happy to accept such a windfall. The 1805 treaty with the Chickasaws marked the first time that the names of individual chiefs appear in the official document as recipients of personal gifts for their part in helping the United States reach a favorable conclusion to the negotiations. Two chiefs, George Colbert and O'Koy, received $1,000 each. Colbert, then in his mid-thirties, was the mixed-blood son of trader James Colbert and an effective spokesman for the Chickasaws. Archaeologist James Atkinson has suggested that O'Koy (Okoye, also known as Tishumustubbee) was the same person as Tishomingo, an important Chickasaw chief in later treaty negotiations. Atkinson notes that "Tishomingo" was an office title for one who speaks for a king or chief. The other chief receiving a special favor was Chinubbee, who received a $100 lifetime annuity. Considering Chinubbee's age (perhaps early sixties), the diplomatic investment must have seemed a bargain. (The chief lived fourteen more years.) Although the 1805 Chickasaw cession was a significant slice out of the tribe's hunting land, the Chickasaws still controlled (on paper, at least) a vast area covering present-day western Kentucky, western Tennessee, northwestern Alabama, and northern Mississippi.[24]

Traders and government officials calculated the Choctaws' debt at more than twice that of the Chickasaws. Armed with this persuasive argument, U.S. commissioners began preliminary land cession negotiations with the Choctaw chiefs and head warriors at St. Stephens in the spring of 1805. These proceedings included plenty of food and liquor, making for a rather raucous atmosphere that came to characterize future treaty negotiations.[25] The commissioners Robertson and Dinsmoor and chiefs led by Apuckshunubee (Pukshunnubbee, Western/Upper Towns Division), Mingo Homastubbee (Eastern/Lower Towns Division), and Pushmataha (Sixtowns Division) reconvened in November at the Choctaw village of Pooshpukanuk (Pooshapukanuk, Pashiakona) in the western part of present-day Noxubee County and signed the Treaty of Mount Dexter on November 16, 1805. Out of the $50,500 treaty settlement, the representatives of Panton, Leslie & Company received $46,000. Two thousand dollars went to pay for "depredations" against white settlers by "evil disposed persons of the Chaktaw [sic] nation," and trader/interpreter John Pitchlynn came away with $2,500 for "certain losses sustained" and "as a grateful testimonial" on behalf of the tribe. The United States gained approximately 4.1 million acres; however, the Choctaws claimed a victory of sorts by refusing to cede the Mississippi River land that Jefferson desired. Instead, the tribe gave up a huge tract along the U.S. border with Spanish West Florida, which roughly corresponds to the present-day Mississippi counties of Lincoln, Pike, Lawrence, Walthall, Jefferson Davis, Lamar, Covington, Perry, Jones, Wayne, and Greene (Figure 10). Also included in the cession was a large tract in present-day Alabama situated north and east of the land the Choctaws ceded in the Treaty of Hoe Buckintoopa. Jefferson was disappointed with the results of the Mount Dexter treaty and delayed its submission to the U.S. Senate for ratification for two years. As for the Choctaws, they had managed to hold on to their hunting land in the Lower Yazoo Basin and the access it provided to more hunting lands west of the Mississippi River.[26]

As the Chickasaw treaty did earlier in the year, the U.S. commissioners at Mount Dexter awarded the Choctaw leaders who helped bring about the land

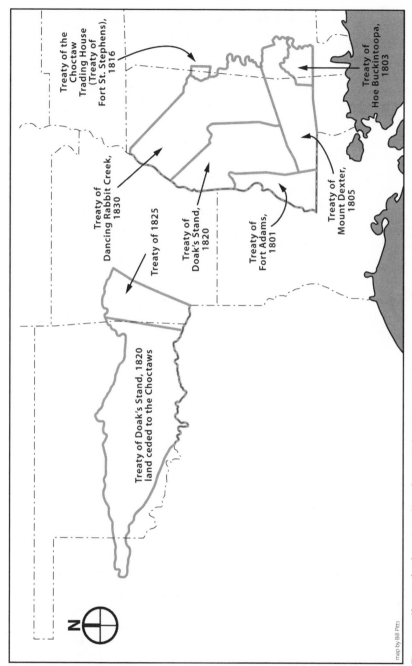

Figure 10. Choctaw land cessions. (Based upon Debo, *Rise and Fall*, 72; DeRosier, *The Removal of the Choctaw Indians*, 29)

cession. Apuckshunubee, Mingo Homastubbee, and Pushmataha, who were flattered with the title of "Great Medal Mingos," each received $500 plus annuities of $150 to continue as long as they held office. The Choctaw tribe as a whole received an annuity of $3,000 worth of merchandise. Other beneficiaries of the treaty included Alzira and Sophia Mitchell, mixed-blood daughters of Samuel Mitchell and his Choctaw wife, Molly, who were awarded a 5,120-acre tract on the Tombigbee River. As mentioned above, Mitchell served briefly as federal agent to the Choctaws before receiving the agent's post with the Chickasaws.[27]

In the years immediately following the Treaty of Mount Dexter, increasing friction with the Spanish gave President Jefferson a better appreciation for the newly acquired buffer zone along the thirty-first parallel. Americans living on both sides of this boundary line pressed for U.S. seizure of West Florida, and Spanish officials looked to the Choctaws for military support. In 1807 Silas Dinsmoor warned territorial governor Robert Williams of Spanish agents promising "large presents" to Choctaw chiefs to maintain the support of the tribe's pro-Spanish faction.[28] After the American takeover of Baton Rouge, Choctaw warriors from the Sixtowns Division responded to Spanish governor Vicente Folch's call for help in the defense of Mobile; however, the garrison there surrendered to American forces without a fight on April 15, 1813.[29]

THE REDSTICK WAR

Three months after the surrender of Mobile, a Mississippi territorial militia force clashed with Redstick warriors at Burnt Corn Creek in present-day Escambia County, Alabama. Although hostilities between Redstick Creeks and encroaching whites had been escalating for more than a year, the Burnt Corn skirmish and the Fort Mims massacre that followed on August 30, 1813, transformed the Creek civil war into a southern front in the War of 1812.[30] As noted by archaeologist Greg Waselkov, the name "Redstick" comes from the wooden war club used by the Creeks, painted red as a sign of war. The internecine hostilities behind the Creek civil war sprang from division within the confederacy over allegiance to the charismatic Shawnee leader Tecumseh and his brother Tenskawatawa (The Prophet).[31]

Reacting to American takeover of tribal land in the Indiana Territory, visionary prophets such as Tenskawatawa called for violent rebellion. In 1811 Tenskawatawa and Tecumseh journeyed south to the Choctaw confederacy, carefully skirting the territory of their old enemies, the Chickasaws. Finding little interest in their message among the Choctaws and resistance from powerful chiefs like Pushmataha, the Shawnees traveled east to the Creek villages. During a council of Creek leaders at the village of Tuckaubatchee (on the Tallapoosa River, present-day Elmore County, Alabama), several thousand Creeks listened to Tecumseh's exhortations. Already hard-pressed by increasing numbers of white settlements in their territory, many Creeks found inspiration in the Shawnee's words and launched the Redstick rebellion.[32]

Alarm spread quickly through the Mississippi Territory, and white settlers on the scattered, isolated farms in the Tombigbee and Tensaw districts above Mobile looked to their volunteer force for protection. Although the real fighting in the War of 1812 was far away, the threat of a British invasion on the Gulf Coast had prompted Generals Andrew Jackson in Tennessee, John Floyd in Georgia, and Ferdinand Claiborne in the Mississippi Territory to form militia units. Now, these volunteer armies mobilized to confront the Redsticks. The Burnt Corn Creek fight was an attempt by a group of Mississippi Territory militiamen and mixed-blood Creeks to intercept a Redstick packhorse train carrying Spanish munitions and other supplies into Creek country from Pensacola. In a show of resolve that gave their movement a needed boost, the Redsticks defeated the poorly trained volunteers.[33]

Both the Redsticks and territorial officials sought alliances with the Choctaws; however, Pushmataha and other chiefs tried to keep the confederacy out of the conflict as tension increased. Despite these efforts to remain neutral, rumors circulated through the territory that a large force of Choctaws had gone over to the Redsticks. In truth, probably fewer than 100 Choctaws joined the insurgency. On the other hand, several hundred Choctaws and Chickasaws eventually entered the war on the side of the Americans and fought alongside militia and regular armies. Many of these Mississippi warriors participated in Andrew Jackson's scorched earth campaign through Creek villages along the Coosa and Tallapoosa rivers during the winter of 1813–1814, which effectively ended the Redstick War.[34]

In the aftermath of the fighting, the Americans punished both the insurgents and friendly Creeks (many of whom fought with Jackson's army) by seizing twenty-three million acres of the confederacy's land, most of which lay in present-day Alabama and Georgia. To America's Indian allies, Jackson's treatment of the Creeks openly revealed the priorities of the U.S. government, although politicians attempted to couch the takeover of Indian land in terms of what was best for the Indians' own survival.[35] For Mississippi's Chickasaws and Choctaws, the Creek Cession of 1814 fell uncomfortably close to their own lands.

The Choctaws and Chickasaws who saw combat in the Redstick War were among the last Mississippi Indians to seek status by way of fighting and earning a war name in the tradition of their forefathers. Indeed, considering the relatively small number of Choctaw and Chickasaw men who took part in the conflict, other ways of making a name for oneself had already replaced the act of killing an enemy. By the early nineteenth century, status and recognition now came through success in ranching and doing business with white merchants and politicians.[36]

For their military service, some of the chiefs earned official recognition and gifts of rifles from the Mississippi territorial legislature. The tribes also assisted the movements of volunteer forces traveling along the roads in their territories, notably Jackson's Tennessee militia. After the conclusion of the War of 1812, these same roads became increasingly crowded with families of settlers arriving in the territory from the Carolinas, Tennessee, Georgia, and Virginia.[37]

TREATY TALKS RESUME

Encroachment was especially troublesome in the Chickasaw hunting lands east of the Tennessee River and along the north-south plateau that divided the drainages of the Tombigbee and Black Warrior rivers. To address this issue, the tribe reluctantly hosted a second land cession treaty in the late summer of 1816 at the home of mixed-blood chief George Colbert. General Andrew Jackson, still riding a crest of popularity from his War of 1812 victories, led the team of U.S. commissioners. By this time, Jackson had publicly advocated the removal of the southeastern tribes to unspecified lands west of the Mississippi River. With the horrors of the Creek War still in recent memory, Jackson found Indian removal to be a popular cause in the Mississippi Territory.[38]

Jackson's co-commissioners were General David Meriwether and Jesse Franklin. Meriwether was former commissioner to the Creeks, and Franklin had served in the U.S. Senate.[39] Chinubbee once again led the Chickasaw delegation, which included Tishomingo and twelve other full-blood chiefs and warriors, along with nine mixed bloods, including four members of the Colbert family. When the United States and the Chickasaws concluded the Treaty of the Chickasaw Council House on September 20, 1816, the tribe ceded approximately six million acres in what is now southwestern Tennessee and northern and western Alabama (Figure 9). Cherokee and Choctaw delegations also attended the negotiations, since the boundaries of the ceded land affected their own tribal boundaries. In return, the Chickasaws received a $12,000 annuity to continue for ten years. An additional $4,500 came to Levi Colbert with instructions that he use the funds to reimburse unspecified tribal members for improvements made on the ceded land.[40]

The treaty's fourth article names twenty-four Chickasaw leaders who received favors for their "conciliatory disposition." Chinubbee and nine other chiefs got $150 in cash or goods, thirteen lesser chiefs and warriors collected $100 each, and the commissioners awarded William Colbert, the oldest of James Colbert's mixed-blood sons, a $100 annuity for life. In addition to cash awards, selected chiefs obtained tracts of land in the ceded area: George Colbert—10,000 acres; Apassantubby—2,560 acres; John McCleish—640 acres; and Levi Colbert—two 40-acre tracts on the Tombigbee River near Cotton Gin Port. The total cash payments to chiefs awarded under the 1816 treaty is only slightly higher than that paid under the 1805 treaty; however, the commissioners wisely spread the funds out so that several chiefs benefited. As James Atkinson points out, one family in particular, the Colberts, was making a small fortune from treaty settlements and using the generous land awards to expand their cattle-ranching business.[41]

One month after the signing of the Treaty of the Chickasaw Council House, Choctaw chiefs and U.S. commissioners signed the Treaty of the Choctaw Trading House (signed October 24, 1816). Leading the Choctaw delegation was Mushulatubbee, Pushmataha, and Apuckshunubee. Since the Treaty of Mount Dexter, Mushulatubbee had succeeded his uncle Mingo Homastubbee as leader of the Eastern, or Lower Towns, Division. Gideon Lincecum, who lived in close proximity to the Choctaws between 1818 and 1848, knew these chiefs and wrote sketches of their appearance and personalities. Mushulatubbee was "a handsome man, about six feet in height and quite corpulent," with "a lively, cheerful disposition." Lincecum described Apuckshunubbee as a "large man, tall and bony, had a down look and was of the religious or superstitious cast of mind. He was, by the people of his district, called a good man, and it was said that he was a man of deep thought and that he was quite intellectual," with a "studiously maintained taciturnity." Another contemporary, George S. Gaines, characterized Apuckshunubbee as "remarkable . . . for his modesty and simplicity." Lincecum provides the following description of Pushmataha, whom he unabashedly admired:

> *The great man of the nation and of the age was the far famed Apushi-*
> *mataha [sic]. He was about five feet ten inches in height, stood very erect,*

full chest, square, broad shoulders and fine front and elevated top head.
His mouth was very large, lips rather thick, eyes and nose very good,
projecting brow, and cheek bones very prominent. He lacked a great deal
of being what the world calls handsome. But he had that inexplicable at-
tribute about which belongs only to the truly great, that which forced the
ejaculation, "who is that?"[42]

The U.S. commissioners were Tennesseans General John Coffee and Congressman John Rhea, and Choctaw agent John McKee.[43] The objective of President James Madison's administration in seeking this treaty was the reconciliation of the Choctaws' eastern boundary with land the United States claimed as spoils of the Creek War. In the cession, the Choctaws relinquished title to all land east of the Tombigbee River between the mouth of Tibbee Creek (called Ooktibbuha Creek in the treaty) near present-day Columbus in Lowndes County and the northern boundary of the Mount Dexter cession in present-day Choctaw County, Alabama. The 1816 cession was modest compared to the Mount Dexter cessions, and historians characterize the gathering of Americans and Choctaws on the banks of the Tombigbee River as amicable. Arthur DeRosier notes that the Choctaws believed that their service in the War of 1812 had earned them exemption from more multimillion-acre land cessions. Due in part to the jovial nature of the treaty negotiations, the Choctaw chiefs apparently did not require personal awards as incentives to sign, and the tribe as a whole received a $6,000 annuity for twenty years plus a one-time payment of $10,000 worth of merchandise.[44]

While the Choctaws and Chickasaws negotiated these 1816 treaties, the U.S. Congress was actively pursuing Mississippi's transition from territory to state. On March 1, 1817, President James Madison signed the act to partition the Mississippi Territory and begin the process toward statehood. Not surprisingly, the constitutional convention held at the territorial capital of Washington in Adams County during the summer of 1817 did not include any tribal representatives. The resulting state constitution contains only an oblique reference to the Choctaws or Chickasaws, stating that "waste or unappropriated lands" are under the "sole and entire disposition of the United States."[45] Statehood required a survey to establish the official boundary between Mississippi and Tennessee, which followed the thirty-fifth parallel, the old line of demarcation separating North Carolina from South Carolina and Georgia. Upon completion of the survey in 1818, the Monroe administration acted to secure for the states of Kentucky and Tennessee all of the Chickasaw tribal land north of the Mississippi-Tennessee line. The U.S. commissioners were Andrew Jackson and Isaac Shelby, former governor of Tennessee. Jackson's popular image as an Indian fighter benefited from large land cessions that he had recently obtained from the Creeks and Cherokees, and only months before taking up his assignment to meet with the Chickasaws the general had been torching Seminole villages in Florida.[46] Once again Chinubbee was a leading chief with the Chickasaw delegation, which included Levi Colbert, Samuel Seeley, Tishomingo, William McGillivray, Apassantubby, and fifteen other chiefs and warriors. By this time the Chickasaw agent William Cocke had partitioned the tribe into four divisions to simplify annuity distributions, with Seeley, Tishomingo, McGillivray, and Apassantubby recognized as the leaders of those divisions.[47]

The treaty, known as Jackson's Purchase (signed October 19, 1818), relieved the Chickasaws of approximately 8.5 million acres of land in present-day western Tennessee and Kentucky, a tract bounded on the south by the thirty-fifth parallel, on the west by the Mississippi River, on the north by the Ohio River, and on the east by the Tennessee River (Figure 9). Under Article 2, the United States agreed to pay the Chickasaws an annuity of $20,000 for fifteen years. The commissioners also agreed to pay a debt of $1,115 owed by William Colbert and paid the Tennessee militia $2,000 for protecting the tribe during the Creek War. Article 4 permitted the tribe to retain and lease out a four-square-mile area within the ceded land containing a salt spring "on or near the River sandy [sic]" (probably the present-day Big Sandy River northeast of Jackson, Tennessee). Under Article 5 Apassantubby (in the treaty as "Oppassantubby" and "Arpashenshtubby") received $500 for the two-square-mile parcel of land (called a "reservation") awarded him in the 1816 treaty. The 1818 treaty also verified the land reservations awarded to George and Levi Colbert in the previous treaty. (As will be seen, this was not the final disposition of these Colbert reservations.) Other awards included $25 for a lost saddle and $1,089 to reimburse the interpreter, James Colbert, who had lost that amount to a thief in a Baltimore music hall. Once again the chiefs received payments of $150 or $100 each, depending upon their ranking, for their "friendly and conciliatory disposition." The 1818 treaty also calls for cash instead of merchandise for all annuities due to the tribe, a concession to traders working among the Chickasaws who would otherwise lose sales on their own merchandise at annuity time.[48]

A journal of the treaty proceedings kept by Robert Butler, adjutant-general and secretary, documents the back-and-forth haggling that was common to Indian land cession negotiations. Cryptically called the "Secret Journal on Negotiations of the Chickasaw Treaty of 1818," the journal also reveals the details of a clandestine bargain between the commissioners and five mixed-blood chiefs. Butler's journal begins with the arrival of the commissioners at the treaty ground near Big Town on September 29, where they found the Chickasaws disgruntled at not having received annuities in two years.[49] Although bureaucratic bumbling may have been at fault, the historian Arrell M. Gibson suggests that withholding the annuities before the 1818 conference was a deliberate attempt on the part of the U.S. government to compel the Chickasaws to negotiate the Tennessee/Kentucky land cession. At any rate, the treaty negotiations stalled for nine days while an agent retrieved the missing annuity funds from a Nashville bank.[50]

When serious talks finally got under way during the week of October 12, the chiefs adamantly refused to accept the government's offer of a cash annuity for their land. The U.S. commissioners also cautiously broached the subject of removal by offering the Chickasaws unspecified land in the West, a proposal the chiefs also refused to consider. Butler's journal entry for October 17 discloses that Jackson and Shelby then opened secret negotiations with mixed-blood chiefs George and Levi Colbert. For their compliance with the land cession, the commissioners offered the Colberts $10,000 for the land reservations they received under the 1816 treaty. When the chiefs refused, the commissioners raised their offer to $17,000. Perhaps sensing desperation on the part of Jackson and Shelby, the Colberts shrewdly threatened to abandon negotiations altogether and appeal directly to the president to reconsider the land cession. Butler wrote that the "Council was about to break up abruptly" when the Colberts suggested that for an additional $3,000 perhaps three other chiefs "who were decidedly hostile to the [treaty]" might also be swayed. Jackson and Shelby may have been irritated, but they saw no recourse except to agree to the chiefs' demands. The three "hostile" chiefs turned out to be James Colbert, Samuel Seeley, and William McGillivray. In dividing the $20,000, the Colberts kept the lion's share for themselves. George and Levi Colbert each received $8,500, James Colbert took $1,666.66, and Seeley and McGillivray each got $666.66. Although Jackson later revealed the details of the secret negotiations in letters justifying his actions, Chinubbee, Tishomingo, Apassantubby, and the other full-blood chiefs were apparently unaware of the secret bargain.[51]

The large Chickasaw cession indicates that the "Indian problem" had moved beyond national defense as the justification behind land acquisition. The rapidly burgeoning cotton industry had transformed Indian removal into a matter of economic urgency. A steady stream of white immigrants after the War of 1812 doubled the region's population between 1810 and 1820, and with the availability of slave labor, hundreds of would-be planters required plenty of land. Likewise, the state legislature needed the land-use taxes these settlers would provide. Mississippi's congressional delegation, led by Representative George Poindexter, looked to the millions of acres belonging to the Choctaws and Chickasaws and declared the status quo to be unacceptable. Although Poindexter and others advocated removing the tribes by force, the federal government continued to adhere to the treaty process in dealing with the Indians.[52]

As secretary of war under President James Monroe, John C. Calhoun inherited the "Indian problem," which was not limited to Mississippi. Across the Southeast, whites chaffed at the presence of Indians on potentially profitable acreage and complained loudly whenever violence arose from settlers encroaching on tribal lands. Rather than attempt to address all of the southeastern tribes at once, Calhoun decided to focus on the Choctaws first. According to Arthur DeRosier, Calhoun believed that the peaceful removal of the Choctaws, a large and respected society, would help convince the other tribes to surrender their lands and accept the government's offer of a place in the Arkansas Territory. Ignoring Poindexter's demands for immediate action, Calhoun approached the situation cautiously, advocating education to instill in the Indians an appreciation for individual ownership of land, while initiating removal discussions with chiefs. Although Calhoun and Poindexter both sought acquisition of tribal land, Calhoun and others in the Monroe administration claimed the high ground in the debate by declaring that they had the Indians' best interests at heart. The Protestant mission among the tribes that began in the early 1800s complemented Calhoun's objectives by providing education and reducing adherence to objectionable traditions such as the law of blood revenge.[53]

MISSIONARIES AND SCHOOLS

The missionaries came as part of the evangelical movement known as the "Second Great Awakening," which originated in New England after the Revolutionary War and accompanied the westward expansion of the United States. Zealously competing for new congregations, Methodist, Baptist, and Presbyterian missionary societies began targeting the southeastern tribes in the late 1700s. Typical of the early efforts to spread the Gospel was the appearance of Rev. Joseph Bullen in the Chickasaw villages in 1799. Bullen, from Vermont, came under the auspices of the New York Presbyterian Churches

Missionary Society. Education was a necessary component of the missionary program, and it was the opportunity to learn to read and write that most interested the Chickasaws. Although Bullen and his associates did some teaching in their homes, they were not prepared to establish a proper school or sustain their mission more than a few years.[54]

Clearly, schools were going to be the missionary societies' key to making inroads with tribes. Some Chickasaw and Choctaw tribal leaders were already using their connections with traders and U.S. military leaders to arrange for the education of their sons and daughters. This meant sending the children to Natchez or sometimes boarding them as far away as Nashville or Pensacola. By 1818 both Choctaws and Chickasaws could attend the new Choctaw Academy established by the Baptist Mission Society of Kentucky in Scott County, just north of Lexington. Around this time, Choctaw mixed-blood chiefs Greenwood Leflore and David Folsom secured an agreement from the American Board of Commissioners for Foreign Missions (ABCFM), an organization founded by Presbyterians, to build a school on the Yalobusha River near present-day Grenada and close to the Choctaw's Western District. In 1820 the Chickasaws also received a missionary school established by the Tennessee-based Cumberland Presbyterian Association. As Choctaw historian Clara Sue Kidwell has noted, missionary outreach complemented the U.S. government's 1819 Civilization Act directing churches and governments to cooperate in merging American Indians with the burgeoning white frontier society. For their part, the missionary societies viewed the civilization process as a way to prevent the destruction of the southeastern tribes.[55]

During the 1820s missionary groups built more schools near the Chickasaw and Choctaw settlements. The tribes' treaty annuities helped to support the missionaries and cover the cost of building and running the schools. The missionary societies also received funds from the federal government under the provisions of the Civilization Act. Although the quality of education provided by the missionaries varied widely, the schools provided training in blacksmithing, leatherworking, sewing, and agricultural techniques in addition to reading and writing. Angie Debo has noted the scholarly contributions of some of the ABCFM missionaries, including Cyrus Byington's *Dictionary of the Choctaw Language*. Horatio Bardwell Cushman, the son of another ABCFM missionary, drew upon his firsthand knowledge of the Choctaws to write his book, *History of the Choctaw, Chickasaw, and Natchez Indians*. As for the missionaries' intent to convert the Indians to Christianity, the Protestant mission program was largely a failure. Despite the lively competition between several denominations, there were few sustained conversions. The Methodists had the most success with their spirited campground meetings in the late 1820s when they claimed to have converted around 1,500 Choctaws; however, this only amounted to about one-tenth of the confederacy's total population. To maintain their traditional rituals, conservative tribal groups held these activities in secret locations, away from the criticism of the missionaries and converted brethren. If most of the Choctaws and Chickasaws never received the Gospel, Christian motifs began to appear in their folklore. Historians have documented the presence of Christian symbolism and characters such as the devil in nineteenth-century tribal mythology. As we will see, mission groups remained with the two Mississippi tribes through removal and emigration to the Indian Territory. Even though their congregations remained small, missionaries played an active role in tribal politics as state and federal pressure for removal grew more intense.[56]

THE FINAL TREATIES

Secretary Calhoun opened removal talks with Choctaw chiefs through a delegation comprised of John McKee, Mississippi state senator Daniel Burnet, and General William Carroll, a former officer in Andrew Jackson's Tennessee militia. The first meeting in October 1818 ended abruptly with the chiefs refusing to consider abandoning their homeland. When removal talks resumed in August of the following year, the Choctaw chiefs met with Calhoun's commissioners on the Yazoo River. This time, the U.S. negotiating team included Andrew Jackson, who replaced General Carroll; however, despite Jackson's bullying, Pushmataha and the other chiefs once again refused to accept any treaty that entailed emigration.[57] The Choctaws' resistance to removal outraged Mississippi politicians like George Poindexter, who had given up his Senate seat to run for governor. Poindexter made much of Calhoun's failure to reach a peaceful agreement with the Choctaws, galvanizing his supporters by accusing the tribe of hoarding land in Mississippi while enjoying hunting access to lands west of the Mississippi River.[58]

Faced with the possibility of losing their land to state annexation without any compensation, the Choctaw chiefs reluctantly consented to further removal discussions with the United States. This time, the location for the treaty talks was Doak's Stand, an inn and tavern on the Natchez-to-Nashville road in present-day Madison County. The spot was conveniently close to the tribe's western towns, and hundreds of Choctaws began arriving at the treaty ground in late September 1820. As the Indians, traders, and camp followers congregated, the grounds around Doak's Stand took on a carnival ambiance fueled by a $20,000 budget for food and liquor. Joining Andrew Jackson as commissioner was General Thomas Hinds, a veteran of the Battle of New Orleans who had lost the 1819 Mississippi governor's race to Poindexter. Pushmataha, Mushulatubbee, and Apuckshunubee once again represented the Choctaw confederacy. Despite Pushmataha's opposition to removal, some Choctaws, including the influential Pitchlynn family, expressed an interest in the western lands and a willingness to consider moving there.[59]

The reservation in the West that the Monroe administration intended as the Choctaws' future home encompassed approximately thirteen million acres stretching from present-day western Arkansas across Oklahoma and into the Texas Panhandle (Figure 10). The Quapaws had ceded this land, hardly empty real estate awaiting settlement, to the United States in 1818 and, by treaty, could hunt there until the U.S. government passed it on to "other friendly Indians." In addition to Quapaw hunters, numerous white families had settled in the eastern portion (present-day western Arkansas), this according to Pushmataha, who had seen the farms and ranches when he had hunted in the region. Other tribes, such as the Osages and Comanches, roamed this area as well.[60]

For three weeks the chiefs listened to Jackson's harangue, which alternated between glowing descriptions of the western reservation and warnings about impending seizure of the tribe's Mississippi land. According to Gideon Lincecum, the chiefs expressed their concerns in private councils about what might happen if they continued to resist federal and state pressure. After all, many Choctaw chiefs and warriors had witnessed firsthand the destruction of Creek and Seminole towns at the hands of Jackson's militia and Indian mercenaries. At the conclusion of negotiations, Pushmataha made it clear to the commissioners that he was familiar with the Quapaw land and considered it to be inferior to the tribe's homeland; however, he and the other chiefs capitulated and signed the Treaty with the Choctaw (later known as the Treaty of Doak's Stand) on October 18, 1820. The Choctaw cession under the Treaty of Doak's Stand comprised some 5.1 million acres (Figure 10), taking in the fertile Lower Yazoo Basin along with much of the Big Black and Pearl river drainages. The cession also contained the future county of Hinds and capital city of Jackson, founded and named for the two commissioners soon after the treaty by a grateful populace. Although not as well documented as with the 1818 Chickasaw treaty, bribery was part of Jackson's strategy at Doak's Stand and may account for Pushmataha's acquiescence. The chief's name is noticeably absent from the treaty text, which contains monetary compensation for both Apuckshunubee and Mushulatubbee, yet it seems odd that Pushmataha would have left the treaty talks empty-handed.[61]

In previous treaties between the United States and the Mississippi tribes, the treaty commissioners worded the documents to read as agreements between nations. In contrast, the removal treaty the Choctaws signed at Doak's Stand represents the tribe's submission to a superior force, and the treaty articles, for the most part, read like terms of surrender. The treaty's preamble reveals the logic by which most whites in Mississippi and Washington justified removal:

> WHEREAS it is an important object with the President of the United States, to promote the civilization of the Choctaw Indians, by the establishment of schools among them; and to perpetuate them as a nation, by exchanging, for a small part of their land here, a country beyond the Mississippi River, where all, who live by hunting and will not work, may be collected and settled together.[62]

Under the treaty's fourth article, Jackson and Hinds (Jackson was probably the treaty's principal author) denigrate the Choctaws by telling them to stay out of the ceded land in Mississippi until they are "civilized and enlightened" enough to become U.S. citizens. To the "poor Indians who wish to remove to the [western land]," the commissioners provided under Article 5 a blanket, kettle, rifle, ammunition, and a year's supply of corn. Article 6 promised to provide a trade factory and a blacksmith in the Arkansas Territory, and, at Pushmataha's request, the commissioners agreed to track down Choctaws who had already dispersed to places west of the Mississippi River—mainly Louisiana and eastern Texas—and unite them with those tribal members who would be settling in the western land.

The subject of missionary schools had been contentious among the chiefs (Pushmataha opposed them, while Apuckshunubee supported them); therefore the treaty's Articles 7 and 8 called for reimbursement of tribal funds that had been used to support these schools. As an alternative plan to provide for schools, the treaty set aside 34,560 acres in the ceded Mississippi land to sell in order to raise funds to support schools "on both sides of the Mississippi River." As an enticement for Choctaws to move to the western land, the commissioners agreed under Article 9 to award families already living within the ceded land an allotment of 640 acres, which the government would purchase for the land's "full value" (to be determined by appointees of President Monroe) if the family moved west within one year.[63]

As mentioned above, any compensation Pushmataha might have received for signing the Treaty of Doak's Stand went unmentioned within the treaty text. Apuckshunubee received $500 for improvements made on the ceded land, and four other chiefs got $200 each for their improvements. The commissioners awarded Mushulatubbee the $150 annuity formerly paid to his now deceased uncle Mingo Homastubbee. The treaty also put in line for payment those Choctaw chiefs and warriors not yet compensated for their service with Jackson in the capture of Pensacola in 1814.[64]

The treaty's Article 12 acknowledges the problems caused by alcohol consumption and gives the Choctaw agent full authority to seize liquor brought into the remaining tribal land in Mississippi. Despite this show of intolerance, the treaty commissioners and the chiefs agreed to liberal exceptions to the prohibition by allowing alcohol sales at public stands in Choctaw territory. The treaty also condoned alcohol sales by white or Indian merchants with permits issued by the tribal agent or any of the three district chiefs. In truth, the provision in the 1820 treaty and similar prohibition laws passed by the U.S. Congress did little to curtail the flow of whiskey into Choctaw villages, which increased with the growth of the white population in the state.[65]

In the wake of the treaty, many tribal members voiced disapproval of the Mississippi land cession and acceptance of the Quapaw land. Confidence in Pushmataha, Apuckshunubee, and Mushulatubbee began to erode, leading to a growing consensus that mixed-blood chiefs might be better equipped to deal with further attempts by the United States to take the Choctaws' remaining Mississippi land. The backlash eventually resulted in the tribe's decision to break with tradition and begin holding elections within division councils to select chiefs.[66] On the other side of the removal issue, many whites in Mississippi were convinced that the Choctaws would not voluntarily surrender their land and leave the state. A growing states' rights coalition in Mississippi openly favored bypassing the federal removal initiative with legislative action to take control of the remaining tribal land in Mississippi.[67]

In the view of the Monroe administration, one of the hindrances in efforts to convince the Choctaws and Chickasaws to emigrate was the continued operation of the Mississippi trading factories. As mentioned above, the Treaty of Doak's Stand provided for the establishment of a trading factory in the Arkansas Territory as an incentive to emigrate. Although the market demand for animal skins had declined substantially since the heyday of the eighteenth-century deerskin trade, the government trading houses still purchased skins and provided a way for those Choctaws without cattle ranches and cotton fields to obtain manufactured goods. Examination of the *Records of the Choctaw Trading House, 1803–1824* shows frequent bartering of skins including deer, bear, raccoon, and otter, along with tallow and beeswax, for guns, powder and lead, needles and thread, fishhooks, brass and tin kettles, and an array of silk, linen, cotton, and wool textiles. Most whites believed that the Indians who were accustomed to hunting and trapping as opposed to farming could do so in the West, and, despite protests from the tribes and the Indian agents, the government factories at Fort Confederation and Chickasaw Bluffs ceased doing business in 1822.[68]

While the government processed the paperwork to close the factories, Calhoun and his staff optimistically assembled supplies and hired managers to oversee what they hoped would be the emigration of a significant portion of the Choctaw confederacy. Instead, most of the Choctaws clung to their homes in Mississippi and ignored the 1820 treaty's enticements for removal. Pushmataha and the other chiefs astutely and repeatedly pointed to the presence of white settlers living on the eastern portion of the Quapaw land and insisted on no more talk of removal until the government addressed this problem. Complaints also came from the Arkansas Territory, where both the settlers and the territorial officials demanded that Calhoun amend the 1820 Choctaw treaty to block Indian settlements in their midst. Since uprooting the white settlers was out of the question, the federal government had no choice except to ask the Choctaws to give back part of the Quapaw land.[69]

When pressed to enter a new round of treaty talks, the Choctaw chiefs refused to meet with commissioners Thomas Hinds and William Woodward, who represented the Arkansas Territory, and instead traveled to Washington, D.C., to negotiate directly with Secretary Calhoun and President Monroe. En route from Mississippi, tragedy struck the small entourage in Kentucky when Apuckshunubee died from injuries he sustained in a fall from a cliff. Shaken by the loss of a senior chief, the Choctaw delegation arrived in Washington on November 1, 1824. During three months of negotiations, Calhoun's staff plied the chiefs and warriors with copious amounts of alcohol and lavish gifts of clothing and jewelry. Tragedy revisited the Choctaw delegation on December 24, 1824, when Pushmataha died, apparently of overexposure to weather and whiskey; the Choctaw delegation's liquor tab for the three-month stay in Washington totaled over $2,000 (much of which was charged to the tribe's annuities). In keeping with the chief's senior rank, President Monroe gave Pushmataha a military funeral and burial at the Congressional Cemetery beside the Anacostia River.[70]

Despite the deaths of the two chiefs and the distractions provided by Calhoun, the rest of the Choctaw delegation negotiated skillfully under the leadership of mixed-blood chief James McDonald. Well aware that the Arkansans were pressing Calhoun and that the federal government was at a disadvantage, McDonald demanded and got a high price for the land in question. The Washington treaty, signed on January 20, 1825, established the eastern boundary of the Choctaws' western land as "a line beginning on the Arkansas River, 100 paces east of Fort Smith, and running thence, due south to the Red River." In exchange, the tribe received a $6,000 perpetual annuity, with the first twenty years dedicated to funding education. Calhoun also allowed the treaty delegation $2,000 to cover unpaid claims against the tribe by whites in Mississippi, and, perhaps most important, the government erased the tribe's trading factory debt. Red tape had stalled the long overdue payments to Choctaws who had served with Jackson in the Pensacola campaign (something Pushmataha had demanded in the 1820 treaty), so the 1825 treaty once again called for the Monroe administration to meet this obligation. Calhoun also agreed to award all Choctaws living on the land ceded at Doak's Stand a one-mile-square tract on which they could continue to live or sell at their discretion. Hoping to override the threat of state annexation of their remaining land in Mississippi, the chiefs obtained the federal government's promise never to consign the Choctaws to individual allotments or bring the tribe under the laws of the U.S. government without the consent of the Choctaws themselves (a promise broken five years later). Even though the treaty does not mention removal, Article 9 served as a reminder to the Choctaws by allowing for the placement of a tribal agent and a blacksmith in the western land. Finally, Calhoun formally recognized the mixed-blood chief Robert Cole as Apuckshunubee's successor and awarded Cole a $150 annuity for life. Curiously, the treaty text makes no mention of Pushmataha's passing. Pushmataha's nephew, the full-blood chief Tapenahomma, succeeded his uncle as leader of the Sixtowns Division. Signing the Treaty of Washington on behalf of the Choctaws were Mushulatubbee, Robert Cole, Daniel McCurtain, Talking Warrior, Red Fort (possibly Red Foot or Red Shoe), Nitakechi (another nephew of Pushmataha), David Folsom, and McDonald.[71]

Chickasaw delegations also traveled to Washington during the 1820s to meet with Calhoun, who was convinced that he could eventually settle both Mississippi tribes on the Quapaw land remaining after the Treaty of Washington. Toward this end, U.S. commissioners William Clark (of Lewis and Clark fame), Thomas Hinds, and John Coffee, with a budget of $20,000 for food and other considerations, scheduled treaty talks with the Chickasaws and Choctaws in the late summer of 1826 to press for removal.

In October of that year, Hinds and Coffee (Clark was delayed in transit and missed most of the negotiations) met at the Chickasaw council house with chiefs Tishomingo, Pisiatantubbe (Pisiatansttubia), William McGillivray, Samuel Seeley, John McCleish, Levi Colbert, Martin Colbert, Emmubbee, Ashtamatatutka, and King Ishtehotopa.[72] After the interpreter, Malcolm McGee, conveyed the customary diplomatic greetings to the chiefs, he told them bluntly: "It is the policy of our government to extinguish the Indian title to all lands on this side of the Mississippi [River]." As in treaty talks going back to the Jefferson administration, the commissioners cited the need for national security as their justification, although the state of Mississippi was hardly in danger of foreign invasion by this time. Resistance would be futile, Hinds and Coffee told the chiefs, because the U.S. government could simply extend its laws over the tribes within its borders; however, President John Quincy Adams was prepared to offer equal land in the West or payment in cash for the Chickasaws' Mississippi land. The commissioners stated disingenuously that the Creeks, Cherokees, and Choctaws had already claimed their land in the West and that the Chickasaws should accept the U.S. proposal before it was withdrawn. The negotiations went on for several days while the commissioners argued that the Chickasaws' Mississippi land was too small for a hunting reserve and too large to make family farming practical. Hinds and Coffee said that as long as the Chickasaws controlled most of north Mississippi, they blocked the state's economic progress and provided a safe haven for criminals. The time had come for the tribe to pay its debt to the United States, or as the commissioners framed the situation: "The indulgence hitherto granted [to the Chickasaws] by this Government was founded more on compassion for your ignorant, helpless, and unprotected condition, than any acknowledged political right upon either its bounty or protection."[73]

Despite the badgering by Hinds and Coffee, the chiefs would not consider leaving their homeland, and they reminded the commissioners that they had already given the United States large land cessions. The following statement by Levi Colbert, Martin Colbert, Emmubbee, Ashtamatatutka, and John McCleish, recorded in the journal of the proceedings by Hinds and Coffee, expresses the tribe's genuine desire to change and become accepted by Mississippi frontier society: "Our father the President introduced missionaries to come amongst us to advance us to a state of civilization; we accepted them, and are making all the progress that people can; we have also been provided means for the support of the missionaries, to enable us to go on with the education of our children and to have them enlightened. Industry is spreading amongst us."[74]

The chiefs also refuted the security issue, citing the roads through their territory, and questioned the accusation that they harbored fugitives: "If there are any such characters amongst us, it is not known to the nation." Finally, the chiefs told the commissioners that if the Chickasaws were to abandon their homeland and move to the west, they would expose themselves to danger from old vendettas held by their former enemies.[75] With both sides at loggerheads, the talks ended in stalemate. The commissioners were quick to blame the mixed-blood chiefs, whom they accused of looking out for their own economic interests and ignoring the inevitability of removal. Also vilified were several white men married to Chickasaw women, who allegedly urged the Indians to resist U.S. domination. Although there was widespread sentiment among the Chickasaws against ceding their remaining land, James Atkinson has noted correspondence between Levi Colbert and Chickasaw agent John D. Terrell indicating that Colbert might have been in favor of removal if the price had been right.[76]

The Choctaws, who had suffered a devastating smallpox epidemic in the spring of 1826, also refused to bend during the removal talks. In addition to weathering the deadly disease, which killed over 400 people, the tribe fell into political turmoil in the wake of the Washington treaty and the deaths of the two district chiefs. Frustrated by empty promises from the U.S. government and apprehensive about what might happen the next time treaty commissioners descended upon the tribe, residents in two of the tribe's districts elected new chiefs. The ambitious mixed-blood chief Greenwood Leflore unseated Robert Cole in the Upper Towns Division, and David Folsom overthrew old Mushulatubbee in the Lower Towns Division. In a cooperative proactive effort to give the Choctaw confederacy more governmental legitimacy, Folsom and Leflore set to work drafting a constitution for the tribe as a whole. Their vision was to accelerate the civilization process so the Choctaws could conform to the white society now surrounding them with provisions for male inheritance, recognition of private property, and language to curb the practice of polygamy. In view of previous treaty negotiations, the constitution included punishments for leaders caught accepting bribes from U.S. officials. Such a document, if adopted by the three divisions, would help streamline U.S. relations with the Choctaws and (in part) address the diplomatic dilemma of dealing with a tripartite confederacy that had complicated the tribe's external relations since Bienville's days.[77]

Meanwhile, the forces determined to eject Mississippi's two tribes gathered strength at both the state and federal levels. Gerard Brandon, who served as Mississippi's governor from 1826 to 1832, supported a bill before the legislature in 1826 to abolish tribal ownership of land in the state. Another bill that made headway in the legislature during this period sought to prevent Indians in Mississippi from carrying firearms. Although these bills failed to pass, the "Indian problem" gave supporters of states' rights a volatile issue around which to rally. In Washington, Mississippi's congressional delegation continued to press for removal, and in 1826 Secretary of War James Barbour told the congressional Committee on Indian Affairs that the separate tribes should be disbanded and all Indians combined into one group to simplify their management, an idea that Congress was still seriously considering as late as the 1870s.[78]

During the following year, Superintendent of Indian Affairs Thomas L. McKenney held prolonged talks with the Choctaws and Chickasaws, trying to convince the chiefs to accept the federal government's plan for a peaceful exodus.[79] McKenney warned the chiefs of both tribes that impending state legislation would soon take control of tribal land, in spite of existing treaties with the United States. In the end the chiefs remained opposed to any removal agreement; however, they did consent to a government-funded expedition to explore the western land. After a series of delays, the exploring party—comprised of six Choctaws, three Creeks, and twelve Chickasaws—departed from St. Louis on October 13, 1828. The Choctaw delegation included Greenwood Leflore and Peter Pitchlynn. Among the Chickasaws were King Ishtehotopa, Tishomingo, and George, James, and Levi Colbert. Captain G. H. Kennerly led the expedition, and Isaac McCoy, a Baptist missionary with the Ottawa tribe in Michigan, served as treasurer, carefully managing the government funds allotted for the trip. McCoy's journal provides a detailed itinerary and description of the land. The tour was ostensibly for the benefit of the Chickasaws, who had not yet received land in the West. Traveling by horseback, Kennerly led the group across Missouri to the Neosho River in present-day Kansas and then south to the Arkansas and Canadian rivers.

McCoy described the landscape as "high rolling country" dominated by prairie and stony hills. The only trees were those along streams. The prairie had recently been burned by the Indians of the region (as noted elsewhere, the Mississippi tribes also followed this practice), and McCoy notes the discomfort experienced by the horses and men in breathing the clouds of windblown ash. Aptly sizing up the Indians on the tour as "agricultural men," McCoy admitted that the chiefs would not be impressed with the country they were seeing. The entourage held a friendly meeting with the Osages at their villages on the Neosho River, and McCoy noted the presence of Kansa and Shawnee villages in the area. According to McCoy, the only threat to the expedition was posed by a group of Pawnee warriors, thought to number around 1,500 men, who were conducting raids in the area. Upon reaching the Arkansas River, the majority of the group elected to return home, even though the expedition had only reached the northern fringe of the Choctaws' lands acquired at the Treaty of Doak's Stand. The Indians were naturally interested in the abundance of river cane, and McCoy's journal mentions the expedition's first encounter with small canebrakes on the lower Neosho River. As they made their way to the lower Canadian River and the Arkansas River they found much more extensive canebrakes, which attracted buffalo seeking to feed on the tender young cane shoots. Most of the entourage returned home after a buffalo hunt, while a few Choctaws remained to spend a few days exploring their land.[80]

While the Mississippi chiefs scouted the western land, mounting pressure from voters in all of the southeastern states where Indians resided resulted in a removal bill before the U.S. Congress in 1828. Although the bill failed to pass, removal advocates gained the momentum they needed later that year with Andrew Jackson's election as president of the United States. In Mississippi, Jackson's election empowered states' righters, and the legislature responded in February 1829 by extending state jurisdiction over Choctaw and Chickasaw land within its borders. If the legislation stopped short of state control of the Indians themselves, the bill was still a brash proclamation of states' rights over the federal treaty process. Within the Choctaw nation, the chiefs argued over how best to respond to the removal issue, and two opposing political parties emerged. The mixed-blood chiefs, some of whom had experienced religious conversion, dominated the so-called Christian party and advocated resistance to removal. By 1829 John Garland had replaced Tapenahomma as leader of the Sixtowns Division, and, with Leflore and Folsom controlling the Upper Towns Division and Lower Towns Division, respectively, the Christian party held sway over tribal government. These men had seen the western land, and they were determined to hold on to their Mississippi plantations. On the other side of the issue was a coalition of full bloods and mixed bloods led by Mushulatubbee and the Pitchlynns, who called their party the Republicans. Mushulatubbee and his followers saw removal as inevitable and were prepared to listen to the U.S. government's terms for purchase of the tribe's Mississippi land.[81]

When the Jackson administration made no effort to contest Mississippi's challenge to the federal treaty process, the emboldened state legislature passed an act "to extend the laws of the State of Mississippi over the persons and property of the Indians, resident within its limits" on January 19,

1830, which summarily abolished the tribes and set fines and imprisonment for anyone calling himself a "chief, mingo, or head-man." In asserting its dominion over tribal land, the Mississippi legislature set an ominous precedent for other states and their resident tribes even though the new law would be impossible to enforce without federal help. To be sure, not everyone in Mississippi agreed with the move, and the law sparked debate around the country.[82]

The January 19 state legislation signaled the beginning of a turbulent year for the Mississippi tribes and an especially intense period for the Choctaws. With the state suddenly threatening to sweep away federal offers of compensation for removal and annex tribal land, Folsom and Leflore abruptly changed their positions in favor of emigration. Behind the scenes, both chiefs were quietly angling for ways to derive profit from the collapse of the Choctaw confederacy. Around the same time that the Mississippi legislature passed the 1830 act, Indian affairs superintendent McKenney offered Leflore a choice of a prominent administrative position in the Choctaws' new western land or a plantation in Mississippi in exchange for using his influence to effect Choctaw removal. Likewise, Folsom was communicating with congressmen and offering to lie to his constituents about what he had seen during his 1828 tour out West.[83]

In March 1830 Leflore held talks with McKenney and Mushulatubbee (who was contemplating parlaying his newfound U.S. citizenship into a bid for Congress) while cobbling together a treaty that Leflore hoped would be favorable to both the tribe and the government. Methodist missionary Alexander Talley assisted Leflore with drafting the treaty, which contained as its main points: allotment of 640 acres in Mississippi to each Choctaw family with children and 320 acres to each single man, which would in turn be purchased by the state; clothes and annuities for tribal leaders; homesteading supplies; transportation and military protection for Choctaws moving west; and a $50,000 annuity for the tribe as a whole.[84] Moving quickly, a combined council of district representatives dominated by the Christian party reviewed the treaty and, in an unprecedented move, elected Leflore chief over all three districts. Obligingly, Folsom and Garland resigned their posts as district chiefs, and runners carried copies of Leflore's treaty to Governor Brandon and President Jackson.[85]

The Choctaws were attempting to bargain from a rapidly weakening position, and the terms that Leflore offered the U.S. government had little chance of acceptance. Not surprisingly, Congress rejected the treaty and moved ahead with legislation that culminated in the Indian Removal Act, which

President Jackson signed on May 28, 1830. The act empowered the president to exchange tracts of land in the West "to which the Indian title has been extinguished" for Indian-controlled land east of the Mississippi River. Like Mississippi's Indian law passed only five months earlier, the Indian Removal Act asserted the United States' control over tribal lands and made the southeastern Indians a promise that would be broken before the end of the nineteenth century: "It shall and may be lawful for the President solemnly to assure the tribe or nation with which the exchange is made, that the United States will forever secure and guaranty to them, and their heirs or successors, the country so exchanged with them."[86] The act goes on to provide for compensation to the tribes for "improvements" on their eastern land as well as assistance and protection for emigrants. No mention is made of forced removal; however, the historian James Taylor Carson has noted that the interlocking state and federal laws of 1830 made it impossible for the Choctaws and Chickasaws to remain in Mississippi and retain their tribal identities.[87]

After the passage of the Indian Removal Act, Jackson proceeded swiftly to secure final removal treaties with the Choctaws and Chickasaws. Accordingly, Secretary of War John H. Eaton summoned the chiefs of both tribes to treaty talks at his residence in Franklin, Tennessee, not far from the president's Nashville home. For reasons discussed below, the Choctaws did not send a delegation to Franklin, leaving Jackson and his two commissioners, Eaton and Coffee, to meet with some twenty Chickasaw chiefs and headmen in August 1830. Importantly, several members of the Chickasaw delegation had participated in the 1828 western tour, including Levi and James Colbert, King Ishtehotopa, Ahtohowoy (Ah to ko wa), and John McCleish. Tishomingo may have been present since his name appears in the text of the Franklin treaty; however, he was not among those who signed the document. In the treaty that resulted from the Franklin negotiations (Treaty with the Chickasaw, signed August 31, 1830), the Chickasaws agreed to cede to the United States their remaining land east of the Mississippi River, but only if suitable land could be found for them in the West. In a set of supplementary articles that the Chickasaw leaders appended to the treaty, the chiefs' words cut to the heart of Jackson's intentions and, in so doing, spoke for all American Indians:

We are informed by our Father the President of the United States, that states have been formed around us and now claim the right of extending her laws through out her territorial limits [and] consequently subject us to her civil and criminal laws. Should we find it expedient to remain where we are [and] the States of Mississippi and Alabama extend their

> *laws over us, we would view it an act of usurpation on their part, unwar-*
> *ranted by the constitution of the United States and treaties that now*
> *exist, unparalleled in history, and in many instances the greatest griev-*
> *ances and hardships would be imposed upon us.*

Leaving nothing unsaid, the chiefs forced the commissioners to hear the truth: "The citizens of the State of Mississippi and Alabama, are perfectly aware that by the extension of their laws over us it would not Benefit them one cent, but to affect an object so desirable to themselves, that is to drive us from our homes and take possession of our lands."

Historians call the Treaty of Franklin a "provisional treaty" because its ratification depended upon the Chickasaws accepting land in the West. To that end, the Jackson administration wasted little time in organizing another western exploring expedition for the Chickasaw chiefs. During October 1830 the chiefs inspected the Choctaw land along the Red River, but considered the country inferior to their Mississippi homeland. Crossing the Red River into present-day Texas, the Chickasaw party ventured down along the Sabine River, where the chiefs found land more to their liking. Unfortunately, the country south of the Red River was under Mexican control at the time, and the Chickasaws made no further effort to secure land there.[88]

When Eaton summoned the Mississippi chiefs to Franklin in the summer of 1830, the Choctaw nation was in too much turmoil to negotiate a treaty. Upon hearing of Jackson's rejection of Leflore's treaty, Mushulatubbee seized the opportunity to lambaste the Christian party (now dubbed the "Despotic party") for placing the Upper Towns Division chief in control of the other two divisions. Extending the blame to the missionaries for assailing the tribe's traditions, Mushulatubbee rallied the full bloods, and he and Nitakechi regained the governorships of the Lower Towns and Sixtowns divisions, respectively. The opposing factions confronted each other on July 14 at St. Stephens, where the Choctaw people assembled for their annuity distribution. In a tense showdown, Leflore's Upper Towns warriors faced off against men from the Lower Towns and Sixtowns led by Mushulatubbee and Nitakechi. The two sides traded threats until nightfall helped diffuse tensions, and Leflore led his group away.[89]

Despite their internal feuding, the Choctaws could not evade Jackson's demands for a meeting to finalize the tribe's removal. Unlike the Chickasaws, the Choctaws already had land in the West that they had accepted by formal treaty. Now all that remained were logistical details and the establishment of a timetable for emigration. Secretary Eaton and the chiefs selected a treaty location on Dancing Rabbit Creek, a tributary of Hashuqua Creek south of present-day Mushulaville in Noxubee County. By mid-September approximately 6,000 Choctaws had converged on the area, with tribal divisions forming separate campgrounds along the creek's two branches, known as Big Rabbit Creek and Little Rabbit Creek. Commissioners Eaton and Coffee organized food for the multitude, and U.S. military troops kept order amid the liquor sales, gambling, and prostitution. In a touch of irony, Eaton barred the missionaries from the proceedings, fearing that their presence might incite the full bloods. Defiantly, some of the clergymen camped outside the treaty grounds with David Folsom and members of the Christian party.[90]

Treaty negotiations began on September 18 and lasted for only ten days. Leflore, Mushulatubbee, and Nitakechi led the Choctaw delegation comprised of twenty chiefs drawn from the three districts. Dissension among the chiefs stemming from the dispute between the Christian and Republican parties weakened Choctaw resistance to the threats and bribes from U.S. commissioners Eaton and Coffee. The terms offered the tribe, a cash payment plus government assistance in moving to the West, left little room for bargaining, and the chiefs' opposition to removal eventually collapsed. The commissioners and 172 chiefs and headmen signed the Treaty of Dancing Rabbit Creek on September 27, 1830, and the Choctaws reluctantly surrendered their homeland. With their mission accomplished, Eaton and Coffee saw no harm in agreeing to a second round of conciliatory bribes. Through a set of supplementary articles approved on September 28, the commissioners rewarded over sixty influential chiefs and individuals who had not been favored in the main treaty.[91]

The text of the Treaty of Dancing Rabbit Creek is presented in Appendix 1. In summary, the Choctaws exchanged their remaining tribal land east of the Mississippi River, an area comprising almost 10.5 million acres in Mississippi and western Alabama, for approximately 13 million acres in the West. As in the Treaty of Franklin with the Chickasaws, the U.S. government in Article 4 made the Choctaws a promise it would not keep: "no part of the land granted [to the Choctaws] shall forever be embraced in any capital Territory or State." Eight of the treaty's twenty-two articles define how the new Choctaw territory would interact legally with the United States. The commissioners seem to have been particularly worried about the Indian land becoming a haven for outlaws. Article 10 promised help from the federal government in policing unsavory traders and alcohol sales in the western land (although one needed only to take an evening walk beyond the torchlights surrounding the treaty ground to judge the government's diligence in this regard). Tribal annuities had become a standard incentive at treaty negotiations, and at Dancing Rabbit Creek the commissioners agreed under Article 17 to pay the Choctaws $20,000 a year for twenty years "commencing after their removal to the west."

The treaty's Articles 15 and 19 contained the most important information for the chiefs in attendance. Under Article 15, Leflore, Nitakechi, and Mushulatubbee each received 2,560-acre reservations in Mississippi to keep or sell, and the commissioners awarded Leflore and Nitakechi annuities of $250 to continue while they held office. Since Mushulatubbee already had a lifetime annuity from a previous treaty, his annuity under this treaty was set at $100 while he remained in office. As mentioned above, dozens more chiefs and lower-ranked individuals fell in line for incentives, awarded in the supplementary articles approved by the commissioners and appended to the treaty. These awards ranged in size from over 1,200 acres down to 160 acres, and the beneficiaries varied from prominent second-tier chiefs like Pierre Juzan, Peter Pitchlynn, and George W. Harkins, to the widows of Pushmataha and Apuckshunubee. In addition to handing out Mississippi land to chiefs and headmen, Article 19 set forth a complicated procedure for dispensing land grants ranging from 160 to 640 acres or more to heads of families with land currently in cultivation (see Appendix 1). The article set limits on the number of family heads who might receive land grants and placed the onus on the division chiefs to decide who would (and who would not) benefit.[92]

It was the U.S. government's intent with the land grants under Article 19 and the supplementary articles that Choctaw recipients would turn around and sell their land to the state of Mississippi or to incoming whites. Another part of the treaty, Article 14, provided a way for Choctaws to remain in Mississippi, albeit without their tribal status. Under this article, heads of Choctaw households could keep their families in Mississippi and receive land reservations of 160 acres or more by registering the intention to do so with William Ward, the tribal agent, within six months of the treaty's ratification. Although seemingly straightforward, this article became a complex issue that troubled the Choctaws and U.S. government for years to come. Eaton had hoped that Article 14 would provide a way for some of the more prosperous mixed-blood Choctaws to remain in Mississippi, where they would acculturate more easily than the full bloods. William Ward, the Choctaw agent in charge of registrations under Article 14, seemed intent on carrying out Eaton's wishes. Although illiteracy and failure to understand the treaty kept some Choctaws from registering to remain in the state, numerous complaints make it apparent that Ward deliberately prevented many tribal members from taking advantage of Article 14. By the deadline, only sixty-nine heads of Choctaw families had successfully registered to remain in Mississippi. Of these, thirty-nine were either mixed blood or white.[93]

Reaction among the general Choctaw population to the Treaty of Dancing Rabbit Creek ranged from confusion to dejection to outright anger as reports circulated through the villages about the behavior of the leading chiefs during the treaty negotiations. Along with talk of the unconcealed bribery, stories surfaced about suspicions of military coercion and even accounts of death threats aimed at keeping certain chiefs from signing the treaty. A rumor that many of the Choctaws left the treaty grounds in disgust before the treaty concluded may have some truth, but it seems to be at odds with the large number of signatures by chiefs and headmen on the September 27 document.[94] Not surprisingly, a power struggle ensued in which chiefs seeking to improve their ranking vilified those who had been part of the negotiating commission. Leflore's support for his claim to the office of overall chief quickly eroded in favor of a return to joint governance by three district leaders. In the Lower Towns Division, Peter Pitchlynn and David Folsom vied for Mushulatubbee's post. Chiefs like Pitchlynn who openly scorned the Treaty of Dancing Rabbit Creek were quite content to accept the rewards it offered. In the Sixtowns Division, Joel H. Nail replaced Nitakechi, and in the Upper Towns Division, Leflore's nephew George W. Harkins claimed leadership of the district. All of these machinations proved useless, however, as the Jackson administration continued to recognize the top three treaty negotiators—Leflore, Nitakechi, and Mushulatubbee—as the chiefs of their respective divisions.[95]

The many land reservations awarded under Articles 14 and 19 had to be located and surveyed before they would be of any use to the recipients, a time-consuming process that soon became problematic for both the Choctaws and the Jackson administration. In fact, before the U.S. Senate ratified the Treaty of Dancing Rabbit Creek, whites began moving into the ceded area, and public land sales commenced in direct violation of the government's agreement with the tribe. Speculators hounded Choctaws who held land claims under the treaty, offering quick cash, or in some cases whiskey, for their reservations. Despite appeals and complaints from Choctaws, local authorities made little effort to discourage the trespassers.[96]

In the face of the white invasion, some Choctaw families gathered what possessions they could carry and set out on their own for a country most of them had never seen. Almost all of these early departures were from Leflore's district. Leflore himself chose to remain in Mississippi and embrace the life of a planter and slave-owner; however, the chief actively followed through on his part of the bargain made at Dancing Rabbit Creek by encouraging around

400 people to sell their livestock and other property to incoming whites and move west. Although Methodist and Baptist missionaries volunteered to help these early emigrants, they were woefully unprepared for the task of moving families with elders and children over 400 miles across rivers and swamps in midwinter. Eaton and the War Department, though not yet prepared for a Choctaw exodus, had little choice but to authorize military assistance for the Indians and missionaries. After suffering cold, starvation, and an unknown number of deaths, these early Choctaw refugees finally settled close to Fort Towson, near the confluence of the Kiamichi and Red rivers.[97]

Also during the closing months of 1830, George S. Gaines organized the government-sponsored exploratory tour of the Indian Territory authorized by the Treaty of Dancing Rabbit Creek (Supplementary Article 3). Gaines, well known among the Choctaws from having formerly served as factor at the St. Stephens trading house, had accepted the War Department's post as civilian manager of the Choctaw removal. The Choctaw party of eighteen chiefs included Mushulatubbee, Nitakechi, George W. Harkins, and Robert Folsom. As discussed above, Leflore had no plans to emigrate and therefore no reason to join the western expedition. A party of Chickasaws, which included Levi, George, and Pitman Colbert, eventually joined the Choctaw tour. For protection against hostile Indians, Gaines's party rendezvoused with a U.S. Cavalry escort at Fort Smith before traveling west along the Arkansas and Canadian rivers, then south to the Red River. In contrast to the plight of the Choctaw refugees making their way west that December, the chiefs riding with Gaines and the soldiers had plenty of provisions and winter clothing.[98]

Upon returning to Mississippi, the Choctaw tribal councils worked out a plan to apportion the new western territory among the three divisions (Figure 11). Nitakechi's Sixtowns Division would be along the north side of the Red River and west of the Kiamichi River. Leflore's Upper Towns Division took the area along the Red River to the east of the Kiamichi. Mushulatubbee's Lower Towns Division bordered the other two divisions on the north, along the south side of the Canadian and Arkansas rivers. After their removal, the Choctaws renamed these western divisions: Sixtowns became Pushmataha, Upper Towns became Oklafalaya and later Apuckshunubbee, and Lower Towns became Mushulatubbee. For protection from the western tribes and access to government assistance, the initial Choctaw settlements in the Indian Territory clustered around Fort Towson and Fort Smith.[99]

On the eve of the 1831 removal, a U.S. Army census of the tribe reported 17,963 Choctaws, 151 whites, and 521 enslaved African Americans. Based on these counts, the War Department resolved to move approximately 6,000

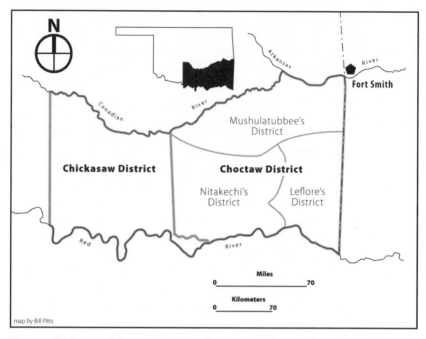

Figure 11. Chickasaw and Choctaw districts in the West. (Based upon Debo, *Rise and Fall*, 72, 153)

Choctaws per year during 1831 through 1833.[100] If the plan looked feasible on paper, its execution would prove to be a catastrophe. John Eaton resigned from his post as secretary of war in April 1831, and his replacement, Lewis Cass, was unfamiliar with the overly ambitious military and civilian partnership that his predecessor had concocted. Eaton's strategy for herding the Choctaws west called for building roads and bridges in Arkansas, engaging steamboats, arranging for hundreds of wagons and teams, and contracting with suppliers of flour, corn, beef, blankets, and other materials to be stockpiled at way stations and at Forts Towson and Smith. As merchants scrambled for the lucrative government contracts, the approaching deadline for the first departure left little time for the kind of oversight the operation required. Eaton also gambled that farmers along the removal route would supply beef and corn to the thousands of people who would soon be passing through.[101]

An estimated 4,000 Choctaws drawn from all three districts reluctantly agreed to join the exodus starting out in October 1831. George Gaines found the uprooting of the Choctaw people "truly painful to witness"; however, like many other sympathetic whites, Gaines thought that removal was the only way to save the tribe. The evacuation plan called for Mushulatubbee's Lower Towns people to depart from Memphis while the people from the Upper Towns and Sixtowns divisions moved out for departure from Vicksburg. Delays in assembling the necessary riverboats forced the Choctaws to wait in makeshift camps at the port towns for over two weeks. As winter descended, five groups of already weary emigrants set out along four routes. Those embarking from Memphis traveled down the Mississippi River and up the Arkansas River to Little Rock, where they followed a 200-mile overland trail to Fort Towson. One group leaving from Vicksburg disembarked at Lake Providence, Louisiana, and trekked some 250 miles overland across the swampy drainages of the Maçon, Boeuf, and Bartholomew bayous. Another group departing from Vicksburg took the Arkansas River–to–Little Rock route, while two other groups from Vicksburg descended the Mississippi River to the Red River and steamed up the Ouachita River to Écore à Fabre (Fabre's Cliffs, present-day Camden, Arkansas). From there, they faced a 150-mile overland journey to Fort Towson.[102]

Under ideal conditions, the sprawling evacuation would have been fraught with hardships, but the crowded boats departing from Memphis and Vicksburg were steaming into a bitter snowstorm that eventually blanketed the whole region. Told that they could not bring baggage that would take up space on the boats, the Choctaws had left their homes with little clothing and were unprepared for the freezing weather. Although they were promised blankets and food, much of the supplies never arrived at the departure points or simply went missing in the confusion of loading the boats. Exposure to the cold, overcrowding, and sickness created miserable conditions aboard the steamboats, and the suffering became worse once the people disembarked to begin their overland march. Miscommunications stranded around 2,500 Choctaws in the snow at Arkansas Post for several desperate days without enough tents and food. The historian Grant Foreman estimates that in addition to the government-organized emigration, as many as 1,000 Choctaws set out independently that winter in numerous groups to make their own way west. For all of the parties following overland routes, the hoped-for wagons and teams were in short supply, forcing most of the people to walk through the snow and spend their nights huddled together for warmth. During February and March 1832 the last of the evacuees finally straggled into the Indian Territory, with most of the survivors dependent upon the government to avoid starvation. There is no reliable record of the total number of Choctaw deaths that winter; however, given the numerous reports of sickness and miscellaneous casualties, all emigrating parties must have suffered multiple fatalities. The historian Arthur DeRosier suggests that the loss of life might have been much worse and notes that many of the agents who led Choctaw groups on the journey made valiant efforts to keep the people in their parties alive.[103]

In the wake of the disastrous first removal, Secretary Cass dismissed Gaines and the other civilian agents, though they had done their best under the circumstances. According to Gaines, Cass was more concerned about the cost of the removal than he was about the suffering inflicted upon the Choctaws. Gaines himself thought that the expense was minimal. At any rate, the War Department placed the subsequent Choctaw removal operation under the charge of the U.S. Army. With lessons learned from the previous winter, the military set about improving the Arkansas roads, replenishing stockpiles of food and blankets, and seeking better cooperation from farmers along the route. Again, the aim was to move around 6,000 people, but under the military's new scheme, the Choctaws would travel in three groups roughly corresponding to the tribal divisions. As in the previous evacuation, Mushulatubbee's people assembled in Memphis, while those from Leflore's and Nitakechi's districts made their way to Vicksburg. Dropping the Red River and Lake Providence routes, army planners arranged for all boats to ascend the White River to the Rock Roe settlement (present-day Monroe County, Arkansas) about fifty miles east of Little Rock. From there the Upper Towns and Sixtowns people would follow an overland trail via Little Rock and Washington (Arkansas, present-day Hempstead County) to Fort Towson. Mushulatubbee's people would travel by boat from Little Rock to Fort Smith.[104]

If the Choctaws had known that cholera was spreading through the Mississippi River towns in the fall of 1832, there would have been no emigration that year. News of the sickness panicked the first groups arriving at Memphis and Vicksburg, and the accompanying soldiers made an effort to protect the people by establishing camps at some distance from the settlements; however, the unsanitary conditions and the inevitable contact with townspeople quickly brought cholera into the Choctaw encampments. The very young and very old were most susceptible, and deaths began to occur while awaiting the steamboats. At Memphis, several hundred terrified Choctaws refused to board the boats, and insisted instead on being ferried across the Mississippi River so that they could travel overland to Rock Roe. The seventy-five-mile trek through the present-day Arkansas counties of Crittenden, St. Francis, Lee, and Monroe meant crossing Fifteenmile Bayou,

Blackfish Bayou, the St. Francis River, L'Anguille Bayou, Big Creek, and numerous smaller watercourses that parallel the drainages of the larger streams. Although these people did not have to contend with snow, a cold front spread heavy rains across the Mississippi Valley, turning the swampy landscape into a quagmire. Those who were herded aboard the steamboats at Memphis and Vicksburg brought the cholera with them to Rock Roe, where all of the groups were gathered before moving overland to Little Rock. At the Arkansas River, some of the evacuees boarded steamboats headed for Fort Smith, while the rest set out across southwest Arkansas toward Fort Towson. As they had the previous year, around 1,000 Choctaws made their way west independently of the military effort, crossing the Mississippi River at Helena and Point Chico. Cholera worked its way through all of these traveling communities that winter and resulted in an unknown number of deaths.[105]

The War Department estimated that a little over 5,000 Choctaws came to the Indian Territory during the winter of 1832–1833. Around 700 of these immigrants crossed the Red River into Texas and eventually settled near Nacogdoches. In the fall of 1833 the remainder of the Choctaws who were willing to emigrate crossed the Mississippi River at Memphis and, under military escort, made the difficult overland journey through Rock Roe to Little Rock and up the Arkansas River to Fort Smith. By the spring of 1834, an estimated 12,500 Choctaws were in the Indian Territory, and approximately 6,000 remained in Mississippi. Some people in the western land set to work clearing fields for planting while others, too discouraged to make the effort, depended more heavily upon government assistance. Unfamiliarity with the new country led some families to place their homes too close to creeks, and they lost what possessions they had in the spring floods. Tragedies like this, along with the widespread sickness and hunger, convinced many Choctaws to return to Mississippi, although conditions back home were in similar chaos.[106]

During the Choctaw removal, Secretary of War Cass was actively pursuing final eastern treaty cessions with the other four southeastern groups that, along with the Choctaws, would eventually become known as the "Five Civilized Tribes." The Creeks and Seminoles gave up the last of their land east of the Mississippi in the spring of 1832, while the Cherokees' final cession came in 1835. For the Chickasaws, the surrender of their homeland, a tenure stretching back into prehistory, came quietly in the fall of 1832.[107] The previous year, Chickasaw agent Benjamin Reynolds began urging the Chickasaw chiefs to continue talks with the Choctaws aimed at convincing the latter to sell the tribe approximately 4.5 million acres of their western land. These talks had begun informally among chiefs of the two tribes during the 1830 tour of the Indian Territory. The Choctaws refused to sell any of their hard-won treaty land, but agreed to allow the Chickasaws to settle with them as guests. Desiring their own territory, the Chickasaws refused the offer. The stalemate prevented the ratification of the Treaty of Franklin, so the Jackson administration appointed General Coffee to make a new treaty with the Chickasaws and try to speed the tribe's emigration.[108]

Coffee met with the Chickasaw chiefs in October 1832 at the tribal council house on Pontotoc Creek, near present-day Pontotoc in Pontotoc County.[109] The principal negotiators for the Chickasaws included King Ishtehotopa, Tishomingo, George Colbert, William McGillivray, Samuel Seeley, Toopulaco, Isaac Albertson, and Emmubbee. The historian Arrell Gibson has charged Coffee with holding back tribal annuities to force Chickasaw compliance; however, James Atkinson notes that the chiefs negotiated the best treaty they could, considering the tribe's weak bargaining position.[110] In the Treaty with the Chickasaw (see Appendix 2), signed on October 20, 1832, also known as the Treaty of Pontotoc Creek, the United States agreed (Article 3) to pay the Chickasaws the proceeds from the sale of their eastern land, after deducting the costs of surveying and selling the land and all expenses connected with the tribe's removal. Under Article 10, the Chickasaws relinquished control of these proceeds for a period of fifty years from the date of the treaty's ratification. At that time, the government could chose to give the tribe the freedom to manage its own funds "if the Chickasaw nation shall have improved in education and civilization, and become so enlightened, as to be capable of managing so large a sum of money to advantage." Under Articles 4 and 5, the Chickasaws agreed to search for their new home; however, if the Chickasaw land sales commenced before a western home could be established, the tribal members could receive temporary allotments in Mississippi ranging from 640 to 2,560 acres, depending on family size and the number of slaves owned. Article 12 provided Tishomingo with a $100 lifetime annuity in recognition of his age and status, and Queen Puc-caun-la, described as "very old and very poor," received a $50 lifetime annuity (to be administered by the tribal agent). Atkinson has identified Queen Puc-caun-la as the widow of King Chinubbee. Surprisingly, the treaty includes no gifts or reservations for the tribe's other ranking chiefs.[111]

Two days after the signing of the Treaty of Pontotoc Creek, Coffee and the chiefs signed a supplementary treaty (October 22, 1832; see Appendix 2) in which the Chickasaws introduced several measures to give the tribe more control over the sale of their ceded land and ensure that all sales benefited the tribe as a whole instead of individuals. As Atkinson has pointed out, the supplementary articles, taken together with the October 20 treaty, seem to represent the wishes of the whole nation and not just those of a few high-ranking chiefs. Another issue amended here was the minimum age for head of family allotments. The supplementary document changes the minimum age from twenty-one to seventeen, stating that "Indians mature earlier than white men, and generally marry younger." Another supplementary measure makes provisions for the assistance of orphans and widows. Although sixty-five chiefs, headmen, and warriors signed both the treaty and supplementary articles, members of the tribe, including Levi Colbert, accused Coffee of coercing the chiefs to conclude the treaty. Despite Coffee's denial of these charges, Colbert and others continued to press for more amendments to the treaty, and Chickasaw delegations journeyed to Washington, D.C., in 1833 and 1834. The resulting treaty (Treaty with the Chickasaw, signed May 24, 1834) awarded reservations in the ceded land ranging from 320 acres up to 2,560 acres to all of the leading chiefs as well as to heads of families and other individuals according to a complex combination of criteria. The treaty also gave the Chickasaws limited authority to manage the sale of these reservations.[112]

During the long delay between the cession of the Chickasaws' eastern lands and their removal, thousands of whites entered the former tribal territory. When the sales of reservations commenced in 1836, some Chickasaws inevitably fell victim to the whiskey merchants, while many others used the money from their land sales to prepare for the journey west, purchasing wagons, oxen, plows, and other items at exorbitant prices.[113] The wait for the tribe to find a western home came to an end with the Treaty of Doaksville, also called the Treaty with the Choctaw and Chickasaw, signed near Fort Towson on January 17, 1837. Under the treaty, the Chickasaws acquired approximately 3.2 million acres from the Choctaws for $530,000. The Chickasaw land, situated to the west of the Choctaw districts (Figure 11), became a fourth Choctaw district administratively, although the two tribes' annuities would remain separate. The treaty also states that Chickasaws and Choctaws could settle anywhere within the four districts. In reaching this historic agreement, the two tribes relinquished any quarrels associated with lingering vendettas from their past wars. For their part, the Chickasaws had made a substantial compromise by accepting minority status in the politics of the newly formed confederacy.[114]

Wasting little time in implementing the Treaty of Pontotoc Creek, the War Department appointed Major A. A. M. Upshaw to direct the Chickasaw removal. Under military oversight, the planned route for the westward emigration was to proceed overland from Memphis to Little Rock and then by boat to Fort Coffee, about ten miles west of Fort Smith on the Arkansas River. According to the 1837 federal census, the Chickasaw population totaled 6,070, of which 1,156 were African American slaves. Accordingly, Upshaw and his officers went about setting up way stations supplied with corn, flour, beef, and pork. The first group of emigrants, numbering around 500, crossed the Mississippi River at Memphis in July 1837 and followed the swampy overland route through Rock Roe taken by the Choctaws a few years earlier. Where the Choctaws had been pressed to bring as few personal items as possible, the Chickasaw emigration was a rambling train of people and dogs, loaded wagons, and herds of horses and cattle strung out for miles across the landscape. Although conditions were not as adverse as those felt by the Choctaws, the Chickasaws soon experienced fever and dysentery under drenching summer rains.[115]

At Little Rock, the careful military planning came unraveled, partially as the result of the murder of Emmubbee, one of the leading Chickasaw chiefs, during an argument with a white man before the emigration began. The Chickasaw leaders announced to John M. Millard, the agent in charge of the removal group, that Emmubbee had instructed them before their departure to proceed overland to Fort Towson from Little Rock, instead of going up the Arkansas River valley as Upchurch had planned. Although Millard was able to convince the chiefs to place the women and children and sick and injured aboard a steamboat, some 300 Chickasaws resolutely headed southwest with their horses and cattle bound for the Red River and Fort Towson. After delivering those aboard the steamboat to Fort Coffee, Millard caught up with the slow-moving Chickasaw party not far from Little Rock. As Millard endeavored to see the stubborn group safely to the Indian Territory, his journal documents the hardships and sickness, made worse by the availability of liquor along the way and the loss of livestock to thieves dogging the procession. After two months on the road, the weary soldiers and Chickasaws reached Fort Towson on September 5.[116]

The second and final wave of Chickasaw immigrants, numbering around 4,000, departed from Memphis in November 1837. Most traveled to Fort Coffee by steamboat, but about one-fourth of the group went overland in a sprawling train herding some 5,000 horses. To the relief of their military escort, the emigrants followed the planned route up the Arkansas River valley. The last members of this group reached Fort Coffee by late January 1838, in time to cope with a withering smallpox epidemic that swept through the Indian Territory, killing over 500 Chickasaws and Choctaws, including the venerable Mushulatubbee. As with the Choctaws, around 1,000 Chickasaws and their slaves journeyed to Indian Territory by way of various routes without the benefit of military escort. Over the next decade, most of the Chickasaws remaining in Mississippi made their way to the new country, where they had to contend with Pawnees, Kiowas, Comanches, and other western tribes whose own hunting lands were now overrun with displaced eastern groups.[117] The removal of the Mississippi tribes accomplished the cruel objective envisioned by the Thomas Jefferson administration some thirty years earlier. Without the use of military force, a combined Indian population of almost 20,000 had surrendered their homeland and voluntarily left the state. Despite the absence of gunfire, the United States did not win its victory without bloodshed, for hundreds perished from smallpox, exposure, starvation, and dysentery.

EPILOGUE

If anything, Greenwood Leflore personified the type of Choctaw that Eaton and Coffee had in mind when they drafted Article 14 of the Treaty of Dancing Rabbit Creek. In the best southern planter tradition, the mixed-blood chief skillfully managed his holdings in Carroll County, and by the 1850s his Malmaison cotton plantation comprised some 15,000 acres worked by over 400 slaves.[1] But Leflore was hardly representative of the approximately 5,000 Choctaws that remained in Mississippi after removal. Choctaw historian Clara Sue Kidwell has characterized the majority of those who stayed behind as traditionalists who clung to their "core identity, language, and customs." Stripped of their tribal organization, these people retreated to the periphery of Mississippi's burgeoning white society and relied on subsistence farming, hunting, and bartering to survive. Depending upon the availability of work, Choctaw men sometimes moved back and forth between Mississippi and the Indian Territory, leaving their women to oversee the families. Without a federal agent, these Mississippi Choctaws were vulnerable to speculators who wanted to press their treaty claims for reservation land, and they endured racial denigration that extended from their white neighbors to the highest levels of the U.S. government.[2]

Although a few Chickasaws resisted removal, the majority of the tribe was in the Indian Territory by 1840. Arrell Gibson has pointed out that Levi Colbert's death in 1834 left the Chickasaws without leadership at this critical time. In fact, King Ishtehotopa and most of the mixed-blood chiefs who had held leadership roles in Mississippi had all migrated west; however, the tribe's reorganization had to await the establishment of new army forts within its district to provide protection from the hostile western tribes and the general lawlessness that prevailed west of the Washita River. The western Chickasaws gained independence from the Choctaws in 1855 in a treaty between the two tribes and the United States. In the treaty, the Choctaws ceded their land west of 100 degrees west longitude and agreed to lease the government their land west of 98 degrees west longitude to be used as reservation land for other tribes. In return, the treaty provided the Choctaws with a course of action to settle unpaid claims remaining from the Treaty of Dancing Rabbit Creek.[3]

During the Civil War most Choctaws and Chickasaws sided with the Confederacy. In Mississippi, Choctaw men formed the First Mississippi Choctaw Infantry Battalion (trained and commanded by whites), reportedly captured at Camp Moore, Louisiana (north of Lake Pontchartrain near present-day Tangipahoa, Louisiana).[4]

The Confederates recruited actively among the slave-holding tribes in the Indian Territory and raised three regiments of Chickasaws and Choctaws, which saw action in the war's western campaigns.[5] After the war, the U.S. government signed Reconstruction treaties with the Indian Territory tribes. For the Chickasaws and Choctaws, perhaps the most contentious issue was the status of their former slaves, now known as "freedmen." These people identified culturally with their former owners, and many of them sought tribal membership. The Chickasaws reluctantly adopted their freedmen in 1873, and the Choctaws did the same in 1883.[6]

In the years following the Civil War, many Mississippi Choctaws found employment as sharecroppers, while others continued to lead a marginal existence in places avoided by whites. Kidwell notes that during this time of poverty and uncertainty, Choctaw communities in Mississippi remained in contact through stickball games and dances. Along with these traditional activities, a critical element in the survival of Choctaw culture in Mississippi was the establishment of Indian churches in the 1880s by Protestant and Catholic missionaries, the former coming mainly from Baptist and Methodist congregations in the Indian Territory. These churches provided the people with much-needed community centers at scattered sharecropper settlements and, as the historian C. Blue Clark has noted, gave the Choctaws a nurturing place for preserving their language and traditional music and dancing.[7]

In the West, the Choctaws and Chickasaws fulfilled their part of the removal bargain with the United States. They founded towns, adopted constitutions, and formed governments, yet despite the predictions of Thomas Jefferson, Andrew Jackson, and all of the other whites who brought about Indian removal, the "Indian problem" had not gone away. After the Civil War, as railroads and wagon trains brought the inevitable tide of white settlers to the Indian Territory, a new generation of politicians looked with disapproval at the vast landholdings that the displaced eastern tribes now owned in the West. In 1887 Congress passed the Dawes Severalty Act, also known as the General Allotment Act, exchanging tribal land held in common for individual ownership of property. Since their removal treaties shielded the Five

Civilized Tribes from the Dawes Severalty Act, Congress created the Dawes Commission in 1893 to pressure the Chickasaws, Choctaws, Seminoles, Cherokees, and Creeks into accepting allotments. The tribes protested; tribal populations were relatively small, and individual allotments would only take up a fraction of the Indian Territory, freeing millions of acres of former tribal property for white settlement. Without a viable position from which to bargain, the Choctaws and Chickasaws ceded all of their western land to the United States in the Muskogee Agreement (1896) and the Atoka Agreement (1897), which, along with similar agreements with the Seminoles, Cherokees, and Creeks, allowed Congress to extend allotments to the Five Civilized Tribes through the Curtis Act in 1898.[8] Between 1898 and 1907 the Dawes Commission determined who would receive allotments under the Curtis Act through tribal enrollment in the Indian Territory and in Mississippi. In 1902 Congress set the allotments for enrolled Choctaws and Chickasaws at 320 acres per person, while freedmen received allotments of 40 acres. The commission enrolled 2,335 Choctaws in Mississippi; however, as many as 500 more may have been overlooked or simply chose not to enroll. Following enrollment, some 300 to 400 Choctaws left Mississippi in 1903 to receive allotments in the Indian Territory, although some eventually returned to the state.[9]

During the twentieth century, the U.S. Congress, through a succession of laws, continued to assert control over the lives of American Indians. The Indian Citizenship Act of 1924 extended U.S. citizenship to any Indian groups not already covered. Although presented as a benevolent gesture on the part of the United States, some tribes considered the Citizenship Act a threat to their autonomy. More far-reaching was the Indian Reorganization Act of 1934, also known as the Wheeler-Howard Act, which imposed the tribal council system of government on federally recognized groups and on tribal groups seeking federal recognition. The Indian Reorganization Act did not include the Five Civilized Tribes; these groups received authorization to form tribal governments under Oklahoma's 1936 Indian Welfare Act. The Indian Claims Commission Act of 1946 ostensibly provided tribes with a procedure to address fraudulent actions on the part of the U.S. government and seek unpaid claims stemming from land cession treaties. In practice, the commission's procedural rules and its findings on numerous claims betray the inherent conflict of interest when the U.S. government sets out to investigate itself. For example, congressional authority limited the commission to acting on group or tribal claims, allowing the commission to dismiss numerous claims by determining them to be personal claims of individuals within the plaintiff group. Furthermore, the Indian Claims Commission Act specified that, by accepting compensation for a claim, the tribe in question forfeited the right to seek additional claims. Consequently, some tribes avoided the commission in order to protect their right to pursue their claims through the court system. When the commission did make awards of compensation, they were often substantially reduced by "offsets," or deductions for miscellaneous government expenses.[10]

During the 1940s and 1950s, the federal government adopted a policy known as "termination," which sought to integrate Indians into American society by withdrawing federal support. In legislation eerily reminiscent of Mississippi's 1830 Indian law, Congress passed the Termination Act of 1953, calling for the abolishment of several specific tribes. The Choctaws and Chickasaws were not included in the Termination Act; however, the legislation set a dangerous precedent. The Relocation Act of 1956 supported termination by providing job training along with decreases in federal funding for tribes. Predictably, opposition to termination was widespread, boosted by the concurrent civil rights movement, and by the 1960s termination had lost its appeal to politicians, as evidenced by the passage of the Indian Civil Rights Act of 1968.[11] During the 1970s, Congress continued to assert its control over American Indians while providing much needed assistance across a wide spectrum of issues through the Indian Education Act (1972), the Indian Self-Determination and Education Act (1975), the American Indian Religious Freedom Act (1978), and the Indian Child Welfare Act (1978).[12] In 1990 Congress passed the Native American Graves Protection and Repatriation Act (NAGPRA), which provides a process for federally recognized tribes to claim their cultural items held by state and federal museums, agencies, and other institutions. According to anthropologists Robert A. Brightman and Pamela S. Wallace, the Chickasaws received Mississippi's first NAGPRA repatriation of sacred objects in 1998.[13]

The Atoka Agreement ended the independent nation status of the Chickasaws and Choctaws in the Indian Territory, and members of these tribes became U.S. citizens when Oklahoma became a state in 1907. As mentioned above, Oklahoma's Indian Welfare Act permitted the reorganization of Chickasaw and Choctaw tribal governments. Both Oklahoma tribes adopted new constitutions in 1983 and have formed effective partnerships with other western tribes.[14] Of those tribal groups that left Mississippi before removal, only a few have managed to maintain their tribal identity. As mentioned in previous chapters, groups of Choctaws emigrated to Louisiana and Texas following the 1763 Treaty of Paris. Some of these people eventually established communities in Grant, La Salle, and Catahoula parishes in east-central Louisiana. According to Louisiana archaeologist Hiram F. Gregory, members of this group journeyed to the Indian Territory around the turn of the twentieth century and enrolled with the Dawes Commission, but returned to Louisiana when they failed to receive allotments. Like so many other southeastern Indians during the postremoval era, the Louisiana Choctaws lived in poverty and isolation. They held their first tribal election in 1974 and, after achieving state recognition, received federal recognition in 1995 as the Jena Band of Choctaw Indians.[15]

The Tunica and Biloxi groups gathered near Marksville, Louisiana, merged in the nineteenth century and received federal recognition in 1981 as the Tunica-Biloxi Tribe of Louisiana.[16] The Alabama and Koasati also united in the nineteenth century near Livingston, Texas, and achieved federal recognition in 1987.[17] As discussed in chapter 7, the large Houma group formed several communities in south Louisiana along Bayou Lafourche and its distributaries in the present-day parishes of Terrebonne, Lafourche, Saint Mary, and Saint Bernard. They organized in 1979 as the United Houma Nation, Inc., and received recognition from the state of Louisiana. Since 1985 the Houmas have been actively seeking federal recognition.[18] At the time of this writing (September 2011), the Houmas are awaiting determination from the Bureau of Indian Affairs on their federal recognition status.[19] The Natchez are currently represented by two separate groups, the Kussoe-Natchez near Charleston, South Carolina, and the Natchez Nation at Gore, Oklahoma. Both organizations are seeking federal recognition.[20]

According to the 1910 census, the Choctaw population in Mississippi was 1,253, although the 1918 influenza pandemic may have killed as many as 20 percent of the tribe. These Mississippi Choctaws experienced the poverty and isolation that were common to the state's expatriate tribes. Based upon reports about the condition of the tribe, a congressional delegation traveled to Mississippi in 1917, and the following year Congress authorized the Bureau of Indian Affairs to place a Choctaw agency at Philadelphia, Mississippi, thereby establishing federal recognition. Subsequent federal assistance helped many Mississippi Choctaws to make the transition from sharecropping to farm ownership, as well as providing the tribe with hospitals and schools. Following the Indian Reorganization Act of 1934, the Mississippi Choctaws elected their first tribal council, called the Choctaw Business Committee.[21] In 1945 the secretary of the interior approved the tribe's constitution and bylaws as the Mississippi Band of Choctaw and released Choctaw land formerly held in trust. The tribe revised its constitution in 1975 to allow for the democratic election of chiefs. Calvin J. Isaac, the first elected chief, served until 1979 and initiated educational, social, and economic development programs. Phillip Martin replaced Isaac and served as chief for twenty-eight years. Martin's administration brought about significant increases in tribal employment through diversification of businesses involving manufacturing, service, retail, and tourism, resulting in an annual impact on Mississippi's economy of over $1 billion. In 2007 the Choctaws entered a new phase of leadership with Beasley Denson's election as chief, or *Miko*. Four years later, Phyliss J. Anderson became the tribe's first female *Miko* when she was sworn into office on October 11, 2011.[22]

Today, the Mississippi Band of Choctaw Indians numbers approximately 9,660 individuals residing in eight communities in the eastern part of the state: Redwater (Leake County), Standing Pine (Leake County), Pearl River (Neshoba County), Bogue Chitto (Kemper County), Tucker (Neshoba County), Conehatta (Newton County), Bogue Homa (Jones County), and Crystal Ridge (Winston County), plus a Mississippi Choctaw community in Henning, Tennessee, about forty miles northeast of Memphis. Other tribal lands include a portion of Greenwood Leflore's Malmaison property in Carroll County and additional properties in Attala and Jackson counties. In 2007 the Mississippi legislature conveyed ownership of the Nanih Waiya mound and cave mound properties to the tribe. The return of these two sites, which figure so prominently in Choctaw origin stories, has special significance, coming 177 years after the same legislative body abolished the Choctaws' tribal status. With courage and determination, Mississippi Choctaws endured invasion and resisted removal to keep their language and culture in the land of their ancestors. As Mississippi's sole remaining indigenous American Indian tribe, they represent all of the tribes that once lived here.[23]

TREATY OF DANCING RABBIT CREEK

A treaty of perpetual friendship, cession and limits, entered into by John H. Eaton and John Coffee, for and in behalf of the Government of the United States, and the Mingoes, Chiefs, Captains and Warriors of the Choctaw Nation, begun and held at Dancing Rabbit Creek, on the fifteenth of September, in the year eighteen hundred and thirty.

WHEREAS the General Assembly of the State of Mississippi has extended the laws of said State to persons and property within the chartered limits of the same, and the President of the United States has said that he cannot protect the Choctaw people from the operation of these laws; Now therefore that the Choctaw may live under their own laws in peace with the United States and the State of Mississippi they have determined to sell their lands east of the Mississippi and have accordingly agreed to the following articles of treaty.

ARTICLE 1. Perpetual peace and friendship is pledged and agreed upon by and between the United States and the Mingoes, Chiefs, and Warriors of the Choctaw Nation of the Red People; and that this may be considered the Treaty existing between the parties all other Treaties heretofore existing and inconsistent with the provisions of this are hereby declared null and void.

ARTICLE 2. The United States under a grant specially to be made by the President of the U.S. shall cause to be conveyed to the Choctaw Nation a tract of country west of the Mississippi River, in fee simple to them and their descendants, to inure to them while they shall exist as a nation and live on it, beginning near Fort Smith where the Arkansas boundary crosses the Arkansas River, running thence to the source of the Canadian fork; if in the limits of the United States, or to those limits; thence due south to Red River, and down Red River to the west boundary of the Territory of Arkansas; thence north along that line to the beginning. The boundary of the same to be agreeable to the Treaty made and concluded at Washington City in the year 1825. The grant to be executed so soon as the present Treaty shall be ratified.

ARTICLE 3. In consideration of the provisions contained in the several articles of this Treaty, the Choctaw nation of Indians consent and hereby cede to the United States, the entire country they own and possess, east of the Mississippi River; and they agree to move beyond the Mississippi River, early as practicable, and will so arrange their removal, that as many as possible of their people not exceeding one half of the whole number, shall depart during the falls of 1831 and 1832; the residue to follow during the succeeding fall of 1833; a better opportunity in this manner will be afforded the Government, to extend to them the facilities and comforts which it is desirable should be extended in conveying them to their new homes.

ARTICLE 4. The Government and people of the United States are hereby obliged to secure to the said Choctaw Nation of Red People the jurisdiction and government of all the persons and property that may be within their limits west, so that no Territory or State shall ever have a right to pass laws for the government of the Choctaw Nation of Red People and their descendants; and that no part of the land granted them shall forever be embraced in any capital Territory or State; but the U.S. shall forever secure said Choctaw Nation from, and against, all laws except such as from time to time may be enacted in their own National Councils, not inconsistent with the Constitution, Treaties, and Laws of the United States; and except such as may, and which have been enacted by Congress, to the extent that Congress under the Constitution are required to exercise a legislation over Indian Affairs. But the Choctaws, should this treaty be ratified, express a wish that Congress may grant to the Choctaws the right of punishing by their own laws, any white man who shall come into their nation, and infringe any of their national regulations.

ARTICLE 5. The United States are obliged to protect the Choctaws from domestic strife and from foreign enemies on the same principles that the citizens of the United States are protected, so that whatever would be a legal demand upon the U.S. for defense or for wrongs committed by an enemy, on a citizen of the U.S. shall be equally binding in favor of the Choctaws, and in all cases where the Choctaws shall be called upon by a legally authorized officer of the U.S. to fight an enemy, such Choctaw shall receive the pay and other emoluments, which citizens of the U.S. receive in such cases, provided, no war shall be undertaken or prosecuted by said Choctaw Nation but by declaration made in full Council, and to be approved by the U.S. unless it be in self defense against an open rebellion or against an enemy marching into their country, in which cases they shall defend, until the U.S. are advised thereof.

ARTICLE 6. Should a Choctaw or any party of Choctaws commit acts of violence upon the person or property of a citizen of the U.S. or join any war party against any neighboring tribe of Indians, without the authority in the preceding article; and except to oppose an actual or threatened invasion or rebellion, such persons so offending shall be delivered up to an officer of the U.S. if in the power of the Choctaw Nation, that such offender may be punished as may be provided in such cases, by the laws of the U.S.; but if such offender is not within the control of the Choctaw Nation, then said Choctaw Nation shall not be held responsible for the injury done by said offender.

ARTICLE 7. All acts of violence committed upon persons and property of the people of the Choctaw Nation either by citizens of the U.S. or neighboring Tribes of Red People, shall be referred to some authorized Agent by him to be referred to the President of the U.S. who shall examine into such cases and see that every possible degree of justice is done to said Indian party of the Choctaw Nation.

ARTICLE 8. Offenders against the laws of the U.S. or any individual State shall be apprehended and delivered to any duly authorized person where such offender may be found in the Choctaw country, having fled from any part of U.S. but in all such cases application must be made to the Agent or Chiefs and the expense of his apprehension and delivery provided for and paid by the U. States.

ARTICLE 9. Any citizen of the U.S. who may be ordered from the Nation by the Agent and constituted authorities of the Nation and refusing to obey or return into the Nation without the consent of the aforesaid persons, shall be subject to such pains and penalties as may be provided by the laws of the U.S. in such cases. Citizens of the U.S. traveling peaceably under the authority of the laws of the U.S. shall be under the care and protection of the nation.

ARTICLE 10. No person shall expose goods or other article for sale as a trader, without a written permit from the constituted authorities of the Nation, or authority of the laws of the Congress of the U.S. under penalty of forfeiting the Articles, and constituted authorities of the Nation shall grant no license except to such persons as reside in the Nation and are answerable to the laws of the Nation. The U.S. shall be particularly obliged to assist to prevent ardent spirits from being introduced into the Nation.

ARTICLE 11. Navigable streams shall be free to the Choctaws who shall pay no higher toll or duty than citizens of the U.S. It is agreed further that the U.S. shall establish one or more Post Offices in said Nation, and may establish such military post roads, and posts, as they may consider necessary.

ARTICLE 12. All intruders shall be removed from the Choctaw Nation and kept without it. Private property to be always respected and on no occasion taken for public purposes without just compensation being made therefor to the rightful owner. If an Indian unlawfully take or steal any property from a white man a citizen of the U.S. the offender shall be punished. And if a white man unlawfully take or steal any thing from an Indian, the property shall be restored and the offender punished. It is further agreed that when a Choctaw shall be given up to be tried for any offence against the laws of the U.S. if unable to imply counsel to defend him, the U.S. will do it, that his trial may be fair and impartial.

ARTICLE 13. It is consented that a qualified Agent shall be appointed for the Choctaws every four years, unless sooner removed by the President; and he shall be removed on petition of the constituted authorities of the Nation, the President being satisfied there is sufficient cause shown. The Agent shall fix his residence convenient to the great body of the people; and in the selection of an Agent immediately after the ratification of this Treaty, the wishes of the Choctaw Nation on the subject shall be entitled to great respect.

ARTICLE 14. Each Choctaw head of a family being desirous to remain and become a citizen of the States, shall be permitted to do so, by signifying his intention to the Agent within six months from the ratification of this Treaty, and he or she shall thereupon be entitled to a reservation of one section of six hundred and forty acres of land, to be bounded by sectional lines of survey; in like manner shall be entitled to one half that quantity for each unmarried child which is living with him over ten years of age; and a quarter section to such child as may be under 10 years of age, to adjoin the location of the parent. If they reside upon said lands intending to become citizens of the States for five years after the ratification of this Treaty, in that case a grant in fee simple shall issue; said reservation shall include the present improvement of the head of the family, or a portion of it. Persons who claim under this article shall not lose the privilege of a Choctaw citizen, but if they ever remove are not to be entitled to any portion of the Choctaw annuity.

ARTICLE 15. To each of the Chiefs in the Choctaw Nation (to wit) Greenwood Laflore, Nutackachie, and Mushulatubbe there is granted a reservation of four sections of land, two of which shall include and adjoin their present improvement, and the other two located where they please but on unoccupied unimproved lands, such sections shall be bounded by sectional lines, and with the consent of the President they may sell the same. Also to the three principal Chiefs and to their successors in office there shall be paid two hundred and fifty dollars annually while they shall continue in their respective offices, except to Mushulatubbe, who as he has an annuity of one hundred and fifty dollars for life under a former treaty, shall receive only the additional sum of one hundred dollars, while he shall continue in office as Chief: and if in addition to this the Nation shall think proper to elect an additional principal Chief of the whole to superintend and govern upon republican principles he shall receive annually for his services five hundred dollars, which allowance to the Chiefs and their successors in office, shall continue for twenty years. At any time when in military service, and while in service by authority of the U.S. the district Chiefs under and by selection of the President shall be entitled to the pay of Majors; the other Chief under the same circumstances shall have the pay of a Lieutenant Colonel. The Speakers of the three districts, shall receive twenty-five dollars a year for four years each; and the three secretaries one to each of the Chiefs, fifty dollars each for four years. Each Captain of the Nation, the number not to exceed ninety-nine, thirty-three from each district, shall be furnished upon removing to the West, with each a good suit of clothes and a broad sword as an outfit, and for four years commencing with the of their removal, shall each receive fifty dollars a year, for the trouble of keeping their people at order in settling; and whenever they shall be in military service by authority of the U.S. shall receive the pay of a captain.

ARTICLE 16. In wagons; and with steam boats as may be found necessary— the U.S. agree to remove the Indians to their new homes at their expense and under the care of discreet and careful persons, who will be kind and brotherly to them. They agree to furnish them with ample corn and beef, or pork for themselves and families for twelve months after reaching their new homes. It is agreed further that the U.S. will take all their cattle, at the valuation of some discreet person to be appointed by the President, and the same shall be paid for in money after their arrival at their new homes; or other cattle such as may be desired shall be furnished them, notice being given through their Agent of their wishes upon this subject before their removal that time to supply the demand may be afforded.

ARTICLE 17. The several annuities and sums secured under former Treaties to the Choctaw nation and people shall continue as though this Treaty had never been made. And it is further agreed that the U.S. in addition will pay the sum of twenty thousand dollars for twenty years, commencing after their removal to the west, of which, in the first year after their removal, ten thousand dollars shall be divided and arranged to such as may not receive reservations under this Treaty.

ARTICLE 18. The U.S. shall cause the lands hereby ceded to be surveyed; and surveyors may enter the Choctaw Country for that purpose, conducting themselves properly and disturbing or interrupting none of the Choctaw people. But no person is to be permitted to settle within the nation, or the lands to be sold before the Choctaws shall remove. And for the payment of the several amounts secured in this Treaty, the lands hereby ceded are to remain a fund pledged to that purpose, until the debt shall be provided for and arranged. And further it is agreed, that in the construction of this Treaty wherever well founded doubt shall arise, it shall be construed most favorably towards the Choctaws.

ARTICLE 19. The following reservations of land are hereby admitted. To Colonel David Fulsom four sections of which two shall include his present improvement, and two may be located elsewhere, on unoccupied, unimproved land.

To I. Garland, Colonel Robert Cole, Tuppanahomer, John Pytchlynn, Charles Juzan, Johokebetubbe, Eaychahobia, Ofehoma, two sections, each to include their improvements, and to be bounded by sectional lines, and the same may be disposed of and sold with the consent of the President. And that others not provided for, may be provided for, there shall be reserved as follows:

First. One section to each head of a family not exceeding Forty in number, who during the present year, may have had in actual cultivation, with a dwelling house thereon fifty acres or more. Secondly, three quarter sections after the manner aforesaid to each head of a family not exceeding four hundred and sixty, as shall have cultivated thirty acres and less that fifty, to be bounded by quarter section lines of survey, and to be contiguous and adjoining.

Third: One half section as aforesaid to those who shall have cultivated from twenty to thirty acres the number not to exceed four hundred.

Fourth; a quarter section as aforesaid to such as shall have cultivated from twelve to twenty acres, the number not to exceed three hundred and fifty, and one half that quantity to such as shall have cultivated from two to twelve acres, the number also not to exceed three hundred and fifty persons. Each of said class of cases shall be subject to the limitations contained in the first class, and shall be so located as to include that part of the improvement which contains the dwelling house. If a greater number shall be found to be entitled to reservations under the several classes of this article, than is stipulated for under the limitation prescribed, then and in that case the Chiefs separately or together shall determine the persons who shall be excluded in the respective districts.

Fifth: Any Captain the number not exceeding ninety persons, who under the provisions of this article shall receive less that a section, he shall be entitled, to an additional quantity of half a section adjoining to his other reservation. The several reservations secured under this article, may be sold with the consent of the President of the U.S. but should any prefer it, or omit to take a reservation for the quantity he may be entitled to, the U.S. be on his removing pay fifty cents an acre after reaching their new homes, provided that before the first of January next they shall adduce to the Agent, or some other authorized person to be appointed, proof of his claim and the quantity of it.

Sixth: likewise children of the Choctaw Nation residing in the Nation, who have neither father or mother, a list of which, with satisfactory proof of Parentage and orphanage being filed with Agent in six months to be forwarded to the War Department, shall be entitled to a quarter section of Land, to be located under the direction of the President, and with his consent the same may be sold and the proceeds applied to some beneficial purpose for the benefit of said orphans.

ARTICLE 20. The U.S. agree and stipulate as follows, that for the benefit and advantage of the Choctaw people, and to improve their condition, there shall be educated under the direction of the President and at the expense of the U.S. forty Choctaw youths for twenty years. This number shall be kept at school, and as they finish their education others, to supply their places shall be received for the period stated. The U.S. agree also to erect a Council House for the Nation at some convenient central point, after their people shall be settled; and a House for each Chief, also a Church for each of the three Districts, to be used also as school houses, until the Nation may conclude to build others; and for these purposes ten thousand dollars shall be appropriated; also fifty thousand dollars (viz.) Twenty-five hundred dollars annually shall be given for the support of three teachers of schools for twenty years. Likewise there shall be furnished to the Nation, three Blacksmiths one for each district for sixteen years, and a qualified Mill Wright for five years; Also there shall be furnished the following articles, twenty-one hundred blankets, to each warrior who emigrates a rifle, moulds, wipers and ammunition. One thousand axes, ploughs, hoes, wheels and cards each; and four hundred looms. There shall also be furnished, one ton of iron and two hundred weight of steel annually to each District for sixteen years.

ARTICLE 21. A few Choctaw Warriors yet survived who marched and fought in the army with General Wayne, the whole number stated not to exceed twenty. These it is agreed shall hereafter, while they live receive twenty-five dollars a year; a list of them to be early as practicable, and within six months, made out, and presented to the Agent, to be forwarded to the War Department.

ARTICLE 22. The Chiefs of the Choctaws who have suggested that their people are in a state of rapid advancement in education and refinement, and have expressed a solicitude that they might have the privilege of a Delegate on the floor of the House of Representatives extended to them. The Commissioners do not feel that they can under a treaty stipulation accede to the request, but at their desire, present it in the Treaty, that Congress may consider of, and decide the application.

(Signed by one hundred and seventy-two chiefs, headmen, and warriors, including Greenwood LeFlore, Mushulatubbee, and Nitaketchie.)

SUPPLEMENTARY ARTICLES TO THE PRECEDING TREATY

Various Choctaw persons have been presented by the Chiefs of the nation, with a desire that they might be provided for. Being particularly deserving, and earnestness has been manifested that provision night be made for them. It is therefore by the undersigned commissioners here assented to, with the understanding that they are to have no interest in the reservations which are directed and provided for under the general Treaty to which this is a supplement. As evidence of the liberal and kind feelings of the President and Government of the United States the Commissioners agree to the request as follows, (to wit) Pierre Juzan, Peter Pitchlynn, G. W. Harkins, Jack Pitchlynn, Israel Fulsom, Louis Laflore, Benjamin James, Joel H. Nail, Hopoynjahubbee, Onorkubbee, Benjamin Laflore, Michael Laflore, and Allen Yates and wife shall be entitled to a reservation of two sections of land each to include their improvement where they at present reside, with the exception of the three first named persons and Benjamin Laflore, who are authorized to locate one of their sections on any other unimproved and unoccupied land, within their respective districts.

ARTICLE 2. And to each of the following persons there is allowed a reservation of a section and a half of land, (to wit) James L. McDonald, Robert Jones, Noah Wall, James Campbell, G. Nelson, Vaughn Brashears, R. Harris, Little Leader, S. Foster, J. Vaughn, L. Durans, Samuel Long, T. Magagha, Thos. Everge, Giles Thompson, Thomas Garland, John Bond, William Laflore, and Turner Brashears, the two first named persons, may locate one section each, and one section jointly on any unimproved and unoccupied land, these not residing in the Nation; The others are to include their present residence and improvement.

Also one section is allowed to the following persons (to wit) Middleton Mackey, Wesley Train, Choclehomo, Moses Foster, D. W. Wall, Charles Scott, Molly Nail, Susan Colbert, who was formerly Susan James, Samuel Garland, Silas Fisher, D. McCurtain, Oklahoma, and Polly Fillecuthey, to be located in entire sections to include their present residence and improvement, with the exception of Molly Nail and Susan Colbert, who are authorized to locate theirs, on any unimproved unoccupied land.

John Pitchlynn has long and faithfully served the nation in character of U. States Interpreter, he has acted as such for forty years, in consideration it is agreed, in addition to what has been done for him there shall be granted to two of his children, (to wit) Silas Pitchlynn, and Thomas Pitchlynn one section of land each, to adjoin the location of their father; likewise to James Madison and Peter sons of Mushulatubbee one section of land each to include the old house and improvement where their father formerly lived on the old military road adjoining a large Prarie. And to Henry Groves son of the Chief Natticache there is one section of land given to adjoin his father's land.

And to each of the following persons half a section of land is granted on any unoccupied and unimproved lands in the Districts where they respectively live (to wit) Willis Harkins, James D. Hamilton, William Juzan, Tobias Laflore, Jo Doke, Jacob Fulsom, P. Hays, Samuel Worcester, George Hunter, William Train, Robert Nail and Alexander McKee.

And there is given a quarter section of land each to Delila and her five father-less children, she being a Choctaw woman residing out of the nation; also the same quantity to Peggy Trihan, another Indian woman residing out of the nation and her two fatherless children; and to the widows of Pushmilaha, and Pucktshenubbee, who were formerly distinguished Chiefs of the nation and for their children four quarter sections of land, each in trust for themselves and their children.

All of said last mentioned reservations are to be located under and by direc-tion of the president of the U. States.

ARTICLE 3. The Choctaw people now that they have ceded their lands are so-licitous to get to their new homes early as possible and accordingly they wish that a party may be permitted to proceed this fall to ascertain whereabouts will be most advantageous for their people to be located.

It is therefore agreed that three or four persons (from each of the three dis-tricts) under the guidance of some discreet and well qualified person or per-sons may proceed during this fall to the West upon an examination of the country.

For their time and expenses the U. States agree to allow the said twelve per-sons two dollars a day each, not to exceed one hundred days, which is deemed to be ample time to make an examination. If necessary, pilots acquainted with the country will be furnished when they arrive in the West.

ARTICLE 4. John Donly of Alabama who has several Choctaw grand children, and who for twenty years has carried the mail through the Choctaw Nation, a desire by the Chiefs is expressed that he may have a section of land, it is accordingly granted, to be located in one entire section, on any unimproved and unoccupied land. Allen Glover and George S. Gaines licensed Traders in the Choctaw Nation, have accounts amounting to upwards of nine thousand dollars against the Indians who are unable to pay their said debts without distressing their families; a desire is expressed by the Chiefs that two sections of land be set apart to be sold and the proceeds thereof to be applied toward the payment of the aforesaid debts. It is agreed that two sections of any unimproved and unoccupied land be granted to George S. Gaines who will sell the same for the best price he can obtain and apply the proceeds thereof to the credit of the Indians on their accounts due to the before mentioned Glover and Gaines; and shall make the application the poorest Indian first.

At the earnest and particular request of the Chief Greenwood Laflore there is granted to David Haley one half section of land to be located in a half section on any unoccupied and unimproved land as a compensation, for a journey to Washington City with dispatches to the Government and returning others to the Choctaw Nation.

(Signed by seventeen chiefs, headmen, and warriors, including Greenwood LeFlore, Mushulatubbee, and Nitaketchie.)

Treaty of Dancing Rabbit Creek with the Choctaw, September 27, 1830. In *Indian Affairs: Laws and Treaties*. Vol. 2, *Treaties*, comp. and ed. Charles J. Kappler, LL. M., Clerk to the Senate Committee on Indian Affairs. Washington, D.C.: Government Printing Office, 1904. http://www.felihkatub be.com/ChoctawNation/treaties/rabbit_creek_1830.htm.

TREATY WITH THE CHICKASAW, OCTOBER 20, 1832 (TREATY OF PONTOTOC CREEK)

A rticles of a treaty made and entered into between Genl. John Coffee, being duly authorized thereto, by the President of the United States, and the whole Chickasaw Nation, in General Council assembled, at the council House, on Pontitock Creek on the twentieth day of October, 1832.

THE Chickasaw Nation find themselves oppressed in their present situation; by being made subject to the laws of the States in which they reside. Being ignorant of the language and laws of the white man, they cannot understand or obey them. Rather than submit to this great evil, they prefer to seek a home in the west, where they may live and be governed by their own laws. And believing that they can procure for themselves a home, in a country suited to their wants and condition, provided they had the means to contract and pay for the same, they have determined to sell their country and hunt a new home. The President has heard the complaints of the Chickasaws, and like them believes they cannot be happy, and prosper as a nation, in their present situation and condition, and being desirous to relieve them from the great calamity that seems to await them, if they remain as they are—He has sent his Commissioner Genl. John Coffee, who has met the whole Chickasaw nation in Council, and after mature deliberation, they have entered into the following articles, which shall be binding on both parties, when the same shall be ratified by the President of the United States by and with the advice and consent of the Senate.

ARTICLE 1. For the consideration hereinafter expressed, the Chickasaw nation do hereby cede, to the United States, all the land which they own on the east side of the Mississippi river, including all the country where they at present live and occupy.

ARTICLE 2. The United States agree to have the whole country thus ceded, surveyed, as soon as it can be conveniently done, in the same manner that the public lands of the United States are surveyed in the States of Mississippi and Alabama, and as soon thereafter as may be practicable, to have the same prepared for sale. The President of the United States will then offer the land for sale at public auction, in the same manner and on the same terms and conditions as the other public lands, and such of the land as may not sell at the public sales shall be offered at private sale, in the same manner that other private sales are made of the United States lands.

ARTICLE 3. As a full compensation to the Chickasaw nation, for the country thus ceded, the United States agree to pay over to the Chickasaw nation, all the money arising from the sale of the land which may be received from time to time, after deducting therefrom the whole cost and expenses of surveying and selling the land, including every expense attending the same.

ARTICLE 4. The President being determined that the Chickasaw people shall not deprive themselves of a comfortable home, in the country where they now are, until they shall have provided a country in the west to remove to, and settle on, with fair prospects of future comfort and happiness—It is therefore agreed to, by the Chickasaw nation, that they will endeavor as soon as it may be in their power, after the ratification of this treaty, to hunt out and procure a home for their people, west of the Mississippi river, suited to their wants and condition; and they will continue to do so during the progress of the survey of their present country, as is provided for in the second article of this treaty. But should they fail to procure such a country to remove to and settle on, previous to the first public sale of their country here then and in that event, they are to select out of the surveys, a comfortable settlement for every family in the Chickasaw nation, to include their present improvements, if the land is good for cultivation, and if not they may take it in any other place in the nation, which is unoccupied by any other person. Such settlement must be taken by sections. And there shall be allotted to each family as follows (to wit): To a single man who is twenty-one years of age, one section—to each family of five and under that number two sections—to each family of six and not exceeding ten, three sections, and to each family over ten in number, four sections—and to families who own slaves, there shall be allowed, one section to those who own ten or upwards and such as own under ten, there shall be allowed half a section. If any person shall now occupy two places and wish to retain both, they may do so, by taking a part at one place, and a part at the other, and where two or more persons are now living on the same section, the oldest occupant will be entitled to remain, and the others must move off to some other place if so required by the oldest occupant. All of which tracts of land, so selected and retained, shall be held, and occupied by the Chickasaw people, uninterrupted until they shall find and obtain a country suited to their wants and condition. And the United States will guaranty to the Chickasaw nation, the quiet possession and uninterrupted use of the said reserved tracts of land, so long as they may live on and occupy the same. And when they shall determine to remove from said tracts of land, the Chickasaw nation will notify the President of the United States of their determination to remove, and thereupon as soon as the Chickasaw people shall remove, the President will proclaim the said reserved tracts of land for sale at public auction and at private sale, on the same terms and conditions, as is provided for in the second article of this treaty, to sell the same, and the net proceeds thereof, to be paid to the Chickasaw nation, as is provided for in the third article of this treaty.

ARTICLE 5. If any of the Chickasaw families shall have made valuable improvements on the places where they lived and removed from, on the reservation tracts, the same shall be valued by some discreet person to be appointed by the President, who shall assess the real cash value of all such improvements, and also the real cash value of all the land within their improvements, which they may have cleared and actually cultivated, at least one year in good farming order and condition. And such valuation of the improvements and the value of the cultivated lands as before mentioned, shall be paid to the person who shall have made the same. To be paid out of the proceeds of the sales of the ceded lands. The person who shall value such land and improvements, shall give to the owner thereof, a certificate of the valuation, which shall be a good voucher for them to draw the money on, from the proper person, who shall be appointed to pay the same, and the money shall be paid, as soon as may be convenient, after the valuation, to enable the owner thereof to provide for their families on their journey to their new homes. The provisions of this article are intended to encourage industry and to enable the Chickasaws to move comfortably. But lest the good intended may be abused, by designing persons, by hiring hands and clearing more land, than they otherwise would do for the benefit of their families—It is determined that no payment shall be made for improved lands, over and above one-eighth part of the tract allowed and reserved for such person to live on and occupy.

ARTICLE 6. The Chickasaw nation cannot receive any part of the payment for their land until it shall be surveyed and sold; therefore, in order to greater facilitate, in surveying and preparing the land for sale, and for keeping the business of the nation separate and apart from the business and accounts of the United States, it is proposed by the Chickasaws, and agreed to, that a Surveyor General be appointed by the President, by and with the advice and consent of the Senate, to superintend alone the surveying of this ceded country or so much thereof as the President may direct, who shall appoint a sufficient number of deputy surveyors, as may be necessary to complete the survey, in as short a time as may be reasonable and expedient. That the said Surveyor General be allowed one good clerk, and one good draftsman to aid and assist him in the business of his office, in preparing the lands for sale. It is also agreed that one land office be established for the sale of the lands, to have one Register and one Receiver of monies, to be appointed by the President, by and with the advice and consent of the senate, and each Register and Receiver to have one good clerk to aid and assist them in the duties of their office. The Surveyor's office, and the office of the Register and Receiver of money, shall be kept somewhere central in the nation, at such place as the President of the United States may direct. As the before mentioned officers, and clerks, are to be employed entirely in business of the nation, appertaining to preparing and selling the land, they will of course be paid out of the proceeds of the sales of the ceded lands. That the Chickasaws, may now understand as near as may be, the expenses that will be incurred in the transacting of this business—It is proposed and agreed to, that the salary of the Surveyor General be fifteen hundred dollars a year, and that the Register and Receiver of monies, be allowed twelve hundred dollars a year each, as a full compensation for their services, and all expenses, except stationary and postages on their official business, and that each of the clerks and draftsman be allowed seven hundred and fifty dollars a year, for their services and all expenses.

ARTICLE 7. It is expressly agreed that the United States shall not grant any right of preference, to any person, or right of occupancy in any manner whatsoever, but in all cases, of either public or private sale, they are to sell the land to the highest bidder, and also that none of the lands be sold in smaller tracts than quarter sections or fractional sections of the same size as near as may be, until the Chickasaw nation may require the President to sell in smaller tracts. The Chiefs of the nation have heard that at some of the sales of the United States lands, the people there present, entered into combinations, and united in purchasing much of the land, at reduced prices, for their own benefit, to the great prejudice of the Government, and they express fears, that attempts will be made to cheat them, in the same manner when their lands shall be offered at public auction. It is therefore agreed that the President will use his best endeavors to prevent such combinations, or any other plan or state of things which may tend to prevent the land selling for its full value.

ARTICLE 8. As the Chickasaws have determined to sell their country, it is desirable that the nation realize the greatest possible sum for their lands, which can be obtained. It is therefore proposed and agreed to that after the President shall have offered their lands for sale and shall have sold all that will sell for the Government price, then the price shall be reduced, so as to induce purchasers to buy, who would not take the land at the Government minimum price;—and it is believed, that five years from and after the date of the first sale, will dispose of all the lands, that will sell at the Government price. If then at the expiration of five years, as before mentioned, the Chickasaw nation may request the President to sell at such reduced price as the nation may then propose, it shall be the duty of the President to comply with their request, by first offering it at public and afterwards at private sale, as in all other cases of selling public lands.

ARTICLE 9. The Chickasaw nation express their ignorance, and incapacity to live, and be happy under the State laws, they cannot read and understand them, and therefore they will always need a friend to advise and direct them. And fearing at some day the Government of the United States may withdraw from them, the agent under whose instructions they have lived so long and happy—They therefore request that the agent may be continued with them, while here, and wherever they may remove to and settle. It is the earnest wish of the United States Government to see the Chickasaw nation prosper and be happy, and so far as is consistent they will contribute all in their power to render them so—therefore their request is granted. There shall be an agent kept with the Chickasaws as heretofore, so long as they live within the jurisdiction of the United States as a nation, either within the limits of the States where they now reside, or at any other place. And whenever the office of agent shall be vacant, and an agent to be appointed, the President will pay due respect to the wishes of the nation in selecting a man in all respects qualified to discharge the responsible duties of that office.

ARTICLE 10. Whenever the Chickasaw nation shall determine to remove from, and leave their present country, they will give the President of the

United States timely notice of such intention, and the President will furnish them the necessary funds, and means for their transportation and journey, and for one year's provisions, after they reach their new homes, in such quantity as the nation may require, and the full amount of such funds, transportation and provisions, is to be paid for, out of the proceeds of the sales of the ceded lands. And should the Chickasaw nation remove, from their present country, before they receive money, from the sale of the lands, hereby ceded; then and in that case, the United States shall furnish them any reasonable sum of money for national purposes, which may be deemed proper by the President of the United States, which sum shall also be refunded out of the sales of the ceded lands.

ARTICLE 11. The Chickasaw nation have determined to create a perpetual fund, for the use of the nation forever, out of the proceeds of the country now ceded away. And for that purpose they propose to invest a large proportion of the money arising from the sale of the land, in some safe and valuable stocks which will bring them in an annual interest or dividend, to be used for all national purposes, leaving the principal untouched, intending to use the interest alone. It is therefore proposed by the Chickasaws, and agreed to, that the sum to be laid out in stocks as above mentioned, shall be left with the government of the United States, until it can be laid out under the direction of the President of the United States, by and with the advice and consent of the Senate, in such safe and valuable stock as he may approve of, for the use and benefit of the Chickasaw nation. The sum thus to be invested, shall be equal to, at least three-fourths of the whole net proceeds of the sales of the lands; and as much more, as the nation may determine, if there shall be a surplus after supplying all the national wants. But it is hereby provided, that if the reasonable wants of the nation shall require more than one fourth of the proceeds of the sales of the land, then they may, by the consent of the President and Senate, draw from the government such sum as may be thought reasonable, for valuable national purposes, out of the three-fourths reserved to be laid out in stocks. But if any of the monies shall be thus drawn out of the sum first proposed, to be laid out on interest, the sum shall be replaced, out of the first monies of the nation, which may come into the possession of the United States government, from the sale of the ceded lands, over and above the reasonable wants of the nation. At the expiration of fifty years from this date, if the Chickasaw nation shall have improved in education and civilization, and become so enlightened, as to be capable of managing so large a sum of money to advantage, and with safety, for the benefit of the nation, and the

President of the United States, with the Senate, shall be satisfied thereof, at that time, and shall give their consent thereto, the Chickasaw nation may then withdraw the whole, or any part of the fund now set apart, to be laid out in stocks, or at interest, and dispose of the same, in any manner that they may think proper at that time, for the use and benefit of the whole nation; but no part of said fund shall ever be used for any other purpose, than the benefit of the whole Chickasaw nation. In order to facilitate the survey and sale of the lands now ceded, and to raise the money therefrom as soon as possible, for the foregoing purpose, the President of the United States is authorized to commence the survey of the land as soon as may be practicable, after the ratification of this treaty.

ARTICLE 12. Chickasaws feel grateful to their old chiefs for their long and faithful services, in attending to the business of the nation. They believe it a duty, to keep them from want in their old and declining age—with those feelings, they have looked upon their old and beloved chief Tish-o-mingo, who is now grown old, and is poor and not able to live, in that comfort, which his valuable life and great merit deserve. It is therefore determined to give him out of the national funds, one hundred dollars a year during the balance of his life, and the nation request him to receive it, as a token of their kind feelings for him, on account of his long and valuable services.

Our old and beloved Queen Puc-caun-la, is now very old and very poor. Justice says the nation ought not to let her suffer in her old age; it is therefore determined to give her out of the national funds, fifty dollars a year during her life, the money to be put in the hands of the agent to be laid out for her support, under his direction, with the advice of the chiefs.

ARTICLE 13. The boundary line between the lands of the Chickasaws and Choctaws, has never been run, or properly defined, and as the Choctaws have sold their country to the United States, they now have no interest in the decision of that question. It is therefore agreed to call on the old Choctaw chiefs, to determine the line to be run, between the Chickasaws and their former country. The Chickasaws, by a treaty made with the United States at Franklin in Tennessee, in Aug. 31, 1830, declared their line to run as follows, to wit: Beginning at the mouth of Oak tibby-haw and running up said stream to a point, being a marked tree, on the old Natches road, one mile southwardly from Wall's old place. Thence with the Choctaw boundary, and along it, westwardly through the Tunicha old fields, to a point on the Mississippi river, about twenty-eight miles by water below where the St. Francis river enter said stream on the west side. It is now agreed, that the surveys of the Choctaw country which are now in progress, shall not cross the line until the true line shall be decided and determined; which shall be done as follows, the agent of the Choctaws on the west side of the Mississippi shall call on the old and intelligent chiefs of that nation, and lay before them the line as claimed by the Chickasaws at the Franklin treaty, and if the Choctaws shall determine that line to be correct, then it shall be established and made the permanent line, but if the Choctaws say the line strikes the Mississippi river higher up said stream, then the best evidence which can be had from both nations, shall be taken by the agents of both nations, and submitted to the President of the United States for his decision, and on such evidence, the President will determine the true line on principles of strict justice.

ARTICLE 14. As soon as the surveys are made, it shall be the duty of the chiefs, with the advice and assistance of the agent to cause a correct list to be made out of all and every tract of land, which shall be reserved, for the use and benefit of the Chickasaw people, for their residence, as is provided for in the fourth article of this treaty, which list, will designate the sections of land, which are set apart for each family or individual in the nation, shewing the precise tracts which shall belong to each and every one of them, which list shall be returned to the register of the land office, and he shall make a record of the same, in his office, to prevent him from offering any of said tracts of land for sale, and also as evidence of each person's lands. All the residue of the lands will be offered by the President for sale.

ARTICLE 15. The Chickasaws request that no persons be permitted to move in and settle on their country before the land is sold. It is therefore agreed, that no person, whatsoever, who is not Chickasaw or connected with the Chickasaws by marriage, shall be permitted to come into the country and settle on any part of the ceded lands until they shall be offered for sale, and then there shall not be any person permitted to settle on any of the land, which has not been sold, at the time of such settlement, and in all cases of a person settling on any of the ceded lands contrary to this express understanding, they will be intruders, and must be treated as such, and put off of the lands of the nation.

In witness of all and every thing herein determined, between the United States and the whole Chickasaw nation in general council assembled, the parties have hereunto set their hands and seals, at the council-house, on Pontitock creek, in the Chickasaw nation, on the twentieth day of October, one thousand eight hundred and thirty-two.

(Signed by sixty-five chiefs, headmen, and warriors, including King Ishtehotopa, Tishomingo, Levi Colbert, George Colbert, William McGillivray, Samuel Seeley, Toopulaco, Isaac Albertson, and Emmubbee.)

Treaty with the Chickasaw, 1832. In *Indian Affairs: Laws and Treaties.* Vol. 2, *Treaties,* comp. and ed. Charles J. Kappler, 356–362. Washington, D.C.: Government Printing Office, 1904. Online, Oklahoma State University Library, http://digital.library.okstate.edu/KAPPLER/Vol2/treaties/chio356.htm#mn1.

TREATY WITH THE CHICKASAW, OCTOBER 22, 1832 (SUPPLEMENTARY ARTICLES TO THE TREATY OF PONTOTOC CREEK)

Articles supplementary to, and explanatory of, a treaty which was entered into on the 20th instant, between General John Coffee on the part of the United States, and the whole Chickasaw nation in General Council assembled.

THE fourth article of the treaty to which this is a supplement, provides that each Chickasaw family, shall have a tract of land, reserved for the use of the family, to live on and occupy, so long as the nation resides in the country where they now are. And the fifth article of the treaty provides that each family or individual shall be paid for their improvements, and the value of their cleared lands, when the nation shall determine to remove and leave the said reserved tracts of land. It is now proposed and agreed to, that no family or person of the Chickasaw nation, who shall or may have tracts of land, reserved for their residence while here, shall ever be permitted to lease any of said land, to any person whatsoever, nor shall they be permitted to rent any of said land, to any person, either white, red, or black, or mixed blood of either. As the great object of the nation is to preserve the land, and timber, for the benefit of posterity, provided the nation shall continue to live here, and if they shall at any time determine to remove and sell the land, it will be more valuable, and will sell for more money, for the benefit of the nation, if the land and timber be preserved.

It is also expressly declared by the nation, that, whenever the nation shall determine to remove from their present country, that every tract of land so reserved in the nation, shall be given up and sold for the benefit of the nation. And no individual or family shall have any right to retain any of such reserved tracts of land, for their own use, any longer than the nation may remain in the country where they now are.

As the reserve tracts of land above alluded to, will be the first choice of land in the nation, it is determined that the minimum price of all the reserved tracts, shall be three dollars an acre, until the nation may determine to reduce the price, and then they will notify the President, of their wishes, and the price to which they desire to reduce it.

The chiefs still express fears that combinations may be formed at the public sales, where their reserved tracts of land shall be offered for sale, and that they may not be sold so high as they might be sold, by judicious agents at private sale. They therefore suggest the propriety of the President determining on some judicious mode of selling the reserves at private sale.

It is therefore agreed that the suggestion be submitted to the President, and if he and the Chiefs can agree on a plan of a sale, different from the one proposed in the treaty, to which this is a supplement, and which shall be approved of by both parties, then they may enter into such agreement and the President shall then be governed by the same, in the sale of the reserved tracts of land, whenever they may be offered for sale.

In the provisions of the fourth article of the treaty to which this is a supplement, for reserves to young men who have no families, it expresses that each young man, who is twenty-one years of age, shall have a reserve. But as the Indians mature earlier than white men, and generally marry younger, it is determined to extend a reserve, to each young man who is seventeen years of age. And as there are some orphan girls in the nation or whose families do not provide for them, and also some widows in the same situation, it is determined to allow to each of them a reservation of one section, on the same terms and conditions in all respects, with the other reservations for the nation generally, and to be allowed to the same ages, as to young men.

Colbert Moore and family have always lived in the Chickasaw nation, and he requests the liberty to continue with the nation. The Chiefs and nation agree to his request, and they also agree to allow him and his family a reserve tract of land to live on and occupy in the same manner, and on the same terms and conditions as is provided for the Chickasaw families, in the nation generally, during his good behavior.

The Chiefs of the nation represent that they in behalf of the nation gave a bond to James Colbert for a debt due to him, of eighteen hundred and eleven dollars, ninety-three and three fourth cents principal, that James Colbert transferred said note to Robert Gordon and that said note, and the interest thereon is yet due and unpaid, and the said Robert Gordon has proposed to take a section of land for said note, and interest up to this date. It is therefore agreed by the nation to grant him a section of land, to be taken any where in the nation, so as not to interfere with any reserve which has been provided as a residence for the Chickasaws, which shall be in full for said note and interest.

The Treaty, to which this is a supplement provides that there shall be offices kept some where central in the nation, at such place as the President shall determine, for transacting the business of the nation in selling their lands &c. It is now agreed to by the nation, that the President may select a section of land, or four quarter sections adjoining, at such place as he may determine agreeably to that provision of the Treaty, to establish the said offices on, and for all the necessary uses thereto attached, and he is permitted to improve the said tract of land in any manner, whatsoever, but when it shall cease to be used for the purposes, for which it is set apart—for offices &c.—then the same shall be sold under the direction of the President—and the proceeds thereof shall be paid to the Chickasaw nation, after deducting therefrom the value of all the improvements on the land, which value shall be assessed by the President, and in no case shall it exceed one half the sale of the land.

The Chickasaw nation request the government to grant them a cross mail route through the nation as follows, one to pass from Tuscumbia in Alabama, by the Agency, and by the place to be selected for the offices to be kept and to Rankin in Mississippi on horse back, once a week each way. The other to run from Memphis in Tennessee, by the offices and to the Cotton Gin in Mississippi—to pass once a week each way. They conceive these mails would be useful to the nation, and indispensable to the carrying on the business of the nation when the offices are established, but they would respectfully solicit the mails to be started as soon as possible, to open the avenues of information into their country.

John Donley has long been known in this nation as a mail carrier; he rode on the mails through our nation when a boy and for many years after he was grown; we think he understands that business as well, if not better than any other man—and we should prefer him to carry our mails to any other person—and if he is given the contract, the nation will set apart a section of land for his use while we remain here in this country, which section he may select with the advice of the Chiefs any where that suits him best, so as not to interfere with any of the reserves, and he may use it in any manner to live on, or make such improvements as may be necessary for keeping his horses, or to raise forage for them. But when the nation shall move away and leave this country this tract of land must be sold for the benefit of the nation, in the same manner that the reserve tracts are sold &c. and he is not to claim of the nation any pay for improving said tract of land.

In witness of all and every thing herein determined between the United States and the whole Chickasaw nation, in general council assembled, the parties have hereunto set their hands and seals at the council house, on Pontitock creek, in the Chickasaw nation, on this twenty-second day of October one thousand eight hundred and thirty

(Signed by the same chiefs who signed the October 20, 1832, treaty.)

Treaty with the Chickasaw, 1832. In *Indian Affairs: Laws and Treaties*. Vol. 2, *Treaties*, comp. and ed. Charles J. Kappler, 362–364. Washington, D.C.: Government Printing Office, 1904. Online, Oklahoma State University Library, http://digital.library.okstate.edu/kappler/Vol2/treaties/chio362.htm.

NOTES

INTRODUCTION

1. Barnett, *Natchez Indians: A History*, xv, 41–44; Lorenz, "Re-Examination of Natchez Sociopolitical Complexity," 97–112; Lorenz, "Natchez of Southwest Mississippi," 158–163; Smith, "Aboriginal Population Movements," 18–19.

2. Gallay, *Indian Slave Trade*; Galloway, *Choctaw Genesis*, 352–360.

3. See Galloway, "Dearth and Bias," for insight into the use of historical materials.

4. Mississippi Band of Choctaw Indians Miko Beasley Denson, "Tribal Profile."

5. As genealogical expressions, the terms "mixed blood" and "full blood" have nothing to do with the actual mixing of human blood. Nevertheless, the ancient concept of blood quantum, expressed as the percentage of one's ethnic ancestry, lives on in twenty-first-century federal laws addressing the rights of American Indians and is used by some modern tribes to determine membership. Livesay, "Understanding the History of Tribal Enrollment"; Wheeler-Howard Act, Article 19. For a discussion of universal blood groups and world populations, see Sykes, *Seven Daughters of Eve*, 33–34, 46–47.

6. O'Brien, *Choctaws in a Revolutionary Age*, 77; Oswalt and Neely, *This Land Was Theirs*, 42–43; Waselkov, *Conquering Spirit*, 12–14; Wright, *Creeks and Seminoles*, 60–62.

7. McWilliams, *Iberville's Gulf Journals*, 47; Martin et al., "Synonymy," 595; Mooney, *Siouan Tribes of the East*, 14–15.

8. Galloway, "Concha," 178.

9. Galloway, "Choctaw Names and Choctaw Roles," 207, 216.

10. Galloway, "Confederacy as a Solution," 393, 395, 399; Galloway and Kidwell, "Choctaw in the East," 499; Swanton, *Source Material*, 55–56.

11. Galloway, *Choctaw Genesis*, 358; Galloway, "Confederacy as a Solution," 399; Swanton, *Source Material*, 56.

12. Brightman and Wallace, "Chickasaw," 478.

13. Galloway and Jackson, "Natchez and Neighboring Groups," 598; Martin, "Languages," 83; McWilliams, *Iberville's Gulf Journals*, 122; McWilliams, *Pénicaut Narrative*, 147; Swanton, *Indian Tribes of the Lower Mississippi Valley*, 181–182, 272.

14. Brain, *Tunica Archaeology*, 284; Galloway et al., "Yazoo," 190; McWilliams, *Iberville's Gulf Journals*, 73; Swanton, *Indian Tribes of the Lower Mississippi Valley*, 307–310, 332–333.

15. Brain et al., "Tunica, Biloxi, and Ofo," 586; Swanton, *Indian Tribes of the Lower Mississippi Valley*, Plate 18a.

16. Jeter, "Shatter Zone Shock Waves," 369–371.

17. Demaillie, "Tutelo and Neighboring Groups," 286, 288; Ethridge, "Introduction," 29–30; Martin, "Languages," 77–78; Mooney, *Siouan Tribes of the East*, 9–10, 12–13.

18. De Reuse, "Biloxi and Ofo," 594–595; Galloway and Goddard, "Ouispé," 183–184; Martin et al., "Synonymy," 596; Swanton, *Indian Tribes of North America*, 235, 273, 314.

19. Campisi, "Houma," 632; Goddard et al., "Small Tribes," 174; Galloway, "Currency of Language," 239–240; Lankford, "Chacato," 664; Martin, "Languages," 81; McWilliams, *Pénicaut Narrative*, 81, 126.

20. Gregory, "Survival and Maintenance," 655.

CHAPTER 1

1. Cross et al., *Atlas of Mississippi*, 3–7, 20–21, 81–84.

2. Prehistoric cultural periods in Mississippi prior to the introduction of pottery are dated according to Samuel O. McGahey's projectile point sequence. McGahey, *Mississippi Projectile Point Guide*.

3. McGahey, *Mississippi Projectile Point Guide*, 1.

4. McGahey, *Mississippi Projectile Point Guide*, 3.

5. The "fluted design" refers to channels or grooves produced by removing large flakes from each face of the flint blade (biface). The flutes extend from the base and usually run halfway or two-thirds the way up the length of the blade.

6. McGahey, *Mississippi Projectile Point Guide*, 1. Most of the Clovis points in McGahey's database were gathered by private collectors.

7. "Chert" is a term for a type of sedimentary rock that includes flint, jasper, chalcedony, and agate. Because chert produces a predictable cone-shaped fracture when struck with a hard object and holds a sharp edge, it served as a preferred raw material for making many types of prehistoric stone tools, including spear and arrow points, knives, and scrapers. The terms "chert" and "flint" are sometimes used interchangeably. Bureau of Economic Geology, University of Texas at Austin, http://www.beg.utexas.edu/mainweb/publications/graphics/chert.htm.

8. McGahey, *Mississippi Projectile Point Guide*, 1–14. McGahey's early Clovis types are I–III and Cumberland.

9. McGahey, *Mississippi Projectile Point Guide*, 1; Jeter and Williams, "Lithic Horizons and Early Cultures," 72; Bense, *Archaeology of the Southeastern United States*, 38–39. Eastern U.S. sites with possible pre-Clovis components include the Meadowcroft rock shelter in Pennsylvania and the Page-Ladson and Little Salt Springs sites in Florida. Anderson et al., "Environmental and Chronological Considerations," 8–9. More recently, the Topper site in South Carolina has been identified as a pre-Clovis location. Carey Geiger, personal communication October 16, 2007.

10. Anderson et al., "Environmental and Chronological Considerations," Figure 1.1; Saucier, *Geologic History of the Lower Mississippi Valley*, 246.

11. Fickle, *Mississippi Forests and Forestry*, 6–7.

12. McGahey, "Paleoindian and Early Archaic Data," 357–361.

13. McGahey, "Paleoindian and Early Archaic Data," Figure 18.6.

14. The Pleistocene epoch, spanning the period from approximately 2.5 million years ago to 12,000 years ago (10,000 B.C.), is the geological time period that immediately precedes the Holocene (modern) epoch. Saucier, *Geologic History of the Lower Mississippi Valley*, 41, Figures 3 and 4.

15. McGahey, *Mississippi Projectile Point Guide*, 2.

16. Anderson et al., "Environmental and Chronological Considerations," 3–4; John Connaway, personal communication February 13, 2008.

17. Quimby, "Locus of the Natchez Pelvis," 77–79. The bone, in the vertebrate biology collection at the Academy of Natural Sciences in Philadelphia, is radiocarbon dated to 5,580 Å 80 B.P. Anonymous, "Natchez Man Gets Younger," 1662. The Natchez Pelvis was first described in 1846 by M. W. Dickeson. Manning and Bograd, *Annotated Bibliography of the Geology of Mississippi*, 62, 69.

18. Anderson and Sassaman, "Early and Middle Holocene Periods," 87.

19. Anderson et al., "Environmental and Chronological Considerations," 6–7.

20. John Connaway, personal communication February 13, 2008; McGahey, *Mississippi Projectile Point Guide*, 1, Figures 3 and 8; McGahey, "Paleoindian and Early Archaic Data," 381–382.

21. McGahey, "Paleoindian and Early Archaic Data," 365, 368–369.

22. McGahey, *Mississippi Projectile Point Guide*, 11–26.

23. McGahey, *Mississippi Projectile Point Guide*, 41; McGahey, "Paleoindian and Early Archaic Data," 354; Brookes, *Hester Site*.

24. McGahey, *Mississippi Projectile Point Guide*, 26–33.

25. Anderson and Sassaman, "Paleoindian and Early Archaic Research in the South Carolina Area," 229; Broster and Norton, "Recent Paleoindian Research in Tennessee," 294; Futato, "Synopsis of Paleoindian and Early Archaic Research," 308, 310, 312, 313; Dunbar and Webb, "Bone and Ivory Tools," 352; McGahey, "Paleoindian and Early Archaic Data," 367, 371–374, 377, 381; Morse, "Arkansas View," 425–429.

26. McGahey, *Mississippi Projectile Point Guide*, 41.

27. Brookes, *Hester Site*, 30.

28. McGahey, "Paleoindian and Early Archaic Data," 374.

29. Brookes, *Hester Site*, Table 4. Brookes has assigned functional labels to the stone tools from the Hester site, while conceding that many of these objects probably served multiple purposes.

30. Brookes, *Hester Site*, 32–41, 47–50. Brookes points out that the Hester site adzes are similar to the Dalton adzes from northeastern Arkansas; however, the Hester adzes were found in post-Dalton context.

31. McGahey, "Paleoindian and Early Archaic Data," 373.

32. Brookes, *Hester Site*, 13–14.

33. McGahey, *Mississippi Projectile Point Guide*, 41.

34. McGahey, "Paleoindian and Early Archaic Data," 373.

35. Anderson and Sassaman, "Early and Middle Holocene Periods," 91–92.

36. McGahey, *Mississippi Projectile Point Guide*, Figures 27, 43, 69, and 77.

37. Saucier, "Geological Analysis," 99.

38. Saucier, *Geologic History of the Lower Mississippi Valley*, 247, Plate 28, Sheets 2–3.

39. McGahey's dates for this period are used here, since he focuses on Mississippi. McGahey, *Mississippi Projectile Point Guide*, 88. For some examples of alternate dates for the Middle Archaic/Hypsithermal in the Southeast, see Anderson and Sassaman, "Early and Middle Holocene Periods," 94; Jeter and Williams, "Lithic Horizons and Early Cultures," 85. The Hypsithermal was a worldwide climatic event. Anderson and Sassaman, "Early and Middle Holocene Periods," 94.

40. Anderson and Sassaman, "Early and Middle Holocene Periods," 94, 96, 98; Jeter and Williams, "Lithic Horizons and Early Cultures," 85–86.

41. McGahey, *Mississippi Projectile Point Guide*, 87.

42. McGahey, *Mississippi Projectile Point Guide*, 87.

43. McGahey, *Mississippi Projectile Point Guide*, 87–88.

44. Saucier, *Geologic History of the Lower Mississippi Valley*, 99.

45. Saucier, *Geologic History of the Lower Mississippi Valley*, 188–191, 194–195.

46. Saucier, *Geologic History of the Lower Mississippi Valley*, 264; Saucier, "Geological Analysis," 99.

47. Crawford, *Archaic Effigy Beads*, 16, 90–91, Tables 1 and 3; John Connaway, personal communications June 29, 2007, and February 13, 2008; McGahey, "Prehistoric Stone Bead Manufacture," 3–4, 16–17.

48. Connaway, *Denton Site*, ix, 1, 6, 137–138.

49. Anderson and Sassaman, "Early and Middle Holocene Periods," 99–100; Connaway, *Archaeological Investigations in Mississippi*, 7–8. Early use of squash (*Cucurbita sp.*) has been noted in southern Illinois (ca. 7,000 B.P.) and Florida (ca. 7,300 B.P.). Jeter and Williams, "Lithic Horizons and Early Cultures," 85–86.

50. Connaway, *Denton Site*, 4.

51. Middens are trash accumulations, sometimes deposited in pits and sometimes piled up to form mounds.

52. Anderson and Sassaman, "Early and Middle Holocene Periods," 94; Claassen, "New Hypotheses," 66, 67.

53. Peacock, "Shellfish Use," 444.

54. Anderson and Sassaman, "Early and Middle Holocene Periods," 95; Jeter and Williams, "Lithic Horizons and Early Cultures," 93–94.

55. Peacock et al., "Confirmation of an Archaic Period Mound," 355–368.

56. Anderson and Sassaman, "Early and Middle Holocene Periods," 95; Jeter and Williams, "Lithic Horizons and Early Cultures," 95–96.

57. Sam Brookes notes a scarcity of archaeological sites in Mississippi dating to the period between ca. 3,000 and ca. 1,700 B.C., representing a mysterious 1,300-year "hiatus." Sam Brookes, personal communication May 14, 2008.

58. Sassaman and Anderson, "Late Holocene Period," 101, 103. Numerous shell midden sites have been recorded in the Yazoo Basin, some of which may date to the Late Archaic. Evan Peacock, personal communication July 3, 2007. See Phillips, *Archaeological Survey in the Lower Yazoo Basin*.

59. Bense, *Archaeology of the Southeastern United States*, 91, 94.

60. Claassen, "New Hypotheses," 69, 71. Claassen also speculates, based upon ethnographic analogy, that the mussels may have been valued for fish bait and not for food. Claassen, "New Hypotheses," 69.

61. Sassaman and Anderson, "Late Holocene Period," 109.

62. Saucier, *Geologic History of the Lower Mississippi Valley*, 248, Plate 28, Sheet 3; Bense, *Archaeology of the Southeastern United States*, 85. Sea level stabilization and occupation of the Gulf Coast marks the beginning of the archaeological period called Gulf Formational. Brown, "Prehistory of the Gulf Coastal Plain," 574.

63. Bruseth, *Poverty Point Development*, 9, 11, 14, 21.

64. Webb, "Poverty Point Culture and Site," 3.

65. Gibson, "Swamp Exchange," 57–63.

66. Webb, *Poverty Point Culture*, 68–73.

67. Webb, *Poverty Point Culture*, 12, 58–60.

68. Gibson, "Swamp Exchange," 58–59.

69. Gibson, "Swamp Exchange," 58.

70. Gibson, "Swamp Exchange," 61–63.

71. The Yazoo River follows a former channel of the Mississippi River. Wasp Lake is part of the Bear Creek Meander Belt, a distributary of the Mississippi River created during the period of activity of Saucier's Stage 4 meander belt of the Mississippi River. Saucier, *Geologic History of the Lower Mississippi Valley*, 258–259, Plate 8.

72. Lehmann, *Jaketown Site*, 4.

73. Arco, "Geoarchaeology of the Buried Poverty Point," 1, 2, 4, 5–6, 8; Ford et al., *Jaketown Site*, 13–14, 117; Lehmann, *Jaketown Site*, 11; Saunders, "Jaketown"; Webb, *Poverty Point Culture*, Table 18.

74. Webb, *Poverty Point Culture*, Figure 3.

75. Brookes, "Prehistoric Exchange in Mississippi," 89–90, 94.

76. Jackson, "Bottomland Resources and Exploitation Strategies," 133, 134–138, 148, 149.

77. Connaway et al., *Teoc Creek*, 32–33, 118

78. Sassaman and Anderson, "Late Holocene Period," 100, 103, 105, 111; Jeter and Williams, "Lithic Horizons and Early Cultures," 96, 106.

79. Sassaman and Anderson, "Late Holocene Period," 100; Bense, *Archaeology of the Southeastern United States*, 64.

80. Connaway et al., *Teoc Creek*, 81–87; Webb, *Poverty Point Culture*, 45.

81. Webb, *Poverty Point Culture*, 44–45.

82. Webb, *Poverty Point Culture*, 4.

83. "Fiber tempering" refers to mixing plant fibers with the clay. Tempering raw clay by mixing in various materials helps to reduce the contraction and expansion of the clay during the crucial firing process. Temper also allows heat to be more evenly distributed through the clay during firing, all of which helps prevent cracking. *ArchNet.*

84. Webb, *Poverty Point Culture*, Table 18.

85. Jackson et al., "Woodland Cultural and Chronological Trends," 239; Jenkins, "Wheeler Series," 48.

86. The sequence of Woodland and Mississippian cultural periods is based largely upon changes in the way pottery was manufactured through time. In Mississippi, the evolution of pottery styles followed different trends in different parts of the state. The cultural periods in the Mississippi River valley were never in sync with developments in the Tombigbee River valley, and both regions were out of step with the Gulf Coast. Therefore, my dates for ceramic cultural periods represent "ballpark" time periods that roughly fit what was going on across the state. My dates for ceramic-using cultures are based on Brown, "Prehistory of the Gulf Coastal Plain," 574, 576; Kidder, "Woodland Period Archaeology," Figure 4.2; Rafferty, "Woodland Period Settlement Patterning," Figure 10.2.

87. Phillips, *Archaeological Survey in the Lower Yazoo Basin*, 876.

88. Phillips, *Archaeological Survey in the Lower Yazoo Basin*, 37–38.

89. Rafferty, "Woodland Period Settlement Patterning," 212. The use of fabric-impressed decorations in this area is diagnostic of the local Miller I period. Rafferty, "Woodland Period Settlement Patterning," 212.

90. Phillips, *Archaeological Survey in the Lower Yazoo Basin*, 162–165.

91. John Connaway, personal communication February 13, 2008.

92. Phillips, *Archaeological Survey in the Lower Yazoo Basin*, 16, 77, 174–175. The decorative technique using cord impressions was achieved by wrapping knotted string or cord around a paddle. Futato, "Continuity and Change," 42.

93. Blitz and Mann, *Fisherfolk*, 98; Brown, "Prehistory of the Gulf Coastal Plain," 574; Brookes and Taylor, "Tchula Period Ceramics," 23–27; Fields, "Contributions," 106, 109–110; Jackson et al., "Woodland Cultural and Chronological Trends," 241; Marshall, *Report on Archaeological Test Excavations*, 62–63; Toth, *Early Marksville Phases*, 23, 25; Weinstein, "Tchefuncte Occupation," 107.

94. Rafferty, "Woodland Period Settlement Patterning," 207.

95. Kidder, "Woodland Period Archaeology," 72.

96. Toth, *Early Marksville Phases*, 26. John Connaway notes the presence of clay cooking balls in Tchula sites in the northern Yazoo Basin. John Connaway, personal communication February 13, 2008.

97. Kidder, "Woodland Period Archaeology," 69.

98. Toth, *Early Marksville Phases*, 21; Brown, "Prehistory of the Gulf Coastal Plain," 576. The Early Archaic in the Lower Mississippi Valley is called the Tchula period. Griffin, "Tchula Period in the Mississippi Valley," 40–42; Wilkins, *Tchula Period in the Natchez Bluffs*, 15, 43–49.

99. Marshall, *Survey and Excavation*, 54.

100. Saucier, *Geologic History of the Lower Mississippi Valley*, 266, Plate 28, Sheet 3.

101. Olsen, "Appendix," 69; Toth, *Early Marksville Phases*, 26; Kidder, "Woodland Period Archaeology," 71.

102. Jeffries, "Regional Cultures," 117.

103. Rafferty, "Woodland Period Settlement Patterning," 220–224.

104. Rafferty, "Woodland Period Settlement Patterning," 220–224; Brown, "Prehistory of the Gulf Coastal Plain," 574.

105. Johnson et al., *Excavations at the Batesville Mounds*, 36, 86, 89, 90, 91, 94.

106. Jeter and Williams, "Lithic Horizons and Early Cultures," 80–81, 100; Jeter and Williams, "Ceramic-Using Cultures," 114, 122, 126.

107. Jeffries, "Regional Cultures," 117; Kidder, "Woodland Period Archaeology," 71–72.

108. Jeffries, "Regional Cultures," 118; Anderson and Mainfort, "Introduction," 6–8.

109. Toth, *Early Marksville Phases*, 44.

110. Hally and Mainfort, "Prehistory of the Eastern Interior," 270–271; Brown, "Prehistory of the Gulf Coastal Plain," 576–577; McNutt, "Central Mississippi Valley," 209; Toth, *Early Marksville Phases*, 29; Reilly and Garber, "Introduction," 1–2.

111. Jeter and Williams, "Ceramic-Using Cultures," 132.

112. Hally and Mainfort, "Prehistory of the Eastern Interior," 269; Brown, "Prehistory of the Gulf Coastal Plain," 580–581.

113. Bense, *Archaeology of the Southeastern United States*, 140–141.

114. Kidder, "Prehistory of the Lower Mississippi Valley," Figure 4.2, 551.

115. Gibson and Shenkel, "Louisiana Earthworks," 14–15; Kidder, "Prehistory of the Lower Mississippi Valley," 549; Toth, *Early Marksville Phases*, 42, 45. The "stamping" decorative technique is achieved by repeatedly pressing a sharp-edged implement such as a stick or bone in the clay surface. A variation known as "rocker-stamping" is made by rocking the implement back and forth in the clay. Brown, *Decorated Pottery of the Lower Mississippi Valley*, 35.

116. Jeter and Williams, "Ceramic-Using Cultures," Figure 13; Kidder, "Prehistory of the Lower Mississippi Valley," 549–550; Phillips, *Archaeological Survey in the Lower Yazoo Basin*, 67–69, 78–81.

117. Futato, "Continuity and Change," 42–47. Hally and Mainfort, "Prehistory of the Eastern Interior," 269; Mainfort, "Pinson Mounds," 132–146; Rafferty, "Woodland Period Settlement Patterning," 222–224. Futato notes that the stamped decorative technique on Copena ceramics is

derived from earlier cord-impressed decoration by replacing cord-wrapped paddles with carved paddles. The carved-paddle treatment is known as "check stamping." Futato, "Continuity and Change," 42–44. Ian Brown defines check stamping as "[a vessel] surface impressed with a waffle grid pattern . . . of different sizes and shapes, represent[ing] in negative form designs carved in wooden or clay paddles." Brown, *Southeastern Check Stamped Pottery Tradition*, 9.

118. Peacock, "Excavations at Stinking Water," 6.

119. Blitz, "McRae Mound," 16–17.

120. Brown, "Prehistory of the Gulf Coastal Plain," 576–578.

121. Blitz and Mann, *Fisherfolk*, 98; Thunen, "Geometric Enclosures in the Mid-South," 98–115; Williams, *Archaeological Excavations*.

122. Brookes, *Grand Gulf Mound*.

123. Brown, "Prehistory of the Gulf Coastal Plain," 577–578, 581; Johnson, "Woodland Settlement in Northeastern Mississippi," 57–59; Kidder, "Woodland Period Archaeology of the Lower Mississippi Valley," Figure 4.1, 74–75.

124. Brown, "Prehistory of the Gulf Coastal Plain," 581; Connaway, *Archaeological Investigations in Mississippi*, 16; Faulkner, "Middle Woodland Community and Settlement Patterns," 94; Jeffries, "Regional Cultures," 122; Kidder, "Prehistory of the Lower Mississippi Valley," 549–550; Wynn and Atkinson, *Archaeology of the Okashua and Self Sites*.

125. McGahey, *Mississippi Projectile Point Guide*, 136–197.

126. McGahey, *Mississippi Projectile Point Guide*, 187–205.

127. Rafferty, "Woodland Period Settlement Patterning," 226–227; Jeffries, "Regional Cultures," 125; Samuel Brookes, personal communication May 14, 2008; John Connaway, personal communication February 13, 2008.

128. Kidder, "Woodland Period Archaeology of the Lower Mississippi Valley," 80; Kidder, "Prehistory of the Lower Mississippi Valley," 552.

129. Brown, "Prehistory of the Gulf Coastal Plain," 578; Jackson et al., "Woodland Cultural and Chronological Trends," 245; Jeter and Williams, "Ceramic-Using Cultures," 152–154.

130. Jackson et al., "Woodland Cultural and Chronological Trends," 245; Rafferty, "Woodland Period Settlement Patterning," 212.

131. Rafferty, "Woodland Period Settlement Patterning," Figures 10.3–6, 217.

132. Rafferty, "Woodland Period Settlement Patterning," 225.

133. Brown, "Prehistory of the Gulf Coastal Plain," 580–581.

134. Galinat, "Domestication and Diffusion of Maize," 245–278.

135. Asch and Asch, "Prehistoric Plant Cultivation," 196–199; Galinat, "Domestication and Diffusion of Maize," 269, 277, Figure 8.7; Hudson, *Southeastern Indians*, 292–293, 297; Kniffin et al., *Historic Indian Tribes of Louisiana*, 191–193; Swanton, *Indian Tribes of the Lower Mississippi Valley*, 73–76.

136. Brown, "Prehistory of the Gulf Coastal Plain," 580–581.

137. Williams and Brain, *Excavations at the Lake George Site*, 364–367.

138. Kidder, "Prehistory of the Lower Mississippi Valley," 553–554.

139. Neuman, *Introduction to Louisiana Archaeology*, 170–172.

140. Jeter and Williams, "Ceramic-Using Cultures," Figures 14–16; John Connaway, personal communication February 13, 2008.

141. Williams and Brain, *Excavations at the Lake George Site*, 317–319, 371–373.

142. Kidder, "Prehistory of the Lower Mississippi Valley," 554–555; Williams and Brain, *Excavations at the Lake George Site*, 405.

143. Brown and Brain, "Archaeology of the Natchez Bluff Region," 5–7.

144. Kidder, "Prehistory of the Lower Mississippi Valley," 555; Williams and Brain, *Excavations at the Lake George Site*, 407–407.

145. Brain, *Winterville*, 14.

146. Blitz and Mann, *Fisherfolk*, 99.

147. Brain, *Winterville*, 108.

148. Kidder, "Prehistory of the Lower Mississippi Valley," 554.

149. Brown, "Prehistory of the Gulf Coastal Plain," 581; Connaway, *Archaeological Investigations in Mississippi*, 23–24, 27–31; Kidder, "Prehistory of the Lower Mississippi Valley," 555; Rafferty, "Woodland Period Settlement Patterning," 226.

150. Jeter and Williams, "Ceramic-Using Cultures," Figure 16, 160; Knight and Steponaitis, "New History of Moundville," 11; Williams, "Paleoethnobotany of the Feltus Mounds Site," 19–41. For readers who are unaccustomed to the admittedly confusing jargon of southeastern archaeology, the final prehistoric time period is called "Mississippi," while the cultural expression of the period (pottery, stone tools, arrow points, mound building, and so forth) is termed "Mississippian."

151. Bense, *Archaeology of the Southeastern United States*, 195–198, 251–253.

152. Anderson, "Role of Cahokia," 248; Emerson, *Cahokia*, 44–46, 59–60; Pauketat and Emerson, "Introduction," 5–6, Figure 1.3.

153. Knight and Steponaitis, "New History of Moundville," 1–15, Figure 1.2; Schoeninger and Schurr, "Human Subsistence at Moundville," 121.

154. Galloway, *Choctaw Genesis*, 39. More information about corn agriculture is presented in chapter 3.

155. Lolly, "Archaeology at the Lyon's Bluff Site"; Rafferty, *Owl Creek Mounds*, Figure 4, 4, 100, 126–132.

156. Knight and Steponaitis, "New History of Moundville," 2–4, 15.

157. Galloway, *Choctaw Genesis*, 59; Peebles, "Foreword," xvi.

158. John Connaway, personal communication February 13, 2008.

159. John Connaway, personal communication February 13, 2008.

160. Winterville is situated on a natural levee associated with Saucier's Stage 1 Mississippi River channel. Saucier, *Geologic History of the Lower Mississippi Valley*, Plate 8.

161. Brain, *Winterville*, 11–14.

162. Philip Phillips, James A. Ford, and James B. Griffin founded the Lower Mississippi Survey (LMS) in 1939. Through the 1980s the LMS was based at Harvard University's Peabody Museum. Along with Brain, other LMS archaeologists include Stephen Williams, Ian W. Brown, Vincas P. Steponaitis, John S. Belmont, David J. Hally, and Tristram R. Kidder. See Williams, "Introduction to 2003 Edition."

163. Brain, *Winterville*, 27, 108, 110–111.

164. Jackson, "Excavations at Winterville."

165. Williams and Brain, *Excavations at the Lake George Site*.

166. McNutt, "Summary," 225–226.

167. Brown, *Decorated Pottery of the Lower Mississippi Valley*.

168. Saucier, *Geologic History of the Lower Mississippi Valley*, 267, Plate 10.

169. Brown, *Excavations at the Anna Site*, 3–6.

170. Brown, *Excavations at the Anna Site*, 4; Brain, "Late Prehistoric Settlement Patterning," 352; Steponaitis, "Late Prehistory of the Natchez Region," 16–22, 27–30, 53, 79–87.

171. Brain, "Late Prehistoric Settlement Patterning," Table 12.2.

172. Connaway, *Archaeological Investigations in Mississippi*, 9–11, 37–40, 41–44, 45–49, 51–55.

173. Connaway, *Wilsford Site*, 93–94, Figure 6.

174. Brown, "Plaquemine Culture Structure Types," 52–70.

175. Calibrated 2_ mean. Connaway, *Fishweirs*, Table 6.2.

176. McGahey, "Compendium of Mississippi Dugout Canoes," 59–60. Since its discovery, the Homochitto River canoe has remained in private ownership, although staff from the Mississippi Department of Archives and History (MDAH) were permitted to examine it and take samples for radiocarbon dating. At this writing, its whereabouts are unknown.

177. McGahey, "Compendium of Mississippi Dugout Canoes," 60–70.

178. Range of calibrated 2_ mean dates. Connaway, *Fishweirs*, 91.

179. Range of calibrated 2_ mean dates. Connaway, *Fishweirs*, 101.

180. Connaway, *Fishweirs*, 77–102.

181. Brown, "Introduction to the Bottle Creek Site," 1, 2, 3–7, Figures 1.1 and 1.2; Scarry, "Food Plant Remains," 107–110, 113, Table 5.5; Quitmyer, "Zooarchaeological Remains," 130–155.

182. Hudson, "Introduction," 1–9; Milanich, "Origins and Prehistoric Distributions of Black Drink," 83–119; Scarry, "Use of Plants," Tables 6.1 and 6.2.

183. Fuller, "Origin and Evolution of Pensacola Culture," 61–62.

184. I. Brown, personal communication June 7, 2007.

185. Blitz and Mann, *Fisherfolk*, 103–104.

186. Widmer, "Structure of Southeastern Chiefdoms," 137–139.

187. Bense, *Archaeology of the Southeastern United States*, 192; Steponaitis, "Location Theory and Complex Chiefdoms," 420.

188. Widmer, "Structure of Southeastern Chiefdoms," 126–127.

189. Galloway, *Choctaw Genesis*, 69–70.

190. Widmer, "Structure of Southeastern Chiefdoms," 127.

191. Swanton, *Indian Tribes of the Lower Mississippi Valley*, 100–108.

192. Widmer, "Structure of Southeastern Chiefdoms," 133.

193. Depratter, "Chiefdom of Cofitachequi," 199; Kelly, "Woodland Period Archaeology in the American Bottom," 156–158.

194. Scarry, "Late Prehistoric Southeast," 30.

195. Brown, "Sequencing the Braden Style," 242; Emerson, "Water, Serpents, and the Underworld," 45–92; Galloway, *Choctaw Genesis*, 136, 282; Lankford, "Great Serpent," 108–109; Lankford, "'Path of Souls,'" 175; Larson, "Etowah Site," 133–141; Muller, "Southern Cult," 11–26; Peterson, "Spiro Mounds Site," 114–121; Reilly, "Petaloid Motif," 39–40; Reilly and Garber, "Introduction," 1–5; Strong, "Mississippian Bird-Man," 211–238; Williams and Brain, *Excavations at the Lake George Site*, 380–381, 417–419.

196. Galloway, "Confederacy as a Solution," 395–396, 401.

197. Bense, *Archaeology of the Southeastern United States*, 201–202; Brose, "From the Southeastern Ceremonial Complex to the Southern Cult," 30, 32; Galloway, *Choctaw Genesis*, 69–70.

198. Kelton, *Epidemics and Enslavement*, 6–12.

199. Galloway, *Choctaw Genesis*, 71; Galloway, "Colonial Period Transformations," 230–231; Fagan, *Little Ice Age*.

200. Bense, *Archaeology of the Southeastern United States*, 243, 246–248, 253; Jeter, "From Prehistory through Protohistory," 197–219.

201. Galloway, *Choctaw Genesis*, 63–66; Knight and Steponaitis, "New History of Moundville," 21–24.

202. Galloway, *Choctaw Genesis*, 64, 142, 288–290.

203. Brown, "Concluding Thoughts," 221–222.

204. Brain, "Late Prehistoric Settlement Patterning," 350–354.

CHAPTER 2

1. Brain, "Late Prehistoric Settlement Patterning," 354–356; Galloway, *Choctaw Genesis*, 67, 73.

2. Bell and Galloway, "Minet," 29–68; Foster, *La Salle Expedition*.

3. Galloway, *Choctaw Genesis*, 27–163; Jeter, "From Prehistory," 177–223; Kelton, *Epidemics and Enslavement*; Kidder, "Prehistory of the Lower Mississippi Valley," 559; Smith, "Aboriginal Depopulation," 257–275.

4. Galloway, *Choctaw Genesis*, 78–80; Kelton, *Epidemics and Enslavement*, 52; Saunt, "History until 1776," 128.

5. Kelton, *Epidemics and Enslavement*, 52.

6. Galloway, *Choctaw Genesis*, 82–85; Hoffman, "Narváez," 63; Saunt, "History until 1776," 128; Smith, "Aboriginal Depopulation," 258.

7. Hoffman, "Hernando De Soto," 421–459.

8. Hudson, *Knights of Spain*, 7–11.

9. Galloway, *Choctaw Genesis*, 111. I refer to De Soto's men as "Spaniards" as a matter of convenience; the expedition included other nationalities, such as Portuguese and Italians.

10. Of the five known narratives of the De Soto expedition, four describe the expedition's adventures in Mississippi. These are the narratives of Luys Hernández de Biedma, The Gentleman from Elvas (anonymous), Rodrigo Rangel, and Garcilaso de la Vega. Rangel's narrative does not cover the activities of the expedition in 1542 and 1543. The fifth narrative is a very brief abstract of a lost account of the expedition by a priest named Sebastián de Cañete, which does not provide any information about the events of interest here. English translations of all of the De Soto narratives are available in Clayton et al., *De Soto Chronicles*.

11. Hudson, "Hernando De Soto Expedition," 78.

12. Clayton et al., *De Soto Chronicles*.

13. Galloway, *Choctaw Genesis*, 129; Hudson, *Knights of Spain*, 243–244.

14. Hudson, *Knights of Spain*, 247–248, 256.

15. Galloway, *Choctaw Genesis* 23, 353, Figure 3.4; Robertson, "Elvas," 105; Worth, "Rangel," 294–296. Because the word *"pafalaya"* is similar to the Choctaw word for long hair and because the Choctaws were sometimes called Long Hair, the ethnohistorian John R. Swanton and others have speculated that these people were one of the groups that eventually became part of the Choctaw confederacy in the seventeenth century. Swanton, *Indians of the Southeastern United States*, 121.

16. Hudson, *Knights of Spain*, 259–260; Morgan, *Mississippi De Soto Trail*, 1–9. Archaeologist Robbie Ethridge has argued that the Chicaza polity was organized as a chiefdom instead of an egalitarian big-man society. Ethridge, *From Chicaza to Chickasaw*, 3.

17. Galloway, "Chakchiuma," 496; Hudson, *Knights of Spain*, 250–267; Robertson, "Elvas," 105–107; Worth, "Rangel," 297. The Saquechuma (or Sacchuma) village was probably located somewhere between the Noxubee and Tombigbee rivers in present-day northern Noxubee County or southern Lowndes County. Ethridge, *From Chicaza to Chickasaw*, 77.

18. Hudson, *Knights of Spain*, 267–269; Robertson, "Elvas," 106–109.

19. May, "Alabama and Koasati," 407; Robertson, "Elvas," 204n.

20. Robertson, "Elvas," 110.

21. Hudson, *Knights of Spain*, 272–274; Robertson, "Elvas," 109–110. According to Robbie Ethridge, the Alibamo villages were north of Line Creek in northeast Mississippi (northern Clay County, southern Chickasaw County, southwestern Monroe County). Elements of this group later moved to present-day central Alabama to become part of the eighteenth-century Alabama confederacy. Ethridge, *From Chicaza to Chickasaw*, 75.

22. Galloway, *Choctaw Genesis*, 122.

23. Morgan, *Mississippi De Soto Trail*, 1–9, Figure 7.

24. Hudson, *Knights of Spain*, 274–278.

25. Shelby and Bost, "Florida," 385–386.

26. Robertson, "Elvas," 111–112; Worth, "Biedma," 238; Worth, "Rangel," 299.

27. Robertson, "Elvas," 112; Shelby and Bost, "Florida," 385; Worth, "Rangel," 271n.

28. Hudson, "Hernando De Soto Expedition," 91.

29. Robertson, "Elvas," 112–113.

30. Robertson, "Elvas," 113; Worth, "Biedma," 238; Worth, "Rangel," 300.

31. Brain, *Tunica Archaeology*, 22–25, 273, 292.

32. Jeter, "From Prehistory through Protohistory," 205–207, 211–213.

33. Brown, "Culture Contact," 375–379.

34. Robertson, "Elvas," 132–134; Shelby and Bost, "Florida," 443–446.

35. Robertson, "Elvas," 134.

36. Hudson, "Hernando De Soto Expedition," 94–98.

37. Worth, "Biedma," 245; Robertson, "Elvas," 151–153.

38. Robertson, "Elvas," 153–154; Worth, "Biedma," 245.

39. Robertson, "Elvas," 155, 156; Shelby and Bost, "Florida," 503; Worth, "Biedma," 245.

40. Hudson, "Hernando De Soto Expedition," 99; Robertson, "Elvas," 157–158; Shelby and Bost, "Florida," 507, 509, 518; Worth, "Biedma," 245. According to Elvas, Chief Quigualtam's men turned their war canoes around at noon on July 5 and headed back upriver, while the forces of a second (unnamed) chiefdom took up the pursuit. However, both Biedma and Garcilaso indicate that Quigualtam's warriors pursued the Spaniards the entire way. Robertson, "Elvas," 158; Shelby and Bost, "Florida," 518; Worth, "Biedma," 245. If a second chiefdom entered the chase in a sort of tag-team strategy, this second chiefdom must have been part of Quigualtam's hegemony.

41. Barnett, *Natchez Indians*, 14–16.

42. Swanton, *Final Report*, 54. For a discussion of Swanton's Natchezan place-names in southeast Arkansas, see Jeter, "From Prehistory through Protohistory," 206–213.

43. Hudson, "Hernando De Soto Expedition," Figure 1.

44. Brain, *Tunica Archaeology*, Figure 201.

45. Brain, "Late Prehistoric Settlement Patterning," 338, 340–343, 349.

46. Brain, "Late Prehistoric Settlement Patterning," 338, 340–343, 349, 356–358; Brain, "Introduction," xl–xlvi; Brain, *Winterville*; I. Brown, personal communication July 31, 2006; Brown, *Excavations at the Anna Site*, 4; Hally, *Plaquemine and Mississippian Occupations*, 347, 480, 533, 536, 580–586, 602; Jackson, "Excavations at Winterville"; Jeter, "From Prehistory through Protohistory," 211–213; Steponaitis et al., *LMS Archives Online*, December 27, 2004, and August 22, 2006, 24-M-1 pages 1–4, 24-M-2 pages 1–33, 22-M-5 page 2; Williams and Brain, *Excavations at the Lake George Site*.

47. Galloway, *Choctaw Genesis*, 143–160.

48. Kelton, "Great Southeastern Smallpox Epidemic," 21; Saunt, "History until 1776," 128; Scarry, "Late Prehistoric Southeast," 26; Smith, "Aboriginal Depopulation," 258.

49. Galloway, *Choctaw Genesis*, 78–80; Kelton, "Great Southeastern Smallpox Epidemic," 22; Saunt, "History until 1776," 128; Smith, "Aboriginal Depopulation," 258.

50. Galloway, *Choctaw Genesis*, 140–143; Kelton, "Great Southeastern Smallpox Epidemic," 21–25.

51. Kelton, *Epidemics and Enslavement*; Mann, *1491*, 96, 102; Saunt, "History until 1776," 128.

52. Galloway, *Choctaw Genesis*, 131–132, 143–160.

53. Kelton, *Epidemics and Enslavement*, 30, 35, 49–50, 56, 61–62, 90, 222.

54. Galloway, *Choctaw Genesis*, 131–134; Kelton, *Epidemics and Enslavement*, 58–59, 66, 77.

55. Galloway, *Choctaw Genesis*, 133–134, Table 4.3; Hudson, *Knights of Spain*, 72–78; Mann, *1491*, 107–110, 176.

56. Smith, "Aboriginal Depopulation," 270.

57. Hudson, *Knights of Spain*, 386, 387; Smith, "Aboriginal Depopulation," 264.

58. Galloway, *Choctaw Genesis*, 143–160.

59. Kelton, *Epidemics and Enslavement*, xxii, 1, 42, 50, 101–159.

60. Brain, "Late Prehistoric Settlement Patterning," 354–356.

61. Galloway, *Choctaw Genesis*, 138–140; Ramenofsky, "Death by Disease," 47–49.

62. Galloway, *Choctaw Genesis*, Figures 8.1 and 8.3; Swanton, *Indian Tribes of the Lower Mississippi Valley*, 44–45, 186–191, 258, 302, 304, 307, 327, 332, Plate 1.

63. Gallay, *Indian Slave Trade*, 102–105; Jeter, "From Prehistory through Protohistory," 188–190; Jeter, "Shatter Zone Shock Waves," 372–374; Swanton, *Indian Tribes of North America*, 213–214. Some archaeologists consider the Quapaws to be among the possible descendants of the Cahokia chiefdom. Pauketat and Emerson, "Introduction," 24.

64. Foster, "Nicolas de La Salle Journal," 98–103.

65. Gallay, *Indian Slave Trade*, 105–110; McWilliams, *Iberville's Gulf Journals*, 46–48. See Brown, "Calumet Ceremony."

66. Foster, "Nicolas de La Salle Journal," 105–107.

67. Unfortunately for historians, the expedition's two chroniclers, Tonti and Nicolas de La Salle, remained at the riverside camp and did not visit the Natchez chief with their leader; therefore, we have no written account of this momentous encounter.

68. Barnett, *Natchez Indians: A History*, 23–26, 40–41; Foster, "Nicolas de La Salle Journal," 108.

69. Foster, "Nicolas de La Salle Journal," 108–109; Swanton, *Indian Tribes of the Lower Mississippi Valley*, 327–328.

70. Foster, "Nicolas de La Salle Journal," 112, 117–118, 120–121; Swanton, *Indian Tribes of the Lower Mississippi Valley*, 328.

71. Foster, "Nicolas de La Salle Journal," 112–114.

72. Foster, "Nicolas de La Salle Journal," 103, 105, 112–114, 117–118.

73. Foster, "Nicolas de La Salle Journal," 103, 107, 123. The Mosopelea, a Siouan-speaking group, were first documented in southwestern Ohio. In the Lower Mississippi Valley, they were more commonly known as the Ofogoula (or Ofo) and were longtime allies of the French. Swanton, *Indian Tribes of North America*, 235, 273, 314.

74. Foster, *La Salle Expedition*, xiii–xiv, 10, 29, 39; Foster, "Nicolas de La Salle Journal," 102.

75. Bell and Galloway, "Minet," 52n, 60.

CHAPTER 3

1. Rowland and Sanders, *Vol. 2*, 86, 153.

2. Nairne, *Muskhogean Journals*, 47–48.

3. Gallay, *Indian Slave Trade*, 311.

4. Atkinson, *Splendid Land, Splendid People*, 25; Crane, *Southern Frontier*, 46; Gallay, *Indian Slave Trade*, 103.

5. Gallay, *Indian Slave Trade*, 41.

6. Crane, *Southern Frontier*, 67.

7. Nairne, *Muskhogean Journals*, 43.

8. Nairne, *Muskhogean Journals*, 41–44.

9. Crane, *Southern Frontier*, 133–135, 134n, 135n; McDowell, *Colonial Records 1750–1754*, 509–514.

10. Bowne, *Westo Indians*, 37; Ethridge, "Introduction," 29–30; Fox, "Events as Seen from the North," 64, 74; Myers, "From Refugees to Slave Traders," 83–84.

11. Bowne, "Caryinge aweay their Corne and Children," 105; Ethridge, *From Chicaza to Chickasaw*, 102; Gallay, *Indian Slave Trade*, 41, 56, 103; Myers, "From Refugees to Slave Traders," 96–97.

12. Ethridge, *From Chicaza to Chickasaw*, 167–168, 256–258; Myers, "From Refugees to Slave Traders," 96–97.

13. Kelton, *Epidemics and Enslavement*.

14. Kelton, *Epidemics and Enslavement*, 50, 143.

15. Kelton, *Epidemics and Enslavement*, 40–42, 107, 147.

16. Barnett, *Natchez Indians: A History*, 40–45; Galloway, *Choctaw Genesis*, 142–143.

17. Kelton, *Epidemics and Enslavement*, 157.

18. Swanton, *Indian Tribes of the Lower Mississippi Valley*, 188–189.

19. Shea, "Letters of J. F. Buisson Saint-Cosme." Both Shea and John R. Swanton assumed that the La Source who accompanied the Seminarian priests that year was the Seminarian Thaumer de La Source, who served in the Illinois country in the 1720s; however, Jeffrey P. Brain points out that it was the lay adult J.-B. La Source who traveled with Davion, Saint-Cosme, and De Montigny during the winter of 1698–1699. Brain, *Tunica Archaeology*, 17.

20. Kelton, *Epidemics and Enslavement*, 143–158; Swanton, *Indian Tribes of the Lower Mississippi Valley*, 308.

21. Swanton, *Indian Tribes of the Lower Mississippi Valley*, 22, 139n, 189.

22. Swanton, *Indian Tribes of the Lower Mississippi Valley*, 39.

23. Brain et al., "Tunica, Biloxi, and Ofo," 586–587; Delanglez, *French Jesuits*, 48; Rowland and Sanders, *Vol. 2*, 346n.

24. Giraud, *Vol. 1*, 9, 55, 57–58.

25. Gallay, *Indian Slave Trade*, 125, 126; Galloway, "Four Ages of Alibamon Mingo," 324; McWilliams, *Iberville's Gulf Journals*, 20n, 45.

26. McWilliams, *Iberville's Gulf Journals*, 45–46, 45n, 67; Swanton, *Indian Tribes of the Lower Mississippi Valley*, 279–281; Waselkov, "Capinan and Moctoby," 176. Members of the Biloxi tribe called themselves Taneks anyadi, which has become garbled into several forms including Istanani, Estananis, Anani, Annochy, and Biloucchy. Lankford, *Cultural Resources Reconnaissance*, 6; Mooney, *Siouan Tribes of the East*, 14–15. Iberville and Bienville were born in New France (Canada). Iberville's reputation as a fighter, made battling the English in King

William's War (1689–1697), earned him the mission to Louisiana in 1699. His younger brother Bienville made his reputation in Louisiana, serving three times as governor of the colony. McWilliams, "Introduction," 1–3; Rowland and Sanders, *Vol. 1*, 193n.

27. Goddard, "Bayogoula," 175–176; Goddard, "Mougoulacha," 181; Goddard, "Quinipissa," 185.

28. McWilliams, *Iberville's Gulf Journals*, 45, 45n; Mooney, *Siouan Tribes of the East*, 18.

29. De Reuse, "Biloxi and Ofo," 593; McWilliams, *Iberville's Gulf Journals*, 92; Waselkov, "Capinan and Moctoby," 176; Waselkov, "Pascagoula," 185;

30. McWilliams, *Iberville's Gulf Journals*, 46.

31. McWilliams, *Iberville's Gulf Journals*, 47–48.

32. McWilliams, *Pénicaut Narrative*, 5, 206; Rowland and Sanders, *Vol. 3*, 535; Rowland, Sanders, and Galloway, *Vol. 4*, 158n6; Waselkov, "Capinan and Moctoby," 176.

33. Goddard, "Washa, Chawasha, and Yakni-Chito," 188–190; McWilliams, *Iberville's Gulf Journals*, 47n.

34. Goddard, "Bayacchyto," 175; McWilliams, *Iberville's Gulf Journals*, 48n.

35. Pénicaut (sometimes given as Pénicault, Pénicaud, or Pénigault) was a ship's carpenter who lived in the Louisiana colony from 1700 to 1721. His published narrative is an important source of information about the Mississippi tribes during this period. Despite Pénicaut's claim of having accompanied Iberville in 1699, he may not have arrived in Louisiana until Iberville's second voyage in 1700. McWilliams, *Pénicaut Narrative*, xxvii–xxviii, xxxi–xxxii, xxxiv–xxxv.

36. Waselkov, "Pascagoula," 185.

37. McWilliams, *Pénicaut Narrative*, 18–20.

38. Kelton, *Epidemics and Enslavement*, 148; McWilliams, *Iberville's Gulf Journals*, 20, 38; McWilliams, *Pénicaut Narrative*, 10–11.

39. McWilliams, *Iberville's Gulf Journals*, 139–140.

40. Brain, *Tunica Archaeology*, 30–31, 150; McWilliams, *Iberville's Gulf Journals*, 67; Swanton, *Indian Tribes of the Lower Mississippi Valley*, 285.

41. Swanton, *Indian Tribes of the Lower Mississippi Valley*, 285.

42. McWilliams, *Iberville's Gulf Journals*, 67–69.

43. Delanglez, *French Jesuits*, 26–29; Kelton, *Epidemics and Enslavement*, 156; McWilliams, *Iberville's Gulf Journals*, 119, 122; Swanton, *Indian Tribes of the Lower Mississippi Valley*, 288–289.

44. McWilliams, *Iberville's Gulf Journals*, 71–74.

45. Jeter, "Grigra," 180–181; Jeter and Goddard, "Koroa," 180; Kidder, "Koroa Indians," 1, Figure 2; La Harpe, *Historical Journal*, 36, 201; McWilliams, *Iberville's Gulf Journals*, 147; McWilliams, *Pénicaut Narrative*, 33; Swanton, *Indian Tribes of the Lower Mississippi Valley*, 327, 330.

46. Brain, *Tunica Archaeology*, 284; Galloway et al., "Yazoo," 190; McWilliams, *Iberville's Gulf Journals*, 73; Swanton, *Indian Tribes of the Lower Mississippi Valley*, 332–333.

47. Brain et al., "Tunica, Biloxi, and Ofo," 586–587; Delanglez, *French Jesuits*, 48; Rowland and Sanders, *Vol. 2*, 346n.

48. Brain et al., "Tunica, Biloxi, and Ofo," 586; Jeter, "From Prehistory through Protohistory," 203–206, Figure 2.

49. Swanton, *Indian Tribes of the Lower Mississippi Valley*, 306–307.

50. De Reuse, "Biloxi and Ofo," 594–595; Galloway and Goddard, "Ouispé," 183–184; Martin et al., "Synonymy," 596; Swanton, *Indian Tribes of North America*, 235, 273, 314. With regard to the translation of the term "Ofogoula," Mississippi Choctaw Brantly Willis has indicated that the expression should be rendered into English as "doglike" instead of "dog people," perhaps lessening the offensiveness of the label. Brantly Willis, personal communication April 29, 2011.

NOTES

51. Anonymous [map ca. 1728], *Cours du fleuve Saint-Louis*; Broutin [map 1731], *Carte partic-ulière du cours du fleuve Missisipy*; Franquelin [map 1686], *Amérique*; Jeter and Goddard, "Tiou," 188; McWilliams, *Iberville's Gulf Journals*, 72, 73, 74n, 143; Vincas P. Steponaitis, personal communication April 10, 2008.

52. James R. Atkinson, personal communication November 11, 2008; Galloway, *Choctaw Genesis*, 182, 312; Galloway, "Henri de Tonti," 154–155, Figure 2.

53. Galloway, "Chakchiuma," 496; Swanton, *Indian Tribes of the Lower Mississippi Valley*, 29, 42, 292–293.

54. Swanton, *Indian Tribes of the Lower Mississippi Valley*, 292–293.

55. Galloway, "Chakchiuma," 496.

56. Galloway, "Taposa," 185; Swanton, *Indians of the Southeastern United States*, 190; Swanton, *Indian Tribes of the Lower Mississippi Valley*, 294, 296.

57. Galloway, "Ibitoupa," 185; Swanton, *Indians of the Southeastern United States*, 140–141; Swanton, *Indian Tribes of the Lower Mississippi Valley*, 297.

58. Galloway, "Choula," 185; La Harpe, *Historical Journal*, 201; Rowland and Sanders, *Vol. 1*, 531; Swanton, *Indian Tribes of the Lower Mississippi Valley*, 297.

59. Alternate spellings of Theloel include Challaouelles, Chelouels, Techloel, Théloël, Theloelles, and Thecoél. See Swanton, *Indian Tribes of the Lower Mississippi Valley*, 25, 45; for de-tails of Iberville's 1700 Mississippi expedition, see Swanton, *Indian Tribes of the Lower Mississippi Valley*, 45–46, 190–191, 219, 277, 286–287, 347; McWilliams, *Iberville's Gulf Journals*, 1–3, 49, 67, 114, 124–127.

60. McWilliams, *Iberville's Gulf Journals*, 72–73.

61. McWilliams, *Iberville's Gulf Journals*, 124–126; Swanton, *Indian Tribes of the Lower Mississippi Valley*, 191.

62. McWilliams, *Iberville's Gulf Journals*, 119, 124–126, 133, 137.

63. McWilliams, *Iberville's Gulf Journals*, 72–73.

64. Barnett, *Natchez Indians: A History*, 37–38.

65. Barnett, *Natchez Indians: A History*, 41; McWilliams, *Pénicaut Narrative*, 84–85, 88–89.

66. Galloway and Jackson, "Natchez and Neighboring Groups," 598; Swanton, *Indian Tribes of the Lower Mississippi Valley*, 181–182. A 1723 map by Ignace-François Broutin shows a small group called "Canard" (Duck) located close to the Flour district and probably considered by the French to have been part of that settlement. Broutin [map 1723], *Carte des environs du fort Rosalie aux Natchez*.

67. Barnett, *Natchez Indians: A History*, 40–45; Brain et al., "Tunica, Biloxi, and Ofo," 586; Brown, *Natchez Indian Archaeology*, 12, 190; Galloway and Jackson, "Natchez and Neighboring Groups," 598, 603; Swanton, *Indian Tribes of the Lower Mississippi Valley*, 334–336.

68. See Barnett, *Natchez Indians: A History*.

69. Barnett, "New Building Location," 2–11; Broutin [map 1723], *Carte des environs du fort Rosalie aux Natchez*; Swanton, *Indian Tribes of the Lower Mississippi Valley*, 190–191.

70. Neitzel, *Archaeology of the Fatherland Site*, 16–26, 64–67, Figures 5–7; Neitzel, *Grand Village Revisited*, Figures 7, 8, 13, and 14.

71. Neitzel quotes all of the French accounts of the Natchez temple in his comparison with the building's archaeological remains. Neitzel, *Archaeology of the Fatherland Site*, 67–72, 77. For descriptions of the Taensa and Bayogoula temples, see Swanton, *Indian Tribes of the Lower Mississippi Valley*, 260, 275.

72. O'Neill and Shea, *Charlevoix's Louisiana*, 137–140 [page numbers referenced for Charlevoix follow O'Neill's numbers at the bottom of each page in this edition]; McWilliams, *Pénicaut Narrative*, 90–92; Swanton, *Indian Tribes of the Lower Mississippi Valley*, 59–60.

73. Barnett, "Natchez House Reconstruction"; Brown, *Natchez Indian Archaeology*, Figures 17, 18, 19, 22, 23, and 70; Brown, "Plaquemine Culture Structure Types," 56–57, 60, Figure 11; Neitzel, *Grand Village Revisited*, Figures 7, 8, 13, and 14.

74. Du Pratz, *History of Louisiana* (Claitor's), 24, 119–120, 164–165; Fickle, *Mississippi Forests*, 9–18; Hitchcock, *Manual of the Grasses*, 2:757–759; McWilliams, *Pénicaut Narrative*, 90–92.

75. Swanton, *Indian Tribes of the Lower Mississippi Valley*, 51–57.

76. Du Pratz, *History of Louisiana* (Claitor's), 318–319. Le Page du Pratz's *Histoire de la Louisiane* (three volumes, Paris: De Bure, Delaguette, Lambert 1758) has become the best-known primary source of information about the Natchez Indians. In 1774 an English-language version of the book was printed to acquaint Britons with the country acquired from France in the Treaty of Paris. The English edition has been reprinted twice in the United States: *The History of Louisiana or of the Western Parts of Virginia and Carolina* (Baton Rouge, La.: Claitor's Publishing Division, 1972) and Joseph G. Tregle Jr., ed., *The History of Louisiana or of the Western Parts of Virginia and Carolina* (facsimile reproduction of the 1774 edition; Baton Rouge: published for the Louisiana American Bicentennial Commission by Louisiana State University Press, 1976). These two reprints are a combination of literal translation and passages that merely paraphrase Du Pratz's original French publication. Literal translations of portions of Du Pratz's French-language narrative are provided by John R. Swanton, Gordon Sayre, and Patricia Galloway. Swanton's excerpts are from his 1911 *Indian Tribes of the Lower Mississippi Valley*. Sayre's translation is available at his website dedicated to Le Page du Pratz: http://www.uoregon.edu/~gsayre/LPDP.html. Galloway's translations stem from her work with an original manuscript in the MDAH's collection. Whenever possible, I rely on the literal translations.

77. Barnett, *Natchez Indians: A History*.

78. Du Pratz, *History of Louisiana* (Claitor's), 307.

79. Brain, "Natchez Paradox"; Galloway and Jackson, "Natchez and Neighboring Groups," 602–603; Quimby, "Natchez Social Structure"; Swanton, *Indian Tribes of the Lower Mississippi Valley*, 107; White et al., "Natchez Class and Rank Reconsidered."

80. Galloway and Jackson, "Natchez and Neighboring Groups," 603. Some scholars make distinctions between classes and moieties among southeastern groups. See Urban and Jackson, "Social Organization," 697–700.

81. Robbie Ethridge, personal communication December 25, 2010; Galloway, "Etouchoco," 179; Rowland and Sanders, *Vol. 2*, 9, 9n3; Patricia Galloway has noted a 1700 map by Claude Delisle listing several small tribes—the Minco, Choila, Etouchoco, Tounia, and Movilla (Mobiles)—on the lower Tombigbee River. Galloway, "Choila," 177; Galloway, "Etouchoco," 179.

82. Brown, "Prehistory of the Gulf Coastal Plain," 585; Robertson, "Elvas," 94–104; Shelby and Bost, "Florida," 334–348; Swanton, *Early History of the Creek Indians*, 151, 159, 160; Worth, "Biedma," 232–236; Worth, "Rangel," 290–294.

83. Swanton, *Early History of the Creek Indians*, 159.

84. Lankford, "Chacato," 666; Lankford, *Cultural Resources Reconnaissance*, 34, 35; McWilliams, *Pénicaut Narrative*, 64–65.

85. Crane, *Southern Frontier*, 68–69; La Harpe, *Historical Journal*, 39–40; McWilliams, *Iberville's Gulf Journals*, 133, 172.

86. Galloway, "Henri de Tonti," 149–151, 158–159; McWilliams, *Iberville's Gulf Journals*, 171–175; Tonti, "Extracts from Letters," 167–169.

87. McWilliams, *Iberville's Gulf Journals*, 171–173.

88. Galloway, "Henri de Tonti," 168.

89. Galloway, "Henri de Tonti," 168–169.

90. Adair, *History*, 69–71; Gibson, *Chickasaws*, 7–8; Nairne, *Muskhogean Journals*, 46.

91. Adair, *History*, 71; Swanton, *Chickasaw Society and Religion*, 50.

92. Adair, *History*, 71, 297; Gibson, *Chickasaws*, 7; Romans, *Concise Natural History*, 56; Swanton, *Source Material*, 42, 56, 57, 116, 118–119, 163; Waselkov and Braund, *William Bartram*, 129.

93. Galloway and Kidwell, "Choctaw in the East," 502–503; Romans, *Concise Natural History*, 57; Swanton, *Indians of the Southeastern United States*, 439, 440, 449, 450, 452–453, 455, 456–457, 471, 473, 476; Swanton, *Source Material*, 43–44.

94. Swanton, *Source Material*, 5.

95. Adair, *History*, 220–221; Galloway and Kidwell, "Choctaw in the East," 504; Swanton, *Chickasaw Society and Religion*, 2–8; Swanton, *Indian Tribes of the Lower Mississippi Valley*, 185, 356.

96. Brinton, *Myths of the New World*, 241–242; Swanton, *Indian Tribes of the Lower Mississippi Valley*, 252. "Nanne," usually spelled "Nanih," is the Choctaw word for mound. Byington, *Dictionary of the Choctaw Language*, 277.

97. Adair, *History*, 119, 374, 540n426; Brown, *Archaeology of Mississippi*, 24; Carlton, "Nanih Waiya," 127; Williamson et al., "Act to Return the Nanih Waiya State Park and Mound."

98. Adair, *History*, 282, 354; Galloway, *Choctaw Genesis*, 335–359; Romans, *Concise Natural History*, 47–48.

99. Carlton, "Nanih Waiya," Tables 1–4, 151; Galloway, "Confederacy as a Solution," 393, 395, 399, 413; Galloway, *Choctaw Genesis*, 63–66, 347–352, 355, 357, Figure 9.1; Knight and Steponaitis, "New History of Moundville," 21–24; Rowland, Sanders, and Galloway, *Vol. 5*, 25n3; Swanton, *Indians of the Southeastern United States*, 151, 196.

100. James Atkinson and Jay Johnson advocate a late Mississippi period arrival onto the Black Prairie of people from collapsing chiefdoms to the east along the Black Warrior River. Atkinson, *Splendid Land, Splendid People*, 6–7; Johnson, "Chickasaws," 88–89. In contrast, Janet Rafferty and Evan Peacock point to archaeological evidence of continuity of settlements in the Black Prairie dating from the Woodland period through the Mississippi period. Evan Peacock, personal communication April 6, 2011; Rafferty and Peacock, "Spread of Shell Tempering," 255, 258.

101. Atkinson, *Splendid Land, Splendid People*, 130; Johnson, "Chickasaws," 88–92, Figure 4.1.

102. Adair, *History*, 397–398, 407; Brightman and Wallace, "Chickasaw," 483; Gibson, *Chickasaws*, 27, 28; Rowland and Sanders, *Vol. 1*, 93; Romans, *Concise Natural History*, 50, 56; Swanton, *Indians of the Southeastern United States*, 400–401; Swanton, *Source Material*, 37–40.

103. Galloway and Kidwell, "Choctaw in the East," Table 2; Usner, *American Indians in the Lower Mississippi Valley*, Table 1.

104. Swanton documented 115 Choctaw village names, but in some cases more than one name may refer to the same place, while some village names denote hamlets that were part of a larger village. Swanton, *Source Material*, 59–75, 95. Spellings for Choctaw town or village names are far from uniform in the colonial sources and in recent scholarly publications. For example, the name of the historically prominent community located near the headwaters of Ponta and Lost Horse

creeks in Lauderdale County is presented by different writers as Kusha, Kunshak, and Concha, all variations on *kuni*, one of the Choctaw words for cane. Blitz, *Archaeological Study*, Map 6; Byington, *Dictionary of the Choctaw Language*, 404; Galloway, "Choctaw Factionalism," 80, 81; O'Brien, *Pre-removal Choctaw History*, x.

105. Adair, quoted by Swanton, *Source Material*, 166.

106. For an early French assessment of the divisions partitioning the Choctaw confederacy and slightly different division names in Choctaw and translations thereof, see Régis du Roullet's 1732 journal of his diplomatic mission, which lists a western part called Goula Falaya (Friends of the Great Band), an eastern part called Goula Tennap (Friends of the Other Side), and a center part called Goula Tchitou (the Great Friends). Rowland and Sanders, *Vol. 1*, 149–154. Other French narratives sometimes recognize only two divisions, Western and Eastern, with the southern Sixtowns grouped with the former and Chickasawhay villages grouped with the latter. Du Roullet and a few others recognized a central division, usually comprising the main town of Concha (Kunshak) and its satellite villages. Galloway, "Confederacy as a Solution," 395, 402; Galloway, "Choctaw Factionalism," 74; Galloway, *Choctaw Genesis*, 273, 276, 353; Galloway and Goddard, "Concha"; Rowland and Sanders, *Vol. 1*, 116–117; Swanton, *Source Material*, 56, 95–96; White, "Roots of Dependency," 37. The six towns for which the Sixtowns Division is named were Yellow Canes, Nachoubanouanya, Tala, Seneacha, Bouctoulouctsi, and Toussana. Galloway, "Choctaw Factionalism," 86–87.

107. Atkinson, *Splendid Land, Splendid People*, 9–10.

108. Stubbs, "Chickasaw Contact with the La Salle Expedition," 42–44.

109. Cook, *Chickasaw Village Sources*, Table 1; Brightman and Wallace, "Chickasaw," Table 1.

110. Adair's tenure with the Chickasaws did not begin until the 1730s, so his 1720 list of villages was provided by tribal informants. Adair, *History*, 354; Braund, "Adair," 3.

111. Atkinson, *Splendid Land, Splendid People*, Figure 6.

112. Atkinson, *Splendid Land, Splendid People*, 9–18; Johnson, "Chickasaws," 98–101; Romans, *Concise Natural History*, 42. Table 1 in Brightman and Wallace, "Chickasaw," presents six lists of Chickasaw towns recorded between 1702 and 1805.

113. O'Brien, *Choctaws in a Revolutionary Age*, 22–23; Swanton, *Source Material*, 77, 103–104, 131.

114. Carlton, "Foreword," viii–ix; O'Brien, *Choctaws in a Revolutionary Age*, 13, 18, 19, 24; Swanton, *Chickasaw Society and Religion*, 25; Swanton, *Source Material*, 77–81.

115. Lankford, *Looking for Lost Lore*, 73. Galloway argues that the colors white and red, which are too often simplified in discussions of southeastern Indians to equate with peace and war, respectively, might better be viewed as shorthand for personality traits usually associated with elder men (white/peace = mature in judgment, cautious, wise, and so forth) and young men (red/war = daring to the point of recklessness, spontaneous, and so forth). Galloway, "Dual Organization Reconsidered," 366.

116. Galloway, *Choctaw Genesis*, 355; Galloway, "Choctaw Factionalism," 74, 75; O'Brien, *Choctaws in a Revolutionary Age*, 15, 17–19, 24–25; Swanton, *Source Material*, 76–78, 83, 89.

117. Swanton, *Source Material*, 84.

118. Swanton, *Source Material*, 162–163.

119. Byington, *Dictionary of the Choctaw Language*, 485, 534; Swanton, *Source Material*, 121–124, 167.

120. Swanton, *Source Material*, 101, 121.

121. Adair, *History*, 415–416; Galloway and Kidwell, "Choctaw in the East," 508; Galloway, "Dual Organization Reconsidered," 367, 369; O'Brien, *Choctaws in a Revolutionary Age*, 27–28, 32, 33–35; Swanton, *Source Material*, 90–98, 165.

122. Rowland and Sanders, *Vol. 1*, 150, 156–158, 194–195.

123. Rowland and Sanders, *Vol. 1*, 156. According to Baudouin, Bienville named Chicacha Oulacta Great Chief around 1708–1712. Rowland and Sanders, *Vol. 1*, 156.

124. Atkinson, *Splendid Land, Splendid People*, 95–96; Galloway, "Medal Chief's *Grosse Lettre*," 296–297, 299, Figures 16.1–3; Rowland, Sanders, and Galloway, *Vol. 4*, 235–236.

125. Swanton, *Chickasaw Society and Religion*, 19–26.

126. Atkinson, *Splendid Land, Splendid People*, 4–5, 27–28; Nairne, *Muskhogean Journals*, 63.

127. Nairne, *Muskhogean Journals*, 41. The English normally used the term "king" to denote hereditary chiefs. War chiefs did sometimes claim this title, and the office could be inherited by a nephew within their matrilineage. Atkinson, *Splendid Land, Splendid People*, 27–28.

128. Nairne, *Muskhogean Journals*, 38–39.

129. Adair, *History*, 415–416.

130. Nairne, *Muskhogean Journals*, 40–41. For an analysis of the office of Fane Mingo, see Ethridge, *From Chicaza to Chickasaw*, 227–229.

131. Giraud, *Vol. 1*, 84–85; La Harpe, *Historical Journal*, 65–66; McWilliams, *Iberville's Gulf Journals*, 97, 176; McWilliams, *Pénicaut Narrative*, 73–79; Rowland and Sanders, *Vol. 2*, 125, 126.

132. Rowland and Sanders, *Vol. 2*, 626; Rowland and Sanders, *Vol. 3*, 31; Swanton, *Indian Tribes of the Lower Mississippi Valley*, 306–315.

133. Crane, *Southern Frontier*, 71–72, 84; McWilliams, *Iberville's Gulf Journals*, 12–13, 13n.

134. Crane, *Southern Frontier*, 74–85; Gallay, *Indian Slave Trade*, 153; Rowland and Sanders, *Vol. 1*, 193n; Rowland and Sanders, *Vol. 3*, 15, 19–22.

135. Lankford, "Chacato," 668; Rowland and Sanders, *Vol. 3*, 24.

136. Lankford, "Chacato," 664, 665, 668; Lankford, *Cultural Resources Reconnaissance*, 45; McEwan, "Apalachee and Neighboring Groups," 673; O'Neill and Shea, *Charlevoix's Louisiana*, 215; Swanton, *Early History of the Creek Indians*, 106, 120–122, 123, 127, 134, 135, 136, 138, 323; Waselkov, "Tawasa," 14, 186.

137. Crane, *Southern Frontier*, 104; La Harpe, *Historical Journal*, 70–71; Rowland and Sanders, *Vol. 3*, 34.

138. Crane, *Southern Frontier*, 85; Gallay, *Indian Slave Trade*, 153; La Harpe, *Historical Journal*, 73.

139. Braund, "Adair," 8; Swanton, *Chickasaw Society and Religion*, 45–46.

140. Foucault established a mission with the Quapaws in 1700. Delanglez, *French Jesuits*, 33–34.

141. Jeter and Goddard, "Koroa," 180; Swanton, *Indian Tribes of the Lower Mississippi Valley*, 331.

142. Jeter and Goddard, "Koroa," 180; La Harpe, *Historical Journal*, 60, 69; McWilliams, *Pénicaut Narrative*, 98–99; Swanton, *Indian Tribes of the Lower Mississippi Valley*, 310–311, 329. Foucault's murder may have prompted Father Davion to temporarily abandon his Tunica mission in 1702, although both Charlevoix and Pénicaut indicate that Davion left after smashing religious objects belonging to either the Tunicas or Yazoos. McWilliams, *Pénicaut Narrative*, 77; O'Neill and Shea, *Charlevoix's Louisiana*, 161; Swanton, *Indian Tribes of the Lower Mississippi Valley*, 309–310.

143. La Harpe, *Historical Journal*, 76–77; Rowland and Sanders, *Vol. 2*, 181n; McWilliams, *Pénicaut Narrative*, 70–72, 101–102, 217–219.

144. Galloway, "Natchez Matrilineal Kinship," 106.

145. The Colapissa-Natchez link is a very tenuous language affiliation. The best source on the Colapissas is Pénicaut, who was fluent in Mobilien. The Colapissas undoubtedly used the trade jargon to communicate with him, leaving the question of their language open to speculation. As discussed in the text, a segment of the Caddoan-speaking Natchitoches tribe lived with the Colapissas temporarily. The historian Ives Goddard has noted that the names of two of the Natchitoches chief's daughters recorded by Pénicaut resemble the Natchez language: Oulchogonime ("good daughter") and Ouilchil ("pretty spinner"). Goddard suggests that, since the Natchitoches are known to have spoken a Caddoan language, the Colapissas might have been Natchez speakers. Goddard, "Colapissa," 178; McWilliams, *Pénicaut Narrative*, 81, 107. Goddard is assuming that the girls' mother was not Natchitoches, but Colapissa, and that she would have given her daughters these names or nicknames. Another possibility is that the girls' mother was Natchez.

146. La Harpe, *Historical Journal*, 21–22; Rowland and Sanders, *Vol. 2*, 9, 9n3; Swanton, *Indians of the Southeast*, 82; Swanton, *Indian Tribes of the Lower Mississippi Valley*, 281.

147. Delanglez, *French Jesuits*, 18.

148. McWilliams, *Pénicaut Narrative*, 100–101, 110.

149. Goddard, "Colapissa," 177–178; La Harpe, *Historical Journal*, 91; McWilliams, *Pénicaut Narrative*, 101, 219, 243; O'Neill and Shea, *Charlevoix's Louisiana*, 25; Rowland and Sanders, *Vol. 3*, 535; Swanton, *Indian Tribes of the Lower Mississippi Valley*, 281.

150. Goddard, "Bayogoula," 175–176; La Harpe, *Historical Journal*, 75–76; McWilliams, *Iberville's Gulf Journals*, 120n42, 163; McWilliams, *Pénicaut Narrative*, 68, 129–130; Swanton, *Indian Tribes of the Lower Mississippi Valley*, 270, 279.

151. Crane, *Southern Frontier*, 46, 90, 90n63; La Harpe, *Historical Journal*, 75; LeMaire 1716 map; Moore, "Introduction," 15; Nairne, *Muskhogean Journals*, 74, 79n3; Rowland and Sanders, *Vol. 2*, 39.

152. Crane, *Southern Frontier*, 95–98; Moore, "Introduction," 9–14; Nairne, *Muskhogean Journals*, 3, 14–16, 73–75.

153. Rowland and Sanders, *Vol. 2*, 60–61.

154. La Harpe, *Historical Journal*, 88.

155. Giraud, *Vol. 2*, 72–99; Rowland and Sanders, *Vol. 2*, 60–61, 219–223, 226–227, 317–319, 404–405.

156. Crane, *Southern Frontier*, 104; La Harpe, *Historical Journal*, 89, 90, 92; Moore, "Introduction," 20; Rowland and Sanders, *Vol. 3*, 183. La Harpe give the names of two of the pro-French villages as "Loucha" and "Echicache." La Harpe, *Historical Journal* 89. Neither of these names matches (with any reasonable certainty) any of the 115 Choctaw village names listed by Swanton. Swanton, *Source Material*, 59–67.

157. Crane, *Southern Frontier*, 102; Gallay, *Indian Slave Trade*, 328; McWilliams, *Pénicaut Narrative*, 159–163; Rowland and Sanders, *Vol. 3*, 182, 186–187.

158. Gallay, *Indian Slave Trade*, 330.

159. Kelton, *Epidemics and Enslavement*, 161–163, 200, 203.

160. Bowne, "Carying awaye their Corne and Children," 107.

161. Crane, *Southern Frontier*, 169–170; La Harpe, *Historical Journal*, 92; Moore, "Introduction," 20–21; Rowland and Sanders, *Vol. 3*, 187–188.

162. Gallay, *Indian Slave Trade*, 334.

CHAPTER 4

1. Crane, *Southern Frontier*, 24–25, 115, 185, 217; Davies, *Europe*, 638.

2. For an overview of these privatization ventures, see Barnett, *Natchez Indians: A History*, 57–59, 75–78.

3. Barnett, *Natchez Indians: A History*, 57–62, 63–72; Crane, *Southern Frontier*, 185; Giraud, *Vol. 2*, 157, 170–171; Rowland and Sanders, *Vol. 2*, 250.

4. Crane, *Southern Frontier*, 111–112; Rowland and Sanders, *Vol. 3*, 538; Usner, *Indians, Settlers, and Slaves*, 246.

5. Saunt, "History until 1776," 133–134; Usner, *Indians, Settlers, and Slaves*, 248–249.

6. Saunt, "History until 1776," 133.

7. Rowland and Sanders, *Vol. 2*, 225. While deerskins dominated the southeastern frontier exchange, European traders in the Illinois country and Great Lakes regions focused on the beaver skin trade that had flourished there since the early seventeenth century.

8. McWilliams, *Iberville's Gulf Journals*, 62; Saunt, "History until 1776," 133–134.

9. Crane, *Southern Frontier*, 192–198; Rowland and Sanders, *Vol. 3*, 303; Usner, *Indians, Settlers, and Slaves*, 245, 249–250.

10. Usner, *Indians, Settlers, and Slaves*, 261; Waselkov, "Exchange and Interaction," 692–693.

11. Usner, *Indians, Settlers, and Slaves*, 245.

12. Johnson, "Chickasaws," 97.

13. Rowland and Sanders, *Vol. 3*, 159–161, 188, 223.

14. Giraud, *Vol. 2*, 157; Rowland, *English Dominion*, 18n.

15. Rowland and Sanders, *Vol. 3*, 183, 185, 185n.

16. McWilliams, *Pénicaut Narrative*, 167–169.

17. Rowland and Sanders, *Vol. 3*, 208–209.

18. Barnett, *Natchez Indians: A History*, 63–65; White et al., "Natchez Class and Rank," 382.

19. Rowland and Sanders, *Vol. 3*, 208.

20. Swanton, *Indian Tribes of the Lower Mississippi Valley*, 197–199. Swanton provides an English translation of Captain Louis Poncereau de Richebourg's detailed account of the 1716 Natchez campaign. Swanton, *Indian Tribes of the Lower Mississippi Valley*, 196–204. The location of the island Bienville fortified in the spring of 1716 remains a mystery. Confusingly, Natchez Island, about five miles south of the present-day Natchez river landing, appears on a few early eighteenth-century maps as "Bienville's Island"; however, Jack D. Elliott Jr. has pointed out that de Richebourg's journal mentioned above and an account of the campaign by Pénicaut both state that Bienville's island was farther downriver near the Tunica villages. Jack D. Elliott Jr., personnel communication November 9, 2009; McWilliams, *Pénicaut Narrative*, 176.

21. See Barnett, *Natchez Indians: A History*, 68 and 150n27, for a discussion of the identities of the Natchez chiefs captured by Bienville.

22. Swanton, *Indian Tribes of the Lower Mississippi Valley*, 200–201.

23. Barnett, *Natchez Indians: A History*, 72–73; Galloway, "Barthelemy Murders," 252–253; Rowland and Sanders, *Vol. 2*, 24, 75, 126–127; Rowland and Sanders, *Vol. 3*, 19–22, 33–34, 113, 114, 128, 136, 139, 161; Swanton, *Indian Tribes of the Lower Mississippi Valley*, 337–342.

24. Giraud, *Vol. 2*, 155; Swanton, *Indian Tribes of the Lower Mississippi Valley*, 204–205.

25. Du Pratz, *History of Louisiana* (Claitor's), 96; Giraud, *Vol. 5*, 392; S. Lehmann, "Problems of Founding a Viable Colony," 360–366.

26. Du Pratz, *History of Louisiana* (Claitor's), 23–24.

27. Barnett, *Natchez Indians: A History*, 78–79; Swanton, *Indian Tribes of the Lower Mississippi Valley*, 210.

28. Galloway and Jackson, "Natchez and Neighboring Groups," 609.

29. Barnett, *Natchez Indians: A History*, 78–79; Du Pratz, *History of Louisiana* (Claitor's), 20, 25. The *commissaire-ordonnateur* assisted the governor with the administration of the colony. See Lemieux, "Office of Commissaire-Ordonnateur," 395–407.

30. McWilliams, *Pénicaut Narrative*, 239.

31. La Harpe, *Historical Journal*, 156.

32. Rowland and Sanders, *Vol. 1*, 53–54, 217.

33. Swanton, *Indian Tribes of the Lower Mississippi Valley*, 210.

34. Barnett, *Natchez Indians: A History*, 84–94; Swanton, *Indian Tribes of the Lower Mississippi Valley*, 207–217.

35. Rowland and Sanders, *Vol. 2*, 421–422; Rowland and Sanders, *Vol. 3*, 386–387; Swanton, *Indian Tribes of the Lower Mississippi Valley*, 214–215.

36. Rowland and Sanders, *Vol. 3*, 343.

37. Crane, *Southern Frontier*, 260; La Harpe, *Historical Journal*, 156; Rowland and Sanders, *Vol. 1*, 193n.

38. Crane, *Southern Frontier*, 174.

39. Rowland and Sanders, *Vol. 2*, 277.

40. Rowland and Sanders, *Vol. 3*, 303. At the time, one ounce of gold was worth about 90 livres.

41. Rowland and Sanders, *Vol. 2*, 277; Rowland and Sanders, *Vol. 3*, 343, 355.

42. Rowland and Sanders, *Vol. 1*, 33, 33n, 34, 46, 159; Rowland, Sanders, and Galloway, *Vol. 4*, 16n, 70–71, 72n, 269, 294n; Swanton, *Indian Tribes of the Lower Mississippi Valley*, 213.

43. Galloway, "Choctaw Names and Choctaw Roles," 207, 216; Rowland and Sanders, *Vol. 1*, 33–34, 41, 44, 188; Rowland, Sanders, and Galloway, *Vol. 4*, 16n.

44. Rowland and Sanders, *Vol. 3*, 343, 457–459, 378–382.

45. Atkinson, *Splendid Land, Splendid People*, 18–21; Crane, *Southern Frontier*, 190; St. Jean, "Squirrel King," 343.

46. Charlevoix, *Letters*, 307.

47. Charlevoix, *Letters*, 306–307.

48. O'Neill and Shea, *Charlevoix's Louisiana*, 131–133; Swanton, *Indian Tribes of the Lower Mississippi Valley*, 333.

49. Swanton, *Indian Tribes of the Lower Mississippi Valley*, 178, 334.

50. Brown, *Early 18th Century French-Indian Culture Contact*, 164–166, 168, 179–180, 198, Figure 10; Brown, *Fort St. Pierre Site*, 4–6.

51. Brain, *Tunica Archaeology*, 204–248, Figure 165; Steponaitis et al., *LMS Archives Online* site files: 23-M-5, 23-M-11, 24-M-12, 24-M-14, 24-M-15, 24-M-16, 24-M-17.

52. Diron d'Artaguiette [map 1719], *Fleuve Saint Louis*; Giraud, *Vol. 5*, 384–385; O'Neill and Shea, *Charlevoix's Louisiana*, 159–162.

53. Brain, *Tunica Archaeology*, 50, 65–151, 152–195.

54. O'Neill and Shea, *Charlevoix's Louisiana*, 162–167, 182; Swanton, *Indian Tribes of the Lower Mississippi Valley*, 278–279, 283, 290. French maps of the period confirm Charlevoix's observations. Anonymous [map ca. 1719], *Carte du cours du Mississipi*; Anonymous [map ca. 1720], *Carte du cours de la rivière du Mississipi*; Diron d'Artaguiette [map 1719], *Fleuve Saint Louis*.

55. O'Neill and Shea, *Charlevoix's Louisiana*, 138–139.

56. Dumont's account of the Tattooed Serpent's funeral was apparently derived from that of Du Pratz. Du Pratz is apparently the first-person narrator in Dumont's account. Compare the two accounts in Swanton, *Indian Tribes of the Lower Mississippi Valley*, 140–157.

57. Swanton, *Indian Tribes of the Lower Mississippi Valley*, 150, 154–155.

58. None of the French informants actually witnessed the strangulation of children by their parents for funeral sacrifice. Given the likelihood of a fairly high infant mortality rate among the Natchez, it is possible that the children's deaths by natural causes may have coincided with the funerals, and their parents used the opportunity to gain prestige for their families.

59. Barnett, *Natchez Indians: A History*, 98; Du Pratz, *Histoire de la Louisiane*, chapters 3–4; Rowland and Sanders, *Vol. 1*, 128; Swanton, *Indian Tribes of the Lower Mississippi Valley*, 138–157.

60. Swanton, *Indian Tribes of the Lower Mississippi Valley*, 140–157.

61. Gregory, "Survival and Maintenance," 655.

62. Brown, "On the Identity of the Birdman," 61–63; Dye, "Ritual, Medicine, and the War Trophy," 153–155.

63. Vomiting induced by swallowing emetic plants was a common approach to purification. Button snakeroot (*Eryngium yuccifolium* and *E. aquaticum*) was reported to have this effect if taken internally. Hudson, "Introduction," 4.

64. Adair, *History*, 77, 165–166, 186, 211, 506n184; Nairne, *Muskhogean Journals*, 39, 48–49.

65. Galloway, *Choctaw Genesis*, 299; O'Brien, *Choctaws in a Revolutionary Age*, 23–24; Swanton, *Source Material*, 170–194.

66. Dart and Cruzat, "Concession at Natchez," 390–391; Delanglez, *French Jesuits*, 99–100, 106–107, 111–112, 378–379, 434–435, 448–449; Giraud, *Vol. 5*, 382–383; Rowland and Sanders, *Vol. 3*, 496.

67. Delanglez, *French Jesuits*, 431, 432–433, 436.

68. Barnett, *Natchez Indians: A History*, 81–82, 99–100, 101–102; Du Pratz, *History of Louisiana* (Claitor's), 29, 70–71; Du Pratz, *Histoire de la Louisiane*, 231–237; Giraud, *Vol. 5*, 390, 391, 393; La Harpe, *Historical Journal*, 170; Rowland and Sanders, *Vol. 2*, 390, 396–397, 398–399, 402, 419–421, 492–493, 503–504, 525, 526, 547, 602, 620, 639, 658, 663; Rowland and Sanders, *Vol. 3*, 520–522, 530; Swanton, *Indian Tribes of the Lower Mississippi Valley*, 221–222.

69. Du Pratz, *Histoire de la Louisiane*, 252–253, 255–258, 266; Le Petit, *Natchez Massacre*; O'Neill and Shea, *Charlevoix's Louisiana*, 87–90; Rowland and Sanders, *Vol. 1*, 54, 58, 62, 63, 122–126; Swanton, *Indian Tribes of the Lower Mississippi Valley*, 224–230.

70. Le Petit, *Natchez Massacre*, 20; O'Neill and Shea, *Charlevoix's Louisiana*, 91–92; Rowland and Sanders, *Vol. 1*, 75; Swanton, *Indian Tribes of the Lower Mississippi Valley*, 229–230, 331. Charlevoix says that Father Souel's death was on December 11 and that the massacre happened the following day. One of the surviving French women reported that these events took place during the week before Christmas. O'Neill and Shea, *Charlevoix's Louisiana*, 91–92; Rowland and Sanders, *Vol. 1*, 99.

71. Rowland and Sanders, *Vol. 1*, 97–99.

72. Rowland and Sanders, *Vol. 1*, 66, 84, 87, 88, 94, 104, 158–159, 162–163.

73. As one of the preeminent Choctaw leaders during the colonial era, Alibamon Mingo deserves more attention than I am able to give him here, so I refer the interested reader to Patricia Galloway's biographical essay, "The Four Ages of Alibamon Mingo." Galloway points out that Alibamon Mingo was most prominent as a peace chief of the Inholahta moiety, but he had also won a warrior name, Alibamon Ajo (Berserker). As Galloway notes, the chief's name also points to a connection to the Alabama tribe, which she speculates might have come from having an

Alabama mother who married into the Choctaw confederacy. Galloway, "Four Ages of Alibamon Mingo," 336–356; Galloway, "Dual Organization Reconsidered," 361.

74. O'Neill and Shea, *Charlevoix's Louisiana*, 90–91; Rowland and Sanders, *Vol. 1*, 79, 80, 88, 100–101, 103, 105–111.

75. Historians continue to keep alive the rumor that the missionary Saint-Cosme fathered the chief called Saint-Cosme in a love affair with a female Natchez chief. Apparently, for some writers this piece of French colonial gossip is too juicy to resist. In fact, the rumor stems from an anonymous 1728 document in the Bibliothéque nationale de France, *Grand Soleil, files d'un français en 1728* (*BNF, manuscripts, nouvelles acquisitions, française, tome 2550, folder 115*). Having been written anonymously over twenty years after the birth in question, this document's veracity is doubtful, to say the least. As I have argued elsewhere, Charlevoix, a Jesuit who might have delighted in exposing the weakness of a Seminarian missionary, wrote that the "woman chief . . . out of respect [for Saint-Cosme] . . . called one of her sons by his name." Barnett, *Natchez Indians: A History*, 55–56; O'Neill and Shea, *Charlevoix's Louisiana*, 157, 157n.

76. Swanton, *Indian Tribes of the Lower Mississippi Valley*, 248.

77. Barnett, *Natchez Indians: A History*, 127–130; Swanton, *Indian Tribes of the Lower Mississippi Valley*, 247–251. For a discussion about Saint-Cosme, the Natchez chief, see Barnett, *Natchez Indians: A History*, 55–56, 148n197.

78. O'Neill and Shea, *Charlevoix's Louisiana*, 92–94, 92n; Rowland and Sanders, *Vol. 1*, 66–67, 75–76, 99–100.

79. Rowland and Sanders, *Vol. 1*, 97; Rowland, Sanders, and Galloway, *Vol. 4*, 33, 41, 70.

80. Rowland and Sanders, *Vol. 1*, 166–167; Rowland, Sanders, and Galloway, *Vol. 4*, 122–123, 213, 290.

81. Bellin, *Carte de la Louisiane*; Broutin et al., *Carte particulère*; O'Neill and Shea, *Charlevoix's Louisiana*, 108; Rowland and Sanders, *Vol. 3*, 755; Rowland, Sanders, and Galloway, *Vol. 4*, 41, 73. The maps also show a Tiou village in present-day Claiborne County or Jefferson County along the Big Black River, which became known in the 1740s as the "river (or bayou) of the Tious." Vincas P. Steponaitis, personal communication April 10, 2008.

82. Barnett, *Natchez Indians: A History*, 90–94, 100, 102; Rowland and Sanders, *Vol. 1*, 54–55.

83. Rowland and Sanders, *Vol. 1*, 159–160; Rowland, Sanders, and Galloway, *Vol. 4*, 37, 38n, 55, 74.

84. Claiborne, *Mississippi*, 47; Du Pratz, *Histoire de la Louisiane*, 193–295; Green, "Perier's Expedition," 556–557.

85. Rowland, Sanders, and Galloway, *Vol. 4*, 70.

86. Atkinson, *Splendid Land, Splendid People*, 37; Rowland, Sanders, and Galloway, *Vol. 4*, 148–149.

87. Rowland, Sanders, and Galloway, *Vol. 4*, 17–18.

88. Atkinson, *Splendid Land, Splendid People*, 37; Rowland, Sanders, and Galloway, *Vol. 4*, 65, 70–71.

89. Rowland and Sanders, *Vol. 1*, 159; Rowland, Sanders, and Galloway, *Vol. 4*, 70–71, 269, 294n.

90. Rowland and Sanders, *Vol. 1*, 166–167, 168, 190, 213, 221, 264–266; Rowland, Sanders, and Galloway, *Vol. 4*, 122.

91. Atkinson, *Splendid Land, Splendid People*, Figure 6; Rowland and Sanders, *Vol. 1*, 164, 165, 189, 198–200, 210–211, 231, 234, 252, 271; Rowland and Sanders, *Vol. 3*, 552, 632–634, 672–673; Rowland, Sanders, and Galloway, *Vol. 4*, 124–125, 139.

92. Rowland and Sanders, *Vol. 1*, 230, 236–237; Rowland and Sanders, *Vol. 3*, 671; Rowland, Sanders, and Galloway, *Vol. 4*, 80–82, 111, 134–135, 137.

93. Rowland and Sanders, *Vol. 1*, 230–231, 278, 293–294. For a detailed discussion of the 1736 war from the Indians' point of view, see Galloway, "Ougoula Tchetoka, Ackia," 3–10.

94. Rowland and Sanders, *Vol. 1*, 261, 279, 289–290, 295.

95. Rowland and Sanders, *Vol. 1*, 311–312, 313, 314. For a detailed discussion of D'Artaguette's attack on the Chickasaws, see Atkinson, *Splendid Land, Splendid People*, 43–50.

96. Atkinson, *Splendid Land, Splendid People*, 43–44, Figure 9; Rowland and Sanders, *Vol. 1*, 312, 357.

97. Atkinson, *Splendid Land, Splendid People*, 46–47; Rowland and Sanders, *Vol. 1*, 312–314; Rowland, Sanders, and Galloway, *Vol. 4*, 141.

98. Atkinson, *Splendid Land, Splendid People*, 44, 55; Rowland and Sanders, *Vol. 1*, 287–288, 293–294, 298–299, 303–304, 316–319.

99. Rowland and Sanders, *Vol. 1*, 314.

100. Rowland and Sanders, *Vol. 1*, 21n, 337–338, 339, 348–349, 350–351, 353–355.

101. Rowland and Sanders, *Vol. 3*, 701, 703–705.

102. Atkinson, *Splendid Land, Splendid People*, 18–21.

103. Rowland and Sanders, *Vol. 1*, 356; Rowland, Sanders, and Galloway, *Vol. 4*, facing 142; Waselkov, "Indian Maps," 440–443, 444, 445.

104. Rowland and Sanders, *Vol. 1*, 367–368, 371; Rowland and Sanders, *Vol. 3*, 719, 723, 724–725, 730, 733–734.

105. Rowland and Sanders, *Vol. 1*, 376–377, 381.

106. Rowland and Sanders, *Vol. 1*, 381, 389–390, 400, 401–403, 408, 410–411, 448.

107. Atkinson, *Splendid Land, Splendid People*, 67, 69–70, 71; Rowland and Sanders, *Vol. 1*, 407–409, 410–413, 419, 421, 428–431, 444, 448, 449, 451–454, 455–456, 458.

108. Rowland and Sanders, *Vol. 3*, 741, 746–747, 758, 769, 773–774; Rowland, Sanders, and Galloway, *Vol. 4*, 212–213, 232, 246.

109. Braund, "Adair," 2; Rowland, Sanders, and Galloway, *Vol. 4*, 253–256.

110. Adair, *History*, 75–241, 247–432; Atkinson, *Splendid Land, Splendid People*, 89; Braund, "Adair," 3, 4–7, 33–34, 35, 43–46; Rowland and Sanders, *Vol. 1*, 305.

111. Rowland and Sanders, *Vol. 3*, 581.

112. Atkinson, *Splendid Land, Splendid People*, 18; Brightman and Wallace, "Chickasaw," 479–480; Lieb, "Grand Village Is Silent," Table 4.1; Swanton, *Indian Tribes of the Lower Mississippi Valley*, 254–255.

113. Swanton, *Indian Tribes of the Lower Mississippi Valley*, 251.

114. Stiggins, *Creek Indian History*, 33, 41; Swanton, *Early History of the Creek Indians*, 313; Swanton, *Indian Tribes of the Lower Mississippi Valley*, 253.

115. Hudson, *Southeastern Indians*, 131, 139; Swanton, *Indian Tribes of the Lower Mississippi Valley*, 254–256.

116. Rowland and Sanders, *Vol. 3*, 538.

117. Giraud, *Vol. 5*, 175, 176, 371, 373; Rowland and Sanders, *Vol. 2*, 537; Rowland and Sanders, *Vol. 3*, 302–303, 538; Rowland, Sanders, and Galloway, *Vol. 4*, 17, 21.

118. Rowland and Sanders, *Vol. 1*, 20n; Rowland and Sanders, *Vol. 2*, 612–614.

119. Delanglez, *French Jesuits*, 453–455; Rowland and Sanders, *Vol. 2*, 594, 613–614; Rowland, Sanders, and Galloway, *Vol. 5*, 226n45.

120. Delanglez, *French Jesuits*, 460; Rowland and Sanders, *Vol. 1*, 85, 95, 108, 155–163, 227, 270, 285, 287; Rowland, Sanders, and Galloway, *Vol. 5*, 226n45.

121. Rowland and Sanders, *Vol. 2*, 206–208, 218–219, 636–637.

122. Nairne, *Muskhogean Journals*, 61.

123. Braund, "Adair," 33–34; Rowland, Sanders, and Galloway, *Vol. 4*, 208–209.

124. Adair, *History of the American Indians*, 398; McDowell, *Colonial Records of South Carolina, 1750–1754*, 384–385.

125. Rowland and Sanders, *Vol. 1*, 17–20, 21–54, 136–154, 158, 170–192; Rowland, Sanders, and Galloway, *Vol. 4*, 26, 41–42.

126. Rowland, Sanders, and Galloway, *Vol. 4*, 53, 208–209.

127. Rowland, Sanders, and Galloway, *Vol. 4*, 225–229, 233–240, 243–246, 249–250, 255–256, 260–262, 263–266, 270–293, 298–304.

128. Galloway, "Choctaw Factionalism," 70, 71. Galloway's article remains the most thorough analysis of the Choctaw civil war.

129. Red Shoe received a French medal for jump-starting the war with the Chickasaws in 1731. Rowland, Sanders, and Galloway, *Vol. 4*, 126. He received his English medal in 1734 for promoting English trade among the Choctaws. Rowland and Sanders, *Vol. 3*, 672–673.

130. Rowland, Sanders, and Galloway, *Vol. 4*, 155–156, 217, 225–229, 233–237.

131. Braund, "Adair," 6; Rowland, Sanders, and Galloway, *Vol. 4*, 298–299.

132. Adair, *History*, 322; Braund, "Adair," 6–7.

133. Galloway, "Choctaw Factionalism," 84; Rowland, Sanders, and Galloway, *Vol. 4*, 280, 282, 284, 295n25, 312.

134. Rowland, Sanders, and Galloway, *Vol. 4*, 270–294.

135. Adair, *History*, 326.

136. Rowland, Sanders, and Galloway, *Vol. 4*, 280.

137. Galloway, "Choctaw Factionalism," 86; Rowland, Sanders, and Galloway, *Vol. 4*, 280–286.

138. Adair, *History*, 334; Galloway, "Choctaw Factionalism," 90; Rowland, Sanders, and Galloway, *Vol. 4*, 312, 324, 329, 333.

139. Rowland, Sanders, and Galloway, *Vol. 5*, 61.

140. Rowland, Sanders, and Galloway, *Vol. 4*, 333.

141. Galloway, "Choctaw Factionalism," 91.

142. Adair, *History*, 336; Rowland, Sanders, and Galloway, *Vol. 4*, 313; Rowland, Sanders, and Galloway, *Vol. 5*, 14.

143. Rowland, Sanders, and Galloway, *Vol. 5*, 62–63.

144. Braund, "Adair," 10, 11–12; Galloway, "Choctaw Factionalism," 95; Rowland, Sanders, and Galloway, *Vol. 4*, 326, 330, 335–336.

145. Galloway, "Choctaw Factionalism," 96; Rowland, Sanders, and Galloway, *Vol. 5*, 16, 18, 60, 64, 62, 218.

146. Rowland, Sanders, and Galloway, *Vol. 5*, 55, 60–61.

147. Rowland, Sanders, and Galloway, *Vol. 4*, 300.

148. Galloway, "Choctaw Factionalism," 75; Rowland, Sanders, and Galloway, *Vol. 5*, 65n2.

149. O'Brien, *Choctaws in a Revolutionary Age*, 15.

150. Rowland, Sanders, and Galloway, *Vol. 4*, 295n23; Rowland, Sanders, and Galloway, *Vol. 5*, 26, 27, 31–33, 62–63.

151. McDowell, *Colonial Records 1750–1754*, 3, 15, 36–40, 364–366, 510.

152. McDowell, *Colonial Records 1750–1754*, 256–257, 289, 364–366; Rowland, Sanders, and Galloway, *Vol. 5*, 31, 32, 46–47, 48–49, 50, 112, 122.

153. Galloway, "Chief Who Is Your Father," 345–370.

154. Rowland, Sanders, and Galloway, *Vol. 5*, 154–155.

155. McDowell, *Colonial Records 1750–1754*, 458–459, 510–512, 513, 514. According to Swanton, the Breed Camp and New Windsor (Augusta, Georgia) settlements were abandoned before the end of the eighteenth century. Swanton, *Early History of the Creek Indians*, 283, 418.

156. McDowell, *Colonial Records 1754–1765*, 111–114; Rowland, Sanders, and Galloway, *Vol. 5*, 143–144.

157. McDowell, *Colonial Records 1754–1765*, 296, 372, 413–414, 415, 422, 445, 446, 458, 459, 475–476; Rowland, Sanders, and Galloway, *Vol. 5*, 184, 189, 190, 193.

158. McDowell, *Colonial Records 1754–1765*, 111–114, 299, 363, 423, 424; Rowland, Sanders, and Galloway, *Vol. 5*, 197–198, 257.

159. Calloway, *Scratch of a Pen*, 136; O'Brien, "Protecting Trade," 103–104.

CHAPTER 5

1. Atkinson, *Splendid Land, Splendid People*, 88, 89, 95–96, 154; Calloway, *Scratch of a Pen*, 66, 102, 103; Galloway, "Choctaw Factionalism," 74–75.

2. Rowland, Sanders, and Galloway, *Vol. 5*, 296. D'Abbadie replaced Kerlérec as director general of Louisiana and presided over the division of the colony between England and Spain. Rowland, Sanders, and Galloway, *Vol. 5*, 275n; Rowland, *English Dominion*, 16, 55. The entire text of the speech is transcribed in Rowland, Sanders, and Galloway, *Vol. 5*, 294–301.

3. Rowland, *English Dominion*, 14, 84–91, 185; Rowland, Sanders, and Galloway, *Vol. 5*, 298. For details on the conflict sometimes known as "Pontiac's War," see Dowd, *War under Heaven*.

4. Rowland, *English Dominion*, 11–12, 13, 150.

5. Rowland, *English Dominion*, 12, 19, 119, 119n, 121–122.

6. Rowland, *English Dominion*, 233, 267.

7. Rowland, *English Dominion*, 232, 260–264, 262n, 266–273, 279–282, 358.

8. Haffner, "Major Arthur Loftus' Journal," 330n.

9. Haffner, "Major Arthur Loftus' Journal," 325–328, 331, 331n, 332–334; Rowland, *English Dominion*, 514.

10. Atkinson, *Splendid Land, Splendid People*, 27, 82, 89, 95–98, 104; Galloway, "Four Ages of Alibamon Mingo," 338; Rowland, *English Dominion*, 184, 187, 202, 215–255. The land the Choctaws ceded to the English in 1765 was later part of the Fort Confederation and Hoe Buckintoopa treaties with the United States (see chapter 6).

11. Galloway, "So Many Little Republics," 320, 326.

12. Calloway, *Scratch of a Pen*, 137; Galloway, "So Many Little Republics," 320–321; Rowland, *English Dominion*, 239.

13. O'Brien, "Protecting Trade," 103–104; Rowland, *English Dominion*, 35, 150, 242.

14. Rowland, *English Dominion*, 237–238.

15. Rowland, *English Dominion*, 219–220, 239–241; Usner, *American Indians in the Lower Mississippi Valley*, 65–66.

16. Atkinson, *Splendid Land, Splendid People*, 91, 92, 96–99, 103–104, 143; Braund, "Adair," 31; Romans, *Concise Natural History*, 46; Usner, *Indians, Settlers, and Slaves*, 268.

17. Rowland, Sanders, and Galloway, *Vol. 4*, 47, 101, 223.

18. McDowell, *Colonial Records 1750–1754*, 86–89, 312, 367; McDowell, *Colonial Records 1754–1765*, 44, 67, 105–106, 192, 231, 296, 354; O'Brien, "Protecting Trade," 104–106; Rowland, *English Dominion*, 241.

19. Galloway, "So Many Little Republics," 327; Rowland, *English Dominion*, 248.

20. St. Jean, "Squirrel King," 350–353.

21. McDowell, *Colonial Records 1750–1754*, 312; Rowland, Sanders, and Galloway, *Vol. 4*, 146; Rowland, Sanders, and Galloway, *Vol. 5*, 47, 212, 224, 226n40; Swanton, *Indian Tribes of the Lower Mississippi Valley*, 290.

22. Kniffin et al., *Historic Indian Tribes of Louisiana*, 78, 83, 90–91; Swanton, *Indians of the Southeastern United States*, 140.

23. Brain et al., "Tunica, Biloxi, and Ofo," 589, 593, 595; Gauld [map 1778], *Plan*; Kniffin et al., *Historic Indian Tribes of Louisiana*, 18–19, 84; May, "Alabama and Koasati," 407; Swanton, *Indians of the Southeastern United States*, 88; Swanton, *Indian Tribes of the Lower Mississippi Valley*, 314–315; Waselkov, "Capinan and Moctoby," 176. Some members of the Alabama and Koasati tribes remained in their homeland and became part of the Creek confederacy. May, "Alabama and Koasati," 407.

24. Kniffin et al., *Historic Indian Tribes of Louisiana*, 84–85, 87.

25. Brain et al., "Tunica, Biloxi, and Ofo," 588; Kniffin et al., *Historic Indian Tribes of Louisiana*, 85–87, 92–96; Swanton, "Historical Sketch," 5–9; Waselkov, "Pascagoula," 14, 185.

26. Brain et al., "Tunica, Biloxi, and Ofo," 589, 593, 595; Gregory, "Survival and Maintenance," 653; Kniffin et al., *Historic Indian Tribes of Louisiana*, 90; Waselkov, "Capinan and Moctoby," 176; Waselkov, "Pascagoula," 185.

27. McDowell, *Colonial Records 1750–1754*, 36–38; McDowell, *Colonial Records 1754–1765*, 415.

28. Galloway, "Ibitoupa," 179–180; Galloway et al., "Yazoo," 190.

29. Jack D. Elliott, personal communication April 8, 2008.

30. Swanton, *Early History of the Creek Indians*, 316.

31. McDowell, *Colonial Records 1750–1754*, 161, 166, 296, 313–314; Rowland, *English Dominion*, 96; Swanton, *Indian Tribes of the Lower Mississippi Valley*, 253.

32. Stiggins, *Creek Indian History*.

33. Stiggins, *Creek Indian History*, 14, 16; Swanton, *Early History of the Creek Indians*, 314, 314n.

34. Dyson, "In Search of Yaneka"; Frank, "Hutchins's Natchez Indian," 7–12; Claiborne, *Mississippi*, 123, 127n.

35. Joseph V. Frank III, personal communication June 7, 2005.

36. Swanton, *Indian Tribes of the Lower Mississippi Valley*, 254–255.

37. McAmis, *Indian People of the Edisto River*, 25–28; Waddell, "Cusabo," 258, 263.

38. Adair, *History*, 282, 284; O'Brien, "Protecting Trade," 106–109, 115; Rowland, *English Dominion*, 17.

39. Adair, *History*, 320–321; O'Brien, "Protecting Trade," 109–111; Rowland, *English Dominion*, 516, 517, 528, 529; Usner, *Indians, Settlers, and Slaves*, 128.

40. Atkinson, *Splendid Land, Splendid People*, 90.

41. Dowd, "American Revolution," 141; Rowland, *English Dominion*, 524, 529–530.

42. Brightman and Wallace, "Chickasaw," Figures 4 and 10; Galloway and Kidwell, "Choctaw in the East," Figures 2, 4, and 8; Gregory, "Survival and Maintenance," 655.

43. Levine, "Music," 720–725, 730, 731.

44. Adair, *History*, 125, 144, 149–151, 494n106, 495n110; Nairne, *Muskhogean Journals*, 48; Swanton, *Chickasaw Society and Religion*, 76, 90; Walker, "Creek Confederacy Before Removal," 387.

45. Galloway and Kidwell, "Choctaw in the East," 509; Swanton, *Source Material*, 21, 38, 169–170, 221–225.

46. Swanton, *Indian Tribes of the Lower Mississippi Valley*, 113–121.

47. Vennum, *Lacrosse*, vi–vii, 33–35.

48. Du Ru, *Journal*, 21.

49. Adair, *History*, 392–393; Brightman and Wallace, "Chickasaw," 488–489; Culin, *Games of the North American Indians*, 562, 597–599; Galloway and Kidwell, "Choctaw in the East," 509; Gregory, "Survival and Maintenance," 655; Hudson, *Southeastern Indians*, 408–411; Romans, *Concise Natural History*, 52–53; Swanton, *Indian Tribes of the Lower Mississippi Valley*, 113–121; Swanton, *Source Material*, 42, 140–141, 155; Vennum, *Lacrosse*, 237, 239, 241–248.

50. Adair, *History*, 393–394; Brightman and Wallace, "Chickasaw," 488–489; Culin, *Games of the North American Indians*, 597–599; Galloway and Kidwell, "Choctaw in the East," 508–509; Hudson, *Southeastern Indians*, 412; Levine, "Music," 720–725; Swanton, *Indian Tribes of the Lower Mississippi Valley*, 117; Vennum, *Lacrosse*, 27–31, 46–51.

51. Adair, *History*, 394–395; Du Ru, *Journal*, 21; Culin, *Games of the North American Indians*, 420–421, 485–488; Romans, *Concise Natural History*, 53–54, 55; Swanton, *Source Material*, 155–157, 158–159.

52. Swanton, *Indian Tribes of the Lower Mississippi Valley*, 90.

53. Brightman and Wallace, "Chickasaw," 495; Galloway and Jackson, "Natchez and Neighboring Groups," 613, Figure 8; King, "Cherokee in the West," 362, 366–367; Levine, "Choctaw at Ardmore, Oklahoma," 531.

54. Culin, *Games of the North American Indians*, 599–602; Debo, *Rise and Fall*, 78, 228; Galloway and Jackson, "Natchez and Neighboring Groups," 611–612, Figures 8–11; Galloway and Kidwell, "Choctaw in the East," 517–518, Figure 12; Levine, "Choctaw at Ardmore, Oklahoma," 531–533, Figure 1. Stickball continues to be an active sport in the twenty-first century. Regular Choctaw and Chickasaw matches include the intratribal competition at the annual Choctaw Fair in Philadelphia, Mississippi.

55. O'Brien, "Protecting Trade," 113; O'Brien, "We are behind you," 108, 109, 110, 111, 112, 115, 116.

56. O'Brien, "Choctaw Defense," 123, 124–125, 126, 139, 140; O'Brien, "We are behind you," 111.

57. Atkinson, *Splendid Land, Splendid People*, 24, 105–112, 115–120.

58. Usner, *American Indians in the Lower Mississippi Valley*, 61, 64, 71, 77, Table 1.

59. Atkinson, *Splendid Land, Splendid People*, 124, 126, 137; Gibson, *Chickasaws*, 88–89.

60. Atkinson, *Splendid Land, Splendid People*, 124; O'Brien, "Conqueror Meets the Unconquered," 150; O'Brien, *Choctaws in a Revolutionary Age*, 1, 56.

61. "Hopewell Treaty," 248–251; Martin, "Appendix A," 237–246; O'Brien, "Conqueror Meets the Unconquered," 148, 150, 152, 159, 161–163; O'Brien, *Choctaws in a Revolutionary Age*, 12, 50, 56.

62. "Hopewell Treaty," 249–250.

63. Martin, "Appendix A," 240–241, 243–246; O'Brien, "Conqueror Meets the Unconquered," 163–168.

64. Atkinson, *Splendid Land, Splendid People*, 128, 129, 133; Gibson, *Chickasaws*, 80–82; "Hopewell Treaty," 250.

65. Atkinson, *Splendid Land, Splendid People*, 129, 133–138, 155–158; Gibson, *Chickasaws*, 83–84, 89; Waselkov, *Conquering Spirit*, 23.

66. Atkinson, *Splendid Land, Splendid People*, 148–149; Gibson, *Chickasaws*, 86.

67. Atkinson, *Splendid Land, Splendid People*, 133–134; O'Brien, "Conqueror Meets the Unconquered," 150, 163, 170–171; Usner, *Indians, Settlers, and Slaves*, 273–274, 275, 278, 284.

68. Atkinson, *Splendid Land, Splendid People*, 143, 144, 183, 184, 185–188; Carson, "Native Americans," 187; Carson, *Searching for the Bright Path*, 42; Gibson, *Chickasaws*, 92–93; Guice, "Face to Face," 162–163; Usner, *American Indians in the Lower Mississippi Valley*, 70–74, 76, 80, 82–83; Usner, *Indians, Settlers, and Slaves*, 284; Waselkov, *Conquering Spirit*, 24, 26, 179.

69. Rowland, *Mississippi*, 1:773–775.

70. Carson, *Searching for the Bright Path*, 40; Malloy and Weeks, "Shuttle Diplomacy," 33–34; O'Brien, *Choctaws in a Revolutionary Age*, 88; Rowland, *Mississippi*, 1:775, 776.

71. Rowland, *Mississippi*, 1:777–779, 2:1003–1013.

72. Carson, *Searching for the Bright Path*, 43–45; Clark and Guice, *Old Southwest*, 75; Malloy and Weeks, "Shuttle Diplomacy," 36–37, 43–47; O'Brien, *Choctaws in a Revolutionary Age*, 88, 89, 90, 92–93.

73. Clark and Guice, *Old Southwest*, 12, 45, 73, 75, 77.

74. Carson, *Searching for the Bright Path*, 46, 48; Dowd, "American Revolution," 143; Claiborne, *Mississippi*, 209, 216–217; Gibson, *Chickasaws*, 91; Guice, "Face to Face," 158–159; Rowland, *Mississippi*, 1:xiii, 675, 778–780, 2:771–772; Jack D. Elliott Jr., personal communication November 29, 2010.

CHAPTER 6

1. Atkinson, *Splendid Land, Splendid People*, 180–181, 190; DeRosier, *Removal of the Choctaw Indians*, 26; O'Brien, "Conqueror Meets the Unconquered," 153; Rowland, *Mississippi*, 2:967–971; Wells, "Federal Indian Policy," 193.

2. Atkinson, *Splendid Land, Splendid People*, 132, 151–152, 189–190; *Chickasaw Indian Treaties*, "Treaty of Chickasaw Bluffs"; Clark and Guice, *Old Southwest*, 85. The Chickasaw chief Chinubbee should not be confused with the Natchez chief of the same name who led a band of Natchez refugees who merged with Creeks. The Natchez chief Chinubbee was an ancestor of Creek/Natchez historian George Stiggins. Rowland, *Mississippi*, 1:77; Wyman, "Introduction," 16.

3. *Treaty of Fort Adams*; *Treaty of Fort Confederation*; *Treaty of Hopewell*.

4. DeRosier, *Removal of the Choctaw Indians*, 29–30; Clark and Guice, *Old Southwest*, 30, 88; Galloway and Kidwell, "Choctaw in the East," 514; O'Brien, *Choctaws in a Revolutionary Age*, 102; O'Brien, "Conqueror Meets the Unconquered," 159; Rowland, *Mississippi*, 1:79; *Treaty of Fort Adams*; *Treaty of Fort Confederation*. Jack D. Elliott Jr. has noted that the 1786 Hopewell Treaty between the Choctaws and the United States excludes the Natchez District from the Choctaws' recognized territory. Therefore the Treaty of Fort Adams simply reaffirmed the United States' claim to the district. Jack D. Elliott Jr., personal communication January 29, 2010.

5. Claiborne, *Mississippi*, 222–223, 232; Gibson, *Chickasaws*, 91; Guice, "Face to Face," 159.

6. DeRosier, *Removal of the Choctaw Indians*, 26; Elliott, "Choctaw Agency," 22–28; Gibson, *Chickasaws*, 93; Guice, "Face to Face," Table 3; O'Brien, *Choctaws in a Revolutionary Age*, 105.

7. Atkinson, *Splendid Land, Splendid People*, 143, 144, 183, 184, 185–188; Galloway and Kidwell, "Choctaw in the East," 514–515; Gibson, *Chickasaws*, 92–93, 138–141, 152; Gilmer, "Chickasaws, Tribal Laws," 134; Guice, "Face to Face," 172; McAlexander, "Saga of a Mixed-Blood Chickasaw

Dynasty," 289–290; O'Brien, *Choctaws in a Revolutionary Age*, 103, 104; Rowland, *Mississippi*, 1:79.

8. Debo, *Rise and Fall*, 36; DeRosier, *Removal of the Choctaw Indians*, 20–22, 24–26; Rowland, *Mississippi*, 1:434; Wells, "International Causes," 178–179.

9. DeRosier, *Removal of the Choctaw Indians*, 30; Wells, "Federal Indian Policy," 181, 185–186, 188–189.

10. DeRosier, *Removal of the Choctaw Indians*, 30; Galloway and Kidwell, "Choctaw in the East," 515.

11. O'Brien, *Choctaws in a Revolutionary Age*, 32, 33, 100. In identifying the division affiliations of the chiefs at the Treaty of Fort Confederation, the first division is given as "lower towns and Chicasawhay." Chicasawhay (more often written as Chickasawhay) is usually associated with the Sixtowns Division (see Figure 6) and may have been Pushmataha's residence at the time. In later years, Pushmataha lived near St. Stephens. Cushman, *History of the Choctaw, Chickasaw, and Natchez Indians*, 231, 260; Debo, *Rise and Fall*, 41.

12. *Treaty of Fort Confederation*; Baird, *Peter Pitchlynn*, 6, 8–10, 19; Elliott, "Plymouth Fort," 338n20.

13. Cushman, *History of the Choctaw, Chickasaw, and Natchez Indians*, 51; DeRosier, *Removal of the Choctaw Indians*, 30; Jack D. Elliott Jr., personal communication September 4, 2009; Ferguson, "Treaties between the United States and the Choctaw Nation," Table 5; *Treaty of Fort Confederation*.

14. DeRosier, *Removal of the Choctaw Indians*, 32–33.

15. MDAH, Special Collections, RG2, Series 488, Box 16618, Document 138.

16. MDAH, Special Collections, RG2, Journal of the Indian Department 1803–1808, Series 488, Box 100, Document 177.

17. Wells, "International Causes," 179–180.

18. Clark and Guice, *Old Southwest*, 32; DeRosier, *Removal of the Choctaw Indians*, 29, 31; O'Brien, *Choctaws in a Revolutionary Age*, 101; *Treaty of Hoe-Buckin-Too-Pa*; Jack D. Elliott Jr., personal communication January 29, 2010.

19. Atkinson, *Splendid Land, Splendid People*, 193; Clark and Guice, *Old Southwest*, 26; DeRosier, *Removal of the Choctaw Indians*, 27–28; Ethridge, *Creek Country*, 129–134; Guice, "Face to Face," 162, 163; MDAH, Special Collections, RG2, Series 488, Box 16618, Document 170; MDAH, Special Collections, Journal of the Indian Department 1803–1808, Document 3; Wells, "International Causes," 182. The Choctaw trading house moved to Fort Confederation in 1818. Pate, *Reminiscences of George S. Gaines*, 9.

20. DeRosier, *Removal of the Choctaw Indians*, 28, 31; Jack D. Elliott Jr., personal communication January 29, 2010.

21. Atkinson, *Splendid Land, Splendid People*, 195–196; Barnhill, "Indian Territory," 149; DeRosier, *Removal of the Choctaw Indians*, 32; Horan, *McKenney-Hall Portrait Gallery*, 39.

22. Atkinson, *Splendid Land, Splendid People*, 110, 149, 195–197, 198; Gibson, *Chickasaws*, 92. Under the Hopewell Treaty, the Chickasaws ceded land for a trading post at Muscle Shoals. Gibson, *Chickasaws*, 103.

23. *Chickasaw Treaty—1805*

24. Atkinson, *Splendid Land, Splendid People*, 93, 198, 212, 302n33; *Chickasaw Treaty—1805*.

25. Clark and Guice, *Old Southwest*, 36.

26. Clark and Guice, *Old Southwest*, 37–38, 269n45; Cushman, *History of the Choctaw, Chickasaw, and Natchez*, 56; DeRosier, *Removal of the Choctaw Indians*, 29, 31–32; McKee and

Schlenker, *Choctaws*, 53–54; *Treaty of Mount Dexter*; Wells, "Federal Indian Policy," 180, 193–194; Wells, "International Causes," 179–180; Jack D. Elliott Jr., personal communication January 29, 2010.

27. *Treaty of Mount Dexter*.

28. MDAH, Special Collections, RG2, Series 488, Box 106, Document 782.

29. Claiborne, *Mississippi*, 304; Clark and Guice, *Old Southwest*, 50–51, 53–54, 55, 57, 65; Rowland, *Mississippi*, 2:270.

30. Waselkov, *Conquering Spirit*, 88–90, 97–98, 100–102, 304n11. For a thorough analysis of the Redstick War and its connection to the larger War of 1812, see Waselkov, *Conquering Spirit*.

31. Waselkov, *Conquering Spirit*, 86–88, 96–99.

32. Waselkov, *Conquering Spirit*, 74–75, 77, 78.

33. Waselkov, *Conquering Spirit*, 99–100.

34. Atkinson, *Splendid Land, Splendid People*, 304n40; Bunn and Williams, *Battle for the Southern Frontier*, 75; Gibson, *Chickasaws*, 96; Lincecum, *Pushmataha*, 90; Waselkov, *Conquering Spirit*, 60, 74–80, 93, 95, 144, 162, 165, 171, 176.

35. Bunn and Williams, *Battle for the Southern Frontier*, 86–87; Waselkov, *Conquering Spirit*, 163–173.

36. Carson, "Greenwood LeFlore," 227.

37. Atkinson, *Splendid Land, Splendid People*, 204–205; Clark and Guice, *Old Southwest*, 167; DeRosier, *Removal of the Choctaw Indians*, 35–36; Guice, "Old Hickory and the Natchez Trace," 181; Acts passed at the first session of the Ninth General Assembly of the Mississippi Territory, begun and held at the Town of Washington, the sixth day of November, one thousand eight hundred and fifteen, published by authority, 53–54.

38. DeRosier, *Removal of the Choctaw Indians*, 27; Waselkov, *Conquering Spirit*, 72–73, 97.

39. "Jesse Franklin," http://bioguide.congress.gov/scripts/biodisplay.pl?index=F000344; "David Meriwether," http://bioguide.congress.gov/scripts/biodisplay.pl?index=M000649.

40. Atkinson, *Splendid Land, Splendid People*, 205–206; *Treaty with the Chickasaw: 1816*.

41. Atkinson, *Splendid Land, Splendid People*, 206; *Treaty with the Chickasaw: 1816*.

42. DeRosier, *Removal of the Choctaw Indians*, 21; Lincecum, *Pushmataha*, 27–29; O'Brien, "Introduction," vii–viii.

43. DeRosier, *Removal of the Choctaw Indians*, 21; "John Rhea," http://bioguide.congress.gov/scripts/biodisplay.pl?index=R000181; Jack D. Elliott Jr., personal communication January 29, 2010. Although Greg O'Brien identifies Mingo Homastubbee as Mushulatubbee's "father," their relationship was more likely that of uncle and nephew with inheritance of tribal office through matrilineal descent. O'Brien, *Choctaws in a Revolutionary Age*, 102.

44. DeRosier, *Removal of the Choctaw Indians*, 36–37; "Treaty of Fort St. Stephens," http://www.choctaw.org/History/Treaties/treaty6.html.

45. *Constitution and Form of Government for the State of Mississippi* [Constitution of 1817]; Rowland, *Mississippi*, 1:499–503, 2:719–725.

46. Wilentz, *Andrew Jackson*, 36–38.

47. Atkinson, *Splendid Land, Splendid People*, 208. Atkinson notes that the four divisions already existed prior to Cocke's giving them formal recognition. Geographically, Tishomingo's was the Northeast Division, McGillivray's the Northwest, Apassantubby's the Southeast, and Seeley's the Southwest. Atkinson, *Splendid Land, Splendid People*, 208.

48. Gibson, *Chickasaws*, 151; *Treaty with the Chickasaw: 1818*.

49. Atkinson, *Splendid Land, Splendid People*, 209.

50. Gibson, *Chickasaws*, 102–103.

51. Atkinson, *Splendid Land, Splendid People*, 210–211; Butler, *"Secret" Journal*; *Treaty with the Chickasaw: 1818*.

52. Carson, "State Rights and Indian Removal," 26–28; Clark and Guice, *Old Southwest*, 164; DeRosier, *Removal of the Choctaw Indians*, 26; Guice, "Face to Face," Table 3; Haynes, "Territorial Mississippi," 289; Wells, "Federal Indian Policy," 203.

53. Carson, "Greenwood Leflore," 228; DeRosier, *Removal of the Choctaw Indians*, 40–43, 46, 48.

54. Atkinson, *Splendid Land, Splendid People*, 216; Clark, "Native Christianity," 742; Kidwell, "Choctaws and Missionaries," 201; Mathews, "Second Great Awakening," 26–27, 33–42.

55. Atkinson, *Splendid Land, Splendid People*, 216–220; Carson, "Greenwood LeFlore," 225–227; Clark, "Native Christianity," 742; Debo, *Rise and Fall*, 41–42; Kidwell, "Choctaws and Missionaries," 201–205, 208, 211, 212.

56. Atkinson, *Splendid Land, Splendid People*, 218–220; Brown, "On the Identity of the Birdman," 59, 69–70; Byington, *Dictionary of the Choctaw Language*; Carson, "Greenwood LeFlore," 228–229; Cushman, *History of the Choctaw, Chickasaw, and Natchez Indians*; Debo, *Rise and Fall*, 43–44; Gregory, "Survival and Maintenance," 655; Kidwell, "Choctaws and Missionaries," 205–206, 215–217; Lankford, "Some Cosmological Motifs," 18.

57. DeRosier, *Removal of the Choctaw Indians*, 46–47, 50–51.

58. Carson, "State Rights and Indian Removal," 28; Claiborne, *Mississippi*, 383; Clark and Guice, *Old Southwest*, 240–241; DeRosier, *Removal of the Choctaw Indians*, 53–58; Rowland, *Mississippi*, 2:441.

59. Baird, *Peter Pitchlynn*, 13–14; Claiborne, *Mississippi*, 383; DeRosier, *Removal of the Choctaw Indians*, 59; *Treaty with the Choctaw, 1820*.

60. "Article 3," *Treaty with the Quapaw, 1818*; Debo, *Rise and Fall*, 41; DeRosier, *Removal of the Choctaw Indians*, 58–59, 65; Lincecum, *Pushmataha*, 81.

61. Baird, *Peter Pitchlynn*, 15, 16; Carson, "State Rights and Indian Removal," 28; Clark and Guice, *Old Southwest*, 242–243; DeRosier, *Removal of the Choctaw Indians*, 29, 62–67; Ferguson, "Appendix: Treaties," 218–219; Lincecum, *Pushmataha*, 79–82; *Treaty with the Choctaw, 1820*.

62. *Treaty with the Choctaw, 1820*.

63. Lincecum, *Pushmataha*, 83–84, 86; *Treaty with the Choctaw, 1820*; Wells, "Federal Indian Policy," 199.

64. *Treaty with the Choctaw, 1820*.

65. Debo, *Rise and Fall*, 47–50; DeRosier, *Removal of the Choctaw Indians*, 22–23; *Treaty with the Choctaw, 1820*.

66. DeRosier, *Removal of the Choctaw Indians*, 74–99; Wells, "Federal Indian Policy," 198–199, 206.

67. Carson, "State Rights and Indian Removal," 28–29.

68. *Records of the Choctaw Trading House, 1803–1824*; *Treaty with the Choctaw, 1820*; Wells, "Federal Indian Policy," 198.

69. Baird, *Peter Pitchlynn*, 16; DeRosier, *Removal of the Choctaw Indians*, 73–78; Wells, "Federal Indian Policy," 199–200.

70. Baird, *Peter Pitchlynn*, 17; DeRosier, *Removal of the Choctaw Indians*, 77–79, 82–83; Ferguson, "Appendix: Treaties," 219; Horan, *McKenney-Hall Portrait Gallery*, 21, 84; O'Brien, "Pushmataha."

71. Baird, *Peter Pitchlynn*, 17, 25; Debo, *Rise and Fall*, 53; DeRosier, *Removal of the Choctaw Indians*, 82, 86, 132–133; *Treaty of Washington D.C. with the Choctaw*.

72. Atkinson, *Splendid Land, Splendid People*, 163, 222; Gibson, *Chickasaws*, 161–162, 163–164, 167; Hinds and Coffee, *Refusal of the Chickasaws and Choctaws*. King Ishtehotopa, a nephew of Chinubbee, inherited the title of "king" upon the death of another of Chinubbee's nephews, Chehopistee, who succeeded Chinubbee when the old king died in 1819. Atkinson, *Splendid Land, Splendid People*, 213.

73. Hinds and Coffee, *Refusal of the Chickasaws and Choctaws*.

74. Hinds and Coffee, *Refusal of the Chickasaws and Choctaws*.

75. Hinds and Coffee, *Refusal of the Chickasaws and Choctaws*.

76. Atkinson, *Splendid Land, Splendid People*, 222–224; Gibson, *Chickasaws*, 163–164; Hinds and Coffee, *Refusal of the Chickasaws and Choctaws*.

77. Baird, *Peter Pitchlynn*, 25–27; DeRosier, *Removal of the Choctaw Indians*, 90–93.

78. Carson, "State Rights and Indian Removal," 29–32; Cockrell, "United States Senators and Representatives," 47–48; MDAH, Special Collections, 970.1 U58p 1826, 8; MDAH, Special Collections, 970.5 M533 1870; Rowland, *Mississippi*, 1:288–289.

79. McKenney is best known for the three volumes of Indian portraits he produced in collaboration with writer James Hall, published between 1836 and 1844. Washington, D.C., artist Charles Bird King painted many of the portraits from life in his studio during diplomatic tribal visits, while others are based upon sketches by other artists, including James Otto Lewis. A fire at the Smithsonian Institution in 1865 destroyed King's original paintings. McKenney and Hall, *History of the Indian tribes of North America*; Horan, *McKenney-Hall Portrait Gallery*, 23. Pushmataha's is the only Mississippi portrait in the McKenney and Hall volumes. Unlike most of the portraits, King's painting, done shortly before Pushmataha's death, shows the Choctaw chief in Anglo-American dress, wearing what appears to be an eighteenth-century military coat with epaulets and a ruffle collar. Horan, *McKenney-Hall Portrait Gallery*, 332–334.

80. Atkinson, *Splendid Land, Splendid People*, 224–225; Baird, *Peter Pitchlynn*, 31–36; Barnes, "Journal of Isaac McCoy," 227; DeRosier, *Removal of the Choctaw Indians*, 96–98; McDermott, "Isaac McCoy's Second Exploring Trip," 400, 407, 409, 411, 416, 419, 423, 425. Isaac McCoy participated in two exploring expeditions for Indians in 1828. Initially, the Choctaws, Chickasaws, and Creeks were to rendezvous with delegations from the Potawatomies and Ottowas in St. Louis in the summer of 1728 for a joint tour. When the southern tribes failed to arrive on time, McCoy and Kennerly toured the Potawatomies and Ottowas over much the same route as that followed by the southern group in October and November. Barnes, "Journal of Isaac McCoy," 227, 228, 267.

81. Baird, *Peter Pitchlynn*, 36–37; Cockrell, "Politics of Land in Jacksonian Mississippi," 2–3; DeRosier, *Removal of the Choctaw Indians*, 98–99; MDAH Special Collections, Laws of the State of Mississippi, Twelfth Session of the General Assembly 1829.

82. Carson, "State Rights and Indian Removal," 32–33, 36–37; DeRosier, *Removal of the Choctaw Indians*, 102, 104–108; MDAH Special Collections, Laws of the State of Mississippi, Thirteenth Session of the General Assembly 1830.

83. Baird, *Peter Pitchlynn*, 25, 37; DeRosier, *Removal of the Choctaw Indians*, 103, 112, 114.

84. Baird, *Peter Pitchlynn*, 37; Debo, *Rise and Fall*, 51–52; DeRosier, *Removal of the Choctaw Indians*, 113–114.

85. Debo, *Rise and Fall*, 52; Haliburton, "Chief Greenwood Leflore," 58.

86. "Section 3, Title Secured to Indians," in An act to provide for the exchange of lands with the Indians residing in any of the states or territories, and for their removal west of the river Mississippi, 412.

87. An act to provide for the exchange of lands with the Indians residing in any of the states or territories, and for their removal west of the river Mississippi, 411–412; Carson, "State Rights and Indian Removal," 36; Debo, *Rise and Fall*, 52, 262; DeRosier, *Removal of the Choctaw Indians*, 116–117; Foreman, *Indian Removal*, 21–23; Galloway and Kidwell, "Choctaw in the East," 527; Satz, "Mississippi Choctaw," 5.

88. Atkinson, *Splendid Land, Splendid People*, 225–227, 234, 319n; Foreman, *Indian Removal*, 193–194; McDermott, "Isaac McCoy's Second Exploring Trip," n51; *Treaty with the Chickasaw: 1830, unratified*.

89. Carson, "Greenwood Leflore," 230; Debo, *Rise and Fall*, 53–54; Foreman, *Indian Removal*, 23–26.

90. Baird, *Peter Pitchlynn*, 39; DeRosier, *Removal of the Choctaw Indians*, 118, 120–121; Ferguson, "Appendix: Treaties," 220–221.

91. Baird, *Peter Pitchlynn*, 39–40; Debo, *Rise and Fall*, 53–55; DeRosier, *Removal of the Choctaw Indians*, 120–124; Foreman, *Indian Removal*, 28, 29; Pate, *Reminiscences of George S. Gaines*, 13; Satz, "Mississippi Choctaw," 5; *Treaty of Dancing Rabbit Creek with the Choctaw*.

92. *Treaty of Dancing Rabbit Creek with the Choctaw*.

93. Debo, *Rise and Fall*, 69; DeRosier, *Removal of the Choctaw Indians*, 135–136; Kidwell, "Choctaw Struggle," 66–80; MDAH, Special Collections, 970.5 M533 1870; Satz, "Mississippi Choctaw," 6–9; *Treaty of Dancing Rabbit Creek with the Choctaw*.

94. Baird, *Peter Pitchlynn*, 39; Choctaw Citizens, *Memorial*, 1–2; DeRosier, *Removal of the Choctaw Indians*, 126–127; Foreman, *Indian Removal*, 27–28.

95. Baird, *Peter Pitchlynn*, 41–42; DeRosier, *Removal of the Choctaw Indians*, 132–133; Foreman, *Indian Removal*, 29–30; Satz, "Mississippi Choctaw," 7.

96. Carson, "State Rights and Indian Removal," 39–40; DeRosier, *Removal of the Choctaw*, 150–151; Foreman, *Indian Removal*, 31; Galloway and Kidwell, "Choctaw in the East," 516; Kidwell, "Choctaw Struggle," 68, 70; Satz, "Mississippi Choctaw," 8–9.

97. Baird, *Peter Pitchlynn*, 41–42; DeRosier, *Removal of the Choctaw*, 129–132; Foreman, *Indian Removal*, 38–41; Haliburton, "Chief Greenwood Leflore," 58.

98. Baird, *Peter Pitchlynn*, 7, 11, 42; Debo, *Rise and Fall*, 37; DeRosier, *Removal of the Choctaw*, 133–135; Foreman, *Indian Removal*, 31–37; Pate, *Reminiscences of George S. Gaines*, 1, 3, 14–16.

99. Baird, *Peter Pitchlynn*, 43–44, 54–55; Debo, *Rise and Fall*, 58, 153.

100. DeRosier, *Removal of the Choctaw*, 137; Pate, *Reminiscences of George S. Gaines*, 17.

101. DeRosier, *Removal of the Choctaw*, 137–139, 140n, 141–147, 152, 159; Foreman, *Indian Removal*, 42–43, 45–48; Pate, *Reminiscences of George S. Gaines*, 16–17. Eaton's untimely resignation resulted from the so-called Peggy Eaton affair, a clash of personalities among the wives of several key members of the Jackson administration. Pate, *Reminiscences of George S. Gaines*, 16–17.

102. DeRosier, *Removal of the Choctaw*, 143–144; Foreman, *Indian Removal*, 40n; Pate, *Reminiscences of George S. Gaines*, 17.

103. DeRosier, *Removal of the Choctaw*, 143–148; Foreman, *Indian Removal*, 44–70.

104. DeRosier, *Removal of the Choctaw*, 149–154; Foreman, *Indian Removal*, 71–75; Pate, *Reminiscences of George S. Gaines*, 19, 125.

105. DeRosier, *Removal of the Choctaw*, 154–158; Foreman, *Indian Removal*, 76–98.

106. DeRosier, *Removal of the Choctaw*, 157–158, 161–162; Foreman, *Indian Removal*, 96–102.

107. *Treaty with the Cherokee, 1835; Treaty with the Chickasaw, 1832; Treaty with the Creeks, 1832; Treaty with the Seminole, 1832*.

108. Atkinson, *Splendid Land, Splendid People*, 227, 228; Foreman, *Indian Removal*, 34–35, 48–49.

109. Pontotoc Creek is not named on some modern maps; James Atkinson describes the creek as "the northern headwater tributary . . . of present-day Chiwapa Creek. Atkinson, *Splendid Land, Splendid People*, 91.

110. Atkinson, *Splendid Land, Splendid People*, 228; Gibson, *Chickasaws*, 175.

111. Atkinson, *Splendid Land, Splendid People*, 213; *Treaty with the Chickasaw, 1832*.

112. Atkinson, *Splendid Land, Splendid People*, 228–229; McAlexander, "Saga of a Mixed-Blood Chickasaw Dynasty," 291; *Treaty with the Chickasaw, 1832*; *Treaty with the Chickasaw, 1832, Supplementary Articles*; *Treaty with the Chickasaw, 1834*.

113. Gibson, *Chickasaws*, 179, 180–182, 213; McAlexander, "Saga of a Mixed-Blood Chickasaw Dynasty," 293.

114. Debo, *Rise and Fall*, 71; Foreman, *Indian Removal*, 194, 200, 203; *Treaty with the Choctaw and Chickasaw, 1837*.

115. Foreman, *Indian Removal*, 206–208; Gibson, *Chickasaws*, 179, 182–185.

116. Foreman, *Indian Removal*, 205–205, 208–213; Gibson, *Chickasaws*, 183–185.

117. Atkinson, *Splendid Land, Splendid People*, 234; Foreman, *Indian Removal*, 213–217, 221, 224; Gibson, *Chickasaws*, 186–188, 191–192; Kidwell, "Choctaw in the West," 522; McAlexander, "Saga of a Mixed-Blood Chickasaw Dynasty," 293, 295; Swanton, *Indian Tribes of North America*, 289, 295, 313.

EPILOGUE

1. Haliburton, "Chief Greenwood Leflore," 58–63. Leflore died in 1865, and his famed Malmaison mansion burned in 1942. Haliburton, "Chief Greenwood Leflore," 62–63.

2. Galloway and Kidwell, "Choctaw in the East," 516; Kidwell, "Choctaw Struggle," 68, 80–81, 86–87; Satz, "Mississippi Choctaw," 8–17.

3. Debo, *Rise and Fall*, 71, 208–211; Gibson, *Chickasaws*, 217, 220–223; Kidwell, "Choctaw in the West," 524–525; *Treaty with the Choctaw and Chickasaw, June 22, 1855*.

4. Satz, "Mississippi Choctaw," 18.

5. Brightman and Wallace, "Chickasaw," 492; Gibson, *Chickasaws*, 264–268.

6. Debo, *Rise and Fall*, 86–87, 99–101; Gibson, *Chickasaws*, 290–293, 303–304; McKee and Schlenker, *Choctaws*, 91.

7. Clark, "Native Christianity since 1800," 748–750; Kidwell, "Choctaw Struggle," 81, 83–85; Roberts, "Second Choctaw Removal," 95; Satz, "Mississippi Choctaw," 19.

8. Brightman and Wallace, "Chickasaw," 492; Debo, *Rise and Fall*, 163–174, 246, 259–260, 262, 273; Galloway and Kidwell, "Choctaw in the East," 527; Gibson, *Chickasaws*, 280; Kidwell, "Choctaw Struggle," 85–86; Oklahoma Historical Society, "Atoka Agreement"; Satz, "Mississippi Choctaw," 20–21.

9. "Agreement with the Choctaws and Chickasaws, approved by Congress July 1, 1902, and ratified by Choctaws and Chickasaws September 25, 1902"; Debo, *Rise and Fall*, 272–276; Kidwell, "Choctaw in the West," 528; Kidwell, "Choctaw Struggle," 86; Roberts, "Second Choctaw Removal," 97–98, 103, 108; Satz, "Mississippi Choctaw," 21.

10. Act to Create an Indian Claims Commission; Brightman and Wallace, "Chickasaw," 494; Churchill and Morris, "Key Indian Laws and Cases," 15; Indian Claims Commission Dockets,

178–194, 304–332, 341–347, 562–572; Wheeler-Howard Act; Kappler, "Indian Citizenship Act," 1165–1166.

11. Churchill and Morris, "Key Indian Laws and Cases," 13–21; Kidwell, "Choctaw in the West," 530; McKee and Murray, "Economic Development since 1945," 124–126.

12. Churchill and Morris, "Key Indian Laws and Cases," 15–17; McKee and Schlenker, *Choctaws*, 150, 154. More recent congressional actions include the Indian Mineral Development Act of 1982, which promotes mining on Indian lands. Churchill and Morris, "Key Indian Laws and Cases," 17.

13. Brightman and Wallace, "Chickasaw," 494; National Park Service, U.S. Department of the Interior, "National NAGPRA."

14. Brightman and Wallace, "Chickasaw," 492–494; Kidwell, "Choctaw in the West," 527–530.

15. Hiram F. Gregory, personal communication August 10, 2009; Jena Band of Choctaw Indians, *Brief Historical Summary*.

16. Brain et al., "Tunica, Biloxi, and Ofo," 589–590.

17. May, "Alabama and Koasati," 407–409; Alabama-Coushatta Tribe of Texas, *Tribal History*.

18. Campisi, "Houma," 636–640, Figure 1.

19. United Houma Nation, *Houma History*.

20. Barnett, *Natchez Indians*, 38–39; Barnett, *Natchez Indians: A History*, 135; McAmis, *Indian People of the Edisto River*, 32–33.

21. Kidwell, "Choctaw Struggle," 87–88; McKee and Murray, "Economic Progress and Development," 122–124; McKee and Schlenker, *Choctaws*, 148, 149; Mississippi Band of Choctaw Indians Miko Beasley Denson, "Choctaw Chronology"; Satz, "Mississippi Choctaw," 22–23.

22. McKee and Schlenker, *Choctaws*, 149, 163; Mississippi Band of Choctaw Indians, "Tribal Profile"; Mississippi Band of Choctaw Indians Miko Beasley Denson, "Choctaw Chronology"; Satz, "Mississippi Choctaw," 22–24.

23. Mississippi Band of Choctaw Indians Miko Beasley Denson, "Choctaw Language"; Mississippi Band of Choctaw Indians Miko Beasley Denson, "Map of Tribal Lands"; Mississippi Band of Choctaw Indians Miko Beasley Denson, "Tribal Profile"; Williamson et al., "Act to Return the Nanih Waiya State Park and Mound."

BIBLIOGRAPHY

Acts passed at the first session of the Ninth General Assembly of the Mississippi Territory, begun and held at the Town of Washington, the sixth day of November, one thousand eight hundred and fifteen, published by authority. Natchez: printed by Peter Isler, 1815. Session 9/1 1815.12.13. Mississippi Department of Archives and History Special Collections.

An Act to Create an Indian Claims Commission [The Indian Claims Commission Act, 1946]. http://www.und.nodak.edu/dept/indian/Treaties/Indian%20Claims%20Commission%20 Act%201946.pdf.

An act to provide for the exchange of lands with the Indians residing in any of the states or territories, and for their removal west of the river Mississippi. Library of Congress, Statutes at Large, Twenty-first Congress, Session I, Chapter CXLVIII, 411–412. Online: American Memory: A Century of Lawmaking for a New Nation: U.S. Congressional Documents and Debates, 1774–1873, http://memory.loc.gov/cgi-bin/ampage?collId=llsl&fileName=004/ llsl004.db&recNum=459.

Adair, James. *The History of the American Indians.* 1775. Reprint, Tuscaloosa: University of Alabama Press, 2005.

"Agreement with the Choctaws and Chickasaws, approved by Congress July 1, 1902, and ratified by Choctaws and Chickasaws September 25, 1902." In *Laws, Decisions, and Regulations Affecting the Work of the Commissioner to the Five Civilized Tribes, 1893 to 1906, together with Maps Showing Classification of Lands in the Chickasaw, Choctaw, Cherokee, Creek, and Seminole Nations, and Bordering Districts, Railroads, and Principal Towns of the Indian Territory, Part 1 Legislation and Agreements.* 32 St. L., 641, compiled by the Commission to the Five Civilized Tribes. Washington, D.C.: Government Printing Office, 1906.

Alabama-Coushatta Tribe of Texas. *Tribal History.* http://www.ac-tribe.com/ac/index .php?option=com_content&task=view&id=24&Itemid=133.

American Southeast Maps, Alabama. http://www.tngenweb.org/cessions/ilcmap1.jpg.

Anderson, David G. "The Role of Cahokia in the Evolution of Southeastern Mississippian Society." In *Cahokia: Domination and Ideology in the Mississippian World*, ed. Timothy R. Pauketat and Thomas E. Emerson, 248–268. Lincoln: University of Nebraska Press, 1997.

Anderson, David G., and Robert C. Mainfort Jr. "An Introduction to Woodland Archaeology in the Southeast." In *The Woodland Southeast*, ed. David G. Anderson and Robert C. Mainfort Jr., 1–19. Tuscaloosa: University of Alabama Press, 2002.

Anderson, David G., and Kenneth E. Sassaman. "Early and Middle Holocene Periods, 9500 to 3750 B.C." In *Southeast*, ed. Raymond D. Fogelson, 87–100. Handbook of North American Indians, Vol. 14. William C. Sturtevant, gen. ed. Washington, D.C.: Smithsonian Institution, 2004.

———. "Paleoindian and Early Archaic Research in the South Carolina Area." In *The Paleoindian and Early Archaic Southeast*, ed. David G. Anderson and Kenneth E. Sassaman, 222–237. Tuscaloosa: University of Alabama Press, 1996.

Anderson, David G., Lisa D. O'Steen, and Kenneth E. Sassaman. "Environmental and Chronological Considerations." In *The Paleoindian and Early Archaic Southeast*, ed. David G. Anderson and Kenneth E. Sassaman, 16–28. Tuscaloosa: University of Alabama Press, 1996.

Anonymous. "The Natchez Man Gets Younger." *Science*, Research News, Briefings (December 21, 1990): 1662.

Anonymous [map ca. 1719]. *Carte du cours du Mississipi depuis La Nouvelle Orléans jusqu'au grand gouffre*. Bibliothèque nationale de France, Département des cartes et plans, Ge DD 2987 [8831]. http://rla.unc.edu/EMAS/regions-ms.html#sec_c.

Anonymous [map ca. 1720]. *Carte du cours de la rivière du Mississipi depuis les Illinois jusqu'à son embouchure*. Bibliothèque nationale de France, Département des cartes et plans, Ge DD 2987 [8819 B]. http://rla.unc.edu/EMAS/regions-ms.html#sec_c.

Anonymous [map ca. 1728]. *Cours du fleuve Saint-Louis depuis le Natchez jusqu'à La Balise*. Harvard Map Collection Karpinski series F 27-2-3; service historique de la Défense, département Marine, Cartes et plans, recueil 69, no. 11; formerly in Bibliothèque de la Service hydrographique, 4040C-11. http://rla.unc.edu/EMAS/regions-ms.html#sec_c.

Anonymous [map 1730]. *Plan des Deux Forts des Natchez Assiegez // au mois de fevrier 1730 Par les Français // Tchactas Tonicas Colapissas et Oumas // La présente carte levée sur les lieux à l'Estime // faite et dessinée a la N.lle Orleans le six avril // mil sept cent trente*. Bibliothèque nationale de France, Estampes, Vd 21 (3) Fol.

ArchNet. Archaeological Research Institute, Arizona State University. http://archnet.asu.edu/archives/ceramic/hgloss/hgloss.html.

Arco, Lee J. "Geoarchaeology of the Buried Poverty Point Landscape at Jaketown." Paper presented at the Southeastern Archaeological Conference, Sixty-sixth Annual Meeting, November 4–7, 2009, Mobile, Ala.

Asch, David L., and Nancy B. Asch. "Prehistoric Plant Cultivation in West-Central Illinois." In *Prehistoric Food Production in North America*, ed. Richard I. Ford, 149–204. Anthropological Papers, Museum of Anthropology, University of Michigan, No. 75. Ann Arbor, Mich., 1985.

Atkinson, James R. *Splendid Land, Splendid People: The Chickasaw Indians to Removal*. Tuscaloosa: University of Alabama Press, 2004.

Baird, W. David. *Peter Pitchlynn: Chief of the Choctaws*. Norman: University of Oklahoma Press, 1972.

Barnes, Lela. "Journal of Isaac McCoy for the Exploring Expedition of 1828." *Kansas Historical Quarterly* 5, no. 3 (August 1936): 227–277. Online as *Kansas Collection: Kansas Historical Quarterlies*, http://www.kancoll.org/khq/1936/36_3_barnes.htm.

Barnett, James F., Jr. "Natchez House Reconstruction, Grand Village of the Natchez Indians." Rev. ed. On file, Grand Village of the Natchez Indians, Mississippi Department of Archives and History, Natchez, 2002.

———. *The Natchez Indians*. Rev. ed. Mississippi Department of Archives and History Popular Report, 2002.

———. *The Natchez Indians: A History to 1735*. Jackson: University Press of Mississippi, 2007.

———. "A New Building Location at the Fatherland Site (Grand Village of the Natchez)." *Mississippi Archaeology* 19, no. 1 (June 1984): 2–11.

———. "The Play Site (22-Ad-812): A Natchez Phase Burial in Natchez, Mississippi." *Mississippi Archaeology* 21, no. 2, (December 1986): 3–11.

Barnhill, J. Herschel. "Indian Territory." In *The Louisiana Purchase: A Historical and Geographic Encyclopedia*, ed. Junius P. Rodriguez, 149–151. Santa Barbara, Calif.: ABC-Clio, 2002.

Bartram, William. *Travels of William Bartram*. Ed. Mark Van Doran. New York: Macy-Masius, 1928. Reprint, New York: Dover, 1955.

Baudier, Roger. *The Catholic Church in Louisiana*. New Orleans: A. W. Hyatt, 1939.

Bell, Ann Linda, trans.; Patricia Galloway, annotations. "Minet: Voyage Made from Canada Inland Going Southward during the Year 1682, By Order of Monsieur Colbert, Minister of State." In *Three Primary Documents, La Salle, the Mississippi, and the Gulf*, ed. Robert S. Weddle, Mary C. Morkovsky, Patricia Galloway, 29–68. College Station: Texas A&M University Press, 1987.

Bellin, Jacques-Nicolas. *Carte de la Louisiane, cours du Mississipi et pais voisins*. Bibliothèque nationale de France, Cote: IFN-6700276, 1744.

Bense, Judith A. *Archaeology of the Southeastern United States: Paleoindian to World War I*. New York: Academic Press, 1994.

Biographical Directory of the United States Congress. http://bioguide.congress.gov/biosearch/biosearch.asp.

Blain, William T. *Education in the Old Southwest: A History of Jefferson College, Washington, Mississippi*. Washington, Miss.: Friends of Jefferson College, 1977.

Blake, Leonard W. "Corn and Other Plants from Prehistory into History in the Eastern United States." In *Protohistoric Period in Mid-South: Proceedings of the 1983 Mid-South Archaeological Conference*, ed. David H. Dye and Ronald C. Bristers, 3–13. Archaeological Report No. 18. Mississippi Department of Archives and History, Jackson, 1986.

Blitz, John H. *An Archaeological Study of the Mississippi Choctaw Indians*. Archaeological Report No. 16. Mississippi Department of Archives and History, Jackson, 1985.

———. "The McRae Mound: A Middle Woodland Site in Southeastern Mississippi." *Mississippi Archaeology* 21, no. 2 (December 1986): 11–39.

Blitz, John H., and C. Baxter Mann. *Fisherfolk, Farmers, and Frenchmen*. Archaeological Report No. 30. Mississippi Department of Archives and History, Jackson, 2000.

Bowne, Eric E. "'Carying awaye their Corne and Children': The Effects of Westo Slave Raids on the Indians of the Lower South." In *Mapping the Mississippian Shatter Zone: The Colonial Indian Slave Trade and Regional Instability in the American South*, ed. Robbie Ethridge and Sheri M. Shuck-Hall, 104–114. Lincoln: University of Nebraska Press, 2009.

———. *The Westo Indians: Slave Traders of the Early Colonial South*. Tuscaloosa: University of Alabama Press, 2005.

Brain, Jeffrey P. "Introduction: Update of De Soto Studies since the United States De Soto Expedition Commission Report." In John R. Swanton, *Final Report of the United States De Soto Commission*, xl–xlvi. Washington, D.C.: Smithsonian Institution Press, 1985.

———. "La Salle at the Natchez: An Archaeological and Historical Perspective." In *La Salle and His Legacy: Frenchmen and Indians in the Lower Mississippi Valley*, ed. Patricia Galloway, 49–59. Jackson: University Press of Mississippi, 1982.

———. "Late Prehistoric Settlement Patterning in the Yazoo Basin and Natchez Bluff Regions of the Lower Mississippi Valley." In *Mississippian Settlement Patterns*, ed. Bruce D. Smith, 331–368. New York: Academic Press, 1978.

———. "The Natchez Paradox." *Ethnology* 10, no. 2 (1971): 215–222.

———. *Tunica Archaeology.* Cambridge, Mass.: Peabody Museum of Archaeology and Ethnology, Harvard University, 1988.

———. *Tunica Treasure.* Papers of the Peabody Museum of American Archaeology and Ethnology, Harvard University 1 (1979). Published jointly by the Peabody Museum, Harvard University, Cambridge, and the Peabody Museum of Salem, Massachusetts.

———. *Winterville: Late Prehistoric Culture Contact in the Lower Mississippi Valley.* Archaeological Report No. 23. Mississippi Department of Archives and History, Jackson, 1989.

Brain, Jeffrey P., George Roth, and Willem J. De Reuse. "Tunica, Biloxi, and Ofo." In *Southeast*, ed. Raymond D. Fogelson, 586–597. Handbook of North American Indians, Vol. 14. William C. Sturtevant, gen. ed. Washington, D.C.: Smithsonian Institution, 2004.

Braund, Kathryn E. Holland. "James Adair: His Life and History." In James Adair, *The History of the American Indians*, 1–53. Tuscaloosa: University of Alabama Press, 2005.

Brightman, Robert A., and Pamela S. Wallace. "Chickasaw." In *Southeast*, ed. Raymond D. Fogelson, 478–496. Handbook of North American Indians, Vol. 14. William C. Sturtevant, gen. ed. Washington, D.C.: Smithsonian Institution, 2004.

Brinton, Daniel G. *The Myths of the New World: A Treatise on the Symbolism and Mythology of the Red Race in America.* 2nd ed., rev. New York: Henry Holt, 1876.

Brookes, Samuel O. *The Grand Gulf Mound: Salvage of an Early Marksville Burial Mound in Claiborne County, Mississippi.* Archaeological Report No. 1. Mississippi Department of Archives and History, Jackson, 1976.

———. *The Hester Site: An Early Archaic Occupation in Monroe County, Mississippi, a Preliminary Report.* Archaeological Report No. 3. Mississippi Department of Archives and History, Jackson, 1979.

———. "Prehistoric Exchange in Mississippi, 10,000 B.C–A.D. 1600." In *Raw Materials and Exchange in the Mid-South*, ed. Evan Peacock and Samuel O. Brookes, 86–94. Archaeological Report No. 29. Mississippi Department of Archives and History, Jackson, 1999.

Brookes, Samuel O., and Cheryl Taylor. "Tchula Period Ceramics in the Upper Sunflower Region." In *The Tchula Period in the Mid-South and Lower Mississippi Valley*, ed. David H. Dye and Ronald C. Brister, 23–27. Archaeological Report No. 17. Mississippi Department of Archives and History, Jackson, 1986.

Brose, David S. "From the Southeastern Ceremonial Complex to the Southern Cult: You Can't Tell the Players without a Program." In *The Southeastern Ceremonial Complex: Artifacts and Analysis, the Cottonlandia Conference*, ed. Patricia Galloway, 27–37. Lincoln: University of Nebraska Press, 1989.

Broster, John B., and Mark R. Norton. "Recent Paleoindian Research in Tennessee." In *The Paleoindian and Early Archaic Southeast*, ed. David G. Anderson and Kenneth E. Sassaman, 288–297. Tuscaloosa: University of Alabama Press, 1996.

Broutin, Ignace-François [map 1723]. *Carte des environs du fort Rosalie aux Natchez 1723.* Bibliothèque nationale de France, http://visualiseur.bnf.fr/Visualiseur?Destination=Gallica &O=IFN-6700314).

———. [map 1731]. *Carte particulière du cours du fleuve Missisipy ou St. Louis à la Lousiane, depuis la Nouvelle Orléans jusqu'aux Natchez, levée par par estime en 1721, 1726, 1731 et dressée au mois d'Aoust 1731, par Broutin.* Bibliothèque nationale de France, Département des cartes et plans, Ge C 5015. http://rla.unc.edu/Natchez/#sec_a.

Broutin, Ignace-François, Bernard de Vergès, and François Saucier [map 1740]. *Carte particulère d'une partie de la Louisianne, où les fleuve & rivierre ont esté relevés à l'estime et les routtes par terre relevées et mesurées aux pas par le Sr. Broutin, de Vergès ingeneurs & Saucier dessinateur. A la Nouvelle-Orléans, ce 27 juin 1740.* Service historique de la défense, département Marine, Cartes et plans, recueil 69, No. 15; formerly in Bibliothèque de la Service hydrographique, 4040C-16.

Brown, Calvin S. *Archaeology of Mississippi.* First published in 1926 for the Mississippi Geological Survey by the University [of Mississippi]. Reprint, Jackson: University Press of Mississippi, 1992.

Brown, Ian W. "An Archaeological Study of Culture Contact and Change in the Natchez Bluffs Region." In *La Salle and His Legacy: Frenchmen and Indians in the Lower Mississippi Valley,* 176–193. Jackson: University Press of Mississippi, 1982.

———. "The Calumet Ceremony in the Southeast and Its Archaeological Manifestations." *American Antiquity* 54 (1989): 311–331.

———. "Concluding Thoughts on Bottle Creek and Its Position in the Mississippian World." In *Bottle Creek: A Pensacola Culture Site in South Alabama,* ed. Ian W. Brown, 205–226. Tuscaloosa: University of Alabama Press, 2003.

———. "Culture Contact along the I-69 Corridor: Prehistoric and Historic Use of the Northern Yazoo Basin, Mississippi." In *Time's River: Archaeological Syntheses from the Lower Mississippi Valley,* ed. Janet Rafferty and Evan Peacock, 357–394. Tuscaloosa: University of Alabama Press, 2008.

———. *Decorated Pottery of the Lower Mississippi Valley: A Sorting Manual.* Jackson: Mississippi Archaeological Association and Mississippi Department of Archives and History, 1998.

———. "Early 18th Century French-Indian Culture Contact in the Yazoo Bluffs Region of the Lower Mississippi Valley." Ph.D. diss., Brown University, 1979.

———, ed. *Excavations at the Anna Site (22Ad500), Adams County, Mississippi: A Preliminary Report, with Contributions by Virgil R. Beasley, Tony Boudreaux, Richard S. Fuller, and John C. Hall.* Tuscaloosa: Gulf Coast Survey, University of Alabama, 1997.

———. *Fort St. Pierre Site.* National Historic Landmark Nomination, U.S. Department of the Interior, National Park Service, 1997.

———. "Introduction to the Bottle Creek Site." In *Bottle Creek: A Pensacola Culture Site in South Alabama,* ed. Ian W. Brown, 1–26. Tuscaloosa: University of Alabama Press, 2003.

———. *Natchez Indian Archaeology: Culture Change and Stability in the Lower Mississippi Valley.* Archaeological Report No. 15. Mississippi Department of Archives and History, Jackson, 1985.

———. "Plaquemine Culture Structure Types in the Natchez Bluffs and Surrounding Regions of the Lower Mississippi Valley." On file, Grand Village of the Natchez Indians, Mississippi Department of Archives and History, Natchez, 1982.

———. "Prehistory of the Gulf Coastal Plain After 500 B.C." In *Southeast,* ed. Raymond D. Fogelson, 574–585. Handbook of North American Indians, Vol. 14. William C. Sturtevant, gen. ed. Washington, D.C.: Smithsonian Institution, 2004.

———. *The Role of Salt in Eastern North American Prehistory.* Anthropological Study No. 3. Department of Culture, Recreation, and Tourism, Louisiana Archaeological Survey and Antiquities Commission, Baton Rouge, 1981.

———. *The Southeastern Check Stamped Pottery Tradition: A View from Louisiana.* Mid-Continent Journal of Archaeology Special Paper 4. Kent, Ohio: Kent State University Press, 1982.

Brown, Ian W., and Jeffrey P. Brain. "Archaeology of the Natchez Bluff Region, Mississippi: Hypothesized Cultural and Environmental Factors Influencing Local Population Movements." Paper presented at the Southeastern Archaeological Conference, Tuscaloosa, Alabama, November 4–6, 1976.

Brown, James A. "Exchange and Interaction until 1500." In *Southeast*, ed. Raymond D. Fogelson, 677–685. Handbook of North American Indians, Vol. 14. William C. Sturtevant, gen. ed. Washington, D.C.: Smithsonian Institution, 2004.

———. "On the Identity of the Birdman within Mississippian Period Art and Iconography." In *Ancient Objects and Sacred Realms: Interpretations of Mississippian Iconography*, ed. F. Kent Reilly III and James F. Garber, 56–106. Austin: University of Texas Press, 2007.

———. "Sequencing the Braden Style within Mississippian Period Art and Iconography." In *Ancient Objects and Sacred Realms: Interpretations of Mississippian Iconography*, ed. F. Kent Reilly III and James F. Garber, 213–245. Austin: University of Texas Press, 2007.

Bruseth, James E. "Poverty Point Development as Seen at the Cedarland and Claiborne Sites, Southern Mississippi." In *The Poverty Point Culture: Local Manifestations, Subsistence Practices, and Trade Networks*, ed. Kathleen M. Byrd, 7–25. Geoscience and Man 29. Geoscience Publications, Department of Geography and Anthropology, Louisiana State University, Baton Rouge, 1991.

Bunn, Mike, and Clay Williams. *Battle for the Southern Frontier: The Creek War and the War of 1812*. Charleston, S.C.: History Press, 2008.

Bureau of Economic Geology, University of Texas at Austin. http://www.beg.utexas.edu/main web/publications/graphics/chert.htm.

Butler, Robert. *"Secret" Journal on Negotiations of the Chickasaw Treaty of 1818*. Yale Law School, Lillian Goldman Law Library, The Avalon Project, Documents in Law, History and Diplomacy. http://avalon.law.yale.edu/19th_century/nt005.asp.

Byington, Cyrus. *A Dictionary of the Choctaw Language*. Ed. John R. Swanton and Henry S. Halbert. Bulletin No. 46. Bureau of American Ethnology, Smithsonian Institution, Washington, D.C., 1915.

Calloway, Colin G. *The Scratch of a Pen: 1763 and the Transformation of North America*. New York: Oxford University Press, 2006.

Campisi, Jack. "Houma." In *Southeast*, ed. Raymond D. Fogelson, 632–641. Handbook of North American Indians, Vol. 14. William C. Sturtevant, gen. ed. Washington, D.C.: Smithsonian Institution, 2004.

Carlton, Kenneth H. "Foreword." In John R. Swanton, *Source Material for the Social and Ceremonial Life of the Choctaw Indians*, v–x. Bulletin No. 103. Bureau of American Ethnology, Smithsonian Institution, Washington, D.C., 1931.

———. "Nanih Waiya (22WI500): An Historical and Archaeological Overview." *Mississippi Archaeology* 34, no. 2 (Winter 1999): 125–155.

Carson, James Taylor "Greenwood LeFlore: Southern Creole, Choctaw Chief." In *Pre-removal Choctaw History: Exploring New Paths*, ed. Greg O'Brien, 221–236. Norman: University of Oklahoma Press, 2008.

———. "Native Americans, the Market Revolution, and Culture Exchange: The Choctaw Cattle Economy, 1690–1830." In *Pre-removal Choctaw History: Exploring New Paths*, ed. Greg O'Brien, 183–189. Norman: University of Oklahoma Press, 2008.

———. *Searching for the Bright Path: The Mississippi Choctaws from Prehistory to Removal*. Lincoln: University of Nebraska Press, 1999.

———. "State Rights and Indian Removal in Mississippi: 1817–1835." *Journal of Mississippi History* 57, no. 1 (February 1995): 25–41.

Charlevoix, Pierre-François-Xavier de. *Letters to the Duchess of Lesdiguieres giving an account of a vouage to Canada, and travels through that vast country, and Louisiana, to the Gulf of Mexico: undertaken by order of the present King of France.* London: printed for R. Goadby 1763.

Chickasaw Indian Treaties. http://www.nanations.com/chickasaw/.

Chickasaw Treaty—1805. Yale Law School, Lillian Goldman Law Library, The Avalon Project, Documents in Law, History and Diplomacy. http://avalon.law.yale.edu/19th_century/nt003 .asp.

Choctaw Citizens of the State of Mississippi. *Memorial of the Choctaw Citizens of the State of Mississippi to the Congress of the United States.* 27th Congress, 2nd Sess., Document No. 15, House of Representatives, referred to the Committee on Indian Affairs, December 15, 1841.

Choctaw Nation Index of Treaties. http://www.felihkatubbe.com/ChoctawNation/treaties/.

Churchill, Ward, and Glenn T. Morris. "Key Indian Laws and Cases." In *The State of Native America: Genocide, Colonization and Resistance,* ed. M. Annette Jaimes, 13–21. Cambridge, Mass.: South End Press, 1992.

Claassen, Cheryl. "New Hypotheses for the Demise of the Shell Mound Archaic." In *The Archaic Period in the Mid-South: Proceedings of the 1989 Mi-South Archaeological Conference, Memphis, Tennessee—July 15, 1989,* ed. Charles H. McNutt, 66–71. Archaeological Report No. 24. Mississippi Department of Archives and History, Jackson. Occasional Papers No. 16, Anthropological Research Center, Memphis State University, 1991.

Claassen, Cheryl, and Rosemary A. Joyce, eds. *Women in Prehistory: North America and Mesoamerica.* Philadelphia: University of Pennsylvania Press, 1997.

Claiborne, J. F. H. *Mississippi as a Province, Territory, and State with Biographical Notices of Eminent Citizens.* 1880. Spartanburg, S.C.: Reprint Company, 1978.

Clark, C. Blue. "Native Christianity since 1800." In *Southeast,* ed. Raymond D. Fogelson, 742–752. Handbook of North American Indians, Vol. 14. William C. Sturtevant, gen. ed. Washington, D.C.: Smithsonian Institution, 2004.

Clark, Thomas D., and John D. W. Guice. *The Old Southwest, 1795–1830: Frontiers in Conflict.* Norman: University of Oklahoma Press, 1996.

Clayton, Lawrence A., Vernon J. Knight Jr., and Edward C. Moore, eds. *The De Soto Chronicles: The Expedition of Hernando De Soto to North America in 1539–1543.* 2 vols. Tuscaloosa: University of Alabama Press, 1993.

Cleland, Charles E., Jr. "Appendix 2. Analysis of the Faunal Remains of the Fatherland Site." In Robert S. Neitzel, *Archaeology of the Fatherland Site: The Grand Village of the Natchez,* 96–101. Anthropological Papers of the American Museum of Natural History 51, Part 1. New York, 1965.

Cockrell, Thomas D. "The Politics of Land in Jacksonian Mississippi." *Journal of Mississippi History* 47, no. 1 (February 1985): 1–14.

———. "United States Senators and Representatives from Mississippi, 1828–1836: An Introduction." *Journal of Mississippi History* 49, no. 1 (February 1987): 35–48.

Collot, Georges-Henri-Victor. *Carte particuliere du cours du Mississippi depuise le Missouri et le pays des Illinois jusqu'a l'embouchure de ce fleuve en 1796.* Harvard Map Collection, Harvard College Library. http://ids.lib.harvard.edu/ids/view/2655331?buttons=y.

Connaway, John M. *Archaeological Investigations in Mississippi: 1969–1977*. Archaeological Report No. 6. Mississippi Department of Archives and History, Jackson, 1981.

——. *The Denton Site: A Middle Archaic Occupation in the Northern Yazoo Basin, Mississippi*. Archaeological Report No. 4. Mississippi Department of Archives and History, Jackson, 1977.

——. *Fishweirs: A World Perspective with Emphasis on the Fishweirs of Mississippi*. Archaeological Report No. 33. Mississippi Department of Archives and History, Jackson, 2007.

——. *The Wilsford Site (22-Co-516), Coahoma County, Mississippi: A Late Mississippi Period Settlement in the Northern Yazoo Basin of Mississippi*. Archaeological Report No. 14. Mississippi Department of Archives and History, Jackson, 1984.

Connaway, John M., Samuel O. McGahey, and Clarence H. Webb. *Teoc Creek: A Poverty Point Site in Carroll County, Mississippi*. Archaeological Report No. 3, Mississippi Department of Archives and History, Jackson, 1977.

Conrad, Glenn R., ed. *The Louisiana Purchase Bicentennial Series in Louisiana History*. Vol. 1, *The French Experience in Louisiana*. Lafayette: Center for Louisiana Studies, University of Southwestern Louisiana, 1995.

Constitution and Form of Government for the State of Mississippi [Constitution of 1817]. *Mississippi History Now*, online publication of the Mississippi Historical Society. http://mshistory.k12.ms.us/articles/100/index.php?s=extra&id=267.

Cook, Stephen R. *The Chickasaw Village Sources*. Table 1. http://www.thechickasawvillages.com/table_1.html.

Crane, Verner W. *The Southern Frontier: 1670–1732*. 1929. Reprint, Tuscaloosa: University of Alabama Press, 2004.

Crawford, Jessica F. "Archaic Effigy Beads: A New Look at Some Old Beads." Master's thesis, University of Mississippi, 2003.

Cross, Ralph D., and Robert W. Wales, eds., Charles T. Traylor, cart. *Atlas of Mississippi*. Jackson: University Press of Mississippi, 1974.

Culin, Stewart. *Games of the North American Indians*. New York: Dover, 1975.

Cushman, H. B. *History of the Choctaw, Chickasaw, and Natchez Indians*. 1899. Reprint, New York: Russell and Russell, 1972.

Dart, Henry P., and Heloise H. Cruzat, trans. "The Concession at Natchez." *Louisiana Historical Quarterly* 8, no. 3 (July 1925): 389–397.

Davies, Norman. *Europe: A History*. Oxford: Oxford University Press, 1996.

Debo, Angie. "Foreword." In H. B. Cushman, *History of the Choctaw, Chickasaw, and Natchez Indians*, 7–10. 1899. Reprint, New York: Russell and Russell, 1972.

——. "Foreword." In Grant Foreman, *Indian Removal: The Emigration of the Five Civilized Tribes of Indians*, 3–6. 1932. Reprint, Norman: University of Oklahoma Press, 1972.

——. *The Rise and Fall of the Choctaw Republic*. 1934. Reprint, Norman: University of Oklahoma Press, 1972

Delanglez, Jean. *The French Jesuits in Lower Louisiana: 1700–1763*. Washington D.C.: Catholic University of America, 1935. Reprint, New York: AMS Press, 1974.

Demallie, Raymond J. "Tutelo and Neighboring Groups." In *Southeast*, ed. Raymond D. Fogelson, 286–300. Handbook of North American Indians, Vol. 14. William C. Sturtevant, gen. ed. Washington, D.C.: Smithsonian Institution, 2004.

Depratter, Chester B. "The Chiefdom of Cofitachequi." In *The Forgotten Centuries: Indians and Europeans in the American South, 1521–1704*, ed. Charles Hudson and Carmen Chaves Tesser, 197–226. Athens: University of Georgia Press, 1994.

De Reuse, William J. "Biloxi and Ofo." In *Southeast*, ed. Raymond D. Fogelson, 593–597. Handbook of North American Indians, Vol. 14. William C. Sturtevant, gen. ed. Washington, D.C.: Smithsonian Institution, 2004.

DeRosier, Arthur H., Jr. *The Removal of the Choctaw Indians*. Knoxville: University of Tennessee Press, 1970. Reprint, New York: Harper Torchbooks, Harper & Row, 1971.

Diron d'Artaguiette, Bernard [map 1719]. *Fleuve Saint Louis cy devant Mississipy relevé à la boussole par le Sr. Diron l'an 1719 depuis la Nouvelle Orléans*. Bibliothèque nationale de France, Département des cartes et plans, Ge C 9120 Rés. http://visualiseur.bnf.fr/CadresFenetre?M=notice&O=IFN-7849849.

Dobyns, Henry. *Their Number Became Thinned: Native American Population Dynamics in Eastern North America*. Knoxville: University of Tennessee Press, 1983.

d'Oney, J. Daniel. "The Houma Nation in Mississippi's Early French Colonial Period: Modern Interpretations and Influences." *Journal of Mississippi History* 68, no. 1 (Spring 2006): 43–64.

Dorsey, James O., and John R. Swanton. *A Dictionary of the Biloxi and Ofo Languages, Accompanied with Thirty-One Biloxi Texts and Numerous Biloxi Phrases*. Bulletin No. 47. Bureau of American Ethnology, Smithsonian Institution, Washington, D.C., 1912.

Dowd, Gregory Evans. "The American Revolution to the Mid-Nineteenth Century." In *Southeast*, ed. Raymond D. Fogelson, 139–151. Handbook of North American Indians, Vol. 14. William C. Sturtevant, gen. ed. Washington, D.C.: Smithsonian Institution, 2004.

———. *War under Heaven: Pontiac, the Indian Nations, & the British Empire*. Baltimore: Johns Hopkins University Press, 2002.

Dumont de Montigny, François-Benjamin. *Regards sur le monde atlantique*. 1753. Reprint, Québec: Septentrion, Sillery, 2008.

Dunbar, James S., and S. David Webb. "Bone and Ivory Tools from Paleoindian Sites in Florida." In *The Paleoindian and Early Archaic in the Southeast*, ed. David G. Anderson and Kenneth E. Sassaman, 331–353. Tuscaloosa: University of Alabama Press, 1996.

Du Pratz, Antoine Simone Le Page. *Histoire de la Louisiane*. 3 vols. Trans. Gordon Sayre. Paris: De Bure, Delaguette, Lambert 1758. http://www.uoregon.edu/~gsayre/LPDP.html.

———. *The History of Louisiana or of the Western Parts of Virginia and Carolina*. 1774. Reprint, Baton Rouge, La.: Claitor's Publishing Division, 1972.

———. *The History of Louisiana or of the Western Parts of Virginia and Carolina*. Ed. Joseph G. Tregle Jr. Facsimile reproduction of the 1774 ed. Baton Rouge: published for the Louisiana American Bicentennial Commission by Louisiana State University Press, 1976.

Du Ru, Paul. *Journal of Paul Du Ru [February 1 to May 8, 1700]: Missionary Priest to Louisiana*. Trans. with introduction and notes from a manuscript in the Newberry Library by Ruth Lapham Butler. Fairfield, Wash.: Ye Galleon Press, 1934.

Dye, David H. "Ritual, Medicine, and the War Trophy Iconographic Theme in the Mississippian Southeast." In *Ancient Objects and Sacred Realms: Interpretations of Mississippian Iconography*, ed. F. Kent Reilly III and James F. Garber, 152–174. Austin: University of Texas Press, 2007.

Dyson, John. "In Search of Yaneka." Paper presented at the 2005 meeting of the Mississippi Archaeological Association, Vidalia, Louisiana, March 5, 2005.

Early, Ann M. "Prehistory of the Western Interior after 500 B.C." In *Southeast*, ed. Raymond D. Fogelson, 560–573. Handbook of North American Indians, Vol. 14. William C. Sturtevant, gen. ed. Washington, D.C.: Smithsonian Institution, 2004.

Elliott, Jack D., Jr. "Choctaw Agency, Natchez Trace Parkway: Archaeological and Historical Investigation, Madison County, Mississippi." SEAC Accessions 1133 and 1205, Cobb Institute of Archaeology/Mississippi State University in cooperation with Southeast Archaeological Center/National Park Service/Tallahassee, Florida, 2000.

———. "Paving the Trace." *Journal of Mississippi History* 64, no. 3 (2007): 199–233.

———. "The Plymouth Fort and the Creek War: A Mystery Solved." *Journal of Mississippi History* 62, no. 4 (2000): 328–372.

Emerson, Thomas E. *Cahokia and the Archaeology of Power.* Tuscaloosa: University of Alabama Press, 1997.

———. "Water, Serpents, and the Underworld: An Exploration into Cahokian Symbolism." In *The Southeastern Ceremonial Complex: Artifacts and Analysis, the Cottonlandia Conference,* ed. Patricia Galloway, 45–92. Lincoln: University of Nebraska Press, 1989.

Ethridge, Robbie. *Creek Country: The Creek Indians and Their World.* Chapel Hill: University of North Carolina Press, 2003.

———. *From Chicaza to Chickasaw: The European Invasion and the Transformation of the Mississippian World, 1540–1715.* Chapel Hill: University of North Carolina Press, 2010.

———. "Introduction: Mapping the Mississippian Shatter Zone." In *Mapping the Mississippian Shatter Zone: The Colonial Indian Slave Trade and Regional Instability in the American South,* ed. Robbie Ethridge and Sheri M. Shuck-Hall, 1–62. Lincoln: University of Nebraska Press.

———. "The Making of a Militaristic Slaving Society: The Chickasaws and the Colonial Indian Slave Trade." In *Indian Slavery in Colonial America,* ed. Alan Gallay, 252–276. Lincoln: University of Nebraska Press, 2009.

Ethridge, Robbie, and Charles Hudson, eds. *The Transformation of the Southeastern Indians, 1540–1760.* Jackson: University Press of Mississippi, 2002.

Ethridge, Robbie, and Sheri M. Shuck-Hall, eds. *Mapping the Mississippian Shatter Zone: The Colonial Indian Slave Trade and Regional Instability in the American South.* Lincoln: University of Nebraska Press, 2009.

Fagan, Brian. *The Little Ice Age: How Climate Made History, 1300–1850.* New York: Basic Books, 2000.

Faulkner, Charles H. "Middle Woodland Community and Settlement Patterns on the Eastern Highland Rim, Tennessee." In *Middle Woodland Settlement and Ceremonialism in the Mid-South and Lower Mississippi Valley,* ed. Robert C. Mainfort Jr., 77–98. Archaeological Report No. 22. Mississippi Department of Archives and History, Jackson, 1988.

Ferguson, Robert B. "Appendix: Treaties between the United States and the Choctaw Nation." In *The Choctaw Before Removal,* ed. Carolyn Keller Reeves, 214–230. Jackson: University Press of Mississippi, 1985.

Fickle, James E. *Mississippi Forests and Forestry.* Jackson: University Press of Mississippi, 2001.

Fields, Rita D. "Contributions to Ceramic Chronology Building in Southeast Mississippi: Prehistoric Ceramics Recovered from 22GN680, 22GN685, and 22GN687, Greene County." *Mississippi Archaeology* 40, no. 2 (Winter 2005): 101–140.

Ford, James A. *Analysis of Indian Village Site Collections from Louisiana and Mississippi.* Anthropological Study, Department of Conservation, Louisiana Geological Survey No. 2, Baton Rouge, 1936.

Ford, James A., Philip Phillips, and William G. Haag. *The Jaketown Site in West-Central Mississippi.* Anthropological Papers of the American Museum of Natural History 45, Part 1. New York, 1955.

Ford, Janet "Introduction." In Calvin S. Brown, *Archaeology of Mississippi,* xi–xxii. First published in 1926 for the Mississippi Geological Survey by the University. Reprint, Jackson: University Press of Mississippi, 1992.

Foreman, Grant. *Indian Removal: The Emigration of the Five Civilized Tribes of Indians.* 1932. Reprint, Norman: University of Oklahoma Press, 1972.

Foster, William C., ed. "Appendix A. Official Report of the Taking Possession of the Acansa Country, 13th and 14th March, 1682." In *The La Salle Expedition on the Mississippi River: A Lost Manuscript of Nicolas de La Salle, 1682,* ed. William C. Foster, 127–130. Austin: Texas State Historical Association, 2003.

———, ed. "Appendix B. Official Report of the Taking Possession at the Mouth of the Sea or the Gulf of Mexico." In *The La Salle Expedition on the Mississippi River: A Lost Manuscript of Nicolas de La Salle, 1682,* ed. William C. Foster, 131–136. Austin: Texas State Historical Association, 2003.

———, ed. "Appendix C. La Salle's 1682 Mississippi River Expedition Itinerary." In *The La Salle Expedition on the Mississippi River: A Lost Manuscript of Nicolas de La Salle, 1682,* ed. William C. Foster, 137–147. Austin: Texas State Historical Association, 2003.

———, ed. *The La Salle Expedition on the Mississippi River: A Lost Manuscript of Nicolas de La Salle, 1682.* Austin: Texas State Historical Association, 2003.

———, ed. "The Nicolas de La Salle Journal." In *The La Salle Expedition on the Mississippi River: A Lost Manuscript of Nicolas de La Salle, 1682,* ed. William C. Foster, 91–125. Austin: Texas State Historical Association, 2003.

Fox, William A. "Events as Seen from the North: The Iroquois and Colonial Slavery." In *Mapping the Mississippian Shatter Zone: The Colonial Indian Slave Trade and Regional Instability in the American South,* ed. Robbie Ethridge and Sheri M. Shuck-Hall, 63–80. Lincoln: University of Nebraska Press, 2009.

Frank, Joseph V., III. "In Defense of Hutchins's Natchez Indian." *Mississippi Archaeology* 10, no. 4 (April 1975): 7–12.

———. "The Rice Site: A Natchez Indian Cemetery." *Mississippi Archaeology* 15, no. 2 (December 1980): 32–41.

Franquelin, Jean Baptiste Louis [map 1686]. *Amérique septentrion.lle [i.e. septentrionale]: composée, corigée, et augme⁻tée, sur les iournaux, mémoires, et observations les plus justes qui en ón'ietes.tes en l'année 1685 & 1686, par plusieurs particuliés / par I Baptiste Louis Franquelin,* g[éographe] du Roy. Bibliothèque du Dépôt des cartes et plans de La Marine, Atlas B4040— piece n. 6. Library of Congress Geography and Map Division call number: G3300 1685 .F7 Vault, Washington, D.C.

Fuller, Richard S. "Out of the Moundville Shadow: The Origin and Evolution of Pensacola Culture." In *Bottle Creek: A Pensacola Culture Site in South Alabama,* ed. Ian W. Brown, 27–62. Tuscaloosa: University of Alabama Press, 2003.

Futato, Eugene M. "Continuity and Change in the Middle Woodland Occupation of the Northwest Alabama Uplands." In *Middle Woodland Settlement and Ceremonialism in the Mid-South and Lower Mississippi Valley,* ed. Robert C. Mainfort Jr., 31–48. Archaeological Report No. 22. Mississippi Department of Archives and History, Jackson, 1988.

——. "A Synopsis of Paleoindian and Early Archaic Research in Alabama." In *The Paleoindian and Early Archaic Southeast*, ed. David G. Anderson and Kenneth E. Sassaman, 298–314. Tuscaloosa: University of Alabama Press, 1996.

Galinat, Walton C. "Domestication and Diffusion of Maize." In *The Paleoindian and Early Archaic Southeast*, ed. David G. Anderson and Kenneth E. Sassaman, 245–278. Tuscaloosa: University of Alabama Press, 1996.

Gallay, Alan, ed. *Indian Slavery in Colonial America*. Lincoln: University of Nebraska Press, 2009.

——. *The Indian Slave Trade: The Rise of the English Empire in the American South, 1670–1717*. New Haven, Conn.: Yale University Press, 2002.

Galloway, Patricia. "The Barthelemy Murders: Bienville's Establishment of the *Lex Talionis* as a Principle of Indian Diplomacy." In *Practicing Ethnohistory: Mining Archives, Hearing Testimony, Constructing Narrative*, ed. Patricia Galloway, 245–258. Lincoln: University of Nebraska Press, 2006.

——. "Chakchiuma." In *Southeast*, ed. Raymond D. Fogelson, 496–498. Handbook of North American Indians, Vol. 14. William C. Sturtevant, gen. ed. Washington, D.C.: Smithsonian Institution, 2004.

——. "The Chief Who Is Your Father: Choctaw and French Views of the Diplomatic Relation." In *Powhatan's Mantle: Indians in the Colonial Southeast*, ed. Gregory A. Waselkov, Peter H. Wood, and Tom Hatley, 344–370. Rev. and expanded ed. Lincoln: University of Nebraska Press, 2006.

——. "Choctaw Factionalism and Civil War, 1746–1750." In *Pre-removal Choctaw History: Exploring New Paths*, ed. Greg O'Brien, 70–102. Norman: University of Oklahoma Press, 2008.

——. *Choctaw Genesis: 1500–1700*. Lincoln: University of Nebraska Press, 1995.

——. "Choctaw Names and Choctaw Roles: Another Method for Evaluating Sociopolitical Structure." In *Practicing Ethnohistory: Mining Archives, Hearing Testimony, Constructing Narrative*, ed. Patricia Galloway, 202–222. Lincoln: University of Nebraska Press, 2006.

——. "Choila." In *Southeast*, ed. Raymond D. Fogelson, 177. Handbook of North American Indians, Vol. 14. William C. Sturtevant, gen. ed. Washington, D.C.: Smithsonian Institution, 2004.

——. "Choula." In *Southeast*, ed. Raymond D. Fogelson, 177. Handbook of North American Indians, Vol. 14. William C. Sturtevant, gen. ed. Washington, D.C.: Smithsonian Institution, 2004.

——. "Colonial Period Transformations in the Mississippi Valley: Dis-integration, Alliance, Confederation, Playoff." In *The Transformation of the Southeastern Indians, 1540–1760*, ed. Robbie Ethridge and Charles Hudson, 225–247. Jackson: University Press of Mississippi, 2002.

——. "Confederacy as a Solution to Chiefdom Dissolution: Historical Evidence in the Choctaw Case." In *The Forgotten Centuries: Indians and Europeans in the American South, 1521–1704*, ed. Charles Hudson and Carmen Chaves Tesser, 393–420. Athens: University of Georgia Press, 1994.

——. "The Currency of Language: The Mobilian Lingua Franca in Colonial Louisiana." In *Practicing Ethnohistory: Mining Archives, Hearing Testimony, Constructing Narrative*, ed. Patricia Galloway, 225–244. Lincoln: University of Nebraska Press, 2006.

——. "Dearth and Bias: Issues in the Editing of Ethnohistorical Materials." In *Practicing Ethnohistory: Mining Archives, Hearing Testimony, Constructing Narrative*, ed. Patricia Galloway, 33–42. Lincoln: University of Nebraska Press, 2006.

———. "Dual Organization Reconsidered: Eighteenth-Century Choctaw Chiefs and the Exploration of Social Design Space." In *Practicing Ethnohistory: Mining Archives, Hearing Testimony, Constructing Narrative*, ed. Patricia Galloway, 357–373. Lincoln: University of Nebraska Press, 2006.

———. "Etouchoco." In *Southeast*, ed. Raymond D. Fogelson, 179. Handbook of North American Indians, Vol. 14. William C. Sturtevant, gen. ed. Washington, D.C.: Smithsonian Institution, 2004.

———. "The Four Ages of Alibamon Mingo, fl. 1700–1766." In *Practicing Ethnohistory: Mining Archives, Hearing Testimony, Constructing Narrative*, ed. Patricia Galloway, 336–356. Lincoln: University of Nebraska Press, 2006.

———. "Henri de Tonti du Village des Chacta, 1702: The Beginning of the French Alliance." In *La Salle and His Legacy: Frenchmen and Indians in the Lower Mississippi Valley*, ed. Patricia K. Galloway, 146–175. Jackson: University Press of Mississippi, 1982.

———, ed. *The Hernando De Soto Expedition: History, Historiography, and "Discovery" in the Southeast*. Lincoln: University of Nebraska Press, 1997.

———, ed. "House Bill No. 533." *Mississippi Archaeological Association Newsletter* 18 (1983): 2–6. Mississippi Archaeological Association, Jackson.

———. "Ibitoupa." In *Southeast*, ed. Raymond D. Fogelson, 179–180. Handbook of North American Indians, Vol. 14. William C. Sturtevant, gen. ed. Washington, D.C.: Smithsonian Institution, 2004.

———. "The Medal Chief's *Grosse Lettre*: A Chapter in French Indian Management Policy." In *Practicing Ethnohistory: Mining Archives, Hearing Testimony, Constructing Narrative*, ed. Patricia Galloway, 292–310. Lincoln: University of Nebraska Press, 2006.

———. "Natchez Matrilineal Kinship: Du Pratz and the Woman's Touch." In *Practicing Ethnohistory: Mining Archives, Hearing Testimony, Constructing Narrative*, ed. Patricia Galloway, 97–108. Lincoln: University of Nebraska Press, 2006.

———. "Ougoula Tchetoka, Ackia, and Bienville's First Chickasaw War: Whose Strategy and Tactics?" *Journal of Chickasaw History* 2 (1996): 3–10.

———, ed. *Practicing Ethnohistory: Mining Archives, Hearing Testimony, Constructing Narrative*. Lincoln: University of Nebraska Press, 2006.

———. "'So Many Little Republics': British Negotiations with the Choctaw Confederacy, 1765." In *Practicing Ethnohistory: Mining Archives, Hearing Testimony, Constructing Narrative*, ed. Patricia Galloway, 311–315. Lincoln: University of Nebraska Press, 2006.

———. "Taposa." In *Southeast*, ed. Raymond D. Fogelson, 186. Handbook of North American Indians, Vol. 14. William C. Sturtevant, gen. ed. Washington, D.C.: Smithsonian Institution, 2004.

———. "Technical Origins for Chickachae Combed Ceramics." *Mississippi Archaeology* 19, no. 2 (December 1984): 58–66.

———. "Where Have All the Menstrual Huts Gone? The Invisibility of Menstrual Seclusion in the Late Prehistoric Southeast." In *Women in Prehistory: North America and Mesoamerica*, ed. Cheryl Claassen and Rosemary A. Joyce, 47–62. Philadelphia: University of Pennsylvania Press, 1997.

Galloway, Patricia, and Ives Goddard. "Concha." In *Southeast*, ed. Raymond D. Fogelson, 178. Handbook of North American Indians, Vol. 14. William C. Sturtevant, gen. ed. Washington, D.C.: Smithsonian Institution, 2004.

———. "Ouispé." In *Southeast*, ed. Raymond D. Fogelson, 183–184. Handbook of North American Indians, Vol. 14. William C. Sturtevant, gen. ed. Washington, D.C.: Smithsonian Institution, 2004.

Galloway, Patricia, and Jason Baird Jackson. "Natchez and Neighboring Groups." In *Southeast*, ed. Raymond D. Fogelson, 598–615. Handbook of North American Indians, Vol. 14. William C. Sturtevant, gen. ed. Washington, D.C.: Smithsonian Institution, 2004.

Galloway, Patricia, and Clara Sue Kidwell. "Choctaw in the East." In *Southeast*, ed. Raymond D. Fogelson, 499–519. Handbook of North American Indians, Vol. 14. William C. Sturtevant, gen. ed. Washington, D.C.: Smithsonian Institution, 2004.

Galloway, Patricia, Marvin D. Jeter, and Ives Goddard. "Yazoo." In *Southeast*, ed. Raymond D. Fogelson, 190. Handbook of North American Indians, Vol. 14. William C. Sturtevant, gen. ed. Washington, D.C.: Smithsonian Institution, 2004.

Gauld, George [map 1778]. *A Plan of the coast of part of west Florida & Louisiana: including the River Yazous / Surveyed by George Gauld M.A. for the Right Honourable the Board of Admiralty.* Library of Congress, G4012.C6 1778 G3 Vault. ield(NUMBER+@band(g4012c+ct000670.

Gibson, Arrell M. *The Chickasaws.* Norman: University of Oklahoma Press, 1971.

Gibson, Jon L. "Swamp Exchange and the Walled Mart: Poverty Point's Rock Business." In *Raw Materials and Exchange in the Mid-South*, ed. Evan Peacock and Samuel O. Brookes, 57–63. Archaeological Report No. 29. Mississippi Department of Archives and History, Jackson, 1999.

Gibson, Jon L., and J. Richard Shenkel. "Louisiana Earthworks: Middle Woodland and Predecessors." In *Middle Woodland Settlement and Ceremonialism in the Mid-South and Lower Mississippi Valley*, ed. Robert C. Mainfort Jr., 7–18. Archaeological Report No. 22. Mississippi Department of Archives and History, Jackson, 1988.

Gilmer, Robert. "Chickasaws, Tribal Laws, and the Mississippi Married Women's Property Act of 1839." *Journal of Mississippi History* 68, no. 2 (Summer 2006): 131–148.

Giraud, Marcel. *A History of French Louisiana.* Vol. 1, *The Reign of Louis XIV, 1698–1715.* Trans. Joseph C. Lambert. Baton Rouge: Louisiana State University Press, 1974.

———. *A History of French Louisiana.* Vol. 2, *Years of Transition.* Trans. Brian Pearce. Baton Rouge: Louisiana State University Press, 1993.

———. *A History of French Louisiana.* Vol. 5, *The Company of the Indies, 1723–1731.* Trans. Brian Pearce. Baton Rouge: Louisiana State University Press, 1991.

Goddard, Ives. "Bayacchyto." In *Southeast*, ed. Raymond D. Fogelson, 175. Handbook of North American Indians, Vol. 14. William C. Sturtevant, gen. ed. Washington, D.C.: Smithsonian Institution, 2004.

———. "Bayogoula." In *Southeast*, ed. Raymond D. Fogelson, 175–176. Handbook of North American Indians, Vol. 14. William C. Sturtevant, gen. ed. Washington, D.C.: Smithsonian Institution, 2004.

———. "Colapissa." In *Southeast*, ed. Raymond D. Fogelson, 177–178. Handbook of North American Indians, Vol. 14. William C. Sturtevant, gen. ed. Washington, D.C.: Smithsonian Institution, 2004.

———. "Mougoulacha." In *Southeast*, ed. Raymond D. Fogelson, 181. Handbook of North American Indians, Vol. 14. William C. Sturtevant, gen. ed. Washington, D.C.: Smithsonian Institution, 2004.

———. "Quinipissa." In *Southeast*, ed. Raymond D. Fogelson, 185. Handbook of North American Indians, Vol. 14. William C. Sturtevant, gen. ed. Washington, D.C.: Smithsonian Institution, 2004.

———. "Washa, Chawasha, and Yakni-Chito." In *Southeast*, ed. Raymond D. Fogelson, 188–190. Handbook of North American Indians, Vol. 14. William C. Sturtevant, gen. ed. Washington, D.C.: Smithsonian Institution, 2004.

Goddard, Ives, Patricia Galloway, Marvin D. Jeter, Gregory Waselkov, and John E. Worth. "Small Tribes of the Western Southwest." In *Southeast*, ed. Raymond D. Fogelson, 174–190. Handbook of North American Indians, Vol. 14. William C. Sturtevant, gen. ed. Washington, D.C.: Smithsonian Institution, 2004.

Green, John A. "Governor Perier's Expedition Against the Natchez Indians: December 1730–January 1731." *Louisiana Historical Quarterly* 19, no. 3 (July 1936).

Gregory, Hiram F., Jr., "Survival and Maintenance among Louisiana Tribes." In *Southeast*, ed. Raymond D. Fogelson, 653–658. Handbook of North American Indians, Vol. 14. William C. Sturtevant, gen. ed. Washington, D.C.: Smithsonian Institution, 2004.

Griffen, James B. "The Tchula Period in the Mississippi Valley." In *The Tchula Period in the Mid-South and Lower Mississippi Valley*, ed. David H. Dye and Ronald C. Brister, 40–42. Archaeological Report No. 17. Mississippi Department of Archives and History, Jackson, 1986.

Guice, John D. W. "Face to Face in Mississippi Territory, 1798–1817." In *The Choctaw Before Removal*, ed. Carolyn Keller Reeves, 157–180. Jackson: University Press of Mississippi, 1985.

———. "Old Hickory and the Natchez Trace." *Journal of Mississippi History* 64, no. 2 (Summer 2007): 167–182.

Haag, William G. "Choctaw Archaeology." *Southeastern Archaeological Conference Newsletter* 3 (1953): 25–28.

Haffner, Gerald O. "Major Arthur Loftus' Journal of the Proceedings of His Majesty's Twenty-Second Regiment up the River Mississippi in 1764." *Journal of the Louisiana Historical Association* 20, no. 3 (Summer 1979): 325–334.

Haliburton, R., Jr. "Chief Greenwood Leflore and His Malmaison Plantation." In *After Removal: The Choctaw in Mississippi*, ed. Samuel J. Wells and Roseanna Tubby, 56–63. Jackson: University Press of Mississippi, 1986.

Hall, Gwendolyn Midlo. *Africans in Colonial Louisiana: The Development of Afro-Creole Culture in the Eighteenth Century*. Baton Rouge: Louisiana State University Press, 1992.

Hally, David J. "The Plaquemine and Mississippian Occupations of the Upper Tensas Basin of Louisiana." Ph.D. diss., Harvard University, 1972.

Hally, David J., and Robert C. Mainfort Jr. "Prehistory of the Eastern Interior after 500 B.C." In *Southeast*, ed. Raymond D. Fogelson, 229–237. Handbook of North American Indians, Vol. 14. William C. Sturtevant, gen. ed. Washington, D.C.: Smithsonian Institution, 2004.

Haynes, Robert V. "Territorial Mississippi, 1798–1817." *Journal of Mississippi History* 65, no. 4 (Winter 2002): 283–305.

Hinds, Thomas, and John Coffee. *Refusal of the Chickasaws and Choctaws to Cede Their Lands in Mississippi: 1826*. Yale Law School, Lillian Goldman Law Library, The Avalon Project, Documents in Law, History and Diplomacy. http://avalon.law.yale.edu/19th_century/nt007.asp.

Hitchcock, A. S. *Manual of the Grasses of the United States, Vols. I and II*. New York: Dover, 1971.

Hoffman, Paul E. "Hernando De Soto: A Brief Biography." In *The De Soto Chronicles: The Expedition of Hernando De Soto to North America in 1539–1543*, ed. Lawrence A. Clayton, Vernon J. Knight Jr., and Edward C. Moore, 1:421–459. Tuscaloosa: University of Alabama Press, 1993.

———. "Lucas Vázquez de Ayllón's Discovery and Colony." In *The Forgotten Centuries: Indians and Europeans in the American South, 1521–1704*, ed. Charles Hudson and Carmen Chaves Tesser, 36–49. Athens: University of Georgia Press, 1994.

———. "Narváez and Cabeza de Vaca in Florida." In *The Forgotten Centuries: Indians and Europeans in the American South, 1521–1704*, ed. Charles Hudson and Carmen Chaves Tesser, 50–73. Athens: University of Georgia Press, 1994.

"Hopewell Treaty Signed by the Choctaws and the United States, Appendix B." In *Pre-removal Choctaw History: Exploring New Paths*, ed. Greg O'Brien, 248–251. Norman: University of Oklahoma Press, 2008.

Horan, James D. *The McKenney-Hall Portrait Gallery of American Indians*. New York: Crown, 1972.

Howe, LeAnne. "Ohoyo Chishba Osh: Woman Who Stretches Way Back." In *Pre-removal Choctaw History: Exploring New Paths*, ed. Greg O'Brien, 26–47. Norman: University of Oklahoma Press, 2008.

Hudson, Charles M., ed. *Black Drink: A Native Tea*. Athens: University of Georgia Press, 1979.

———. "The Hernando De Soto Expedition, 1539–1543." In *The Forgotten Centuries: Indians and Europeans in the American South, 1521–1704*, ed. Charles Hudson and Carmen Chaves Tesser, 74–103. Athens: University of Georgia Press, 1994.

———. "Introduction." In *Black Drink: A Native Tea*, ed. Charles M. Hudson, 1–9. Athens: University of Georgia Press, 1979.

———. *Knights of Spain, Warriors of the Sun: Hernando De Soto and the South's Ancient Chiefdoms*. Athens: University of Georgia Press, 1997.

———. *The Southeastern Indians*. Knoxville: University of Tennessee Press, 1976.

Indian Claims Commission Docket No. 16. *The Choctaw Nation, Petitioner vs. The United States of America, Defendant*, 304–332. Oklahoma State University Digital Library. http://digital .library.okstate.edu/icc/vo1/iccvo1p304.pdf.

Indian Claims Commission Docket No. 39. *Marguerite J. Underwood, on the Relation of an Identifiable Group of Choctaw and Chickasaw Petitioners, et. al. vs. The United States of America, Defendant*, 178–181. Oklahoma State University Digital Library. http://digital.li brary.okstate.edu/icc/vo1/iccvo1p178.pdf.

Indian Claims Commission Docket No. 51. *The Choctaw Nation, Petitioner vs. The United States of America, Defendant*, 182–194. Oklahoma State University Digital Library. http://digital .library.okstate.edu/icc/vo1/iccvo1p182.pdf.

Indian Claims Commission Docket No. 55. *The Choctaw Nation, Petitioner vs. The United States of America, Defendant*, 562–572. Oklahoma State University Digital Library. http://digital .library.okstate.edu/icc/vo1/iccvo1p562.pdf.

Indian Claims Commission Docket No. 56. *The Choctaw Nation, Petitioner vs. The United States of America, Defendant*, 341–347. Oklahoma State University Digital Library. http://digital .library.okstate.edu/icc/vo1/iccvo1p341.pdf.

Ingraham, Joseph Holt. *The Southwest by a Yankee, Volumes I & II*. 1835. Reprint, Naples, Fla.: Readex Microprint, 1966.

Jackson, H. Edwin. "Bottomland Resources and Exploitation Strategies during the Poverty Point Period: Implications of the Archaeological Record from the J. W. Copes Site." In *Poverty Point Culture: Local Manifestations, Subsistence Practices, and Trade Networks*, ed. Kathleen M. Byrd, 131–158. Geoscience and Man 29. Baton Rouge: Geoscience Publications, Department of Geology and Anthropology, Louisiana State University, 1991.

———. "The 2005 Excavations at Winterville Mounds (22Ws500), Washington County, Mississippi." Report submitted to the Mississippi Department of Archives and History, Jackson, 2005.

Jackson, H. Edwin, Melissa L. Higgins, and Robert E. Reams. "Woodland Cultural and Chronological Trends on the Southern Gulf Coastal Plain: Recent Research in the Pine Hills of Southeastern Mississippi." In *The Woodland Southeast*, ed. David G. Anderson and Robert C. Mainfort Jr., 228–248. Tuscaloosa: University of Alabama Press, 2002.

Jackson, Jason Baird, Raymond D. Fogelson, and William C. Sturtevant. "History of Ethnological and Linguistic Research." In *Southeast*, ed. Raymond D. Fogelson, 31–47. Handbook of North American Indians, Vol. 14. William C. Sturtevant, gen. ed. Washington, D.C.: Smithsonian Institution, 2004.

Jeffries, Richard W. "Regional Cultures, 700 B.C.–A.D. 1000." In *The Woodland Southeast*, ed. David G. Anderson and Robert C. Mainfort Jr., 115–127. Tuscaloosa: University of Alabama Press, 2002.

Jena Band of Choctaw Indians. *Brief Historical Summary*. http://www.jenachoctaw.org/history .html.

Jenkins, Ned. J. "The Wheeler Series: Space, Time, and External Relationships." In *The Tchula Period in the Mid-South and Lower Mississippi Valley*, ed. David H. Dye and Ronald C. Brister, 43–51. Archaeological Report No. 17. Mississippi Department of Archives and History, Jackson, 1986.

Jeter, Marvin D. "From Prehistory through Protohistory to Ethnohistory in and near the Northern Lower Mississippi Valley." In *The Transformation of the Southeastern Indians, 1540–1760*, ed. Robbie Ethridge and Charles Hudson, 177–223. Jackson: University Press of Mississippi, 2002.

———. "Grigra." In *Southeast*, ed. Raymond D. Fogelson, 179. Handbook of North American Indians, Vol. 14. William C. Sturtevant, gen. ed. Washington, D.C.: Smithsonian Institution, 2004.

———. "Shatter Zone Shock Waves along the Lower Mississippi." In *Mapping the Mississippian Shatter Zone: The Colonial Indian Slave Trade and Regional Instability in the American South*, ed. Robbie Ethridge and Sheri M. Shuck-Hall, 365–387. Lincoln: University of Nebraska Press, 2009.

Jeter, Marvin D., and Ives Goddard. "Koroa." In *Southeast*, ed. Raymond D. Fogelson, 180–181. Handbook of North American Indians, Vol. 14. William C. Sturtevant, gen. ed. Washington, D.C.: Smithsonian Institution, 2004.

———. "Tiou." In *Southeast*, ed. Raymond D. Fogelson, 188. Handbook of North American Indians, Vol. 14. William C. Sturtevant, gen. ed. Washington, D.C.: Smithsonian Institution, 2004.

Jeter, Marvin D., and G. Ishmael Williams Jr. "Ceramic-Using Cultures, 600 B.C–A.D. 700." In Marvin D. Jeter, Jerome C. Rose, G. Ishmael Williams Jr., and Anna M. Harmon, *Archeology and Bioarcheology of the Lower Mississippi Valley and the Trans-Mississippi South*, 111–170. Arkansas Archeological Survey Research Series No. 37. Final Report Submitted to the U.S. Army Corps of Engineers, Southwestern Division Study Unit 6 of the Southwestern Division Archeological Overview, Contract No. DACW63-84-C-0149, 1989.

————. "Late Prehistoric Cultures, A.D. 1000–1500." In Marvin D. Jeter, Jerome C. Rose, G. Ishmael Williams Jr., and Anna M. Harmon, *Archeology and Bioarcheology of the Lower Mississippi Valley and the Trans-Mississippi South*, 171–220. Arkansas Archeological Survey Research Series No. 37. Final Report Submitted to the U.S. Army Corps of Engineers, Southwestern Division Study Unit 6 of the Southwestern Division Archeological Overview, Contract No. DACW63-84-C-0149, 1989.

————. "Lithic Horizons and Early Cultures." In Marvin D. Jeter, Jerome C. Rose, G. Ishmael Williams Jr., and Anna M. Harmon, *Archeology and Bioarcheology of the Lower Mississippi Valley and the Trans-Mississippi South*, 71–110. Arkansas Archeological Survey Research Series No. 37. Final Report Submitted to the U.S. Army Corps of Engineers, Southwestern Division Study Unit 6 of the Southwestern Division Archeological Overview, Contract No. DACW63-84-C-0149, 1989.

Jeter, Marvin D., Jerome C. Rose, G. Ishmael Williams Jr., and Anna M. Harmon. "Adaptation Types." In Marvin D. Jeter, Jerome C. Rose, G. Ishmael Williams Jr., and Anna M. Harmon, *Archeology and Bioarcheology of the Lower Mississippi Valley and the Trans-Mississippi South*, 355–378. Arkansas Archeological Survey Research Series No. 37. Final Report Submitted to the U.S. Army Corps of Engineers, Southwestern Division Study Unit 6 of the Southwestern Division Archeological Overview, Contract No. DACW63-84-C-0149, 1989.

Jewell, Joseph D. "Appendix C: Fishing on the Mississippi Coast—Vertebrate Faunal Remains." In John H. Blitz and C. Baxter Mann, *Fisherfolk, Farmers, and Frenchmen*, 156–167. Archaeological Report No. 30. Mississippi Department of Archives and History, Jackson, 2000.

Johnson, Jay K. "The Chickasaws." In *Indians of the Greater Southeast: Historical Archaeology and Ethnohistory*, ed. Bonnie G. McEwan, 85–121. Gainesville: University Press of Florida, 2000.

————. "Woodland Settlement in Northeastern Mississippi: The Miller Tradition." In *Middle Woodland Settlement and Ceremonialism in the Mid-South and Lower Mississippi Valley*, ed. Robert C. Mainfort Jr., 49–60. Archaeological Report No. 22. Mississippi Department of Archives and History, Jackson, 1988.

Johnson, Jay K., Gena M. Aleo, Rodney T. Stuart, and John Sullivan. *The 1996 Excavations at the Batesville Mounds: A Woodland Period Platform Mound Complex in Northwest Mississippi*. Archaeological Report No. 32. Mississippi Department of Archives and History, Jackson, 2002.

Johnson, Jay K., Abigayle Robbins, and Andrea Brewer Shea. "Prehistoric Subsistence in the Natchez Bluffs, Jefferson County, Mississippi." *Mississippi Archaeology* 18, no. 2 (December 1983): 4–12.

Johnson, Jay K., Susan L. Scott, James R. Atkinson, and Andrea Brewer Shea. "Late Prehistoric/ Protohistoric Settlement and Subsistence on the Black Prairie: Buffalo Hunting in Mississippi." *North American Archaeologist* 15, no. 2 (1994): 167–179.

Johnson, Walter. *Soul By Soul: Life Inside the Antebellum Slave Market*. Cambridge, Mass.: Harvard University Press, 1999.

Kappler, Charles J. "Indian Citizenship Act, 1924." In *Indian Affairs, Laws and Treaties*. Vol. 4, *Laws*, comp. and ed. Charles J. Kappler, 1165–1166. Washington, D.C.: Government Printing Office, 1929. Online, Oklahoma State University Library. http://digital.library.okstate.edu/ kappler/vol4/html_files/v4p1165.html.

Kelly, John E. "Woodland Period Archaeology in the American Bottom." In *The Woodland Southeast*, ed. David G. Anderson and Robert C. Mainfort Jr., 134–161. Tuscaloosa: University of Alabama Press, 2002.

Kelton, Paul. *Epidemics and Enslavement: Biological Catastrophe in the Native Southeast, 1492– 1715.* Lincoln: University of Nebraska Press, 2007.

———. "The Great Southeastern Smallpox Epidemic, 1696–1700: The Region's First Major Epidemic?" In *The Transformation of the Southeastern Indians, 1540–1760*, ed. Robbie Ethridge and Charles Hudson, 21–37. Jackson: University Press of Mississippi, 2002.

Kent, Timothy J. *Ft. Pontchartrain at Detroit: A Guide to the Daily Lives of Fur Trade and Military Personnel, Settlers, and Missionaries at French Posts.* Vol. 2. Detroit: Wayne State University Press, 2001.

Kidder, Tristram R. "The Koroa Indians of the Lower Mississippi Valley." *Mississippi Archaeology* 23, no. 2 (December 1988): 1–42.

———. "Prehistory of the Lower Mississippi Valley after 800 B.C." In *Southeast*, ed. Raymond D. Fogelson, 545–559. Handbook of North American Indians, Vol. 14. William C. Sturtevant, gen. ed. Washington, D.C.: Smithsonian Institution, 2004.

———. "Woodland Period Archaeology of the Lower Mississippi Valley." In *The Woodland Southeast*, ed. David G. Anderson and Robert C. Mainfort Jr., 66–90. Tuscaloosa: University of Alabama Press, 2002.

Kidwell, Clara Sue. "Choctaw in the West." In *Southeast*, ed. Raymond D. Fogelson, 520–530. Handbook of North American Indians, Vol. 14. William C. Sturtevant, gen. ed. Washington, D.C.: Smithsonian Institution, 2004.

———. "Choctaws and Missionaries in Mississippi Before 1830." In *Pre-removal Choctaw History: Exploring New Paths*, ed. Greg O'Brien, 200–220. Norman: University of Oklahoma Press, 2008.

———. "The Choctaw Struggle for Land and Identity in Mississippi: 1830–1918." In *After Removal: The Choctaw in Mississippi*, ed. Samuel J. Wells and Roseanna Tubby, 64–93. Jackson: University Press of Mississippi, 1986.

King, Duane H. "Cherokee in the West: History since 1776." In *Southeast*, ed. Raymond D. Fogelson, 354–372. Handbook of North American Indians, Vol. 14. William C. Sturtevant, gen. ed. Washington, D.C.: Smithsonian Institution, 2004.

King, Thomas F., Patricia P. Hickman, and Gary Berg. *Anthropology in Historic Preservation: Caring for Culture's Clutter.* New York: Academic Press, 1977.

Kniffin, Fred B., Hiram F. Gregory, and George A. Stokes. *The Historic Indian Tribes of Louisiana.* Baton Rouge: Louisiana State University, 1987.

Knight, Vernon J., Jr., and Vincas P. Steponaitis. "A New History of Moundville." In *Archaeology of the Moundville Chiefdom*, ed. Vernon J. Knight Jr. and Vincas P. Steponaitis, 1–25. Washington, D.C.: Smithsonian Institution Press, 1998.

La Harpe, Jean-Baptiste Bénard de. *Historical Journal of the Settlement of the French in Louisiana.* Ed. Glenn R. Conrad, trans. Virginia Koenig and Joan Cain. Lafayette: University of Southwestern Louisiana, 1971.

Lankford, George E. "Chacato, Pensacola, Tohomé, Naniaba, and Mobila." In *Southeast*, ed. Raymond D. Fogelson, 664–668. Handbook of North American Indians, Vol. 14. William C. Sturtevant, gen. ed. Washington, D.C.: Smithsonian Institution, 2004.

———. *Cultural Resources Reconnaissance Study of the Black Warrior-Tombigbee System Corridor, Alabama.* Vol. 2, *Ethnohistory, A Documentary Study of Native American Life in the*

Lower Tombigbee Valley. Contract DACW01-81-C-0001, Submitted to the U.S. Army Corps of Engineers, Mobile District by the Department of Geology and Geography, University of South Alabama, Mobile, 1983.

———. "The Great Serpent in Eastern North America." In *Ancient Objects and Sacred Realms: Interpretations of Mississippian Iconography*, ed. F. Kent Reilly III and James F. Garber, 107–135. Austin: University of Texas Press, 2007.

———. *Looking for Lost Lore: Studies in Folklore, Ethnology, and Iconography.* Tuscaloosa: University of Alabama Press, 2008.

———, ed. *Native American Legends, Southeastern Legends: Tales from the Natchez, Caddo, Biloxi, Chickasaw, and Other Nations.* Little Rock, Ark.: August House, 1987.

———. "The 'Path of Souls': Some Death Imagery in the Southeastern Ceremonial Complex." In *Ancient Objects and Sacred Realms: Interpretations of Mississippian Iconography*, ed. F. Kent Reilly III and James F. Garber, 174–212. Austin: University of Texas Press, 2007.

———. "Some Cosmological Motifs in the Southeastern Ceremonial Complex." In *Ancient Objects and Sacred Realms: Interpretations of Mississippian Iconography*, ed. F. Kent Reilly III and James F. Garber, 8–38. Austin: University of Texas Press, 2007.

Larson, Lewis H., Jr. "The Etowah Site." In *The Southeastern Ceremonial Complex: Artifacts and Analysis, the Cottonlandia Conference*, ed. Patricia Galloway, 133–141. Lincoln: University of Nebraska Press, 1989.

Lee, Dayna Bowker. "The Ties That Bind: Cane Basketry Traditions among the Chitimacha and the Jena Band of Choctaw." In *The Work of Tribal Hands: Southeastern Split Cane Basketry*, ed. Dayna B. Lee and H. F. Pete Gregory, 43–71. Natchitoches, La.: Northwestern State University Press, 2006.

Lehmann, Geoffrey R. *The Jaketown Site: Surface Collections from a Poverty Point Regional Center in the Yazoo Basin, Mississippi.* Archaeological Report No. 9. Mississippi Department of Archives and History, Jackson, 1982.

Lehmann, Susan Gibbs. "The Problems of Founding a Viable Colony: The Military in Early French Louisiana." In *The Louisiana Purchase Bicentennial Series in Louisiana History.* Vol. 1, *The French Experience in Louisiana*, ed. Glenn R. Conrad, 360–367. Lafayette: Center for Louisiana Studies, University of Southwestern Louisiana, 1995.

Le Maire, François [map 1716]. *Carte nouvelle de la Lousiane et pais circonvoisins dressée sur les lieux pour être présentée à S. M[ajes]té T[très] C[hrétienne] par F. Le Maire prêtre parisien et missionn[air]e apostolique.* Harvard Map Collection, Karpinski series F 32-1-6. Service historique de la Défense, département Marine, Cartes et plans, recueil 68, no. 57. Formerly in Bibliothèque de la Service hydrographique, 4044C-46a.

Lemieux, Donald J. "Some Legal and Practical Aspects of the Office of Commissaire-Ordonnateur of French Louisiana." In *The Louisiana Purchase Bicentennial Series in Louisiana History.* Vol. 1, *The French Experience in Louisiana*, ed. Glenn R. Conrad, 395–407. Lafayette: Center for Louisiana Studies, University of Southwestern Louisiana, 1995.

Le Petit, Mauthurin. *The Natchez Massacre.* Trans. Richard H. Hart. New Orleans: Poor Rich Press, 1950.

Levine, Victoria Lindsay. "Choctaw at Ardmore, Oklahoma." In *Southeast*, ed. Raymond D. Fogelson, 531–533. Handbook of North American Indians, Vol. 14. William C. Sturtevant, gen. ed. Washington, D.C.: Smithsonian Institution, 2004.

———. "Music." In *Southeast*, ed. Raymond D. Fogelson, 720–733. Handbook of North American Indians, Vol. 14. William C. Sturtevant, gen. ed. Washington, D.C.: Smithsonian Institution, 2004.

Lieb, Brad R. "The Grand Village Is Silent: An Archaeological and Ethnohistorical Study of the Natchez Indian Refuge among the Chickasaws in the Eighteenth Century." Master's thesis, University of Alabama, 2005.

Lincecum, Gideon. *Pushmataha: A Choctaw Leader and His People.* Tuscaloosa: University of Alabama Press, 2004.

Linklater, Andro. *An Artist in Treason: The Extraordinary Life of General James Wilkinson.* New York: Walker, 2009.

Livesay, Nora. "Understanding the History of Tribal Enrollment." American Indian Policy Center, St. Paul, Minn. http://www.airpi.org/pubs/enroll.html.

Lolly, Terry. "Archaeology at the Lyon's Bluff Site, a Mississippian and Protohistoric Settlement in Oktibbeha County, Mississippi." *Mississippi Archaeology* 35, no. 1 {Summer 2000): 1–14.

Lorenz, Karl G. "The Natchez of Southwest Mississippi." In *Indians of the Greater Southeast: Historical Archaeology and Ethnohistory,* ed. Bonnie G. McEwan, 142–177. Gainesville: University Press of Florida, 2000.

———. "A Re-Examination of Natchez Sociopolitical Complexity: A View from the Grand Village and Beyond." *Southeastern Archaeology* 16, no. 2 (Winter 1997): 97–112.

Mainfort, Robert C., Jr. "Pinson Mounds: Internal Chronology and External Relationships." In *Middle Woodland Settlement and Ceremonialism in the Mid-South and Lower Mississippi Valley,* ed. Robert C. Mainfort Jr., 132–146. Archaeological Report No. 22. Mississippi Department of Archives and History, Jackson, 1988.

Malloy, Christopher J., and Charles A. Weeks. "Shuttle Diplomacy Eighteenth-Century Style: Stephen Minor's First Mission to the Choctaws and Journal, May–June, 1791." *Journal of Mississippi History* 55, no. 1 (February 1993): 31–51.

Mann, Charles C. *1491: New Revelations of the Americas Before Columbus.* New York: Vintage Books, 2005.

Manning, Earl M., and Michael B. E. Bograd. "Annotated Bibliography of the Geology of Mississippi to 1850." *Mississippi Geology* 20, no. 4 (1999). Department of Environmental Quality, Office of Geology, Jackson.

Marshall, Richard A. *A Report on Archaeological Test Excavations at Goode Lake, Jackson County, Mississippi.* Archaeological Report No. 10. Mississippi Department of Archives and History and Jackson County Port Authority, 1982.

———. *Survey and Excavation along Archusa Creek.* Archaeological Report No. 11. Mississippi Department of Archives and History, Jackson, 1982.

Martin, Jack B. "Languages." In *Southeast,* ed. Raymond D. Fogelson, 68–86. Handbook of North American Indians, Vol. 14. William C. Sturtevant, gen. ed. Washington, D.C.: Smithsonian Institution, 2004.

Martin, Jack B., Willem J. de Reuse, and Ives Goddard. "Synonymy: Tunica, Biloxi, Ofo." In *Southeast,* ed. Raymond D. Fogelson, 595–596. Handbook of North American Indians, Vol. 14. William C. Sturtevant, gen. ed. Washington, D.C.: Smithsonian Institution, 2004.

Martin, General Joseph. "Appendix A. Choctaw Negotiations with the United States at Hopewell, South Carolina, 1785–1786; Journal kept by General Joseph Martin describing the Hopewell Treaty Negotiations with the Southern Indian Nations." In *Pre-removal Choctaw History: Exploring New Paths,* ed. Greg O'Brien, 237–247. Norman: University of Oklahoma Press, 2008.

Mathews, Donald G. "The Second Great Awakening as an Organizing Process, 1780–1830: An Hypothesis." *American Quarterly* 21, no. 1 (Spring 1969): 23–43.

May, Stephanie A. "Alabama and Koasati." In *Southeast*, ed. Raymond D. Fogelson, 407–414. Handbook of North American Indians, Vol. 14. William C. Sturtevant, gen. ed. Washington, D.C.: Smithsonian Institution, 2004.

McAlexander, Hubert H. "The Saga of a Mixed-Blood Chickasaw Dynasty." *Journal of Mississippi History* 64, no. 4 (November 1987): 288–300.

McAmis, Herb. *Indian People of the Edisto River: A Brief History of the Kusso-Natchez Indians, Often Called "Edistos."* Four Holes Indian Organization, Edisto Tribal Council, with assistance from the Men's Club of Bethany United Methodist Church, n.d.

McDermott, John F. "Isaac McCoy's Second Exploring Trip in 1828." *Kansas Historical Quarterly* 13, no. 7 (August 1945): 400–462. Online as *Kansas Collection: Kansas Historical Quarterlies* http://www.kancoll.org/khq/1945/45_7_mcdermott.htm.

McDowell, William L., Jr., ed. *Colonial Records of South Carolina, Documents relating to Indian Affairs, May 21, 1750-August 7, 1754*. Columbia: South Carolina Archives Department, 1958.

———., ed. *Colonial Records of South Carolina, Documents relating to Indian Affairs, 1754–1765*. Columbia: South Carolina Department of Archives and History, and University of South Carolina Press, 1970.

McEwan, Bonnie G. "Apalachee and Neighboring Groups." In *Southeast*, ed. Raymond D. Fogelson, 669–676. Handbook of North American Indians, Vol. 14. William C. Sturtevant, gen. ed. Washington, D.C.: Smithsonian Institution, 2004.

———. *Indians of the Greater Southeast: Historical Archaeology and Ethnohistory*. Gainsville: University Press of Florida, 2000.

McGahey, Samuel O., ed. "The Archaeological Resources Protection Act of 1979." *Mississippi Archaeology* 14, no. 1 (1979): 5–18.

———. "A Compendium of Mississippi Dugout Canoes Recorded since 1974." *Mississippi Archaeology* 21, no. 1 (1986): 58–70.

———. *Mississippi Projectile Point Guide*. Archaeological Report No. 31. Mississippi Department of Archives and History, Jackson, 2004.

———. "Paleoindian and Early Archaic Data from Mississippi." In *The Paleoindian and Early Archaic Southeast*, ed. David G. Anderson and Kenneth E. Sassaman, 354–384. Tuscaloosa: University of Alabama Press, 1996.

———. "Prehistoric Stone Bead Manufacture: The Loosa Yokena Site, Warren County, Mississippi." *Mississippi Archaeology* 40, no. 1 (Summer 2005): 3–30.

McKee, Jesse O., and Steve Murray. "Economic Development of the Choctaw since 1945." In *After Removal: The Choctaw in Mississippi*, ed. Samuel J. Wells and Roseanna Tubby, 122–136. Jackson: University Press of Mississippi, 1986.

McKee, Jesse O., and Jon A. Schlenker. *The Choctaws: Cultural Evolution of a Native American Tribe*. Jackson: University Press of Mississippi, 1980.

McKenney, Thomas L., and James Hall. *History of the Indian tribes of North America, with biographical sketches and anecdotes of the principal chiefs. Embellished with one hundred and twenty portraits from the Indian gallery in the Department of War at Washington*. 3 vols. E. C. Biddle, 1836–1844.

McNutt, Charles H. "The Central Mississippi Valley: A Summary." In *Prehistory of the Central Mississippi Valley*, ed. Charles H. McNutt, 187–257. Tuscaloosa: University of Alabama Press, 1996.

McWilliams, Richebourg G., trans. and ed. *Fleur de Lys and Calumet: Being the Pénicaut Narrative of French Adventure in Louisiana*. Tuscaloosa: University of Alabama Press, 1953.

——, trans. and ed. *Pierre Le Moyne d'Iberville, Iberville's Gulf Journals*. Tuscaloosa: University of Alabama Press, 1981.

McWilliams, Tennant S. "Introduction: Pierre Le Moyne d'Iberville and the Competition for Empire." In *Pierre Le Moyne d'Iberville, Iberville's Gulf Journals*, trans. and ed. Richebourg G. McWilliams, 1–16. Tuscaloosa: University of Alabama Press, 1981.

Merrill, William L. "The Beloved Tree: *Ilex vomitoria* among the Indians of the Southeast and Adjacent Areas." In *Black Drink: A Native Tea*, ed. Charles M. Hudson, 40–82. Athens: University of Georgia Press, 1979.

Meyers, Maureen. "From Refugees to Slave Traders: The Transformation of the Westo Indians." In *Mapping the Mississippian Shatter Zone: The Colonial Indian Slave Trade and Regional Instability in the American South*, ed. Robbie Ethridge and Sheri M. Shuck-Hall, 81–103. Lincoln: University of Nebraska Press, 2009.

Milanich, Jerald T. "Franciscan Missions and Native Peoples in Florida." In *The Forgotten Centuries: Indians and Europeans in the American South, 1521–1704*, ed. Charles Hudson and Carmen Chaves Tesser, 276–303. Athens: University of Georgia Press, 1994.

——. "Origins and Prehistoric Distributions of Black Drink and the Ceremonial Shell Drinking Cup." In *Black Drink: A Native Tea*, ed. Charles M. Hudson, 83–119. Athens: University of Georgia Press, 1979.

Mississippi Band of Choctaw Indians.
http://www.choctaw.org/.

——. "Choctaw Chronology."
http://www.choctaw.org/History/Chronology/chronology.html.

——. "Choctaw Language."
http://www.choctaw.org/Culture/The%20Choctaw%20Language/The%20Choctaw%20Language
.html.

——. "Map of Tribal Lands."
http://www.choctaw.org/doc/MBCI%20LOCATION.PDF.

——. "Tribal Profile."
http://www.choctaw.org/Government/Tribal%20Profile/Tribal%20Profile.html.

Mississippi Band of Choctaw Indians. *Treaties between the United States and the Choctaw Nation*. http://www.choctaw.org/History/Treaties/Treaties.html.

Moerman, Daniel E. *Native American Ethnobotany*. Portland, Ore.: Timber Press, 1998.

Mooney, James. *The Siouan Tribes of the East*. Washington, D.C.: Smithsonian Institution Bureau of Ethnology, 1894. Reprint, New York: Johnson Reprint, 1970.

Mooney, Timothy Paul. *Many Choctaw Standing: An Archaeological Study of Culture Change in the Early Historic Period*. Archaeological Report No. 27. Mississippi Department of Archives and History, Jackson, 1997.

Moore, Alexander. "Introduction." In Thomas Nairne, *Nairne's Muskhogean Journals: The 1708 Expedition to the Mississippi River*, ed. Alexander Moore, 3–31. Jackson: University Press of Mississippi, 1988.

Moore, Clarence B. "Certain Aboriginal Remains of Mobile Bay and Mississippi Sound." *Journal of the Academy of Natural Sciences of Philadelphia* 13, no. 2 (1905): 279–299.

——. "Certain Mounds of Arkansas and of Mississippi, Parts I–III." *Journal of the Academy of Natural Sciences of Philadelphia* 13 (1908): 480–600.

——. "Some Aboriginal Sites on the Mississippi River." *Journal of the Academy of Natural Sciences of Philadelphia* 14 (1911): 367–478.

Moorehead, Warren K. *Explorations of the Etowah Site in Georgia.* Etowah Papers 1. Department of Archaeology, Phillips Academy, Andover, Mass., 1932.

Morgan, David. *The Mississippi De Soto Trail Mapping Project.* Archaeological Report No. 26. Mississippi Department of Archives and History, Jackson, 1996.

Morgan, David W. "Historic Period Chickasaw Indians: Chronology and Settlement Patterns." *Mississippi Archaeology* 31, no. 1 (1996): 1–39.

Morse, Dan F. "An Arkansas View." In *The Paleoindian and Early Archaic Southeast,* ed. David G. Anderson and Kenneth E. Sassaman, 425–429. Tuscaloosa: University of Alabama Press, 1996.

Morse, Dan F., and Phyllis A. Morse, eds. *The Lower Mississippi Valley Expeditions of Clarence Bloomfield Moore.* Tuscaloosa: University of Alabama Press, 1998.

Muller, Jon. "The Southern Cult." In *The Southeastern Ceremonial Complex: Artifacts and Analysis, the Cottonlandia Conference,* ed. Patricia Galloway, 11–26. Lincoln: University of Nebraska Press, 1989.

Nairne, Thomas. *Nairne's Muskhogean Journals: The 1708 Expedition to the Mississippi River.* Ed. Alexander Moore. Jackson: University Press of Mississippi, 1988.

National Park Service, U.S. Department of the Interior. "National NAGPRA." http://www.nps .gov/nagpra/INDEX.HTM.

Neitzel, Robert S. *Archaeology of the Fatherland Site: The Grand Village of the Natchez.* Anthropological Papers of the American Museum of Natural History 51, Part 1. New York, 1965.

——. *The Grand Village of the Natchez Revisited: Excavations at the Fatherland Site, Adams County, Mississippi, 1972.* Archaeological Report No. 12. Mississippi Department of Archives and History, 1983.

Neuman, Robert W. *An Introduction to Louisiana Archaeology.* Baton Rouge: Louisiana State University Press, 1984.

O'Brien, Greg. "The Choctaw Defense of Pensacola in the American Revolution." In *Pre-removal Choctaw History: Exploring New Paths,* ed. Greg O'Brien, 123–147. Norman: University of Oklahoma Press, 2008.

——. *Choctaws in a Revolutionary Age, 1750–1830.* Lincoln: University of Nebraska Press, 2002.

——. "The Conqueror Meets the Unconquered." In *Pre-removal Choctaw History: Exploring New Paths,* ed. Greg O'Brien, 148–182. Norman: University of Oklahoma Press, 2008.

——. "Introduction." In Gideon Lincecum, *Pushmataha: A Choctaw Leader and His People,* vii–xviii. Tuscaloosa: University of Alabama Press, 2004.

——, ed. *Pre-removal Choctaw History: Exploring New Paths.* Norman: University of Oklahoma Press, 2008.

——. "Protecting Trade through War: Choctaw Elites and British Occupation of the Floridas." In *Pre-removal Choctaw History: Exploring New Paths,* ed. Greg O'Brien, 103–122. Norman: University of Oklahoma Press, 2008.

——. "Pushmataha: Choctaw Warrior, Diplomat, and Chief." *Mississippi History Now,* online publication of the Mississippi Historical Society. http://mshistory.k12.ms.us/articles/14/ pushmataha-choctaw-warrior-diplomat-and-chief.

——. "'We are behind you': The Choctaw Occupation of Natchez in 1778." *Journal of Mississippi History* 64, no. 2 (Summer 2002): 107–124.

Oklahoma Historical Society. "Atoka Agreement." In *Encyclopedia of Oklahoma History and Culture.* tries/A/AT004.html.

Olsen, Stanley J. "Appendix: Boyd Site Report of Faunal Analysis." In John M. Connaway and Samuel O. McGahey, *Archaeological Excavation at the Boyd Site, Tunica County, Mississippi*, ed. Elbert R. Hilliard, 65–77. Jackson: National Park Service, Southeast Region, U.S. Department of the Interior and the Mississippi Department of Archives and History, 1971.

O'Neill, Charles E., ed., and John Gilmary Shea, trans. *Charlevoix's Louisiana: Selections from the History and the Journal, Pierre F. X. de Charlevoix*. Baton Rouge: Louisiana State University Press, 1977.

Oswalt, Wendall H., and Sharlotte Neely. *This Land Was Theirs: A Study of Native Americans*. 6th ed. Mountain View, Calif.: Mayfield, 1999.

Parkman, Francis. *La Salle and the Discovery of the Great West: France and England in North America*. 1877. Reprint, Williamstown, Mass.: Corner House, 1980.

Pate, James P., ed. *The Reminiscences of George S. Gaines: Pioneer and Statesman of Early Alabama and Mississippi, 1805–1843*. Tuscaloosa: University of Alabama Press, 1998.

Pauketat, Timothy R., and Thomas E. Emerson. "Introduction: Domination and Ideology in the Mississippian World." In *Cahokia: Domination and Ideology in the Mississippian World*, ed. Timothy R. Pauketat and Thomas E. Emerson, 1–29. Lincoln: University of Nebraska Press, 1997.

Peabody, Charles. *Exploration of Mounds, Coahoma County, Mississippi*. Papers of the Peabody Museum of American Archaeology and Ethnology, Harvard University 3, no. 2 (1904): 27–57.

Peacock, Evan. "Excavations at Stinking Water (22WI515/516), a Prehistoric Habitation Site in the North Central Hills Physiographic Province of Mississippi." *Mississippi Archaeology* 38, no. 1 (Summer 2003): 3–91.

———. "Shellfish Use during the Woodland Period in the Middle South." In *The Woodland Southeast*, ed. David G. Anderson and Robert C. Mainfort Jr., 444–460. Tuscaloosa: University of Alabama Press, 2002.

Peacock, Evan, Philip J. Carr, Sarah E. Price, John Underwood, William L. Kingery, and Michael Lilly. "Confirmation of an Archaic Period Mound in Southwest Mississippi." *Southeastern Archaeology* 29, no. 2 (Winter 2010): 355–368.

Peebles, Christopher S. "Foreword." In *Archaeology of the Moundville Chiefdom*, ed. Vernon J. Knight Jr. and Vincas P. Steponaitis, xi–xx. Washington, D.C.: Smithsonian Institution Press, 1998.

Penman, John T. "Appendix II. Faunal Remains." In Robert S. Neitzel, *The Grand Village of the Natchez Revisited: Excavations at the Fatherland Site, Adams County, Mississippi, 1972*, 146–165. Archaeological Report No. 12. Mississippi Department of Archives and History, Jackson, 1983.

Peterson, Dennis A. "A History of Excavations and Interpretations of Artifacts from the Spiro Mounds Site." In *The Southeastern Ceremonial Complex: Artifacts and Analysis, the Cottonlandia Conference*, ed. Patricia Galloway, 114–121. Lincoln: University of Nebraska Press, 1989.

Phillips, Philip. *Archaeological Survey in the Lower Yazoo Basin, Mississippi, 1949–1955, Parts One and Two*. Papers of the Peabody Museum of Archaeology and Ethnology, Harvard University 60 (1970).

Post, Lauren C. "The Domestic Animals and Plants of French Louisiana as Mentioned in the Literature with Reference to Sources, Varieties, and Uses." *Louisiana Historical Quarterly* 16, no. 4 (1933): 554–586.

Quimby, George I., Jr. "The Locus of the Natchez Pelvis." *American Antiquity* 22 (1956): 77–79.

———. "The Natchezan Culture Type." *American Antiquity* 7 (1942): 255–275.

———. "Natchez Social Structure as an Instrument of Assimilation." *American Anthropologist* 48 (1946): 134–137.

Quitmyer, Irvy R. "Zooarchaeological Remains from Bottle Creek." In *Bottle Creek: A Pensacola Culture Site in South Alabama*, ed. Ian W. Brown, 130–155. Tuscaloosa: University of Alabama Press, 2003.

Rafferty, Janet. *Owl Creek Mounds: Test Excavations at a Vacant Mississippian Mound Center.* Prepared for the USDA Forest Service, Report of Investigations 7, Cobb Institute of Archaeology, Mississippi State University, 1995.

———. "Woodland Period Settlement Patterning in the Northern Gulf Coastal Plain of Alabama, Mississippi, and Tennessee." In *The Woodland Southeast*, ed. David G. Anderson and Robert C. Mainfort Jr., 204–227. Tuscaloosa: University of Alabama Press, 2002.

Rafferty, Janet, and Evan Peacock. "The Spread of Shell Tempering in the Mississippi Black Prairie." *Southeastern Archaeology* 27, no. 2 (2008): 253–264.

Ramenofsky, Ann F. "Death by Disease." *Archaeology* 45, no. 2 (March/April 1992): 47–49.

Records of the Choctaw Trading House, Under the Office of Indian Trade, 1803–1824, Daybooks, 1808–1813. National Archives, National Archives and Records Service, General Services Administration, Washington, D.C., 1960, Microcopy No. T-500, Roll 4; accessed in the Archives Library, Roll 4816, Mississippi Department of Archives and History, Jackson.

Reeves, Carolyn Keller, ed. *The Choctaw Before Removal.* Jackson: University Press of Mississippi, 1985.

Reilly, F. Kent, III. "The Petaloid Motif: A Celestial Symbolic Locative in the Shell Art of Spiro." In *Ancient Objects and Sacred Realms: Interpretations of Mississippian Iconography*, ed. F. Kent Reilly III and James F. Garber, 39–55. Austin: University of Texas Press, 2007.

Reilly, F. Kent, III, and James F. Garber. "Introduction." In *Ancient Objects and Sacred Realms: Interpretations of Mississippian Iconography*, ed. F. Kent Reilly III and James F. Garber, 1–7. Austin: University of Texas Press, 2007.

Reitz, Elizabeth J., and C. Margaret Scarry. *Reconstructing Historic Subsistence with an Example from Sixteenth-Century Spanish Florida.* Special Publication Series No. 3, ed. Ronald L. Michael, published by the Society for Historical Archaeology, 1985.

Roberts, Charles. "The Second Choctaw Removal, 1903." In *After Removal: The Choctaw in Mississippi*, ed. Samuel J. Wells and Roseanna Tubby, 94–111. Jackson: University Press of Mississippi, 1986.

Robertson, James Alexander, trans. and ed. "The Account by a Gentleman from Elvas." In *The De Soto Chronicles: The Expedition of Hernando De Soto to North America in 1539–1543*, ed. Lawrence A. Clayton, Vernon J. Knight Jr., and Edward C. Moore, 1:19–220. Tuscaloosa: University of Alabama Press, 1993.

Romans, Bernard. *A Concise Natural History of East and West Florida.* Vol. 1. 1775. New Orleans: Pelican Publishing, 1961.

Rowland, Dunbar. *Mississippi: Comprising Sketches of Counties, Towns, Events, Institutions, and Persons, Arranged in Cyclopedic Form.* 2 vols. 1907. Reprint, Spartanburg, S.C.: Reprint Company, 1976.

———, ed. *Mississippi Provincial Archives, 1763–1766, English Dominion.* Vol. 1. Nashville, Tenn.: Press of Brandon, 1911.

Rowland, Dunbar, and Albert G. Sanders, eds. and trans. *Mississippi Provincial Archives, 1729–1740, French Dominion.* Vol. 1. Mississippi Department of Archives and History, Jackson, 1927.

———, eds. and trans. *Mississippi Provincial Archives, 1701–1729, French Dominion*. Vol. 2. Mississippi Department of Archives and History, Jackson, 1929.

———, eds. and trans. *Mississippi Provincial Archives, 1704–1743, French Dominion*. Vol. 3. Mississippi Department of Archives and History, Jackson, 1932.

Rowland, Dunbar, Albert G. Sanders, and Patricia Galloway, eds. and trans. *Mississippi Provincial Archives, 1729–1748, French Dominion*. Vol. 4. Baton Rouge: Louisiana State University Press, 1984.

———, eds. and trans. *Mississippi Provincial Archives, 1749–1763, French Dominion*. Vol. 5. Baton Rouge: Louisiana State University Press, 1984.

Rushforth, Brett. "'A Little Flesh We Offer You': The Origins of Indian Slavery in New France." In *Indian Slavery in Colonial America*, ed. Alan Gallay, 353–389. Lincoln: University of Nebraska Press, 2009.

Saade, R. Lira, and S. Montes Hernández. "Cucurbits (*Cucurbita spp.*)." http://www.hort.purdue .edu/newcrop/1492/cucurbits.html.

St. Jean, Wendy. "Squirrel King and the Eastern Chickasaw Band." *Journal of Mississippi History* 65, no. 4 (Winter 2003): 343–354.

Sassaman, Kenneth E., and David G. Anderson. "Late Holocene Period, 3750 to 650 B.C." In *Southeast*, ed. Raymond D. Fogelson, 101–114. Handbook of North American Indians, Vol. 14. William C. Sturtevant, gen. ed. Washington, D.C.: Smithsonian Institution, 2004.

Satz, Ronald N. "The Mississippi Choctaw: From the Removal Treaty to the Federal Agency." In *After Removal: The Choctaw in Mississippi*, ed. Samuel J. Wells and Roseanna Tubby, 3–32. Jackson: University Press of Mississippi, 1986.

Saucier, Roger T. "Geological Analysis." In John M. Connaway, Samuel O. McGahey, and Clarence H. Webb, *Teoc Creek: A Poverty Point Site in Carroll County, Mississippi*, 90–105. Archaeological Report No. 3. Mississippi Department of Archives and History, Jackson, 1977.

———. *Geomorphology and Quaternary Geologic History of the Lower Mississippi Valley*. Vol. 1. Prepared for the president of the Mississippi River Commission, Vicksburg, December 1994.

Saunders, Joe W. "Jaketown (22HU505)." On file, Grand Village of the Natchez Indians, Mississippi Department of Archives and History, Natchez, 2004.

Saunt, Claudio. "History until 1776." In *Southeast*, ed. Raymond D. Fogelson, 128–138. Handbook of North American Indians, Vol. 14. William C. Sturtevant, gen. ed. Washington, D.C.: Smithsonian Institution, 2004.

Scarry, C. Margaret. "Appendix D: Foraging and Gardening on the Mississippi Coast—Plant Food Remains." In John H. Blitz and C. Baxter Mann. *Fisherfolk, Farmers, and Frenchmen*, 168–175. Archaeological Report No. 30. Mississippi Department of Archives and History, Jackson, 2000.

———. "Food Plant Remains from Excavations in Mounds A, B, C, D, and L at Bottle Creek." In *Bottle Creek: A Pensacola Culture Site in South Alabama*, ed. Ian W. Brown, 103–113. Tuscaloosa: University of Alabama Press, 2003.

———. "The Use of Plants in Mound-Related Activities at Bottle Creek and Moundville." In *Bottle Creek: A Pensacola Culture Site in South Alabama*, ed. Ian W. Brown, 114–129. Tuscaloosa: University of Alabama Press, 2003.

Scarry, John F. "The Late Prehistoric Southeast." In *The Forgotten Centuries: Indians and Europeans in the American South, 1521–1704*, ed. Charles Hudson and Carmen Chaves Tesser, 17–35. Athens: University of Georgia Press, 1994.

Schoeninger, Margaret J., and Mark R. Schurr. "Human Subsistence at Moundville: The Stable-Isotope Data." In *Archaeology of the Moundville Chiefdom*, ed. Vernon J. Knight Jr. and Vincas P. Steponaitis, 120–132. Washington, D.C.: Smithsonian Institution Press, 1998.

Shea, John Gilmary, ed. and trans. "Journal of the Voyage of Father Gravier." In *Early Voyages Up and Down the Mississippi*. Albany, N.Y.: Joel Munsell, 1861.

———, ed. and trans. "Letters of J. F. Buisson Saint-Cosme, Mr. De Montigny, and La Source." In *Early Voyages Up and Down the Mississippi*. Albany, N.Y.: Joel Munsell, 1861.

Shelby, Charmion, trans., and David Bost, ed. "La Florida by Garcilaso de la Vega, the Inca." In *The De Soto Chronicles: The Expedition of Hernando De Soto to North America in 1539–1543*, ed. Lawrence A. Clayton, Vernon J. Knight Jr., and Edward C. Moore, 2:25–559. Tuscaloosa: University of Alabama Press, 1993.

Smith, Marvin T. "Aboriginal Depopulation in the Postcontact Southeast." In *The Forgotten Centuries: Indians and Europeans in the American South, 1521–1704*, ed. Charles Hudson and Carmen Chaves Tesser, 257–275. Athens: University of Georgia Press, 1994.

———. "Aboriginal Population Movements in the Postcontact Southeast." In *The Transformation of the Southeastern Indians, 1540–1760*, ed. Robbie Ethridge and Charles Hudson, 3–20. Jackson: University Press of Mississippi, 2002.

Spiess, Arthur. "Appendix H: Archaeology of a Trudeau Trash Pit." In Jeffrey P. Brain, *Tunica Archaeology*, 418–422. Cambridge, Mass.: Peabody Museum of Archaeology and Ethnology, Harvard University, 1988.

Squier, Ephraim G., and Edwin H. Davis. *Ancient Monuments of the Mississippi Valley*. 1848. Reprint, Washington, D.C.: Smithsonian Institution Press, 1998.

Steponaitis, Vincas P. "The Late Prehistory of the Natchez Region: Excavations at the Emerald and Foster Sites, Adams County, Mississippi." B.A. thesis, Harvard University, 1974.

———. "Location Theory and Complex Chiefdoms: A Mississippian Example." In *Mississippian Settlement Patterns*, ed. Bruce D. Smith, 417–454. New York: Academic Press, 1978.

Steponaitis, Vincas P., Jeffrey P. Brain, and Ian W. Brown. "Appendix I. Glossary of Ceramic Types and Varieties." In Robert S. Neitzel, *The Grand Village of the Natchez Revisited: Excavations at the Fatherland Site, Adams County, Mississippi, 1972*, 139–145. Archaeological Report No. 12. Mississippi Department of Archives and History, Jackson, 1983.

Steponaitis, Vincas P., Stephen Williams, R. P. Davis Jr., Ian W. Brown, Tristram R. Kidder, and Melissa Salvanish, eds. *LMS Archives Online*. www.http://rla.unc.edu/archives/lms1/ site files.

Steward, Julian H. "The Direct Historical Approach to Archaeology." *American Antiquity* 7 (1942): 337–343.

Stiggins, George. *Creek Indian History: A Historical Narrative of the Genealogy, Traditions and Downfall of the Ispocoga or Creek Indian Tribe of Indians by One of the Tribe*. Ed. Virginia Pounds Brown. Tuscaloosa: Published for the Birmingham Public Library by the University of Alabama Press 1989.

Strong, John A. "The Mississippian Bird-Man Theme in Cross- Cultural Perspective." In *The Southeastern Ceremonial Complex: Artifacts and Analysis, the Cottonlandia Conference*, ed. Patricia Galloway, 211–238. Lincoln: University of Nebraska Press, 1989.

Stubbs, John D., Jr. "The Chickasaw Contact with the La Salle Expedition in 1682." In *La Salle and His Legacy: Frenchmen and Indians in the Lower Mississippi Valley*, ed. Patricia K. Galloway, 41–48. Jackson: University Press of Mississippi, 1982.

———. "A Preliminary Classification for Chickasaw Pottery." *Mississippi Archaeology* 12, no. 2 (1982): 50–57.

Swanton, John R. *Chickasaw Society and Religion*. Forty-Second Annual Report of the U.S. Bureau of American Ethnology, Washington, D.C., 1928. Reprint, Lincoln: University of Nebraska Press, 2006.

———. *Early History of the Creek Indians and Their Neighbors*. Bulletin No. 73. Bureau of American Ethnology, Smithsonian Institution, Washington, D.C. Reprint, New York: Johnson Reprint, 1970.

———. *Final Report of the United States De Soto Expedition Commission*. Washington, D.C.: Smithsonian Institution Press, 1985.

———. "Historical Sketch of the Biloxi and Ofo." in James O. Dorsey and John R. Swanton, *A Dictionary of the Biloxi and Ofo Languages, Accompanied with Thirty-One Biloxi Texts and Numerous Biloxi Phrases*, 5–12. Bulletin No. 47. Bureau of American Ethnology, Smithsonian Institution, Washington, D.C., 1912.

———. *The Indians of the Southeastern United States*. Washington, D.C.: Smithsonian Institution Press, 1979.

———. *The Indian Tribes of North America*. 1952. Reprint, Washington, D.C.: Smithsonian Institution Press, 1984.

———. *Indian Tribes of the Lower Mississippi Valley and Adjacent Coast of the Gulf of Mexico*. Bulletin No. 43. Bureau of American Ethnology, Smithsonian Institution, Washington, D.C., 1911. Reprint, Mineola, N.Y.: Dover, 1998.

———. *Source Material for the Social and Ceremonial Life of the Choctaw Indians*. Bulletin No. 103. Bureau of American Ethnology, Smithsonian Institution, Washington, D.C., 1931.

Sykes, Bryan. *The Seven Daughters of Eve: The Science That Reveals Our Genetic Ancestry*. New York: W. W. Norton, 2001.

Thunen, Robert L. "Geometric Enclosures in the Mid-South: An Archaeological Analysis of Enclosure Form." In *Middle Woodland Settlement and Ceremonialism in the Mid-South and Lower Mississippi Valley*, ed. Robert C. Mainfort Jr., 99–115. Archaeological Report No. 22. Mississippi Department of Archives and History, Jackson, 1988.

Toth, Edwin Alan. *Early Marksville Phases in the Lower Mississippi Valley: A Study of Culture Contact Dynamics*. Archaeological Report No. 21. Mississippi Department of Archives and History in cooperation with the Lower Mississippi Survey, Harvard University, Jackson, 1988.

Tonti, Henri de. "Extracts from Letters, February 23 and March 14, 1702." In "Henri de Tonti du Village des Chacta, 1702: The Beginning of the French Alliance." Trans. Patricia K. Galloway. In *La Salle and His Legacy: Frenchmen and Indians in the Lower Mississippi Valley*, ed. Patricia K. Galloway, 166–173. Jackson: University Press of Mississippi, 1982.

Treaties Between the United States and the Choctaw Nation. http://www.choctaw.org/History/Treaties/treaties.html.

Treaty of Choctaw Trading House with the Choctaw, October 24, 1816. http://www.felihkatubbe.com/ChoctawNation/treaties/trading_house_1816.htm. In *Indian Affairs: Laws and Treaties*. Vol. 2, *Treaties*, comp. and ed. Charles J. Kappler, LL. M., Clerk to the Senate Committee on Indian Affairs. Washington, D.C.: Government Printing Office, 1904.

Treaty of Dancing Rabbit Creek with the Choctaw, September 27, 1830. http://www.felihkatubbe.com/ChoctawNation/treaties/rabbit_creek_1830.htm. In *Indian Affairs: Laws and Treaties*. Vol. 2, *Treaties*, comp. and ed. Charles J. Kappler, LL. M., Clerk to the Senate Committee on Indian Affairs. Washington, D.C.: Government Printing Office, 1904.

Treaty of Fort Adams with the Choctaw, December 17, 1801. http://www.felihkatubbe.com/ChoctawNation/treaties/fort_adams_1801.htm. In *Indian Affairs: Laws and Treaties.* Vol. 2, *Treaties,* comp. and ed. Charles J. Kappler, LL. M., Clerk to the Senate Committee on Indian Affairs. Washington, D.C.: Government Printing Office, 1904.

Treaty of Fort Confederation on the Tombigbee River with the Choctaw, October 17, 1802. http://www.felihkatubbe.com/ChoctawNation/treaties/fort_confederation_1802.htm. In *Indian Affairs: Laws and Treaties.* Vol. 2, *Treaties,* comp. and ed. Charles J. Kappler, LL. M., Clerk to the Senate Committee on Indian Affairs. Washington, D.C.: Government Printing Office, 1904.

Treaty of Hoe-Buckin-Too-Pa with the Choctaw, August 31, 1803. http://www.felihkatubbe.com/ChoctawNation/treaties/hoe_1802.htm. In *Indian Affairs: Laws and Treaties.* Vol. 2, *Treaties,* comp. and ed. Charles J. Kappler, LL. M., Clerk to the Senate Committee on Indian Affairs. Washington, D.C.: Government Printing Office, 1904.

Treaty of Hopewell, on the Keowee, near Seneca Old Town with the Choctaw, January 3, 1786. http://www.felihkatubbe.com/ChoctawNation/treaties/1786_hopewell.htm. In *Indian Affairs: Laws and Treaties.* Vol. 2, *Treaties,* comp. and ed. Charles J. Kappler, LL. M., Clerk to the Senate Committee on Indian Affairs. Washington, D.C.: Government Printing Office, 1904.

Treaty of Mount Dexter, in Pooshapukanuk, in Choctaw [sic] with the Choctaw, November 16, 1805. http://www.felihkatubbe.com/ChoctawNation/treaties/mt_dexter_1805.htm. In *Indian Affairs: Laws and Treaties.* Vol. 2, *Treaties,* comp. and ed. Charles J. Kappler, LL. M., Clerk to the Senate Committee on Indian Affairs. Washington, D.C.: Government Printing Office, 1904.

Treaty of Washington D.C. with the Choctaw, January 20, 1825. http://www.felihkatubbe.com/ChoctawNation/treaties/washington_1825.htm. In *Indian Affairs: Laws and Treaties.* Vol. 2, *Treaties,* comp. and ed. Charles J. Kappler, LL. M., Clerk to the Senate Committee on Indian Affairs. Washington, D.C.: Government Printing Office, 1904.

Treaty with the Cherokee, 1835. In *Indian Affairs, Laws and Treaties.* Vol. 2, *Treaties,* comp. and ed. Charles J. Kappler. Washington, D.C.: Government Printing Office, 1904. Online, Oklahoma State University Library, http://digital.library.okstate.edu/kappler/Vol2/treaties/che0439.htm.

Treaty with the Chickasaw: 1816. Yale Law School, Lillian Goldman Law Library, The Avalon Project, Documents in Law, History and Diplomacy. http://avalon.law.yale.edu/19th_century/nt004.asp.

Treaty with the Chickasaw: 1818. Yale Law School, Lillian Goldman Law Library, The Avalon Project, Documents in Law, History and Diplomacy. http://avalon.law.yale.edu/19th_century/nt006.asp.

Treaty with the Chickasaw: 1830, unratified. Yale Law School, Lillian Goldman Law Library, The Avalon Project, Documents in Law, History and Diplomacy. http://avalon.law.yale.edu/19th_century/nt008.asp.

Treaty with the Chickasaw, 1832. In *Indian Affairs, Laws and Treaties.* Vol. 2, *Treaties,* comp. and ed. Charles J. Kappler. Washington, D.C.: Government Printing Office, 1904. Online, Oklahoma State University Library, http://digital.library.okstate.edu/KAPPLER/Vol2/treaties/chi0356.htm#mn1.

Treaty with the Chickasaw, 1832, Supplementary Articles. In *Indian Affairs, Laws and Treaties.* Vol. 2, *Treaties,* comp. and ed. Charles J. Kappler, 362–364. Washington, D.C.: Government

Printing Office, 1904. Online, Oklahoma State University Library, http://digital.library.ok state.edu/kappler/Vol2/treaties/chio362.htm.

Treaty with the Chickasaw, 1834. In *Indian Affairs, Laws and Treaties.* Vol. 2, *Treaties,* comp. and ed. Charles J. Kappler, 418–425. Washington, D.C.: Government Printing Office, 1904. Online, Oklahoma State University Library, http://digital.library.okstate.edu/kappler/Vol2/ treaties/chio418.htm.

Treaty with the Choctaw, 1820 [also known as the "Treaty of Doak's Stand"]. http://www.feli-hkatubbe.com/ChoctawNation/treaties/choctaw_treaty_1820.html. In *Indian Affairs: Laws and Treaties.* Vol. 2, *Treaties,* comp. and ed. Charles J. Kappler, LL. M., Clerk to the Senate Committee on Indian Affairs. Washington, D.C.: Government Printing Office. 1904.

Treaty with the Choctaw and Chickasaw, 1837. In *Indian Affairs: Laws and Treaties.* Vol. 2, *Treaties,* comp. and ed. Charles J. Kappler, 486–488. Washington, D.C.: Government Printing Office, 1904. Online, Oklahoma State University Library, http://digital.library.okstate.edu/ kappler/Vol2/treaties/chio486.htm.

Treaty with the Choctaw and Chickasaw, June 22, 1855. Extracted from *Indian Treaties: Acts and Agreements.* http://www.accessgenealogy.com/native/treaty/; http://www.accessgenealogy .com/scripts/data/database.cgi?file=Data&report=SingleArticle&ArticleID=0040171.

Treaty with the Creeks, 1832. In *Indian Affairs: Laws and Treaties.* Vol. 2, *Treaties,* comp. and ed. Charles J. Kappler, 341–343. Washington, D.C.: Government Printing Office, 1904. Online, Oklahoma State University Library, http://digital.library.okstate.edu/kappler/Vol2/treaties/ creo341.htm.

Treaty with the Quapaw, 7 Stat. 176, August 24, 1818, Proclaimed January 5, 1819. http://www.utul sa.edu/law/classes/rice/Treaties/07_Stat_176_QUAPAW.htm. In G. William Rice, College of Law, University of Tulsa, Oklahoma.

Treaty with the Seminole, 1832. In *Indian Affairs: Laws and Treaties.* Vol. 2, *Treaties,* comp. and ed. Charles J. Kappler, 344–345. Washington, D.C.: Government Printing Office, 1904. Online, Oklahoma State University Library, http://digital.library.okstate.edu/kappler/Vol2/ treaties/semo344.htm.

United Houma Nation, Inc. *Houma History.* http://www.unitedhoumanation.org/node/13.

U.S. Department of Agriculture, Natural Resources Conservation Service. *Plants Database.*

Urban, Greg, and Jason Baird Jackson. "Social Organization." In *Southeast,* ed. Raymond D. Fogelson, 697–706. Handbook of North American Indians, Vol. 14. William C. Sturtevant, gen. ed. Washington, D.C.: Smithsonian Institution, 2004.

Usner, Daniel H. *American Indians in the Lower Mississippi Valley: Social and Economic Histories.* Lincoln: University of Nebraska Press, 1998.

——. *Indians, Settlers, and Slaves: The Lower Mississippi Valley Before 1783.* Chapel Hill: University of North Carolina Press, 1992.

Vennum, Thomas, Jr. *American Indian Lacrosse: Little Brother of War.* Washington, D.C.: Smithsonian Institution Press, 1994.

Vogel, Virgil J. *American Indian Medicine.* Norman: University of Oklahoma Press, 1970.

Voss, Jerome A., and John H. Blitz. "An Archaeological Survey in the Choctaw Homeland." *Mississippi Archaeology* 18, no. 2 (December 1983): 49–56.

Waddell, Gene. "Cusabo." In *Southeast,* ed. Raymond D. Fogelson, 254–264. Handbook of North American Indians, Vol. 14. William C. Sturtevant, gen. ed. Washington, D.C.: Smithsonian Institution, 2004.

Walker, Willard B. "Creek Confederacy Before Removal." In *Southeast*, ed. Raymond D. Fogelson, 373–392. Handbook of North American Indians, Vol. 14. William C. Sturtevant, gen. ed. Washington, D.C.: Smithsonian Institution, 2004.

Ward, Rufus. "Choctaw Farmsteads in Mississippi, 1830." In *After Removal: The Choctaw in Mississippi*, ed. Samuel J. Wells and Roseanna Tubby, 33–41. Jackson: University Press of Mississippi, 1986.

———. "Nineteenth-Century Choctaw Indian Reservation Sites in Lowndes County, Mississippi." *Mississippi Archaeology* 19, no. 2 (December 1984): 39–45.

Waselkov, Gregory A. "Capinan and Moctoby." In *Southeast*, ed. Raymond D. Fogelson, 176. Handbook of North American Indians, Vol. 14. William C. Sturtevant, gen. ed. Washington, D.C.: Smithsonian Institution, 2004.

———. *A Conquering Spirit: Fort Mims and the Redstick War of 1813–1814*. Tuscaloosa: University of Alabama Press, 2006.

———. "Exchange and Interaction since 1500." In *Southeast*, ed. Raymond D. Fogelson, 696. Handbook of North American Indians, Vol. 14. William C. Sturtevant, gen. ed. Washington, D.C.: Smithsonian Institution, 2004.

———. "Indian Maps of the Colonial Southeast." In Gregory A. Waselkov, Peter H. Wood, and Tom Hatley, *Powhatan's Mantle: Indians in the Colonial Southeast*, 435–502. Rev. and expanded ed. Lincoln: University of Nebraska Press, 2006.

———. "Pascagoula." In *Southeast*, ed. Raymond D. Fogelson, 185. Handbook of North American Indians, Vol. 14. William C. Sturtevant, gen. ed. Washington, D.C.: Smithsonian Institution, 2004.

———. "Tawasa." In *Southeast*, ed. Raymond D. Fogelson, 186–187. Handbook of North American Indians, Vol. 14. William C. Sturtevant, gen. ed. Washington, D.C.: Smithsonian Institution, 2004.

Waslekov, Gregory A., and Kathryn E. Holland Braund, eds. *William Bartram on the Southeastern Indians*. Lincoln: University of Nebraska Press, 1995.

Webb, Clarence H. *The Poverty Point Culture*. 2nd ed., rev. Geoscience and Man 17. Baton Rouge: Geoscience Publications, Department of Geography and Anthropology, Louisiana State University, 1982.

———. "Poverty Point Culture and Site: Definitions." In *The Poverty Point Culture: Local Manifestations, Subsistence Practices, and Trade Networks*, ed. Kathleen M. Byrd, 3–6. Geoscience and Man 29. Baton Rouge: Geoscience Publications, Department of Geography and Anthropology, Louisiana State University, 1991.

Weinstein, Richard A. "Tchefuncte Occupation in the Lower Mississippi Delta and Adjacent Coastal Zone." In *The Tchula Period in the Mid-South and Lower Mississippi Valley*, ed. David H. Dye and Ronald C. Brister, 102–127. Archaeological Report No. 17. Mississippi Department of Archives and History, Jackson, 1986.

Wells, Samuel J. "Federal Indian Policy: From Accommodation to Removal." In *The Choctaw Before Removal*, ed. Carolyn Keller Reeves, 181–213. Jackson: University Press of Mississippi, 1985.

———. "International Causes of the Treaty of Mount Dexter, 1805." *Journal of Mississippi History* 48, no. 3 (August 1986): 177–186.

———. "The Role of Mixed-Bloods in Mississippi Choctaw History." In *After Removal: The Choctaw in Mississippi*, ed. Samuel J. Wells and Roseanna Tubby, 42–55. Jackson: University Press of Mississippi, 1986.

Wells, Samuel J., and Roseanna Tubby, eds. *After Removal: The Choctaw in Mississippi*. Jackson: University Press of Mississippi, 1986.

Wheeler-Howard Act, June 18, 1934 [The Indian Reorganization Act]. http://www.uintahbasin tah.org/papers/indianreorganizationact.pdf.

White, Douglas R., George P. Murdock, and Richard Scaglion. "Natchez Class and Rank Reconsidered." *Ethnology* 10, no. 2 (1971): 369–388.

White, Richard. *The Roots of Dependency: Subsistence, Environment, and Social Change among the Choctaws, Pawnees, and Navajos*. Lincoln: University of Nebraska Press, 1983.

Widmer, Randolph J. "The Structure of Southeastern Chiefdoms." In *The Forgotten Centuries: Indians and Europeans in the American South, 1521–1704*, ed. Charles Hudson and Carmen Chaves Tesser, 125–155. Athens: University of Georgia Press, 1994.

Wilentz, Sean. *Andrew Jackson*. New York: Times Books, Henry Holt, 2005.

Wilkins, James C. "The Tchula Period in the Natchez Bluffs: The Grace MacNeil Site and the Homochitto Phase." Master's thesis, University of Alabama, 2004.

Williams, G. Ishmael, Jr. "Historic European Period." In Marvin D. Jeter, Jerome C. Rose, G. Ishmael Williams Jr., and Anna M. Harmon, *Archeology and Bioarcheology of the Lower Mississippi Valley and the Trans-Mississippi South*, 249–290. Arkansas Archeological Survey Research Series No. 37. Final Report submitted to the U.S. Army Corps of Engineers, Southwestern Division Study Unit 6 of the Southwestern Division Archeological Overview, Contract No. DACW63-84-C-0149, 1989.

Williams, Leah. "The Paleoethnobotany of the Feltus Mounds Site." Honor's thesis, University of North Carolina at Chapel Hill, 2008.

Williams, Mark. *Archaeological Excavations at the Jackson Landing/Mulatto Bayou Earthwork*. Archaeological Report No. 19. Mississippi Department of Archives and History, Jackson, 1987.

Williams, Stephen. "Introduction to 2003 Edition." In Philip Phillips, James A. Ford, and James B. Griffin, *Archaeological Survey in the Lower Mississippi Alluvial Valley, 1940–1947*, xi–xxxii. 1951. Reprint, Tuscaloosa: University of Alabama Press 2003.

Williams, Stephen, and Jeffrey P. Brain. *Excavations at the Lake George Site, Yazoo County, Mississippi, 1958–1960*. Papers of the Peabody Museum of Archaeology and Ethnology, Harvard University 74 (1983).

Williamson, Gloria C., Bob M. Dearing, Lynn Posey, Jack Gordon, Gary Jackson, Hillman T. Frazier, John Horhn, Kelvin E. Butler, Charles W. Pickering, Charlie Ross, and Terry Burton. "An Act to Return the Nanih Waiya State Park and Mound to the Mississippi Band of Choctaw Indians." Senate Bill 2732, Regular Session 2007 of the Mississippi Legislature, Public Property, signed by Governor Haley Barbour, March 2007.

Worth, John E., trans. and ed. "Account of the Northern Conquest and Discovery of Hernando De Soto by Rodrigo Rangel." In *The De Soto Chronicles: The Expedition of Hernando De Soto to North America in 1539–1543*, ed. Lawrence A. Clayton, Vernon J. Knight Jr., Edward C. Moore, 1:247–306. Tuscaloosa: University of Alabama Press, 1993.

———, trans. and ed. "Luys Hernández de Biedma." In *The De Soto Chronicles: The Expedition of Hernando De Soto to North America in 1539–1543*, ed. Lawrence A. Clayton, Vernon J. Knight Jr., and Edward C. Moore, 1:221–246. Tuscaloosa: University of Alabama Press, 1993.

Wright, J. Leitch, Jr. *Creeks and Seminoles: The Destruction and Regeneration of a Muscogulge People*. Lincoln: University of Nebraska Press, 1986.

Wyman, William S. "Introduction." In George Stiggins, *Creek Indian History: A Historical Narrative of the Genealogy, Traditions and Downfall of the Ispocoga or Creek Indian Tribe of Indians by One of the Tribe*, ed. Virginia Pounds Brown, 13–20. Tuscaloosa: Published for the Birmingham Public Library by the University of Alabama Press, 1989.

Wynn, Jack T., and James R. Atkinson. *Archaeology of the Okashua and Self Sites, Mississippi*. Final Report for Department of the Interior, National Park Service, Mississippi State University, Starkville, 1976.

INDEX